COMMERCIAL BANKING

fourth edition

COMMERCIAL BANKING

Edward W. Reed, Ph.D.
Senior Vice President
and Economist, Retired
United States National Bank of Oregon

Edward K. Gill, Ph.D.
Boise State University

Prentice Hall
Englewood Cliffs, New Jersey 07632

LIBRARY OF CONGRESS
Library of Congress Cataloging-in-Publication Data

Reed, Edward Wilson
    Commercial banking. -- 4th ed. / Edward W. Reed, Edward K. Gill.
        p.   cm.
    Rev. ed. of: Commercial banking / Edward W. Reed ... et al. 3rd
    ed. c1984.
    Includes bibliographies and index.
    ISBN 0-13-154360-1
    1. Banks and banking--United States.   I. Gill, Edward K.
II. Commercial banking.   III. Title.
HG2491.C64 1989
332.1'2'068--dc19   88-15735
                                                            CIP

Editorial/production supervision and
    interior design: *Nancy Savio-Marcello*
Cover design: *Ben Santora*
Manufacturing buyer: *Ed O'Dougherty*

Cover photos courtesy of Library of Congress and Citibank, N.A.

© 1989, 1984, 1980, 1976 by Prentice-Hall, Inc.
A Division of Simon & Schuster
Englewood Cliffs, New Jersey 07632

Printed in the United States of America

10 9 8 7 6 5 4 3 2 1

ISBN 0-13-154360-1   01

PRENTICE-HALL INTERNATIONAL (UK) LIMITED, *London*
PRENTICE-HALL OF AUSTRALIA PTY. LIMITED, *Sydney*
PRENTICE-HALL CANADA INC., *Toronto*
PRENTICE-HALL HISPANOAMERICANA, S.A., *Mexico*
PRENTICE-HALL OF INDIA PRIVATE LIMITED, *New Delhi*
PRENTICE-HALL OF JAPAN, INC., *Tokyo*
SIMON & SCHUSTER ASIA PTE. LTD., *Singapore*
EDITORA PRENTICE-HALL DO BRASIL, LTDA., *Rio de Janeiro*

CONTENTS

12 INTERMEDIATE-TERM BUSINESS LOANS   289

13 REAL ESTATE LENDING   308

16 THE INVESTMENT ACCOUNT: POLICIES AND MANAGEMENT 371

17 INVESTMENT SECURITIES 389

18 TRUST SERVICES OF COMMERCIAL BANKS 406

PREFACE

This book is about the business of commercial banking—and that business has undergone rapid change in recent years as banks have confronted volatile economic conditions and revised regulations. Banks are seeking profits and accessing funding sources in ways new to them. At the same time, nonbank competition in traditional banking activities has increased dramatically. This revision of *Commercial Banking* attempts to depict the new environment in which bank management must operate.

There is a danger, however, that writers of textbooks on banks will focus too extensively on the new elements in banking, forgetting that most of what banks do is what they have done for many years: accept deposits and make loans and investments. New methods may have some influence on how these activities are carried out, but the basic business is unchanged.

Nor has the importance of commercial banks diminished because of changes in the environment. Commercial banks make funds available to meet the needs of individuals, businesses, and governments. In so doing, they facilitate the flow of goods and services and the activities of governments. The commercial banking system provides a large portion of our medium of exchange and is the primary instrument through which monetary policy is conducted.

The ability of our commercial banking system to perform its tasks efficiently and in harmony with our needs and economic goals depends in large measure on effective management. Banks must be managed prudently, safely, and profitably if we are to have a strong, adaptable banking system capable of meeting the needs of society.

This book reviews the management aspects of commercial banks. It has been written with the objective of providing students and professionals with a description and analysis of the operations of commercial banks. It is an investigation into the techniques and principles employed by commercial banks in the performance of their many functions. Although the focus is on management and the individual bank, the book does not lose sight of the social and monetary importance of the banking system.

Lending is the major business of commercial banks, and more bank personnel are involved in the lending activity than in any other. In recognition of its importance, we devote seven of the nineteen chapters to lending. In addition, the text covers structure, organization and management, deposits, cash and liquidity management, investments, trust services, and international banking. Two chapters are devoted to two areas of vital importance, profitability and bank capital. Because of the quasi-public nature of banking, we consider each of these topics in light of the laws and regulations under which banks operate.

We are indebted to many people, both practitioners and academicians. We are particularly grateful to Richard V. Cotter and Richard K. Smith. Information and suggestions have been provided by so many people that we are reluctant to attempt to list all of them, but to each one we owe a debt of gratitude.

COMMERCIAL BANKING

1

COMMERCIAL BANKING: AN OVERVIEW

Commercial banking is one of our oldest industries. The first bank was organized in 1782 before the adoption of our federal Constitution, and many of the banks that were organized in the 1800s are still in operation. Commercial banks are the most important type of financial institution in the nation in terms of aggregate assets. The growth of their assets and liabilities is presented in Figures 1-1 and 1-2. Total assets approximate $3 trillion. In terms of employment, banking is one of our largest industries, with over 1.5 million employees.

FUNCTIONS OF COMMERCIAL BANKS

The business of banking is very broad and far-reaching; with the introduction of the one-bank holding company and the possibility of relaxation of some of the restrictions imposed on banking, the number and variety of services provided by commercial banks and their affiliates have expanded. Recent innovations in banking include the introduction of credit cards, accounting services for business firms, factoring, leasing, automated teller machines, discount brokerage, participation in the Eurodollar market, and lock box banking. The importance of commercial banks can best be illustrated by a brief explanation of their major functions.

1

FIGURE 1-1 Principal Assets of Commercial Banks (seasonally adjusted, quarterly averages)

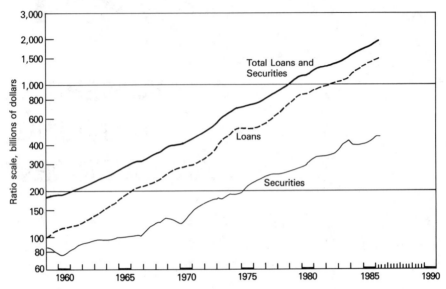

SOURCE: Board of Governors of the Federal Reserve System, *Historical Chartbook, 1986* (1987).

FIGURE 1-2 Principal Liabilities of Commercial Banks (seasonally adjusted, quarterly averages)

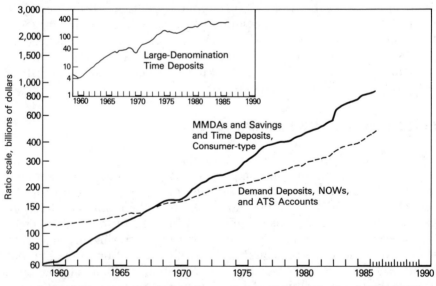

SOURCE: Board of Governors of the Federal Reserve System, *Historical Chartbook, 1986* (1987).

Creating Money

One of the major functions of commercial banks is *the ability to create and to destroy money.*[1] This is accomplished by the lending and investing activities of commercial banks in cooperation with the Federal Reserve System. The power of the commercial banking system to create money is of great economic significance. It results in the elastic credit system that is necessary for economic progress at a relatively steady rate of growth. If bank credit were not available, the expansion of our productive facilities and operations would in many cases be impossible and in other instances delayed until funds could be accumulated from profits or obtained from other outside sources. Moreover, productive units would be forced to maintain larger working balances to meet the fluctuating requirements for funds. Such a practice would be uneconomic since large sums would have to be held idle for some periods, while during the seasonal peaks of business activity such sums might be insufficient.

Our economy needs an adequate but not excessive money supply. If the money supply increases too rapidly, inflation is the result, with all of its ill effects on the various economic processes. Conversely, if the money supply lags production, the economy may suffer from deflation with equally undesirable effects. The objective of Federal Reserve policy is to provide a money supply commensurate with the national objectives of stable prices, sound economic growth, and a high level of employment. Commercial banks play a very important role in the implementation of these policies. They serve as a conduit through which the money supply is increased or decreased in an effort to attain these worthy objectives.

Payments Mechanism

Providing for a payments mechanism, or the *transfer of funds,* is one of the important functions performed by commercial banks, and it is increasing in importance as greater reliance is placed on the use of checks and credit cards.

Most of the checks in the nation are cleared through the commercial banking system. Checks drawn on and deposited in the same bank merely transfer funds from one account to another. If only two banks are involved in the same town, there is a direct exchange of checks. When several banks are involved within the same city, a clearinghouse arrangement is usually employed. The process becomes a bit more complicated, time consuming, and expensive when checks are cleared between banks located in different parts of the country. Such clearings are often handled

---

[1] The money supply is defined by the Board of Governors of the Federal Reserve System. See the current issue of the *Federal Reserve Bulletin* for the most recent definition.

through the correspondent banking system. Banks located on the West Coast, for example, might send checks drawn on East Coast banks to banks in New York City, which would in turn route the checks to the banks in their area on which the checks were drawn. Checks may also be cleared through regional banks of the Federal Reserve System in a manner similar to clearings through the correspondent banking system. Less than half the checks are cleared through the Federal Reserve System, and the dollar amount is even less.

Banks have employed computers and other sophisticated equipment to speed the clearing process, reduce costs, and improve accuracy. In recent years considerable thought and research have been given to what has become known as *checkless banking* or the *checkless society,* that is, the use of some form of *electronic transfer of funds* that would eliminate the bank check and most of the work attendant to it. Experiments have already been made with a system that would involve placing a card similar to a bank credit card into a terminal at a retail store. This would activate computers in banks throughout the nation and thus transfer funds from the purchaser's account to the seller's account. A forerunner of this system is the use of automated teller machines now installed by many banks, whereby a bank credit card can be used to withdraw cash from a depositor's account, make deposits and loan payments, and transfer funds between a depositor's savings and checking accounts. A fuller discussion on the transfer of funds is found in Chapter 6.

Pooling of Savings

Commercial banks perform a very important service to all sectors of the economy by providing facilities for the pooling of savings and making them available for economically and socially desirable purposes. The saver is rewarded by the payment of interest on his or her savings, which are safe and in a highly liquid form. These pooled funds are made available to businesses that may use them for the expansion of their productive capacity and to consumers for such items as housing and consumer goods. A large part of these savings flows into the savings departments of commercial banks.

Extension of Credit

The primary function of commercial banks is the extension of credit to worthy borrowers. From the beginning of time, organizers of banks have been motivated by the opportunities presented by the lending function, and charters have been granted by governments primarily because there was a need for credit in a particular community. In making credit available, commercial banks are rendering a great social service; through their actions, production is increased, capital investments are expanded, and a higher standard of living is realized.

Bank lending is very important to the economy, for it makes possible the financing of the agricultural, commercial, and industrial activities of the nation. It makes possible what economists have called indirect or roundabout production, as compared with direct production, where consumable goods are secured by the direct application of labor to land or natural wealth. Bank loans also make possible production for inventory. The food industry provides us with an excellent example: all the food that is harvested and processed cannot be consumed immediately. Loans to canners enable them to purchase, process, can, and store the food that may at a later time be sold to retailers and ultimately to consumers. During this interval of time—from producer to canner, to wholesaler, to retailer, and finally to consumer—bank loans have made possible the economic handling of the food crop.

The farmer, because of the availability of bank loans, is able to purchase seed, feed, fertilizer, and the many other items necessary for raising and harvesting the agricultural commodities that feed our expanding population. Bank loans to manufacturers make possible the purchase of raw materials and machinery and the employment of labor that in time produce goods demanded by industry, government, and consumers. Retailers and wholesalers are able to stock their shelves and move goods for people to consume because of the funds made available in the form of loans by commercial banks. Goods can be transported from producers to the ultimate consumers because of the financial assistance of banks to transportation enterprises. In addition to financing the agricultural, commercial, and industrial activities of the nation, commercial banks facilitate consumption by making consumer loans. Funds may be extended to consumers by banks for the purchase of such items as houses, automobiles, and appliances.

Although the investment activities of commercial banks are usually considered separately from lending, the economic effects and social results are the same. Because government receipts are not always equal to expenditures, temporary borrowing from commercial banks is not uncommon; therefore, the provision of bank credit enables the smooth operation of government. In general, capital improvements made by governments are not financed out of operating revenue but out of bond issues. Thus, when banks purchase municipal securities, they are providing funds for such capital improvements as the building of schools and hospitals and the purchasing of fire trucks. Because of these expenditures, our standard of living is improved. When securities issued by the federal government are purchased, these funds are used for a multitude of purposes, such as the construction of highways and dams and for national defense.

Facilities for the Financing
of Foreign Trade

Although foreign trade is basically the same as domestic trade, some differences necessitate that international banking services be provided by commercial banks. These differences arise because of the existence of national monetary systems, unfamiliarity with the financial ability of buyers and sellers in foreign countries, and, in some cases, language barriers. A person who orders wine from France, a car from Germany, shoes from Italy, or a subscription to the *Economist* from England may discover that foreign sellers are not willing to take American dollars in payment. Therefore, arrangements must be made to pay in the currency of the foreign country, for example, in francs, marks, lira, or pounds. To do this, the purchaser can go to a commercial bank and quickly and efficiently arrange for the amount of foreign exchange needed. The bank may have foreign currency of these countries on hand but, if not, can arrange for it quickly through another bank. The purchaser may encounter a situation in which the foreign seller is not willing to place the goods on a ship and wait for payment to arrive in the next mail. In fact, the purchaser might not want this type of loose arrangement but would prefer something more binding and businesslike. The transaction might be handled more satisfactorily through the issuance of a commercial letter of credit, which is a written statement on the part of a bank to an individual or firm guaranteeing that the bank will accept and pay a draft, up to a specified sum, if presented to the bank in accordance with the terms of the letter of credit. When a commercial letter of credit is issued, both seller and purchaser are protected; the type and condition of the goods are specified, and the credit of the bank has been substituted for that of the purchaser whose financial standing is not known to the seller. Much of our international trade is financed on this basis.

Many Americans who travel abroad demand the foreign banking services of a commercial bank. Although travelers might want to convert a few dollars into a foreign currency, they would probably purchase traveler's letters of credit or traveler's checks. The financing of foreign trade and travel by commercial banks contributes to a freer flow of trade between nations and at lower prices than if these services did not exist. As foreign trade has increased throughout the world, so have the foreign banking services of commerical banks.

Trust Services

Increased incomes have made possible the accumulation of wealth, which, in turn, has contributed to the growth of the trust services of commercial banks. Individuals who have accumulated an estate, even of moderate size, have an interest in providing for the distribution of the assets before death. Many of these individuals have made wills and have asked trust departments to act as executor. Moreover, many of these wills have provided for the creation of personal trusts under which trust departments have the responsibility of investing and caring for the funds and distributing the proceeds as established by the trust agreement.

Trust departments provide many services for corporations. One such service is the administration of pension and profit-sharing plans, which have grown rapidly in recent years. In addition to this important function, trust departments serve as trustees in connection with bond issues and as transfer agents and registrars for corporations. They may also administer sinking funds and perform other activities associated with the issuance and redemption of stocks and bonds.

Safekeeping of Valuables

The safekeeping of valuables is one of the oldest services provided by commercial banks. They have vaults that are difficult to enter even by the best of burglars and have established a record of proper custody. The protection of valuables falls into two areas or departments of a bank: safe deposit boxes and safekeeping. Safe deposit boxes are made available to customers on a rental basis. Under such an arrangement, customers have control of their valuables at all times. The bank merely provides the vault, the box, and the other facilities necessary for a proper safe deposit box operation. Finally, and most important, the bank controls access to the vault; that is, the bank guarantees that the customer who has rented the box or an authorized representative is the only one permitted access. The procedure consists of proper identification, double locks, and very careful supervision by cautious attendants. A safe deposit box provides a place for securities, deeds, insurance policies, and personal items that may be of value only to the owner. There is no way of estimating the value of all the articles in bank safe deposit boxes. How would a person place a value on the contents of another's safe deposit box: a love letter, a Purple Heart, a Congressional Medal of Honor, a wedding ring, a bit of lace, a rare coin, or a lock of hair? Items of this nature are sometimes found in safe deposit boxes when they are opened with the approval of legal authorities upon the death of a customer.

Safekeeping differs from safe deposit box services in that the bank has custody of the valuables and acts as an agent for the customer. Although the services as well as the items accepted vary considerably, safe-keeping is concerned primarily with caring for securities such as stocks and bonds. This department, for example, would be concerned with the holding of securities that have been pledged as collateral for a loan. Securities that are held in trust by the trust department of a bank would also be cared for in safekeeping. Relatively small banks that do not have facilities for the safekeeping of securities might use those of a larger bank. It is common practice for corporations, both financial and nonfinancial, that own securities to keep them with a bank. Sometimes holders of securities will ask a bank not only to hold their securities in safekeeping while they are away from their home for a prolonged period but also to clip and cash bond coupons and receive dividends and credit them to their accounts.

Brokerage Services

Many commercial banks provide brokerage services, that is, the buying and selling of securities for customers. Although this authority increases the range of financial services that can be offered by banks, it does not expand underwriting activities or include the offering of investment advice and research services normally associated with brokerage activities. The authorization to provide these services was introduced in early 1983, so there has not been sufficient experience with these services to make a thorough evaluation of their potential. Many banks have expressed an interest in providing such services, and it is fairly evident that bank participation in the brokerage business will be expanded in the future, especially by the large banks of the nation.

The need for experience and expertise in this field has prompted some banks and bank holding companies to purchase established brokerage companies. For example, Bankamerica Corporation, the holding company of Bank of America, purchased Charles Schwab Corporation, the largest discount broker in the nation (but later sold); and Security Pacific Bank purchased Fidelity Brokerage Services, Inc., of Boston, which in turn became a part of the bank.

The authority to provide brokerage services is a break with tradition in that the Glass-Steagall Act of 1933 prohibited this activity. The justification of the prohibition rested on the belief that excessive bank credit for speculative purposes, especially loans to brokers and to the public for carrying securities in the 1920s, was a cause of the Great Depression as well as of many of the bank failures that the nation experienced in the early 1930s. All of the provisions of the Glass-Steagall Act have not been repealed, which means that banks at the moment do not possess all the powers normally exercised by investment bankers. The act separated commercial banking from investment banking in that banks were denied the authority to underwrite securities issued by private corporations and revenue bonds of state and local governments. Banks, however, have for many years had the authority to underwrite general obligation bonds of state and local governments and U.S. government securities. The recent authorization regarding brokerage services does not liberalize the underwriting authority of banks, although there is considerable interest on the part of banks in underwriting municipal revenue bonds and other securities. However, as the banking industry is further deregulated, we are likely to see a liberalization of the restrictions surrounding the investment banking activities of commercial banks.

A BRIEF LOOK AT ASSETS AND LIABILITIES

Many of the functions of commercial banking can be illustrated by reviewing the major assets and liabilities of all insured commercial banks of the nation presented in Table 1-1; in fact, much of the subject matter of the following chapters can be highlighted by examining these items. Of the *assets* shown in this table, the entry "Cash and due from depository institutions," which accounted for nearly 12 percent of total assets, includes a variety of items such as currency and coin kept in banks' vaults for customers who need cash for the usual small transactions. Because of the protective measures that must be observed, banks keep the amount of coin and currency to a minimum and rely when possible on the various Federal Reserve banks as a source of supply. Large banks in some areas of the country serve as warehouses for smaller banks. Included in this item are checks drawn on other banks that have been presented to the bank by depositors or other banks for payment. Through a clearing process provided by the correspondent banking system and the Federal Reserve System, these checks are routed to the drawee banks and the paying bank is finally reimbursed. Banks usually refer to this important category of bank assets as *float*. Steps are being taken to reduce the amount of float in the commercial banking system. As the electronic transfer of funds becomes more common, this sizable figure will be reduced substantially.

Banks are required to carry with a Federal Reserve bank reserves equal to a certain percentage of their time and demand deposits, and these reserves must be in the form of cash in the vault or deposits. Banks may also carry balances with other commercial banks commonly referred to as correspondent banks. Banks that provide international banking services carry accounts with foreign banks just as domestic banks for the same reasons carry deposits with larger city correspondent banks.

Approximately 16 percent of all bank assets are invested in securities—of which there are several categories—that banks own for income and liquidity. U.S. Treasury securities represent the direct debt of the United States and are considered by banks and regulatory authorities as prime investments. U.S. Treasury securities account for about 40 percent of the securities portfolio of all banks. Agency securities are those issued by the various agencies of the federal government, such as the Federal Home Loan Bank and the Federal Farm Credit Bank. State and local issues account for about one-third of the investment securities of commercial banks. As the name implies, these securities are issues of state and local

TABLE 1-1 Assets and Liabilities of FDIC-Insured Commercial Banks, December 31, 1986 (in millions of dollars)

Assets
Cash and due from depository institutions	$ 379,153
Securities	485,031
Federal funds sold and securities purchased under agreement to resell	139,301
Loans and leases, total	1,727,776
Plus: allowance for losses	28,937
unearned income	16,242
Loans and leases, gross	1,722,850
Commercial and industrial	600,858
Real estate	515,317
Loans to individuals	335,737
All other	320,938
Bank premises and fixed assets	42,634
Other real estate owned	9,126
All other assets	162,021
Total	$2,941,119

Liabilities

Deposits
Individual, partnerships, and corporations	$1,753,849
U.S. government	5,323
State and political subdivisions	104,922
Deposits in foreign offices	313,795
All other	105,573
Total	$2,283,462

Deposits by type
Demand deposits	$ 510,747
Savings deposits	712,386
Time deposits	746,531
Total	$1,969,664

Deposits by purpose
Transaction accounts	$ 685,997
Nontransaction accounts	1,283,670
Total	$1,969,667

Federal funds purchased and securities sold under agreement to repurchase	$ 248,383
Liability on acceptances outstanding	40,441
Subordinated notes and debentures	16,912
All other liabilities	169,505
Total Liabilities	$2,758,708
Total equity capital	182,329
Total Liabilities and Equity Capital	$2,941,119

NOTE: Details may not add to totals because of rounding.

SOURCE: Federal Deposit Insurance Corporation, *Annual Report, 1986.*

governments, such as schools, counties, and cities. Banks are attracted to these securities because they normally provide a higher after-tax yield than do U.S. government securities. Two of the following chapters are devoted to the investment activities of commercial banks. "Other securities" include those issued by the International Development Bank, the World Bank, and similar institutions. Banks frequently underwrite general obligation securities of state and local governments, make a market in such issues, and sell them to customers, including other banks; hence, the term "Trading account securities." The item "Corporate stock" includes the amount of stock held in the Federal Reserve banks by member banks and other stocks that banks have acquired through foreclosure.

"Federal funds sold and securities purchased under agreement to resell" arise from the sale of excess reserves of member banks held in the Federal Reserve System. These represent funds purchased by banks that are short of required reserves and have decided to buy funds in the federal funds market rather than sell securities or call loans to correct their reserve position. One method of selling (lending) federal funds is to purchase securities under a repurchase agreement from a bank that needs funds. Under such agreements the borrower of the funds (seller of the securities) agrees to repurchase the securities at a specified price on a specified date. Management of the liquidity position of a commercial bank is important, as is the management of the investment portfolio, both of which are discussed in later chapters.

"Loans" account for the largest percentage of bank assets. There are many types of loans as the student will realize after reading the chapters on lending. Here they have been classified into only four categories. From the total amount of commercial and industrial loans, it is fairly obvious why we refer to banks as commercial banks. Lending to business has been the major lending activity from the beginning of banking. Real estate and consumer lending have increased over the years, however. In Table 1-1, the "Allowance for losses" shows the amount set aside to cover potential losses. "Unearned income" on loans arises when the amount of the loan recorded on the books of the bank includes the interest on the loan as well as the amount advanced to the borrower. As interest is earned and loan payments received, appropriate amounts are transferred from unearned income to current income.

"Bank premises and fixed assets" includes the depreciated value of bank buildings, furniture, fixtures, and various pieces of equipment necessary for the bank's operation. Some banks lease part of their equipment, such as computers, and some lease their building or buildings. This is especially true of banks in the larger cities that are housed in very large buildings, the cost of which may exceed the capital account that serves as a limit on the amount of assets that can be invested in real estate. Unless special permission is granted, a bank can invest in bank premises only an amount equal to its capital stock. "Other real estate owned" includes such items as parking lots. "All other assets" include a multitude of items that do not fit into the above categories, such as income accrued but not collected and prepaid expenses.

By far the largest *liability* of commercial banks is deposits. In the table, deposits are listed according to ownership and by type. The greatest proportion of bank deposits is owned by individuals and business firms. "Deposits in foreign offices" includes deposits of American individuals and business firms who have need for such deposits abroad in their business dealings and the deposits of foreigners who have similar needs. "Demand deposits," as the name implies, are deposits that are withdrawable on demand. Some identify these deposits as checking deposits, meaning that they are normally withdrawn by the use of a bank check. "Savings deposits" are the most common consumer type of savings account and are frequently called passbook savings. These deposits can normally be withdrawn anytime, but technically a waiting period could be imposed since banking rules and regulations provide for this treatment. "Time deposits" may take several forms and are for stated periods of time. Time deposits may be held by individuals, corporations, partnerships, or governments and are usually in larger denominations than savings deposits. Time deposits are also known as certificates of deposits or, simply, CDs. They are normally evidenced by a certificate rather than a passbook. The deposits in foreign branches and international subsidiaries are both demand and time deposits, but the breakdowns are not indicated in Table 1-1.

Bank deposits are frequently classified as "transaction accounts" and "nontransaction accounts." As the term implies, transactions accounts are those that are readily available to owners to be used in the settlement of accounts. Obviously those that are classified as nontransaction accounts are not immediately available for that purpose. This classification of deposits is very similar to the classification by type. The major difference is that transaction accounts not only include demand deposits but those that earn interest and are also immediately available for the settlement of accounts.

"Federal funds purchased and securities sold under agreement to repurchase" is the opposite of the item "Federal funds sold and securities purchased under agreement to resell" under assets. The reason for funds purchased being larger than funds sold is that these transactions occur not only with domestic commercial banks but also with brokers and dealers in securities as well.

"Liability on acceptances outstanding" includes those letters of credit and time drafts that banks have issued in favor of customers primarily involved in foreign trade. These instruments will be discussed in greater detail in the chapter on international banking. Letters of credit are sometimes issued to domestic firms to support some special type of credit. A business firm might, for example, issue commercial paper and ask a bank to extend to it a letter of credit that would be used only in the event the funds were not available to redeem the commercial paper at its due date. In this example the bank might never advance any funds but the promise to do so would increase the credit strength of the business firm; consequently, such an arrangement would result in a more favorable rate on the commercial paper. "Subordinated notes and debentures" includes debt instruments issued by banks, a portion of which is considered by regulatory authorities as part of bank capital. This subject will be covered in detail in Chapter 7. "All other liabilities" includes a variety of items, such as expenses accrued and unpaid, minority interest in consolidated subsidiaries, and deferred income taxes.

"Equity capital" in Table 1-1 represents the sum of preferred and common stock outstanding, surplus, undivided profits, reserve for contingencies, and other capital reserves.

COMPETITIVE ENVIRONMENT

Although commercial banks have always operated in a competitive environment, in recent years the competition has become even more intense. In fact, competitive forces due to technological, demographic, and regulatory changes will very likely contribute to changes in the services offered by banks, reduce the role of banks in the financial system, and alter the structure of commercial banking. Competitive pressures in the 1980s have adversely affected the performance of commercial banks. This fact was recognized by a recent study made by the Federal Deposit Insurance Corporation:

> It has become increasingly apparent that our banking system is in need of major reform. The rapidly changing environment, in combination with the existing restrictions on banking activities, has resulted in the inability of banks to remain competitive players in our financial system. This has been characterized as a form of banking crisis—not like the type that occurred during the early 1930s, but one that will slowly erode the viability of banks and ultimately lead to a weak and noncompetitive system.[2]

Commercial banks face competition from a variety of sources, not only from the long-established *thrift institutions*[3] but from sales and consumer finance companies as well. Relatively new competition now comes

---

[2] Federal Deposit Insurance Corporation, *Mandate for Change: Restructuring the Banking Industry*, Staff Study (Washington, D.C., September 21, 1987).

[3] Thrift institutions include savings and loan associations, mutual savings banks, and credit unions.

from brokerage houses that offer *money market accounts*,[4] retail concerns such as Sears, Roebuck that have entered the consumer finance field, and American Express, which provides traveler's checks, cash, and credit to those who carry what was once considered an entertainment and travel card only. In addition to these activities, Sears, Roebuck acquired the brokerage firm of Dean Witter & Co., and American Express purchased the brokerage firm of Shearson Hammill. Many of these competitors operate nationally, whereas banks for the most part have been restricted to operating within one state. Merrill, Lynch, Pierce, Fenner & Smith, for example, has outlets throughout the nation that can accept money market accounts and offer cash management services, and Sears has nearly 1,000 retail stores and 3,000 sales offices through which various financial services can be provided. American Express has offices in all major cities of the country.

This new competition appeared in the late 1970s, but it was not until the early 1980s that Congress responded to the demands of commercial banks for a "more level playing field" and permitted banks to offer money market accounts and brokerage services. As a result of these important developments, competition will intensify in the financial sector, and there will likely be an increasing demand for the banking industry to engage in interstate banking.

For most of the nineteenth century and until the Great Depression of the 1930s, banks enjoyed a near monopoly in the financial sector since they were the only financial institutions that offered demand deposits, and savings of individuals and business firms had not attained their present position of importance. To be sure, there were savings banks and savings and loan associations, but their impact on the financial sector was less significant than that at the present time. Banks were considered to be local in nature and subject to state law as far as location was concerned. They were protected from each other in that new banks were not chartered unless it could be shown that existing banks would not be adversely affected. Moreover, before a charter was forthcoming, promoters of a new bank had to prove that the new bank would be financially successful in a relatively short time.

The role of banks was influenced by a series of laws, some of which were enacted in the depression of the 1930s, that imposed place, price, and product restrictions on commercial banks. They were

1. The McFadden Act of 1927, which prohibited banks from branching across state lines unless states approve
2. The Glass-Steagall Act of 1933, which limited the securities activities of

---

[4] Money market accounts are diversified and highly liquid portfolios of investments in short-term securities such as U.S. government securities, certificates of deposit, bankers' acceptances, and prime commercial paper.

commercial banks, banned interest payments on demand deposits, gave the Federal Reserve System the right to set reserve requirements, and prohibited interest payments on savings and time deposits in excess of those established by the regulatory authorities (Regulation Q)

3. The Banking Act of 1933, which restricted banks from underwriting and dealing in securities except for U.S. government securities and general obligation bonds of state and local governments

4. The Douglas Amendment of 1956, which banned bank holding companies from purchasing banks in another state

Some of these restrictions have been removed in the last few years, and even greater relaxation may occur in the future. As we shall see, the McFadden Act has been bypassed to some degree, and Regulation Q, which established maximum interest rates that could be paid on time and savings deposits, has been removed. The provision of the Douglas Amendment has also been bypassed by state legislation. The major restrictions that still exist and that bankers are demanding Congress remove, are the provisions of the Glass-Steagall Act that separate the activities of commercial banking from investment banking.

Several factors have contributed to the recent increase in competition. Economic forces as every student knows have a sharp impact on established patterns of economic behavior. The volatility that has characterized our economy in recent years has altered the market for financial services. Although low rates of inflation were the norm throughout the 1950s and 1960s, they were considerably higher in the 1970s. During the 1950s, the average growth rate in the consumer price index was 2.1 percent followed by a 2.7 percent rise in the 1960s. In the 1970s, however, consumer prices rose at a 7.8 percent rate, and in the early 1980s double-digit rates were not uncommon.

Inflation had a profound impact on interest rates. By the early 1980s, long-term corporate bond rates were nearly triple the level of ten years earlier, and the bank prime rate rose to nearly 21 percent compared with a level of approximately 7 percent ten years before. High inflation and interest rates and the expectation of a continuation of an upward trend altered the public's demand for savings and investments. Declines in the savings rate occurred as more and more people discovered that their savings were being depleted by inflation. When the market rate of interest exceeded the rate that banks and thrift institutions were permitted to pay, *disintermediation* occurred.[5] Money market funds and direct investments in money market instruments have been the chief beneficiaries of disintermediation since such funds in the past have yielded two or three times the amount paid by banks and thrift institutions on passbook savings accounts.

---

[5] Disintermediation occurs when depositors take their funds out of savings accounts in banks and thrift institutions and invest them in higher-yielding assets.

Demographics and changes in consumer preferences cannot be overlooked when evaluating the transformation of the financial services environment. The population of our nation has maintained its mobility. This fact plus the economic forces mentioned have contributed to a clientele that is not tied to any financial institution. Convenience and location of financial services seem to be uppermost in the minds of many customers. People are not "turned on," it seems, by the bank advertisements of many years ago that emphasized the fact that the bank was "friendly." Banks use computers and computers deal in numbers; unfortunately, many think of themselves as numbers in the eyes of a financial institution. Personal attachment and allegiance appear less strong today; hence the increased shopping for financial services. Moreover, with high rates of inflation and interest, the rates paid on deposits and charged on loans become quite important in selecting a financial institution. Nonprice competition strategies such as advertising and professional competence appear to be less attractive to consumers than in past years.

The many changes that have occurred in the area of financial services have also contributed to greater competition among financial institutions. The use of computer systems (in house and/or services from other banks and nonbanking firms) has become available to almost every financial institution in the nation. Such devices have reduced the cost of providing various financial services and have made possible competitive pricing. Because of demographic shifts in the nation, branching and drive-in banking were looked upon for many years as great innovations. To be sure, they were; but some observers now contend that this "brick and mortar" system of providing banking services may be on the decline. Increased attention is being placed on the automated teller machine (ATM), which has become a very popular way of offering banking services. ATMs can be located economically in a number of places, such as shopping centers, airports and other transportation centers, and recreation facilities, assuming that regulatory authorities permit off-premises location. Point-of-sale (POS) terminals are now a reality, although the adoption of this new technology has not spread rapidly. POS facilities provide for a transfer of funds from a purchaser to the seller at the checkout counter immediately. It indeed has several important advantages over the use of cash and checks. It reduces the need to carry substantial amounts of cash, eliminates float (which purchasers may not like), reduces the use of paper, and eliminates the acceptances of checks that might be drawn on insufficient funds.

Bank credit cards have proved to be a desirable way of transferring funds and securing credit, and it is now possible for any bank to participate in a credit card program through a licensing arrangement with a major credit card. Credit cards are not, however, limited to commercial banks, since other financial institutions provide this service.

The "videotex revolution" that seems to be sweeping the country has an applicability to banking. In fact, national and regional shared networks of electronic banking machines are now being tested. If such programs prove to be feasible and economical, people can not only play video games but, with the flick of a switch or the push of a few buttons, can bank and pay bills from the comfort of their living rooms.

Electronic devices are available not only to banks but to all financial institutions. To be sure, costs will be an important factor in the extensive use of this innovation. However, from past experience with the introduction and use of computers, costs of home banking will very likely decline and make possible the widespread use of this new technique. This, of course, will contribute to increased competition not only among banks but between the banking industry and other financial sectors of the nation.

It is interesting to review how the financial system has changed over the years. Financial services of all kinds have been provided by individuals and commercial enterprises since ancient history. It was not uncommon for these to be furnished in conjunction with other activities. In the last few centuries some business firms began to specialize and supply only financial services. Later the offerings of these were narrowed even more, and firms started to provide only one kind of service. Insurance is a classic example. Home mortgage lending became a special type of financial service, as was consumer lending and brokerage services. Commercial banking was also a special type of financial service, and for many years banks confined their activities to commercial lending.

Over the years these activities have been broadened. Banks expanded into consumer lending after the depression of the 1930s and entered the home mortgage market after World War II. During the last decade several trends have reshaped the financial service industry. Many of the specialized firms have sought diversification and now offer a much wider range of services. Savings and loan associations now offer consumer and commercial loans plus a variety of deposit instruments, and insurance companies have acquired securities companies, consumer finance companies, and banks. Nonfinancial companies have also entered the financial arena by owning consumer and sales finance companies and banks, both unrelated to their product line. It appears that we will experience a continuation of the present trend, and financial institutions will become more and more alike.

Deregulation of Banking

The belief that the regulation of business, which had been on the increase for the past half-century, should be reversed to foster greater economic growth culminated in some degree in the deregulation of several sectors of the economy at the beginning of the 1980s. The financial sector was one of them, along with trucking, the airlines, railroads, and brokerage firms. The Depository Institutions Deregulation and Monetary Control Act (DIDMCA) was enacted into law on March 31, 1980. It has been described by some as the most significant piece of financial legislation since the 1930s. Although it did relax many regulations, it did not completely deregulate the financial sector. The act includes a number of provisions that have had a major impact on the competitive position of commercial banks, the structure of the banking industry, and the performance of all financial institutions.

The major provisions of the act that have influenced the competitive position of commercial banks are the following:

1. Phasing in of reserve requirements for all federally insured depository institutions—savings and loan associations, mutual savings banks, and credit unions. Banks have been subject to reserve requirements for years.
2. Phasing out over a six-year period interest rate ceilings imposed on depository institutions (Regulation Q).
3. Allowing all federally insured depository institutions to borrow at the Federal Reserve's discount window.
4. Authorizing interest-earning checking accounts commonly called NOW accounts.
5. Pricing of Federal Reserve interbank services such as check clearing and collection, coin and currency, wire transfer of funds, Federal Reserve float, and use of automated clearinghouse facilities.
6. Preempting for three years state usury laws for business and agricultural loans in excess of $25,000 while allowing any state to exempt itself at any time.
7. Authorizing state-chartered depository institutions to make any loan at 1 percent above the Federal Reserve discount rate regardless of state usury laws and without permission for state exemption.
8. Authorizing savings and loan associations to engage in credit card operations, exercise trust powers, and make consumer loans; expanding their authority to make real estate, acquisition, development, and construction loans.
9. Authorizing federal mutual savings banks to make commercial, corporate, and business loans and to accept demand deposits in connection with commercial, corporate, and business loan relationships. They were also authorized to make consumer loans and offer trust services.

The nature of financial institutions has been changed by this piece of legislation. Since early in the nineteenth century, the chartering of financial institutions has been based on the idea of specialization. The types of depository institutions have provided the basic financial needs of the nation—commercial banks and thrift institutions. Commercial banks descended from the English commercial bank, which can be traced to the

House of Rothschild in France and the House of Medici in Italy. Historically, such institutions engaged in the financing of production and trade on a short-term basis. They did not nor were they supposed to engage in long-term financing such as the financing of plant and equipment and the purchase of corporate securities—stocks and bonds. As the debt of the nation increased, however, banks were permitted to purchase some securities, but they were expected to concentrate on short-term securities that would contribute to the bank's liquidity.

Savings and loan associations and mutual savings banks are descendants of the English building societies. Traditionally, these institutions were supposed to place the bulk of their funds in mortgages. This was especially true of savings and loan associations. Mutual savings banks had greater flexibility in their investing, but they too were heavily invested in real estate loans. Mortgages are long-term instruments, but this kind of investing was considered appropriate, since the deposits of thrift institutions represented the savings of individuals and were expected to be stable and turn over very slowly. Although credit unions were from the standpoint of size less significant than savings and loan associations and mutual savings banks, deposits of these institutions were considered relatively stable and could be used to make both short- and intermediate-term consumer loans along with some secured by real estate.

The basic reason behind the specialization in lending by the various depository institutions was the different characteristics of their liabilities. The principal liabilities of thrift institutions came from savers and took the form of savings and time deposits. Such deposits were thought to be quite stable; consequently, it was expected that loans of thrift institutions would be long term. On the other hand, commercial banks were expected to rely primarily on demand deposits, which are highly liquid; therefore, bank lending should be relatively short term in nature. Banking legislation, regulations, and examinations reflected this view. Real estate lending as we have today was denied commercial banks for years, and investment activities were prohibited to banks in the Glass-Steagall Act.

As the economy changed, so did the depository institutions. Commercial banks were attracted to the rise in the amount of savings after World War II and aggressively sought savings and time deposits and made real estate loans. Thrift institutions offered transaction accounts and clamored for the right to make consumer loans, and in some cases, savings banks invested in municipal securities. Thrift institutions first experienced disintermediation in the 1960s and since that time have sought lending powers designed to improve their liquidity.

In the 1930s, commercial banks encountered a liquidity problem to which Congress responded by limiting their activities. In the last few years, the liquidity problem has descended on the thrifts, and again Congress has responded not by limiting their activities but by expanding their powers. Moreover, savings and loan associations have been permitted to merge more freely than previously and even to merge across state lines. DIDMCA liberalized their lending powers, and subsequent legislation has further liberalized their authority to make commercial, consumer, and commercial real estate loans. They have also been permitted to offer interest-bearing checking accounts to government agencies and to business customers and to offer money market funds. Savings and loan associations may also issue credit cards and exercise trust powers. Federal mutual savings banks were already permitted to invest in corporate and government securities. The new act, however, permits them to invest 5 percent of their assets in business loans and to accept demand deposits from these business borrowers. They too may issue credit cards and engage in trust activities. The objective of these broadened powers is to permit the earning assets of thrift institutions to reflect market rates more closely, which will, it is hoped, protect them from rising market interest rates.

It is fairly obvious that commercial banks and thrift institutions are becoming more and more alike. DIDMCA was an attempt to rectify errors of overregulation based on the belief that specialization was highly desirable. This approach was quite successful for many years. As long as the amount of inflation in the economy was minimal and interest rates were relatively stable, the system worked. In recent years, as the economy changed, trouble was encountered. The thrift industry that held a very substantial portion of its assets in low, fixed rate, long-term mortgages faced troublesome times as disintermediation mounted in the late 1970s and early 1980s. The severe earnings squeeze from the low return on assets and the high cost of funds resulted in huge losses in the early 1980s. Under such conditions, net worth and liquidity are placed in jeopardy.

A very important restriction imposed on banking in the early 1930s appears to be on its way out at the moment. This restrictive piece of legislation known as the Glass-Steagall Act prohibited banks from underwriting and dealing in securities other than municipal general obligation bonds, U.S. government bonds, private placements, and real estate loans. Underwriting and dealing in corporate securities—stocks, bonds, and commercial paper—and government revenue bonds were denied commercial banks primarily because of the belief that such activities contributed to the stock market crash of 1929 and the Great Depression of the 1930s. Although more recent evidence points to the restrictive monetary policies and the Smoot-Hawley tariff as the real culprits, this attitude prevailed in Congress for more than a half-century.

Because of a decline in income from traditional bank activities compared to permitted nonbank activities, banks began to smart under the restrictions imposed by Glass-Steagall and to urge the relaxation of the established rules. Banks, therefore, requested and lobbied Congress for the right to enter the underwriting and distribution of corporate securities and government revenue bonds. Commercial lending, which has long been a major source of income, has shrunk because many business firms have turned to the commercial paper market as a source of credit. This market has increased substantially from about $15 billion to $330 billion in the last two decades. The blue chip companies, especially, have found that this is a cheaper source of funds than loans at commercial banks. Consequently, relative to the total demand for credit by business firms, commercial loans at banks have declined, a development that has slowed the increase in bank income. Moreover, the income from underwriting and distribution of general obligation bonds of states and municipalities has also declined as this market has contracted. The shrinking of this market has been brought about by the opposition and defeat of many bond issues by voters on both the state and local levels. Local governments have turned to the issuance of revenue bonds as a source of funds for various activities, but banks are not permitted to underwrite and distribute these securities, hence another decline in income.

In its opposition to bank underwriting, the securities industry has brought up the age-old criticism of granting such powers to banks and bank holding companies, namely, it would result in a conflict of interest and self-dealing. To be sure, the potential conflict of interest is present in virtually all buyer-seller relationships, but with the advancements in management controls and information technology these dangers could be minimized. Moreover, bank regulators should be able to devise a monitoring system that would ensure proper performance.

There are some advantages in permitting banks and bank holding companies to enter the corporate securities market. Increased competition would likely lower the high underwriting fees, and it would probably ease the access of small business firms into the capital market. It might also contribute to more stable income of bank holding companies, as well as diversification.

Although Congress until recently has been reluctant to remove the provisions of Glass-Steagall, banks have found sympathy and help from the Board of Governors of the Federal Reserve System. In fact the Board of Governors has been in the forefront in recommending changes in the Glass-Steagall Act. In its annual report, for example, the board made the following recommendations:

> Plainly, the time has arrived to clarify and expand certain securities powers of bank holding companies, a matter that cannot be dealt with reasonably and rationally without congressional action.
>
> The Board believes that it would be appropriate, as a matter of good public policy, to permit bank holding companies to underwrite municipal revenue bonds, mortgage-backed securities, commercial paper, and mutual funds. The Board would also encourage the Congress to consider other financial areas appropriate for bank holding companies, including insurance and real estate brokerage and insurance underwriting.

The Federal Reserve would also urge the Congress to undertake hearings of other studies in the area of corporate underwriting—a process that the Board would be pleased to support. The issues in this area are more complicated because of the greater potential for conflict of interest. However, a substantial amount of such activity is already conducted by bank holding companies abroad, and the increased securitization of financial assets by banks and others requires fresh consideration of how banks may participate in that process.[6]

The Board of Governors has permitted a holding company to operate a banking subsidiary that traded securities and offered investment advice for institutional customers. This activity was challenged in court by the securities industry. In a very important decision by the United States Court of Appeals of the District of Columbia, the court held that this activity was not in conflict with the provisions of the Glass-Steagall Act,[7] and about a year later the U.S. Supreme Court let the decision stand.[8] The board also permitted nearly a dozen large banking organizations to deal in and underwrite four types of securities through subsidiaries, namely, municipal revenue bonds, mortgage-related securities, commercial paper, and securities backed by mortgages and consumer loans. This new line of business was limited to 5 percent of gross income. These permissive activities were upheld by the U.S. Supreme Court.[9]

In the meantime it is highly likely that Congress will soon remove the restrictions imposed by the Glass-Steagall Act since there is a very strong sentiment in Congress that from the standpoint of fairness and the free flow of economic activity, banking organizations should be permitted to enter the securities and insurance business. Consequently, we will probably see banking organizations with the power to underwrite mortgage-backed securities, commercial paper, and municipal revenue bonds. Banking organizations are likely to be permitted to deal in mutual funds and corporate bonds. Moreover, the sale of insurance may also be forthcoming. The underwriting of corporate stock might be withheld by Congress for a while because many of our lawmakers consider such activity to be surrounded by considerable risk.

When these powers are granted, we will probably see a cautious and orderly entry by banking organizations into offering these services since they require considerable start-up costs, plus capable and knowledgeable personnel with expertise in the fields of finance and financial markets. Because of these factors, we are likely to see larger banking organizations

---

[6] Board of Governors of the Federal Reserve System, *Seventy-third Annual Report* (1987), p. 177.

[7] *Securities Industry Association v. Board of Governors of the Federal Reserve System, et al.* No. 86-1412, July 7, 1987.

[8] Certiorari denied January 7, 1988.

[9] *Wall Street Journal*, June 14, 1988, p. 3.

expanding into these activities. With these added powers, the growth of the banking system should accelerate, the public should be well served, and profitability of the industry should be improved.

SELECTED REFERENCES

BAUGHN, WILLIAM H., AND CHARLES E. WALKER, eds. *The Bankers' Handbook*, rev. ed. Homewood, Ill.: Dow Jones-Irwin, 1978.

CANDILIS, WRAY O. *The Future of Commercial Banking*. New York: Praeger, 1975.

COMPTON, ERIC N. *Inside Commercial Banking*. New York: John Wiley, 1980.

FEDERAL DEPOSIT INSURANCE CORPORATION. *Mandate for Change: Restructuring the Banking Industry*. Staff Study. Washington, D.C., September 1987.

FEDERAL RESERVE BANK OF KANSAS CITY. *Restructuring the Financial System*, a symposium sponsored by the Federal Reserve Bank of Kansas City (Jackson Hole, Wyo., August 20–22, 1987).

McKINNEY, GEORGE W., JR., AND WILLIAM J. BROWN. *Management of Commercial Bank Funds*. Washington, D.C.: American Institute of Banking–American Bankers Association, 1974.

SIMPSON, THOMAS D. "Developments in the U.S. Financial System Since the Mid-1970s." *The Federal Reserve System*, Board of Governors of the Federal Reserve System (January 1988), pp. 1–12.

2

STRUCTURE
OF THE BANKING
SYSTEM

The structure of banking is determined by two basic forces—economic and legal. As in any market, the demand for the final product influences the number of sellers. The demand for banking services also affects bank size. In addition, government regulations have a great impact on bank structure. These regulations may be classified as (1) those that restrict the formation of new banks and (2) those that affect structure through the impact on bank organization.

EARLY HISTORY OF BANKING

Many factors have influenced our banking structure, among them war, economic crisis, constitutional authority, and fiscal leadership. During the colonial period, very little money circulated in the American colonies. Money brought from Europe by the settlers soon flowed back because of an unfavorable balance of trade. At the beginning of the American Revolution, there was less than $12 million in coin in circulation—a little less than $5 per person. Barter was common, and commodities such as corn in Massachusetts and tobacco in Virginia were legal tender. In 1690 Massachusetts printed "bills of credit" to finance King William's war, a practice that was adopted by some of the other colonies. These bills of credit became the first paper money introduced in the British Empire. A few "land banks," which issued bank notes secured by real estate, were established. The creation of these banks, as well as the issuance of bills of credit, raised the ire of the British Parliament, which insisted on "sound" money throughout the empire.

In 1782 the Continental Congress granted a charter to the Bank of North America. Doubts concerning the authority of the Continental Congress to grant a charter to a financial institution led the bank to seek a charter from the state of Pennsylvania and later from New York, Massachusetts, and Delaware. In 1784 the Bank of New York and the Bank of Massachusetts were organized. All these banks are still in operation, although under different names. A significant development was the 20-year chartering of the Bank of the United States by Congress in 1791. Alexander Hamilton, our first secretary of the treasury, promoted the creation of the bank, a proposal that started an important and lasting controversy as to the proper roles of the federal government and the states. Supporters of the bank pointed out the need for such an institution and held that Article 1, Section 8, of the Constitution, which states the "Congress shall have the power . . . To coin money and regulate the Value thereof, and of foreign Coin . . . ," was an implied power sufficient to justify the creation of a bank. Although the bank performed many functions, probably the most important was to regulate the money supply and thus protect the economy from inflation. Since the bank served as the depository for the federal government, it could present bank notes for payment in gold and silver to the bank of issue. In the performance of this function, the bank served as a central bank and regulated the amounts of money in circulation—a role not welcomed by those who favored an expanding money supply.

The First Bank of the United States grew and prospered and at the time of its expiration in 1811 operated nationwide, with branches in the major port cities. When the bank passed from the scene, the number of state banks increased rapidly, as did the amount of their bank notes. Unfortunately, the value of their notes declined even more rapidly. This situation plus the economic impact of the War of 1812 set the stage for the return of a national bank.

In 1816 the Second Bank of the United States was chartered. Although it performed the same basic function as the First Bank, it lacked sound management and became embroiled in politics; consequently, in 1832 President Jackson vetoed a bill that would have extended its life beyond its original 20 years. In his criticism Jackson referred to "the 'moneyed aristocracy' and described the bank as an 'odious monopoly' operating 'to make the rich richer and the potent more powerful.' "[1] Opposition to the bank was so great that the state of Maryland imposed a tax on

[1] Paul B. Trescott, *Financing American Enterprise: The Story of Commercial Banking* (New York: Harper & Row, 1963), pp. 27–28.

a branch of the bank to force it out of business. The Supreme Court held such a tax unconstitutional in the celebrated case of *McCulloch* v. *Maryland* and paved the way for an increasing role of the federal government in the area of money and banking.

Following the demise of the Second Bank of United States, there was a substantial increase in the number of state banks. In too many instances, unsound banking practices prevailed, including excessive issue of bank notes and little or no provision for note redemption. Commenting on the shortcomings of our monetary system, Senator John Sherman stated: "In 1862 there were fifteen hundred banks, the notes of 253 of which had not been counterfeited. The variety of imitations was 1,861; of alterations, 3,039; of spurious notes, 1,685."[2]

The very unsatisfactory condition of the currency, together with the needs associated with the financing of the Civil War, led to the passage of the National Bank Act of 1863. This act created the Office of the Comptroller of the Currency whose responsibility it was to charter and regulate national banks. In an effort to create a uniform currency and to help finance the war, banks were encouraged to purchase government bonds, which could then be used as the basis for the issuance of national bank notes. Further, a tax of 10 percent was imposed on all state bank notes in the hope that this would render such issues unprofitable and drive the state banks out of existence. Although their notes disappeared, the state banks did not, since by then note circulation was not essential to banking. Deposit banking had come of age; consequently, state banks remained in existence, which ensured a dual banking system.

Although relatively unimportant in number and in assets held, a few private banks—those that have neither a federal nor a state charter—have continued to exist. Most private banks have operated informally, often in conjunction with the operation of a general store. The National Bank Act and the tax levied on bank notes forced many private banks into the national banking system and restricted the activities of those that remained. At the present time, there are less than a dozen private banks in the nation, and the formation of others is not possible since all states now require newly organized banks to have a charter.

DUAL BANKING

A unique feature of the dual banking system is that both the states and the federal government have rights regarding the chartering, supervision, and examination of commercial banks. Several features of the system are responsible for its uniqueness. Although banking is recognized as a very

[2] Ibid, p. 47.

important industry nationally and one that affects interstate commerce, it is subject to state regulation. With the exception of a few industries, such as oil production and insurance, business activity involving interstate commerce is usually subject to federal regulation. Since both state and federal bank regulatory agencies are concerned with chartering, regulation and supervision, and examination of bank management, the dual system results in a competitive rather than cooperative federalism that is found in so many areas of government such as welfare and education. Another unusual feature is that banks may select the jurisdiction that will regulate and supervise them, a practice not found elsewhere in government regulation. Some delegation of policy decisions exists in the dual banking system, the most important of which is branch banking. Here the states have supreme authority in that they determine whether banks— state or federally chartered—can engage in branch banking. Despite these unique features, a considerable amount of cooperation exists between state and national banking authorities. This cooperation is found in several areas, including examinations and financial reporting.

The efficiency of the dual banking system has been debated for years. Some observers hold that it has created *competition in laxity* between national and state governments, that is, as one regulatory agency lowers its standards to maintain its membership or to attract additional banks, the other is forced to follow, since it is possible for banks to switch charters from one regulatory agency to the other. Some, however, look upon the dual banking system as desirable, believing that it reduces the possibility of overburdensome control. This point of view is expressed in a publication of the American Bankers Association, which states that "the historical value of dual banking lies in its ability to provide an escape valve from arbitrary or discriminatory chartering and regulatory policies at either the state or federal level."[3] This statement raises a question that is fundamental to our political system: Are many facets of our society overregulated? This statement also implies that equity and justice may not always be forthcoming from one regulatory agency and that some degree of competition in government is desirable. It has served as a check and balance system that has probably deterred unduly restrictive legislative and regulatory action by both levels of government.

Although the strength of the dual banking system is dwindling, it still plays an important role in our banking structure. It has survived because it was once a logical arrangement and over time has become entrenched. Once an industry becomes adjusted to a particular arrangement, vested interests develop and become surrounded by political clout, which makes change difficult.

---

[3] William J. Brown, *The Dual Banking System in the United States* (Washington, D.C.: American Bankers Association, 1968), p. 29. Excerpted with permission.

ORGANIZATION OF BANKING

The organization of banking has changed significantly in recent years. Before 1911, unit banking dominated the American scene, but over the years branch banking has become a much more popular form of organization. At the present time about half of the banks operate branches, and some form of branch banking is found in every state.

Unit banking exists when banking services are provided by a single-office institution. About one-fourth of the banking offices are unit banks. The presence of unit banking in our banking system is a result of tradition, law, vested interests, and the ability of this type of organization to meet the demands of banking customers. Because of inadequate transportation and communication facilities when the country was young, the most practical banking organization was unit banking. The First and Second Banks of the United States provided for branches, but few branch systems existed on the state level. When communities were more homogeneous and smaller than they are at present, and small business and farming were more dominant, unit banking worked well. However, with the economic interdependence of large geographic areas, the importance of transportation and communication, the growth of big business firms, a more mobile population, and increasing emphasis placed on location and convenience, unit banking is giving way to branch banking in many parts of the country.

Branch Banking

Branch banking exists when a single banking firm conducts operations at two or more places. The branches are controlled from one location, referred to as the head office. The branch offices may be located in the same city, county, state, and, if permitted, across state and even national lines. The head office and all the branches are controlled by the same board of directors and are owned by the same stockholders. The affairs of the branches are directed by their managers in accordance with the regulations and policies of the head office. Although some banking services are basic, the extent and variety performed at the branch level vary. Such activities as the management of the reserve position and of the investment account are performed at the head office.

Presently there are different degrees of branching throughout the country. Some states permit statewide branching; some limit branching to areas such as towns, cities, or the county in which the head office is located; and in some states banks are permitted to branch only within their home county and in contiguous counties. Nearly three-fourths of the banking offices throughout the nation are branches. The largest number of branches is found in California, where Bank of America leads all banks with more than 1,000 domestic and 100 foreign branches. To be sure, this number is quite impressive, but it is considerably less than the nearly 6,000 domestic and foreign branches of Barclays Bank of England.

NUMBER OF COMMERCIAL BANKS AND COMMERCIAL BANKING OFFICES

The growth of banks and branches is presented in Figure 2-1. The number of banks has remained relatively stable since 1945, but the number of branches has shown a noticeable increase in the past two decades. The shift of population from rural areas to urban centers has reduced the need for many rural banks. The productivity and efficiency of banking offices, resulting from their ability to handle an increased volume of business, have also reduced the need for banks. This increased productivity has stemmed from improved physical layouts, increased automation of operations, drive-in teller windows, the use of bank-by-mail facilities, specialization on the part of bank personnel, and improved organization and management. The introduction of electronic data processing machines is an example of an innovation that has greatly increased the efficiency of banks.

The most important factor responsible for the growth of branch banking has probably been a change in attitude toward branch banking,

FIGURE 2-1   Commercial Banks in the United States

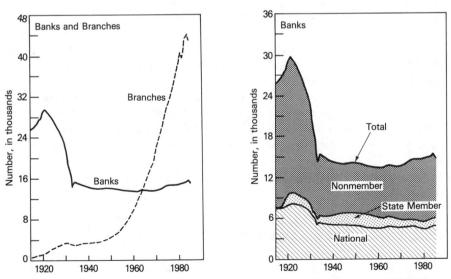

SOURCE: Board of Governors of the Federal Reserve System, *Historical Chartbook, 1986* (1987).

which has been reflected in the liberalization of state banking laws. Other factors include the growth of suburbs, the increased congestion of city traffic, and the movement of industry out of the central cities. Banks have followed the population and the demand for banking services. From information available on the granting of new charters and the establishment of branches, it appears that regulatory agencies regard new branches with greater favor than new unit banks.

The consolidation of banks through purchase has been responsible for a great part of this branch banking growth. The financial return on funds invested in a new unit bank has been lower than alternative investments; therefore, few unit banks have been organized in the past 30 years. Since it takes time for a newly organized bank to operate at a profit, investors have been reluctant to invest their funds in new banks. Established banks are in a better position to expand their banking services into a new community. Some communities are too small to support a full-service unit bank, but a branch bank can provide the necessary services since it can be operated at less cost than a unit bank.

The slight increase in the number of banks in recent years has all occurred in state banks. Although state banks account for two-thirds of the banks of the nation, they hold less than half of the bank assets. National banks have held the majority of bank assets since the mid-1930s.

Member and Nonmember Banks

Banks are frequently classified as *member* or *nonmember banks* to identify their relationship with the Federal Reserve System, which is optional for state banks but mandatory for national banks. This classification is less significant than formerly since all banks must now carry reserves on deposits with the Federal Reserve System in accordance with DIDMCA enacted in 1980. Less than 7 percent of the state banks are members of the Federal Reserve System. In general, state nonmember banks are relatively small in terms of assets and are found in the small communities and rural areas of the nation. A final classification is *insured banks*. As the term implies, insured banks are those whose deposits are insured by the Federal Deposit Insurance Corporation (FDIC). Practically all banks in this nation are insured banks. In fact, 98 percent of the banks are now insured by the FDIC, and these hold approximately 99.5 percent of the bank assets of the nation.

INCORPORATION OF COMMERCIAL BANKS

As outlined earlier, those who wish to engage in commercial banking must either secure a charter or license from the appropriate state agency or request and receive a federal charter from the Comptroller of the Currency. Certain rules and regulations must be complied with regarding board of directors, capitalization, quality of management, location, and so on, at either governmental level. For many years, it was not necessary in many states to receive government sanction to engage in banking. Those banks without a government charter were referred to as private banks. The major reason for requiring incorporation was to provide for closer, more efficient control of banking activities to ensure higher safety and liquidity standards. For a time, the issuance of bank charters was a prerogative of the legislative body on the state as well as the federal level. Under such an arrangement politics crept in, abuses were prevalent, and in many instances qualified persons were prohibited from entering the banking business.

Any group may now apply for permission to engage in commercial banking activities, but an application does not necessarily mean that a charter will be granted. The granting of bank charters has taken on the public utility concept; that is, banks are natural monopolies, and charters are granted only if banking services are needed and banks can operate profitably and in a safe manner.

CORRESPONDENT BANKING

Correspondent banking is an arrangement that exists among banks throughout the country based on the practice of smaller banks carrying deposits with larger banks in exchange for the performance of various services. This arrangement originated in colonial times and developed because of the need for redemption centers for bank notes. Later, as deposits became more acceptable and popular, the major service performed was the clearing of checks. As the banking system developed further, additional services were performed. This cooperative mechanism contributes to more efficient services, greater fluidity of funds, and higher banking standards. Two basic reasons support the existence of correspondent banking: banks find it impossible in many instances to provide certain services that they consider important, or, if these services are provided, the banks find them quite expensive. This is another way of saying that banks can purchase certain services more economically than they can produce them, primarily as a result of the economies of scale in the production of banking services. Although all banks derive benefits from correspondent banking, small banks probably derive the greater benefit.

Banks that receive checks drawn on other banks must arrange for presentation either to the bank on which they are drawn or to some location where the drawee bank maintains an account. Sometimes it is desirable for the receiving bank to keep an account with the paying bank, especially if the volume of checks is quite sizable. Although the Federal Reserve System provides a check clearing service for member banks, many rely instead on the correspondent banking system for this service since the process is faster in many instances. Only about 45 percent of the checks in the nation are cleared through the Federal Reserve facilities. For many years a bank had to be a member of the Federal Reserve System to use its clearing facilities, but in recent years this requirement has been relaxed, in part, to encourage membership. Nonmember banks are permitted to use the clearing facilities of the Federal Reserve Regional Check Processing Centers. If a nonmember bank wants to clear beyond the center, however, it must rely on the correspondent banking system.

In addition to clearing checks, correspondent banking provides some useful asset management services. Small banks encounter two basic limitations in this area. The staff of a small bank often has insufficient expertise, and the relatively small units—loans, investments, deposits, and the like—in which small banks are forced to deal tend to be expensive. It is not uncommon for them to be confronted with a loan request by a valued customer in excess of their legal limit. Such a loan in excess of the small bank's limit can be carried by a correspondent bank, however. The correspondent bank may also share a portion of its loan portfolio with its country cousin if the latter needs an increased loan portfolio and the larger bank is just about "loaned up." In addition, the correspondent bank may serve as an investment counselor and purchase, sell, and hold securities for the small bank.

The correspondent bank is also a source of information and help on various phases of bank operation and may dispatch one of its technicians to the smaller bank to aid in the installation of new machines and equipment or in the introduction of an improved method of operation. The correspondent bank with a foreign department may make its services available to a smaller bank that is called upon to perform such services only occasionally. The larger bank with an extensive credit department may share some of its information if asked to do so.

A very valuable service performed by correspondent banks is lending to banks to enable them to increase their reserves. This service is especially important to those banks that are not members of the Federal Reserve System. Correspondent banks that are located in the large money market centers of the country also assemble and make federal funds available to their smaller correspondents during tight money periods. During periods when small banks have excess reserves, the larger correspondent banks stand ready to purchase their federal funds. Since small banks sometimes find the demand for federal funds greater on the national level than locally and the rate on these funds is relatively high, their sale becomes an important source of revenue.

Correspondent banking relations are both regional and national.

Smaller banks usually carry an account with larger banks that are located at the center of the area's economic activity and are able to provide the services desired. These correspondent banks in turn carry deposits with banks in larger cities. Banks may also carry accounts with major banks beyond the immediate area if the latter are in a position to provide some special banking services. For example, banks in New York have enjoyed correspondent bank relations with many banks throughout the nation, in part because of their location in the heart of the export and import center of the nation. The correspondent banking system is not limited to banks within the United States, but includes foreign banks as well. Many U.S. banks that do not have branches abroad carry accounts with foreign banks to provide foreign trade services for their customers. Foreign banks carry deposits with American banks for the same reason.

For many years, payment for services of correspondent banks has often been in the form of a deposit, which can be invested in earning assets. Since it is difficult sometimes to measure the actual value of correspondent bank services, these deposits may be larger than necessary to cover all costs and provide a reasonable profit. Although deposits are still employed as a means of payment, a shift has occurred toward the use of a specific service charge that actually covers the cost of providing a correspondent bank service. The reasons for this change are the desire to control costs; greater reliance on computerization of certain functions, which has resulted in more accurate measurements of services performed; and improved cost accounting. Although actual payment may not be made for the various services, the cost is expressed in the amount of deposit balances at a stipulated earnings rate that would cover the costs. For example, if the services performed by a correspondent bank were valued at $400,000 and an earnings rate of 8 percent were agreed upon, a deposit of $5 million would be required.

When the Federal Reserve System was introduced, it was thought that correspondent banking would decline in importance or fail completely because the legal reserves of member banks were required to be maintained at the Federal Reserve banks. However, correspondent banking continues since it provides a number of useful services in our banking system.

SUPERVISION OF COMMERCIAL BANKING

Commercial banking is one of the most closely regulated businesses. Few businesses are examined as often and as meticulously by supervisory and regulatory authorities to determine whether they are operating in accordance with the various laws and administrative rulings. This close regulation and supervision reflect their quasi-public nature. Commercial banks hold deposits of millions of people, which may be requested on demand; they can withhold or make credit available to individuals and businesses; and they are closely involved with the nation's money supply. Because of these factors, banks are vested with a public interest and are regulated to ensure that these very basic functions are adequately performed.

Nearly every phase of banking activity is regulated by federal and state banking laws. The numerous regulations can be categorized as follows:

1. Restrictions on the right of entry into the banking business
2. Restrictions on expansion via branching and merging
3. Curbs on the competition for earning assets by prohibiting and restricting both the volume and composition of assets
4. Reserve requirements on deposits, most of which have been phased out
5. Requirements regarding bank capital

From the standpoint of regulation, banks can be divided into four groups: national banks, state member banks, nonmember banks that are members of the Federal Deposit Insurance Corporation, and noninsured nonmember banks. National banks are under the control of the Comptroller of the Currency, a part of the Treasury Department, and are subject to all federal banking laws and regulations, including those imposed by the Federal Reserve System and the FDIC. State member banks are subject to the laws and regulations of the state in which they are chartered and operate and to applicable federal laws since they are members of the Federal Reserve System and the FDIC. Nonmember insured banks are subject to state regulations plus the rules and regulations of the FDIC, and noninsured government nonmember banks are subject to state banking laws only. On the state level, the government officer responsible for the supervision and regulation of banks is known by such titles as state bank commissioner, commissioner of banks, and superintendent of banks.

The functions of banking supervisors such as the Comptroller of the Currency and Superintendent of Banks (or whatever title may be used on the state level) are

1. Passing on applications for charters for new banks, applications for branch permits, proposed mergers and consolidations, and proposed changes in banks' capital structures
2. Liquidation of closed banks
3. Issuance of regulations, rulings, and instructions to supplement or clarify legislation
4. Periodic detailed examinations of the condition, operations, and policies of individual banks
5. Taking corrective action
6. Counsel and advice to bankers
7. Compilation of reports and statistical data

Although these functions vary in some details between the federal and state governments, the general objective is the same: to establish and maintain a sound banking system.

The most important and effective tool of bank supervision and control is the bank examination. An examination is conducted by regulatory officials usually twice a year and may require anywhere from a few days to several weeks, depending on the size of the bank. The agencies that perform examinations are individual state regulatory agencies, the FDIC, the Federal Reserve System, and the Comptroller of the Currency.

The objectives of the agencies are similar, especially on the federal level. A look at the examination procedures of the FDIC will give us an understanding of this important tool employed by regulatory authorities. The FDIC conducts four principal types of examinations for the following purposes.

1. Safety and soundness
2. Compliance with consumer and civil rights laws and regulations
3. Proper performance of fiduciary responsibilities in trust departments
4. Adequacy of internal controls in electronic data processing operations

Great emphasis is placed on the examination for safety and soundness and is one that has been performed the longest. This examination consists of a detailed analysis and assessment of all the relevant characteristics of a bank's financial structure and operations. A composite rating is assigned to the bank after each examination. The factors that serve as a basis of this rating were adopted in 1980 by the five regulatory agencies represented on the Federal Financial Institutions Examinations Council (FFIEC): the FDIC, the Office of the Comptroller of the Currency, the Board of Governors of the Federal Reserve System, the Federal Home Loan Bank Board, and the National Credit Union Administration. These factors include the following:

1. The adequacy of the capital base, net worth, and reserves for supporting present operations and future growth plans
2. The quality of loans, investments, and other assets
3. The ability to generate earnings to maintain public confidence, cover losses, and provide adequate security and return to depositors
4. The ability to manage liquidity and funding
5. The ability to meet the community's legitimate needs for financial services and cover all maturing deposit obligations
6. The ability of management to administer properly all aspects of the financial business and plan for future needs and changing circumstances

To identify those institutions with financial, operating, and compliance weaknesses that might require special supervisory attention, each bank is assigned a composite rating on a scale of 1 to 5. A rating of 1 indicates the lowest level of supervisory concern and 5 the highest. Banks that receive a rating of 4 or 5 are generally referred to as "problem" banks. This is a way of saying that banks with such a rating are operating in an unsafe manner and are subject to failure. Such banks would be monitored closely and might be required to make some changes in operating procedures and financial management. Even though a composite rating may be desirable, it may not be foolproof, since a great deal of subjective evaluation is involved and the economic and financial environment can change rapidly.

Although a bank examination involves all aspects of bank operations, the most significant is the appraisal of assets, especially loans and securities. Assets that do not meet acceptable standards are placed in specific categories and must be treated differently from assets in general. Those, for example, that involve a loss must be charged off—that is, charged to a reserve account specifically created for that purpose—or deducted from the capital account. Sometimes only a portion of a questionable asset is charged off. Other questionable assets may be designated as below standard and require careful supervision.

The supervision and regulation of banks appear to be complicated because of overlapping state and federal laws and the many agencies with authority. Cooperation among the various regulatory agencies has reduced some of this overlapping, however, particularly in the field of examinations, a uniform classification of securities, and the exchange of information regarding chartering and branching. Regulatory authorities get different evaluations, which is highly desirable since examinations by the agencies are available to each other.

Compliance examinations are designed to determine whether or not banks are complying with a host of regulations imposed by federal legislation, including the Trust-in-Lending, Fair Credit Reporting, Fair Housing, Equal Credit Opportunity, Community Reinvestment, Home Mortgage Disclosure, and Fair Debt Collection Practices acts. An electronic data processing examination assesses every aspect of data processing operations. This is a very important examination, since about 90 percent of the banks have some part or all of their operations automated. Trust examinations are concerned with the detection of acts that could result in losses or surcharges, such as the violation of the governing accounting instruments involved in a fiduciary relationship, court orders, laws and regulations imposed by states and the federal government, and acts that deviate from the acceptable fiduciary standards.

A look at the history of banking shows that regulations are a product of financial crises instead of constructive planning. Examples are those arising out of the Civil War years, the period from 1907 to 1914, and that between 1927 and 1935. Although some changes were made, for the most part the structure of regulation until very recently has been the same as was established in the 1930s when the safety of the depositor was uppermost in the minds of legislators. It was not until the enactment of DIDMCA in 1980 that the regulatory climate was relaxed. The factors contributing to this change were high interest rates, tight money, and the disintermediation (outflow of funds from financial institutions into higher yielding assets) that was experienced especially by thrift institutions in recent years. Moreover, there is a ground swell of support for heavier reliance on market forces rather than additional governmental regulations. Changes in banking rules and regulations come slowly; however, because of the many technological developments that now appear on the horizon, changes may be more rapid in the future. Legislators should remember the words of the Hunt Commission:

> The Commission is concerned with achieving a regulatory framework that allows adequate freedom for financial firms to adjust to new technological possibilities, encourages new types of financial firms to emerge, and at the same time assures that resulting benefits will flow to the public.[4]

The regulation of commercial banks is based on several generally accepted objectives. First, the government should control the supply of the nation's medium of exchange. Second, since banks hold a large portion of the business and personal assets of the country, the safety of banks should be given high priority. Third, the government should prohibit anticompetitive market practices. Finally, the government should take steps to ensure that fair and equitable treatment is extended to those seeking credit.

To attain these objectives, the breadth of coverage and the intensity of bank regulation increased considerably from the 1930s until 1980. Not only banks but other financial institutions of the nation have been closely regulated. The result of such regulations was to carve out various areas of financial activity. Artificial differences were delegated by legislation not market forces. Regulations dictated how funds would be invested, and legislated interest rate ceilings influenced the availability and cost of funds. Recent deregulation departs from this basic philosophy by imparting greater freedom and reliance on the market system. The full impact of this legislation has resulted in changes, some probably unwelcomed, in structure and performance of the various intermediaries. The changes will, however, result in a more competitive, viable, and efficient financial system.

FOREIGN BANKS IN THE UNITED STATES

In addition to the domestic banks and offices in the United States, there were 259 banks operating 398 state-licensed branches and agencies by

---

[4] *The Report of the President's Commission on Financial Structure and Regulation* (Washington, D.C.: Government Printing Office, December 1971), pp. 8–9.

year-end 1986. Foreign banks also owned 19 Edge corporations and 11 commercial lending institutions and held a majority interest in 72 U.S. commercial banks. These foreign banks at year end controlled approximately 12 percent of the banking assets of the nation in slightly more than 1,000 offices. Japan has the largest foreign presence in the United States, followed by the United Kingdom. By far the largest concentration of foreign banks is found in New York City, followed by Los Angeles. The rapid growth of foreign banking in the United States has been brought about by the sale of business loan participations by domestic banks to foreign banks and, most importantly, foreign banks being permitted to engage in activities that are denied to domestic banks. The most important of these is investment banking. Foreign banks are not hampered by the finance-commerce separation that is imposed on U.S. banks. This subject will be discussed in more detail in the following chapter.

Since the early 1970s, the number of foreign banks in this country has increased substantially, and their assets have risen at four times the rate of the 300 largest banks in the United States. These foreign banks are concentrated in about a dozen states; about 90 percent of their assets are located in California, Illinois, and New York. These banks provide a wide range of services, including what we normally regard as commercial banking, investment banking, venture capital financing, and real estate development.

A *foreign branch* is a banking office of a foreign-owned bank that performs the usual banking services such as accepting deposits, making loans, and financing international trade. A *subsidiary* is not a branch but a separate entity and may be owned in whole or in part by a foreign bank or a bank holding company. It, too, may perform a wide range of banking services. An agency differs from a foreign branch and a subsidiary in the breadth of services performed. Although an agency may finance international trade and make loans, it does not have legal permission to accept deposits. The funds that an agency employs in the performance of its functions are derived from the home country. A *foreign affiliate* is not owned by a foreign bank, but the foreign bank and its affiliate may have common ownership in that stock of both may be owned by a holding company. A foreign affiliate may perform broad or limited banking services, depending on the permission granted by the state in which it operates.

For many years the entry of foreign banks was controlled exclusively by the states since no federal legislation had been enacted governing entry. Foreign banks were touched by federal law only if they became members of the Federal Reserve System or controlled a subsidiary bank, in which case the Bank Holding Company Act applied. The lack of a national policy regarding foreign banks gave them a competitive advantage over domestic banks, which in recent years became a matter of concern in the domestic banking community. Foreign banks were permitted to branch across state lines, a privilege denied domestic banks by the McFadden Act of 1927. They were also permitted to operate security affiliates to underwrite and sell stocks in the United States, an activity that was denied domestic banks by the Glass-Steagall Act of 1933. Finally, foreign banks have not been subject to Federal Reserve requirements imposed by the Federal Reserve System since they were not required to join.

Because of the unequal impact of the various banking rules and regulations, foreign banks have been in a position to enter choice markets. This is evidenced by the fact that half of the foreign banks operated in two or more states and approximately one-fourth of their assets were found outside their home state. Although foreign banks, like branches of U.S. banks abroad, are interested primarily in financing foreign trade, some have engaged in domestic banking, aggressively seeking deposits of U.S. businesses and residents and making loans domestically. Since foreign banks were not subject to the same reserve requirements as domestic banks, their lending costs were lower, which made them strong competitors for loans.

The rapid growth in the number of foreign banks and foreign bank assets culminated in the International Banking Act of 1978, which was designed to remove some of the competitive inequities that existed. A foreign bank must now select one state as its "home state" of operation and can establish a new branch or agency outside the home state only with that state's express permission. Although the new branch or agency located outside the home state may conduct full banking services in accordance with state law, the new branches may accept deposits only from nonresidents or from activities related to international trade financing. The new legislation provides that all banks shall be subject to reserve requirements imposed by the Federal Reserve System if the parent bank has worldwide assets of $1 billion or more. Although foreign banks operating in the United States are not required to be members of the Federal Reserve System, they may enjoy the services of the central bank on terms comparable with those of member banks.

This legislation is a step toward the removal of inequities. Foreign banks still have important advantages over domestic banks, however, because of a "grandfather" provision, that is, the exemption of existing out-of-state branches, agencies, and subsidiary banks. Moreover, state-chartered subsidiary banks of foreign banks are exempt from this new legislation. The existing operations of security affiliates of foreign banks are also "grandfathered," but new entries are prohibited. Although a national policy for the regulation of foreign banks has been developed for the first time, it falls short of equal treatment of foreign and domestic banks. This is probably not the end of close scrutiny and legislation in this area. Moreover, assets have continued to increase at a rate far in excess of the growth of domestic banks.

BANK HOLDING COMPANIES

The growth of bank holding companies has been phenomenal in recent years. In fact, their influence is one of dominance in the banking industry. At the end of 1986, for example, both multibank and one-bank holding companies held nearly 66 percent of the banks of the nation, and approximately 92 percent of the deposits. The banks owned by a holding company may be unit banks or banks with branches. Such banks retain their own boards of directors, responsible to the stockholders and regulatory authorities for the proper operation of their banks. The two general types of bank holding companies are the *multibank* and the *one-bank holding company*.

Multibank Holding Companies

A multibank holding company is defined by law as one that controls two or more banks. Multibank holding companies have existed since the turn of the century and have developed primarily in states that limit or prohibit branch banking. In essence, the same reasons that contributed to the growth of branch banking also contributed to the growth of group banking. Although group banking has become a significant force on the American banking scene, it has not developed without opposition. The critics have pointed out that group banking tends to lessen competition, is not sufficiently concerned with the needs of local communities, and is a subterfuge employed to evade state banking laws. Federal regulation was introduced in 1933, but it proved relatively ineffective. Consequently, additional legislation was enacted in 1956.

The Bank Holding Company Act of 1956 defines a holding company as one that controls two or more banks by the ownership of 25 percent of the voting shares or controls in any manner the election of a majority of the directors of two or more banks. The law prohibits new acquisitions outside the state of the holding company's principal place of business, unless the company is authorized to make the acquisition by the state in which it is desired. An important provision of the 1956 act, with certain exceptions, prohibits bank holding companies from owning voting shares in nonbanking corporations and from acquiring such interests in the future. Furthermore, they were given the choice of relinquishing all their banking interests with the exception of a single bank or relinquishing their nonbanking interests.

The Board of Governors of the Federal Reserve System is charged with the responsibility of administering the Bank Holding Company Act and in so doing supervises the formation and expansion of bank holding companies. Organizers of a holding company are required to have board approval before a holding company is formed, before a company can acquire over 5 percent of the voting stock of any bank, and before bank holding companies can merge. The act sets forth the five factors that the board is required to consider before granting approval of these actions:

1. The financial history and condition of the company or companies and the banks concerned
2. Their prospects
3. The character of their management
4. The convenience, needs, and welfare of the communities and areas concerned
5. Whether the effect of the acquisition, merger, or consolidation would be to expand the bank holding company system involved beyond limits consistent with adequate and sound banking, the public interest, and preservation of competition in the field of banking.[5]

In 1966 an amendment to the act clarified the last factor with the following language:

1. Any acquisition . . . which would result in a monopoly, or which would be in furtherance of any combination or conspiracy to monopolize or attempt to monopolize the business of banking in any part of the United States.
2. Any other proposed acquisition . . . whose effect in any section of the country may be substantially to lessen competition, or tend to create a monopoly, or which in any manner would be in restraint of trade, unless it finds that the anti-competitive effects of the proposed transaction are clearly outweighed in the public interest by the probable effect of the transaction in meeting the convenience and needs of the community to be served.[6]

The Bank Merger Act of 1966, discussed in the following chapter, included the same provision.

In 1970 several legislative developments contributed to the growth of multibank holding companies. The Bank Holding Company Act of 1956 was amended in a manner that erased for all practical purposes the regulatory distinction between corporations holding one bank and those holding two or more banks. Furthermore, some states liberalized their legislation as it applied to multibank holding companies.

Since bank holding companies range greatly in size, it is difficult to discuss a typical group system. Many bank holding companies control banks with aggregate total assets of less than $100 million, and many have resources in excess of $1 billion. Some bank holding companies operate in a local area only, some statewide, and some across state lines. Citicorp

---

[5] Public Law 89-356, Sec. 1, 80 Stat. 7; 12 U.S. Code 1828.

[6] Bank Holding Company Act of 1956 as amended by Act of July 1, 1966, Sec. 8(b), Stat. 239; and Act of Dec. 31, 1970, Sec. 103, 84 Stat.

of New York (principal asset, Citibank) is the largest multibank holding company in the nation and holds banks with assets of nearly $200 billion. The largest multibank holding company in regard to area covered is First Interstate Corporation of Los Angeles. At the end of 1986, this banking organization controlled 24 banks in 12 western states with 976 domestic offices that held $55 billion in assets.

The success of group banking stems in large part from the services provided by bank holding company offices to their subsidiary banks. Such services include auditing, investment counseling, the purchasing of supplies, data processing equipment, insurance, research on operating methods and procedures, advertising, tax guidance, personnel recruitment and transfer between banks, and advisory services for building and remodeling. These services, and possibly many others, permit a certain degree of personnel specialization and free local bank personnel to carry on other banking services.

Group banking does not have the advantages of mobility of funds, larger lending limits to one borrower, and availability of funds in excess of local deposits to the same extent that branch banking does. Neither does group banking offer the same economy of operations or the same specialized management to the extent offered by branch banking. The history of bank holding companies indicates that their opening of new banks is not as common as is their acquiring control of already established and successful banks. In group banking, less flexibility exists in management, so vital in financial institutions, than in branch banking. This is evidenced by the fact that holding company banking is not nearly so prevalent in those states where branch banking is permitted.

One-Bank Holding Companies

An important development in banking has been the formation of one-bank holding companies, which offer certain economic advantages as do branch banking and the multibank holding company type of organization. Faced with rising costs, bank management relied on several avenues to maintain profit margins in the 1960s. One of these was an increase in earning assets evidenced by a substantial rise in the loan-deposit ratio. This method cannot be used indefinitely since there is a point beyond which the loan-deposit ratio cannot be increased.

Another method of increasing bank earnings is to place bank funds into high-earning assets commensurate with prudent banking practices. This was done by bank management and took many forms, one of which was investing increasing amounts in municipal securities providing tax-free income. An excellent way of increasing profits is increasing loan rates. This was also done, especially in the late 1960s, as interest rates soared due to the great demand for credit and to monetary and fiscal policies. Of course, this method cannot be relied upon forever as a means of solving the pressure on profits. Although keeping expenses down is a worthwhile objective of any business enterprise, banks found this difficult to accomplish with rising inflation, especially in the late 1960s. The two largest expense items of commercial banks are salaries and wages and interest paid on time deposits, both of which have increased rapidly in recent years. The final avenue available to any business firm that desires to increase its profits is to increase its output, that is, produce more goods and/or services and hope that increased sales will result in additional income. Banks that formed one-bank holding companies were following this approach to the problem of profit maximization. In a sense they attempted to form a supermarket of financial services.

Banks were encouraged to broaden their financial services by a changing attitude and administrative rulings on the part of the Comptroller's Office, the regulatory agency that supervises national banks. In the early 1960s, a new Comptroller of the Currency adopted policies permitting banks to perform financial services that were "closely related to banking" if in so doing they did not impair their solvency and liquidity. This attitude was well received by most bankers as evidenced by the large number of banks that exchanged their state charters for national charters. The Federal Reserve System and several state regulatory agencies soon began to relax some of their restrictions. Although banks welcomed this change in attitude, the less restrictive environment was not as free as some had hoped, since many newly adopted services were challenged by politicians and various competitors on the grounds that banks were exceeding their authority. In many instances the courts agreed. This was especially true in the areas of travel and messenger services, service bureaus, and mutual funds. It was fairly obvious, therefore, that if banks were to broaden their services, a different organizational arrangement would be needed; hence the formation of the one-bank holding company.

The one-bank holding company involves the formation of a corporation with broad business powers. Stock in a bank is exchanged for stock in a newly formed corporation, and the bank thus becomes a wholly owned subsidiary. A bank might also be acquired by a tender offer. The holding company can then purchase stock in approved corporations that engage in activities from which banks are either barred or seriously restricted or organize new corporations to perform certain desired services. Firms that are owned and operated by a holding company may engage in such activities as factoring, data processing, and leasing. Although some of these activities could be performed by a bank, because of a multiplicity of regulations, these services are provided with greater flexibility by subsidiaries of a holding company. An example of regulations that restrict a bank in providing a particular service, in contrast to the holding company, is mortgage financing. If funds are needed for this service in addition to those derived from the deposit function, a bank could raise funds in the open market by the issuance of debt claims. These claims would have to be subordinated to the claims of depositors, however, which in all likelihood would result in higher interest costs to the bank and in turn to the borrower. However, a mortgage firm owned by a holding company could issue debt claims that would not be subordinated, leading to lower rates for borrowers, assuming competitive conditions. Moreover, such a separation would permit a mortgage subsidiary to engage in more risky lending than could a bank lending directly.

As far as services performed are concerned, one-bank holding companies in most instances are *congeneric* rather than *conglomerate*; that is, the subsidiaries of the holding companies provide services that are similar rather than unrelated. Bank personnel are knowledgeable in the area of finance, and although lending, leasing, and factoring are not the same, they are certainly similar. Customer demand has also contributed to banks broadening their services. If banks do not maintain their competitive position, customers will turn to other institutions for financial services. This is one reason banks entered the credit card field. Other financial congeneric businesses such as national sales finance companies have demonstrated a wide array of financial services that have proved to be appealing to customers.

In 1970 amendments to the Holding Company Act of 1956 reaffirmed the principle of separation of banking and commerce that was embodied in the 1956 legislation. The definition of a bank holding company was extended to bring in all companies (corporations, partnerships, business trusts, and associations) that directly or indirectly own 25 percent of the stock or exercise a controlling influence over the management or policies of one or more banks as interpreted by the Board of Governors of the Federal Reserve System. The Federal Reserve System is authorized to review all nonbanking subsidiaries of the bank holding companies regardless of the date they were acquired and to determine whether any of them are logically and closely related to banking.

One-bank holding companies are permitted to own or retain shares of companies whose activities the Board of Governors of the Federal Reserve System determines

> to be so closely related to banking or managing or controlling banks as to be a proper incident thereto. In determining whether a particular activity is a proper incident to banking or managing or controlling banks, the Board shall consider whether its performance by an affiliate of a holding company can reasonably be expected to produce benefits to the public, such as greater convenience, increased competition, or gains in efficiency, that outweigh possible adverse effects, such as undue concentration of resources, decreased or unfair competition, conflicts of interest, or unsound banking practices.

Activities of Bank Holding Companies

The Board of Governors of the Federal Reserve System has approved an extended list of activities in which bank holding companies may engage. Some of the most important are

1. Making and servicing loans
2. Industrial banking
3. Trust company functions
4. Investment or financial advice
5. Leasing personal or real property
6. Community development
7. Data processing
8. Insurance agency underwriting—credit insurance
9. Courier services
10. Management consulting to depository institutions
11. Real estate appraising
12. Money orders, savings bonds, and traveler's checks
13. Real estate and personal property appraising
14. Arranging commercial real estate equity financing
15. Securities brokerage
16. Underwriting and dealing in government obligations and money market instruments
17. Foreign exchange advisory and transactional services
18. Future commission merchant
19. Investment advice on financial futures and options on futures
20. Consumer financial counseling
21. Tax planning and preparation
22. Check guarantee services
23. Operating collection agency
24. Operating credit bureau
25. Printing and selling checks that carry coded information
26. Providing investment advice in connection with securities brokerage, subject to certain conditions
27. Placement of commercial paper to a limited extent[7]

One-bank holding companies may engage in any of these financial activities by purchasing existing businesses or by starting up the operation independently. Starting an activity is looked upon with greater favor by regulatory authorities, however, than is purchasing a going concern. If a one-bank holding company acquires more than 5 percent of a going

---

[7] Federal Banking Law Reports, Regulation Y.

TABLE 2-1 Bank Holding Companies Having a Presence in Pennsylvania

Holding Company	Activity				
	Mortgage Banking	Consumer Lending	Commercial Lending	Leasing	Representative Offices
Fleet Financial Group —Rhode Island	✓	✓	✓	✓	
Chase Manhattan Corporation —New York	✓		✓		✓
First Maryland Bancorporation —Maryland	✓		✓		✓
Security Pacific Corporation —California	✓	✓	✓	✓	
BankAmerica Corporation —California	✓	✓	✓		
Manufacturers Hanover Corporation —New York	✓	✓	✓		

NorWest Corporation
—Minnesota

Beneficial Corporation
—Delaware

BarclaysAmerican Corporation
—North Carolina

Bank of Boston Corporation
—Massachusetts

Citicorp
—New York

First Interstate Bancorporation
—California

Marine Midland Banks, Inc.
—New York

Midlantic Banks
—New Jersey

SOURCE: Paul Calem, "Interstate Bank Mergers and Competition in Banking." *Business Review*, Federal Reserve Bank of Philadelphia (January/February 1987), p. 11.

concern engaged in permissible nonbanking activities, it must first obtain the approval of the Board of Governors of the Federal Reserve System. The law requires that the board analyze the competitive effects of the proposal as well as a number of other public interest considerations, such as the efficiencies that would be forthcoming from such ownership and management, convenience to the public, conflict of interest, and undue concentration. A relatively sensitive area in an acquisition is the competitive aspect; if a proposed acquisition were to reduce existing competition or thwart future competition, the board would be reluctant to extend approval.

As more experience is gained from the operation of bank holding companies under the amended Holding Company Act, other activities may be added. There are some activities in addition to those listed earlier in which bank holding companies may participate. They may own shares in companies whose activities are closely related to the primary function of banking. These are functions that could be carried on by banks, including holding properties for the use of a holding company's subsidiary, conducting a safe deposit business, or liquidating assets acquired from the holding company or its banks.

Congress was concerned that unfair competition might arise from the expansion of bank holding companies into related areas and therefore added what has become known as the anti-tie-in provision. This provision prohibits any bank (whether or not it is a holding company subsidiary) from requiring a customer purchasing one of its services to obtain another service from the bank, its holding company, or affiliates. A bank is also prohibited from requiring a customer to refrain from doing business with competitors of the bank or its holding company affiliates unless reasonably imposed to ensure soundness in a credit transaction. This provision bars banks from packaging their services or tying one of their services to the activities of their affiliates. The only exceptions to this rule are transactions exclusively involving the traditional banking services of loans, discounts, deposits, and trusts. One-bank holding companies have entered many areas of financial activity, the most important of which are mortgage banking, consumer financing, factoring, and leasing. Despite the rapid entry into many areas and the successful operation of those endeavors, the assets of nonbanking affiliates account for less than 5 percent of the consolidated assets of bank holding companies.

An indication of the magnitude of nonbanking subsidiaries throughout the nation may be garnered from Table 2-1, which is a partial list of the out-of-state bank holding companies having a nonbanking presence in the state of Pennsylvania. Note that there were subsidiaries from nine different states and that the most popular activity was commercial lending, followed by mortgage banking and consumer lending.

CHAIN BANKING

Another form of bank organization is chain banking, which is usually defined as the control of two or more commercial banks by the same individual or group of individuals. Control may be accomplished through stock ownership, common directors, or any other manner permitted by law. Each bank that is a member of the chain maintains its own identity and has a separate board of directors. Although this type of organization has been around for years, comprehensive information about its size and operation is fragmentary, primarily because it is not regulated as are multibank and one-bank holding companies; hence, there are no published reports on chain organizations. There have been, however, some special studies on chain banking over the years that are quite helpful to students of banking.[8]

Chain banking was introduced in this country near the end of the nineteenth century, and most of the early development was found in the northwestern and southern agricultural states. Chain banking has expanded in states that prohibit branching and multibank holding companies. Banks that are members of a chain are relatively small, and the chain operates in a relatively small area. This has not kept some chains from moving across state lines, however. Usually chain organizations are built around a key bank that is considerably larger than the others in the organization. One study of chain banking in the Seventh Federal Reserve District,[9] a stronghold of this type of banking, showed that there were 86 chains, 70 of which were located in the states of Illinois and Iowa, both of which prohibited branch banking for many years. These chains controlled 322 banks, which held around $14 billion in deposits or 11 percent of the total deposits in the district. Although information regarding the performance of chains is not known, it appears that a philosophy of management, common goals, and objectives could be introduced via the board of directors. Moreover, banks within the chain organization that have personnel with special management techniques and expertise could share this with other members and thus increase the overall efficiency of the organization. Despite these possible advantages, one study in the late 1960s that examined the profitability of chain and nonchain banks revealed that chain banks were less profitable.

---

[8] C. E. Cagle, "Branch Chain and Group Banking," *Banking Studies*, Board of Governors of the Federal Reserve System (August 1941); Jerome C. Darnell, "Profitability Comparisons Between Chain and Non-Chain Banks," *The Bankers Magazine* (Spring 1968); Joseph T. Keating, "Chain Banking in the District," *Economic Perspectives*, Federal Reserve Bank of Chicago (September–October 1977).

[9] Includes the states of Illinois, Iowa, Wisconsin, Indiana, and Michigan.

NONBANKS

To define a nonbank we must first review the definition of a commercial bank. Technically, a commercial bank is a financial institution that accepts demand deposits and makes commercial loans and, because of these characteristics, is regulated by a bank regulatory agency. A nonbank is a financial institution that performs only one of these commercial bank functions—not both—and consequently is not regulated by a bank supervisory agency. Since nonbanks are not, in a technical sense, banks and are not regulated, they have been able to skirt the restrictions imposed on interstate banking. As would be suspected, nonbanks had their origin in the early 1980s when interstate banking became a burning issue.

Some bank holding companies formed nonbanks in an effort to get a foothold in another state where interstate banking was not permitted. It was also a way of gaining entry into the retail banking market. In fact, some commercial firms have formed nonbanks; Prudential Insurance Company, J. C. Penney, Gulf + Western, Beneficial Corporation, Merrill Lynch, Drexel Burnham Lambert, and Sears are examples.

Although the Comptroller's Office received applications for about 400 charters from nonbanks in the early 1980s, many bankers voiced their opposition to this type of financial institution and the concept was not fully accepted by regulatory agencies. This issue was settled by the enactment of the Competitive Equality Banking Act of 1987, which changed the definition of a bank to an institution that has FDIC insurance or accepts deposits and makes commercial loans. By extending to all FDIC-insured institutions, Congress in effect eliminated the chartering of nonbanks in the future.

QUESTIONS

1. If you had been a member of the British Parliament during the colonial period, what would have been your attitude toward the organization of banks in America? Would you have favored restrictions? What kind? Why?

2. Do you think a dual banking system is desirable or undesirable? Why or why not?

3. Discuss how the taxation of state bank notes by the federal government contributed to the organization of national banks.

4. How do you account for the difference in the size of banks in the United States?

5. If you were to recommend the type of banking the nation should have, what would you suggest—unit or branch banking? Why? Would you suggest more or less restrictions on entry? Why?

6. Why did correspondent relationships develop between banks? How would you evaluate the performance of the correspondent banking system? Would it be advisable to permit this system to perform many of the services that are now a responsibility of the Federal Reserve System such as clearance of checks, transfer of funds, safekeeping, providing the nation with coin and currency, and so on?

7. Why have governments chartered and regulated commercial banking? What are the objectives of bank supervision?

8. A multitude of recommendations has been made regarding the structure of commercial banking and how and by whom banks should be regulated. What would you recommend in these two areas?

9. From the standpoint of a free competitive market, how would you evaluate the International Banking Act of 1978? Explain.

10. Why the rise of multibank and one-bank holding companies? Do you consider these developments to be desirable? Explain.

SELECTED REFERENCES

BOARD OF GOVERNORS OF THE FEDERAL RESERVE SYSTEM. "Developments in Banking Structure, 1970–81." *Federal Reserve Bulletin* (February 1982), pp. 77–85.

———. "Financial Developments of Bank Holding Companies in 1981." *Federal Reserve Bulletin* (June 1982), pp. 335–340.

FEDERAL DEPOSIT INSURANCE CORPORATION. *Mandate for Change: Restructuring the Banking Industry.* Staff Study. Washington, D.C., September 1987.

FEDERAL RESERVE BANK OF CHICAGO. *Proceedings of the Conference on Banking Structure and Competition.* Annual.

———. *Toward National Banking: A Guide to the Issues.* Chicago, 1986.

FINE (Financial Institutions and the Nation's Economy). *Compendium of Papers Prepared for the FINE Study.* Books 1 and 2. Committee on Banking, Currency and Housing, U.S. House of Representatives, 94th Cong., 2d sess., June 1976.

"SYMPOSIUM ON THE FINE STUDY." *Journal of Money, Credit and Banking,* 9, no. 4 (November 1977), 605–661.

U.S. DEPARTMENT OF THE TREASURY. *The Report of the President, Geographic Restrictions on Commercial Banking in the United States.* Washington, D.C.: Government Printing Office, January 1981.

3

EXPANSION
OF COMMERCIAL
BANKING

Economic forces, constantly at work, contribute to changes in the commercial banking structure. On a systemwide basis, expansion is largely a product of how rapidly the policymakers at the national level allow the money supply to expand. If decisions in Washington, D.C., result in a rapid growth of the money supply, a concomitant expansion of the banking system occurs. The extent of the expansion that results at an individual bank depends on its own local economy, its competitive environment, and its objectives.

There are many other determinants of an individual bank's ability to expand. Economic activity quickens in some areas of the country and declines in others. Population increases and shifts. New business firms come into being, some pass from the scene, and others change location. Traffic patterns are altered, and business firms—including banks—that were once accessible may encounter difficulties in keeping or attracting customers. To increase earning assets and improve profitability, banks may change their organizational form. The avenues of expansion or structural change that are open to banks are merging, branching, and the formation of holding companies.

MERGERS OF COMMERCIAL BANKS

The two types of business combinations that are available to business firms in general are also available to banks, namely, *mergers* and *consoli-*

dations. A merger occurs when one bank ceases to exist and its assets are combined with those of another. A consolidation results when two or more banks combine to form a new one and the participating banks lose their individual identities. Most combinations in banking are mergers. Although the term "merger" has a technical meaning, it is used here, as it is in most discussions of the concentration of banking, to mean any form of combination whereby two or more operating banks are joined under a single management.

Reasons for Merging

Several factors motivate banks to merge. Cutting the costs of operation and increasing volume to increase profits are the two most important reasons. Population shifts to suburban areas stimulate expansion as banks make an effort to increase deposits and loans and thus increase earnings. Another reason for expanding is to diversify banking operations. Some banks engaged in wholesale banking—catering to large depositors and borrowers—branch out into consumer and other forms of lending.

The size of loan requests has grown, and since the size of loans to any one borrower is limited by the size of a bank's capital and surplus, banks have combined to increase loan limits. In this manner, old customers can be held and new ones attracted. The prestige associated with "bigness" has probably contributed to the desire to expand also. In states that permit branch banking, the purchase of a bank may be less expensive than setting up a new office, with its construction and promotional costs and personnel recruitment problems. The absorption of another bank may eliminate some competition also.

Banks that have agreed to be absorbed by larger banks have done so for a variety of reasons. Some have agreed because of difficulties in raising needed capital, and others to avoid failure. One very important reason has been the problem of management. Many small banks, realizing that competent management is not available to replace present personnel who may be nearing retirement age, decide to merge, consolidate, or sell to a larger bank. An attractive offer also motivates small banks to sell out to larger banks. The stock for small banks usually has a limited market and often sells at a price below book value. In addition, some small banks have conservative management, and as a result, growth is stifled and earnings are impaired. If stockholders exchange their stock for shares in the purchasing bank, often more diversified and progressive, they may enjoy a broader market for their stock and receive larger dividends. Competition from other banks and financial institutions has also encouraged some smaller banks to unite with others.

Although mergers occur every year, a very large number, approximately 1,600, took place during the 1950s. Most of the banks involved were relatively small institutions that became branches of the acquiring bank, but mergers did occur between billion-dollar banks, some of the largest in the nation. This increase in mergers caused some legislators to become concerned about the concentration of banking.

For many years, the task of making rules governing bank mergers was assigned to the various banking agencies, but no specific standards were established for exercising this authority. It was assumed that since banks were closely regulated, banking agencies would approve only those mergers that were desirable from the standpoint of banking competition and the needs and convenience of the public.

Because of the impact of bank mergers on banking competition, the Bank Merger Act of 1960 was enacted. This made all bank mergers involving insured banks subject to one of the three federal agencies. Mergers that would result in national banks were placed under the Comptroller of the Currency. Mergers involving banks that were to be state member banks were under the jurisdiction of the Board of Governors of the Federal Reserve System. If a bank were to be a state nonmember, insured bank, authority to merge would be vested with the FDIC. The act departed from previous legislation on bank mergers by listing criteria to be used in the evaluation of merger applications, but it did not assign relative weights to the individual factors. The factors to be considered were

1. The financial history and condition of each bank involved
2. The adequacy of each bank's capital structure
3. The merged bank's earnings prospects
4. The general character of its management
5. The convenience and needs of the community to be served
6. Whether the merged bank's corporate powers are consistent with the purposes of the Federal Deposit Insurance Corporation Act
7. How the merger will affect competition

In addition to these requirements, each agency was required in the interest of uniform standards to request a report from the other two agencies and from the attorney general on the competitive factors involved. The agency concerned, however, was not bound by these reports. Although there was nothing in the act that required or authorized the attorney general to make an antitrust attack if evidence indicated this should be the proper procedure, he was certainly not barred from doing so.

It soon became evident that the Bank Merger Act of 1960 was not only unclear but also confusing. The wording of the act was very general, allowing great flexibility. No time limit was set for the reports the various agencies were to file with the banking agency supervising a merger. No weight was given to the various criteria set forth. The role of the attorney general was not specific. It was not long, however, before bank mergers were to play a central role in our banking history.

Merging and the Courts

Since it was accepted that the various banking agencies would handle bank mergers, the courts were not involved in bank combinations of any kind until 1962. At that point the courts became quite active and remained so until about the mid-1970s. However, due to changes in banking legislation and bank markets, the courts are now considerably less active in bank mergers.

In a series of Supreme Court decisions,[1] it was held that banking is subject to the provisions of the Sherman Act of 1890 and the Clayton Act of 1914, the cornerstones of federal antitrust legislation. In the *Philadelphia* case, the first and probably the most celebrated case involving a bank merger, the Court ruled that banking was a line of commerce and that, even though a merger was approved by the federal banking agencies, it could be challenged under the antitrust laws. The Court held that the proposed merger of two large Philadelphia banks, which would have resulted in a single bank controlling 36 percent of the deposits in a four-county area, was sufficiently anticompetitive to be in violation of the Clayton Act. Thus banks were declared subject to the same antitrust rules as other business firms.

The Bank Merger Act of 1966, an amendment to the act of 1960, was enacted primarily to reconcile the differences between the courts and the banking agencies. The courts stressed competitive factors, while banking agencies placed greater emphasis on the convenience and needs of the public. It was a compromise between two views: that the antitrust laws should be rigorously applied to bank mergers and that banking agencies should have exclusive control of bank mergers. In this compromise the 1966 act assigned greater weight to the competitive factors than did the 1960 act. It provided, for example, that

> The responsible agency shall not approve . . . any proposed merger transaction which would result in a monopoly, or would be in furtherance of any combination or conspiracy to monopolize or attempt to monopolize the business of banking in any part of the United States.[2]

A review of a few cases, once the courts became active in bank mergers, is helpful in understanding the reasoning on the subject. In the first two cases,[3] the Court's decisions relied heavily on concentration

---

[1] *United States v. Philadelphia National Bank* et al., 210 F. Supp. 348 (1962), 83 S. Ct. 1715, (1963); *United States v. First National Bank and Trust Company of Lexington* et al., 208 F. Supp. 457 (1962), 84 S. Ct. 1033 (1964).

[2] Bank Merger Act of 1966, 80 Stat. 7; Public Law 356, 89th Cong., 2d sess., 1966.

[3] *United States v. Provident National Bank* et al., 262 F. Supp. 297 (1966), 87 S. Ct. 1088 (1967); *United States v. First City National Bank of Houston* et al., Supp. 397 (1966), S. Ct. 1088 (1967).

ratios as an indication of bank competition. In the first case, the merging banks accounted for only 14 percent of the commercial bank deposits in a market in which the five largest commercial banks controlled 71 percent, yet the merger was denied. In the other case, the market share of the proposed merging banks would have been 32 percent while the five largest banks in the area accounted for 66 percent of the deposits. In both cases, the district courts did not see this amount of concentration to be in violation of the antitrust laws. Two major procedural questions were answered in these early cases. The Court asserted that the Justice Department need only challenge a bank merger on the grounds of a violation of the antitrust laws. The Court was not required to prove a violation of the Bank Merger Act of 1966, and an opinion of a banking agency was not binding on the courts. The Court also ruled that the burden of proof that the convenience and needs consideration outweighed the anticompetitive effects rested with the defendant banks.

The first case involving relatively large branch banks was the *Crocker-Anglo Citizens Bank* case in 1967.[4] This case involved the fifth and seventh largest banks in California, where branch banking is widespread. The Court approved the merger on the grounds that the new bank would be in a stronger position to compete with the largest bank in the state. Before the merger, one bank operated in northern California and the other in the southern part of the state with some overlapping in only one county. After the merger, Crocker-Citizens was the fourth largest bank in the state.

A very interesting case, because of the competitive weakness of one of the banks involved, was the *Third National Bank* case in 1968.[5] The Third National Bank of Nashville, the second largest bank in Davidson County, wanted to merge with the fourth largest bank in the area, which held only 4.83 percent of the deposits in the county, a percentage that had been declining since 1960. If the merger had been allowed, the new combination would have held nearly 40 percent of the deposits of the commercial banks in the county. Prior to the merger, the three largest banks controlled 93 percent of the deposits. The lower court had approved the merger on the grounds that the bank being acquired held a relatively small amount of deposits in the area and that it was not a vigorous competitor because of the lack of aggressive management. In other words, the merger would not have resulted in weakened bank competition in the area. For several years banking agencies had approved mergers when one of the banks was in a similar situation. They had also approved mergers when

---

[4] *United States v. Crocker-Anglo National Bank* et al., 263 F. Supp. 125 (1966), 277 F. Supp. 133 (1967).

[5] *United States v. Third National Bank of Nashville* et al., 260 F. Supp. 869 (1966), 88 S. Ct. 882 (1968).

the acquired bank was in a floundering or failing condition. Although the acquired bank in the *Third National Bank* case was not failing, the district court had termed it a *stagnant* or floundering bank. Despite this description the Supreme Court denied the merger, pointing out that the defendant did not show that the gains expected from the merger could not have been attained through other means.

The Court has not been reluctant to reject proposed mergers of relatively small banks. This was evident in the *Phillipsburg National Bank* case, which involved two banks, each with deposits of less than $30 million, that when merged would control only 23 percent of the total deposits of a two-city area, while the remaining two banks controlled 56 percent. In deciding upon the relevant geographic area the Supreme Court considered the two-city area of Phillipsburg, New Jersey, and Easton, Pennsylvania, separated by the Delaware River.[6]

From these decisions, it is fairly easy to conclude that the test of convenience and needs of the public so long relied upon by banking agencies is a less powerful force than is the competitive factor in bank mergers. Moreover, the courts are not bound by the opinions of the banking agencies in their analysis of mergers. For many years, regulatory authorities would approve a merger if one of the banks were on the verge of failing. This is no longer true unless it is the only realistic solution.

The role of the courts in bank mergers has declined considerably in recent years and that of banking agencies has increased. The reason for these significant changes is that the antitrust standards, as applied to mergers and acquisitions, have become less restrictive because of the provisions of DIDMCA and the Garn-St Germain Act of 1982, both of which increased the powers of thrift institutions. Thrift institutions are now considered a part of the financial market when analyzing the competitive effects of proposed bank acquisitions and mergers. Moreover, the Garn-St Germain Act specifically permits the acquisition by out-of-state thrift institutions or bank holding companies of insured savings and loan associations, closed insured commercial banks with assets of $500 million or more, and insured savings banks with the same amount of assets that have failed or are in danger of failing.

The very narrow concept that banking is a "distinct line of commerce" has given way and, rightly so, to a broader interpretation of financial markets. This change in philosophy is well illustrated in the recent merger of Wells Fargo National Bank and Crocker National Bank in California, which was approved by the Board of Governors of the Federal Reserve System and the Office of the Comptroller of the Currency. This was the largest merger ever and joined two banks with combined assets of

---

[6] *United States v. Phillipsburg National Bank and Trust Company* et al., 306 F. Supp. 645 (1969), 90 S. Ct. 2035 (1970).

nearly $47 billion. After the merger, Wells Fargo ranked third in assets in California and ninth in the nation. This merger probably would have been denied before 1980, but in analyzing market conditions and bank concentration, the regulatory agencies gave equal weight of one-half to thrift deposits in the market.

No longer are extension mergers and bank holding company acquisitions denied with the frequency that existed before 1980. In fact, no banking agency has denied a market extension merger since then. In a very important court decision in 1981, the U.S. Fifth Circuit Court of Appeals rendered a decision that has established new antitrust standards in banking.[7] In this case, the court overturned a rejection by the Board of Governors of the Federal Reserve System to a market extension in Texas and pointed out that no banking acquisition or merger could be denied by regulatory agencies unless the acquisition or merger constituted an antitrust violation. Thus the court established the rule that antitrust standards could not be more strict than those of the Department of Justice. It seems, therefore, that the legislation enacted in the early 1980s plus recent court decisions have not only been significant but also have introduced new standards in the area of mergers and acquisitions in banking.

Is Banking a Line of Commerce?

One of the most debated topics in bank merger discussions is the determination of the relevant market. In the *Philadelphia* case, the Supreme Court took a narrow view of the relevant market and in so doing precluded any evaluation of the competition that arose from other financial institutions or financial markets. The defendants held that banking consisted of two main functions: the securing of deposits and the granting of loans, both of which could be further subdivided into areas or markets. The banks, in their defense, further pointed out that each type of deposit or loan attracted different customers, some located in different geographic areas. The banks also held that varying degrees of competition existed in each of these markets. For example, in the competition for funds, banks compete with savings and loan associations, mutual savings banks, and, during tight money periods, even with U.S. Treasury securities for time deposits. In the large certificate of deposit market, banks compete locally as well as nationally for funds. Banks also compete with other institutions for all types of loans.

The concepts of *markets* and *industries* have fundamentally changed over the years. The Court's concept of industry and market as it applies to a segment of the banking industry is quite archaic and applica-

---

[7] *Mercantile Texas Corporation v. Board of Governors of the Federal Reserve System,* 638 F. 2nd 1255 (1981).

ble to a great extent only to small banks, which provide a limited number of services. To say, as the Court has, that banking is a single line of commerce implies that an analysis of local market conditions is not necessary in merger considerations. This seems to have been the Court's position in the *Philadelphia* case when it said that "so also we must be alert to the danger of subverting congressional intent by permitting too broad an economic investigation."[8]

Two authorities in the field of bank competition summarized a more realistic view:

> The Supreme Court view of commercial banking as a "distinct line of commerce" no longer reflects market realities in many sections of the United States. The argument used by the Court to support its findings were not universally endorsed at the time. Today they have been sufficiently eroded by changing competitive conditions and financial innovations in the markets for financial services to require a reassessment of the competitive position of commercial banks.
>
> ***
>
> Commercial banking has been treated as a separate line of commerce because it was thought to offer a unique package or "cluster" of independent depository and credit services to bank customers. This treatment has the effect of excluding from definitions of product markets firms that compete with banks in some but not all service lines. For example, in their role as financial intermediaries, banks face competition for funds from other depository institutions as well as from a myriad of liability instruments offered in the money market. Moreover, on the asset side of the balance sheet, bank credit is offered in competition with thrift institutions, nonbank firms such as finance and insurance companies, and retailers, as well as the markets for securities and commercial paper. Exclusion of this competition may at times result in overstatements of anticipated anticompetitive results from bank consolidations.[9]

Competition in Banking

Economists hold that competition refers to rivalry among firms in a given market. Theory tells us that the strength of this rivalry depends on the number and size of the buyers and sellers in a given market. In fact, pure competition could be defined as a situation in which we have so many buyers and sellers that one can enter or leave the market without having an appreciable effect on it.

The many advantages to competition can be summarized by saying that an industry that is highly competitive is efficient—the smaller the

---

[8] *United States v. Philadelphia National Bank.*

[9] Henry C. Wallich and Walter A. Varvel, "Evolution in Banking Competition," *The Bankers Magazine.* Reprinted by permission from *The Bankers Magazine,* Vol. 163, No. 6, November–December 1980. Copyright © 1980, Warren, Gorham and Lamont, Inc., 210 South Street, Boston, Mass. All rights reserved.

number of sellers or the greater the concentration of business firms, the lower the quality of services and the higher the price for goods and services. Based on this reasoning, it would seem that in highly concentrated banking markets interest on loans would be higher than in areas where there was less concentration, lower rates of interest would be paid on various classes of time deposits, the ratio of time to total deposits would be lower, and earnings would be higher. Moreover, less emphasis would be placed on direct lending, especially in small amounts, than on the purchase of securities. These hypotheses are not fully supported by the research on competition in banking: the results have been inconclusive, and complete agreement on many issues has not been reached. Research on bank competition has been hampered by the unavailability of data, and, more important, by the inability to hold other things equal when measuring the effects of specific factors in different market situations.

Some studies on the relationship of banking markets to loan rates show that the larger the number of banks, the lower the rates of interest, and others have found just the opposite. One study concluded that "no easily identifiable relationship exists between concentration ratios and the level of interest rate charged by commercial banks on business loans."[10]

With the growth of branch banking, there has been great interest in its effect on market conditions. Most research on this subject indicates that when banks acquire additional branches through merger, consumers of banking services are benefited. Several studies show that interest rates paid on savings accounts were higher after a merger and several loan rates were lower, including residential real estate and automobile loans.[11] The maturities of these loans were also more liberal than before the merger. The results of research that relates performance to size are not as convincing as we would like. The reason is largely conceptual in that concluding what banks produce is difficult. Banks of different size and location cater to different clienteles and produce different services. It is difficult to measure these services, and, in many instances, comparison is impossible. Studies have shown, however, that large banks paid higher interest rates on savings than did small banks and also charged lower rates on loans. Large banks had a higher ratio of time to total deposits, were more aggressive in their lending, and had a higher ratio of loans to deposits. Several factors are responsible for some of these developments. Loans made by large banks to large business firms entail less credit risk and require less administration than do many small loans made by small

---

[10] Theodore G. Fleching, *Banking Market Structure & Performance in Metropolitan Areas* (Washington, D.C.: Board of Governors of the Federal Reserve System, 1965).

[11] Larry R. Mote, "The Perennial Issue: Branch Banking," *Business Conditions*, Federal Reserve Bank of Chicago (February 1974). This publication contains an excellent bibliography on branch banking.

FIGURE 3-1 Bank Mergers and Assets Acquired

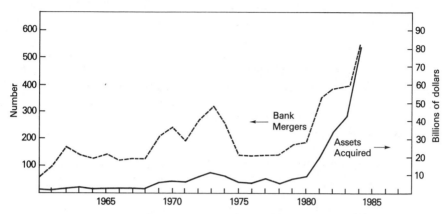

SOURCE: Board of Governors of the Federal Reserve System, *Mergers and Acquisitions by Commercial Banks, 1960–1983*, Staff Study 142, 1985.

banks. Moreover, large banks, in general, have a greater share of their time deposits in large certificates of deposit, which require fewer administrative costs and on which relatively higher rates are paid. Large banks tend to be more aggressive and innovative in new bank services and in the employment of a larger amount of their assets in loans and investments.

Bank size is an important factor in efficiency and the capacity to provide a wide range of banking services to the public. This was recognized by George W. Mitchell of the Board of Governors of the Federal Reserve System when he said

> A competitive banking system must be based on the *capacity* to compete. For many types of services this capacity requires large size. It also requires considerable talent. An arena of sufficient scope must be provided for the exercise of that talent and for its development. The alternative is some sort of sheltering—the kind exemplified by statutory home office protection and regulatory prescription of over-banking. If we believe that competition will provide higher quality and lower prices for banking services, then we cannot assume that the requisite competitive talent will be attracted by a dead-end future.[12]

Increase in Mergers

Although bank mergers have occurred in banking for years, as in other areas of businesses, there has been a substantial increase since 1980 (see Figure 3-1). From 1960 to 1969 bank mergers averaged around 150

[12] George W. Mitchell, "The Changing Structure of Banking," speech delivered to the Graduate School of Banking at the University of Wisconsin, Madison, August 16, 1972.

annually. There was an increase in the first half of the 1970s, then a decline, followed by a sharp increase beginning in 1980.

Mergers tend to rise during periods of structural changes, which in banking are brought about by new regulations and technology. The recent increase was encouraged by two forces: first, the desire of banking organizations to position themselves in anticipation of interstate banking and, second, the less restrictive antitrust policy toward mergers since about 1980.

A recent study of more than 4,000 bank mergers covering the period 1960–83 revealed the following:

1. In general the acquired firms were relatively small—86 percent of the banks had assets of less than $25 million and only 2.5 percent had assets in excess of $500 million.
2. The acquiring firms were generally large—over two-thirds had assets in excess of $200 million and 25 percent in excess of $1 billion.
3. Slightly more than half of the mergers occurred in SMSAs.
4. Multibank holding companies accounted for an increasing proportion of acquisitions, especially after 1969.
5. Banking organizations in four states—Pennsylvania, Florida, Texas, and Ohio—accounted for 31 percent of all acquisitions. Twenty-seven percent of the mergers were found in the states of New York, Virginia, New Jersey, Missouri, and Michigan. A total of 58 percent of the mergers occurred in these nine states. All of these states had one thing in common in that each state had during the period restrictive branching laws; consequently, multibank holding companies were the only vehicle for geographic expansion.
6. The ten leading acquirers accounted for about 10 percent of the banks and bank assets that were absorbed. Very few of the largest banking organizations of the nation were among the ten most active acquirers.
7. Nearly 52 percent of the banks were acquired by bank holding companies, nearly 40 percent by independent banks, and the remainder by one-bank holding companies.[13]

These trends in merger activity will probably continue as more regulatory changes are made and implemented, technology improves, and the efficiency and profitability of small banks turn downward.

Although there has been a significant increase in bank mergers, there is no evidence that it has resulted in a marked reduction in the competitiveness of bank markets. This is the conclusion of bank researchers, bank regulatory agencies, and the courts. One of the reasons for this conclusion is that there has not been a marked decline in the granting of bank charters, and the number of banks has not declined appreciably. Moreover, the

[13] Board of Governors of the Federal Reserve System, *Mergers and Acquisitions by Commercial Banks, 1960–1983*, Staff Study 142, 1985.

number of bank offices has increased as branch banking has flourished. The asset size of banks and branches has increased in recent years, and the efficiency of the banking system has improved. A final factor pointing to increased mergers is the broadening of interstate branching laws, which is well underway throughout the nation. The ultimate result of these forces will be fewer banking organizations, increased banking assets, and improved efficiency of the banking system.

Merger Guidelines

Because of the change in antitrust standards, it should not be assumed that all mergers will be approved in the future. Bank regulatory agencies and the Department of Justice are especially concerned with competition in local banking markets. The Bank Merger Act of 1960 and the Bank Holding Company Act of 1956 require that federal bank regulatory agencies take into account the likely effect on competition when making a decision on merger and acquisition applications from banks and bank holding companies. An evaluation of a proposed merger involves a close examination of the market structure in which the merger would occur. The greater the supply of banking services the more likely the regulatory agencies would approve a merger. Several methods have been designed over the years to measure concentration. One that has long been employed is the three-firm or four-firm concentration ratio. As the name implies, this measure is the aggregate market share of the three or four firms in a particular market. If the three largest banks in the banking market each held 25 percent of the market, the concentration ratio would be 75 percent. If two of the banks wanted to merge in this example, it would probably be denied because the concentration would increase.

Bank regulatory agencies presently employ merger guidelines established by the Department of Justice in 1982 and refined two year later. These guidelines establish a level of market concentration that the Department of Justice is likely to challenge as anticompetitive unless there are some extenuating circumstances. The concentration measure now in vogue gauges the market concentration in terms of the Herfindahl-Hirschman Index (HHI). This index is the sum of the squares of the market shares of each of the banks competing in a given market. If there is only one banking organization in the market, the index would be 10,000 (100% × 100%); if there were ten, the index would be 1,000. As the number of firms increase, the index would be less and approach zero; and as the number of firms decrease, the index would rise. In general, the fewer the number of firms in a given market and the more skewed the distribution of their market share, the higher the index.

If, for example, we assume that there are eight firms in a market area of which two held 20 percent of the market and six held 10 percent each, the index would stand at 1,400: $(20)^2 + (20)^2 + (10)^2 + (10)^2 + (10)^2 + (10)^2 + (10)^2 + (10)^2$. If we assume further that two of the firms holding 10 percent each wanted to merge, the index in the postmerger period would rise to 1,600: $(20)^2 + (20)^2 + (10)^2 + (10)^2 + (10)^2 + (10)^2 + (2 \times 10)^2$. Since at the present time the Department of Justice is concerned about concentration in bank markets, if the index rises more than 200 points in the postmerger period and the total index rises to 1,800, the proposed merger would not be contested. Above these amounts a merger would probably be questioned unless there were some other mitigating factors that should be considered, such as competition from thrifts or other nonbank financial firms, a weakening financial condition of the financial institution being acquired, or prior common control.

ESTABLISHING BRANCHES

Banks that are permitted to engage in branch banking on either a state-wide or a limited basis expand their plant capacity by establishing new branches or by absorbing smaller independent unit banks. Banks engaged in branch banking are, in general, guided in their expansion decisions by the same factors as are the organizers of a new unit bank: the potential growth of the area and an analysis of present banking facilities. They may take a long-run view of their actions because of their pool of capital. For example, a bank might take the view that it can afford to operate a particular branch at a loss for three years, whereas organizers of a unit bank might decide that if the location were not to be completely self-supporting at the end of two years it would not be a good investment. This difference has probably been recognized by supervisory and regulatory agencies and has also contributed to the expansion of branch banking.

A significant piece of legislation that restricted national banks from branching was the McFadden Act of 1927, which allowed national banks to establish branches only in their home office city, if branches were permitted by state law. The act encouraged many states to enact legislation against branching, and such laws were upheld by the courts. This antibranching attitude, which was quite strong in the 1920s, softened somewhat in the early 1930s during the collapse of the banking system. Shortly thereafter many states revised their branching laws to permit statewide or limited branching. In the Banking Act of 1933, national banks were placed on a par with state banks; that is, if state banks were permitted to branch statewide, so were national banks. The legislation regarding branching is quite interesting in that the federal government, which has the authority to charter national banks and permit branching by these institutions, turned over to the states the responsibility of deciding whether branching will be permitted.

Despite a growing interest in branching, state legislatures have been slow to revise their branching laws until recently, with few notable exceptions such as New Jersey and New York. Moreover, no movement has been organized to promote branch banking on the federal level. The Congress has been satisfied, it seems, to permit the states to determine the kind of multioffice banking structure each desires. This reluctance to change our banking structure, primarily established in the 1930s, has continued despite many significant changes in our economy and social patterns. The 1971 Commission on Financial Institutions seemed to accept this position but did indicate that branching was a desirable development when it said, "The public should benefit from the option granted financial institutions to branch statewide."[14] Statewide branching would rule out *home office protection* statutes in many states that prohibit banks from establishing new branches in communities already served by other banks. Obviously, this type of legislation is designed to limit the entry of banks in the area and is certainly anticompetitive.

Several arguments have been set forth against branch banking. One of the oldest is that it is monopolistic and will tend to develop a *money trust*. A second argument is that a branch bank will become impersonal in its activities and that the needs of the small communities and small borrowers will be neglected, as a result. However, no convincing evidence exists that such has happened. Among the arguments advanced in favor of branch banking, the most important is that it leads to better bank management. Because of greater resources and better training facilities, branch banking probably does have an advantage in the development of better management. More skilled people can be employed, and there are greater opportunities for specialization. Another argument is that a greater diversification of assets can take place, allowing a greater diversification of risks. Advocates of branch banking contend that geographic mobility of funds to meet emergencies and seasonal needs and larger amounts of deposits and capital than unit banks usually have are definite advantages. Communities may need funds in excess of the deposits of a unit bank, and the lending limit of branch banks may be greater than that of unit banks. With branch banking, these demands can be met, and larger loans can be made to one borrower. Advocates of branch banking often state that a branch office can be organized more quickly and economically than can a new bank in a rapidly developing area and that there can be more diversified banking services. It is true that branching has made banking facilities available in areas where unit banks would have difficulty surviving. Moreover, branch banking has demonstrated economies of scale that have benefited the banking public. The basic reason for opposing branch bank-

---

[14] *The Report of the President's Commission on Financial Structure and Regulation* (Washington, D.C.: Government Printing Office, 1971), pp. 61–62.

ing is that small banks fear they will be placed at a competitive disadvantage and ultimately be forced from the market.

The form that branching takes in the future may be quite different from the one we have experienced in the past. At the present time, branching has involved the construction of buildings equipped with furniture and fixtures, office machines, and numerous employees. With the rise in technology, this type of "brick and mortar" branch may give way to one that is completely automated. Automated teller machines may be the forerunner of the type of branches we may have in the future. With ATMs, deposits can be accepted, cash disbursed, loan payments made, and funds transferred from one account to another. With the advancements in electronics, why not make use of closed-circuit television in the making of loans and the rendering of other financial advice? It is not difficult to visualize an electronic branch with only one or two persons to welcome customers, explain the use of the equipment, and answer questions relating to the use of the bank's services. The cost of such banking services would be considerably less than that of the present type, and in a competitive system, the cost of bank services to bank customers would be lowered.

The manner in which banking services have been provided in the past and what may occur in the future according to one bank marketing officer are presented in Figure 3-2. Note that the main office was the dominant bank delivery system in the early 1950s. This delivery system gave way to branching and drive-in banking, which are now peaking in importance and will decline during the balance of this century. Electronic

FIGURE 3-2   Delivery System Life Cycle

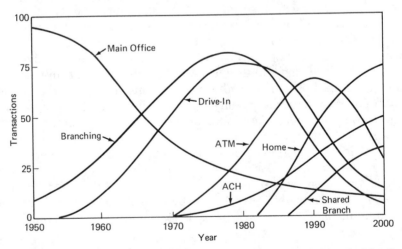

SOURCE: John F. Fisher, "In-Home Banking Today and Tomorrow," *Journal of Retail Banking,* 4, no. 2 (June 1982), 25. Reprinted with permission. © Copyright 1982 by the Consumer Bankers Association. All rights reserved.

delivery systems arrived in the early 1970s in the form of automatic teller machines and the automated clearinghouse (ACH). These systems are spreading rapidly and are logical forerunners of in-home banking, which will be the dominant delivery system in the foreseeable future. Note that shared banking will also play a role in bank delivery systems according to this marketing officer. A shared branch is a location that is shared by a bank with some other related business such as real estate or insurance. The reason for such an arrangement stems from costs of operation. Forecasting the structural arrangement for such an industry as banking is not an exact science, but the technology and other environmental factors that shape the banking industry certainly point to such an arrangement as described in the figure.

THE ISSUE OF INTERSTATE BANKING

One of the debatable issues in commercial banking is that of interstate branching. With the passage of DIDMCA, many assumed that interstate branching would soon be forthcoming, and some banks and bank holding companies took steps to place themselves in a more favorable position should this occur. Some holding companies purchased minority interests in banks, established Edge Act offices across state lines, and a few formed nonbanks.

Most of the opposition to interstate banking comes from small banks that are fearful of increased competition. They are also concerned with increased concentration, which they consider undesirable. The president of the Independent Bankers Association, a trade association of relatively small banks, summarized the association's position when he said

> A principal focus of concern with the proposal to removing existing barriers to geographic expansion of banking is the threat it poses for a substantial increase in concentration. . . . Higher levels of concentration in these markets would not only reduce the vigor of competition in banking but also increase the ability of giant banking institutions to utilize their economic power to exercise significant influence over the political process. . . . It seems clear that repeal of the Douglas Amendment would set off an uncontrollable wave of mergers and acquisitions of large multibank holding companies by megabanks, which would rapidly increase concentration nationwide. The consolidation movement would place community banks across the country in direct competition with the megabanks on very unequal terms. Furthermore, the consolidation of multibank holding companies would present very limited opportunities for independent banks to sell out to a multibank holding company.[15]

---

[15] Thomas F. Bolger, "The McFadden Study: An Unsound Proposal for Community Banks," *Journal of Retail Banking*, 3, no. 1 (March 1981), 42–44. Reprinted with permission. © Copyright 1981 by the Consumer Bankers Association. All rights reserved.

Interstate branching is prohibited by two federal laws, the Douglas Amendment to the Bank Holding Company Act of 1956 and the McFadden Act of 1927. The Douglas Amendment prohibits the acquisition of banks by bank holding companies unless permitted to do so by state law. The McFadden Law authorizes national banks to establish full-service branches only in states where state banks can branch. The limitation of interstate branching has a long history.

In the National Bank Act of 1863, national banks were required to restrict their banking to one office. In 1916 the American Bankers Association went on record in opposition to branch banking in any form. In 1922 the Comptroller of the Currency became concerned that national banks were at a competitive disadvantage in states where state banks were permitted to branch and reversed the established pattern dictated by previous comptrollers and permitted national banks to branch within a bank's home office city. In 1927 Congress enacted the McFadden Act, which authorized national banks to establish branches in states where state banks are permitted but at first national banks were limited to the home office city. In 1933 the McFadden Act was modified to permit national banks to open offices outside the home office city and gave to the states the right to dictate branching for national as well as state-chartered banks. Part of the reasoning behind this decision stemmed from the financial problems encountered by banks. Prior to 1933 bank failures and banking crises were not uncommon, and it was felt that the states were in a position to ensure the performance of the banking system. It was also a way of ensuring the survival of small banks by limiting banking competition from out-of-state banking organizations.

The legislation regarding branching is quite interesting in that the federal government, which has the authority to charter national banks and permit branching by these institutions, turned over to the states the responsibility of deciding whether branching will be permitted. It demonstrates the political power of the supporters of small banks. In fact, much of the banking legislation of the 1930s was a result of political horse trading. Small banks were very much concerned about their future since over a third of the banks that failed from 1930 through 1933 were small rural banks. Small banks clamored for deposit insurance, which was provided by the FDIC and was paid for in large part by the large banks. For many years, individual deposits were insured for $5,000, but the premium for insurance was assessed on all deposits; hence, the banks with a large portion of individual deposits in excess of that amount were forced to pay a disproportionate amount for insurance protection. The large banks succeeded in securing the prohibition of interest on demand deposits, and investment brokers did not oppose the Securities Act of 1933 since the banks were prohibited from engaging in investment banking.

Although a great deal of emotion surrounds the issue of interstate banking, from the standpoint of an efficient banking system, a ban on banking across state lines cannot be supported. The restrictions are anachronistic since they restrict banks to geographic areas that are not consistent with those of their customers and competitors. Borrowers of bank funds located in New York, Chicago, and San Francisco do not necessarily restrict their productive activities to these particular locations. Moreover, depositors may not always live where they carry a deposit. As we have already learned, banks compete with a variety of financial institutions, some of which are not restricted by state boundaries.

Restrictions on bank entry are inconsistent with the concept of competition, which is the very essence of a free market economy. Economists would say that we do not increase competition by restricting entry but by permitting the market to determine whether or not the supply of banking services should be increased.

Although the prohibition against interstate branching has a long history and has proved to be a formidable plug in the dike, it has weakened in recent years. Banks are permitted to have *production offices* across state lines. A production office is one that makes loans but does not accept deposits. Banks are also permitted to have offices in other states for the purpose of providing international banking services. These offices are known as *Edge Act offices* and will be discussed in more detail in the chapter on international banking. Edge Act offices, as is true for production offices, are not permitted to accept deposits. This prohibition against the acceptance of deposits is something of a sham since mail services are available to customers of such offices.

The existence of troubled financial institutions has also contributed to the support of interstate branching. The Depository Institutions Act of 1982, for example, recognized the problem and permits acquisition of both commercial and insured savings banks by out-of-state institutions. In addition to the activities of bank holding companies across state lines and state legislation permitting the entry of out-of-state bank holding companies, changes in the structure of the savings and loan industry have established precedents for interstate banking. The Home Loan Bank Board, the federal agency that supervises the activities of savings and loan associations, has permitted the acquisition of numerous savings and loan associations that were in financial distress located across state lines from the acquiring institution. In fact, Citicorp, headquartered in New York, was permitted to acquire Fidelity Savings and Loan Association of California.

An underlying reason for the opposition to interstate banking stems from the long-held fear of increased concentration of banking resources. Our history reflects our aversion to the concentration of financial and economic power. It is the basic philosophy that served as the impetus for the Sherman and Clayton acts, the Bank Holding Company acts, the Glass-Steagall Act, and the use of the then frequently used term "money trust" in the nineteenth and early twentieth centuries.

The fear held by many who oppose banking across state lines that the large banks and bank holding companies will take over the industry appears to be unwarranted. The purchase of a bank and the establishment of branches require capital, and the reservoir of bank capital for this purpose is not unlimited. Bank capital is derived from retained earnings, the sale of new stock, or the issuance of some form of debt instruments. In the final analysis, bank earnings support all these sources. Moreover, stockholders must approve acquisitions, and their decision rests primarily on what is expected to happen to bank earnings. They are not interested in financial arrangements that will reduce earnings or dilute their equity. The fear of predatory competition and limited opportunity for the sale of small banks also seems to be overemphasized. There has only been one legal action that involved alleged predatory competition in the past 20 years.[16] The construction and staffing of a branch is an expensive process, and if an opportunity to purchase a bank presents itself, rational business judgment would certainly be exercised. From the information available on the sale and purchase of banks, stock premiums have been quite common.

Present Status of Interstate Branching

Despite the long debate surrounding branching across state lines, it has been accomplished in most states by the passage of state laws permitting entry of out-of-state banks and in all probability will become universal in the very near future. In enacting such laws, the states exercised an option provided by the Bank Holding Company Act of 1956, which stated that interstate branching was unlawful unless approved by the state in which a bank was to be acquired. However, no state enacted such legislation until Maine did in 1974, and not until 1982 was another enacted. Since that time nearly all of the states have such a law. Recent interstate branching laws may be categorized as follows:

Nationwide Laws.   Nationwide laws are the most liberal, as well as the most simple, interstate banking laws and allow entry by banking organizations from any state in the nation. The states of Alaska, Arizona, Maine, Oklahoma, and Texas fall into this category.

Nationwide Reciprocal.   These laws are somewhat less liberal than the nationwide laws in that they allow banking organizations from any state to acquire instate banks only if the acquiring bank's state grants similar privileges to banking organizations of the host state. The states of

---

[16] Alan C. McCall and Donald T. Savage, "The Interstate Banking Debate: Another Viewpoint," *Journal of Retail Banking*, 3, no. 3 (September 1981), 36.

Kentucky, New York, Washington, and West Virginia have laws of this kind.

Specialized Laws. These laws authorize some specialized form of entry by out-of-state bank holding companies. Within this broad category are found "limited purpose laws," which permit out-of-state banks to establish special purpose facilities such as credit card operations. These laws generally prohibit out-of-state banks from competing with host state organizations for retail customers. In this category is also found what is commonly termed a "troubled institutions" law. As the name implies, entry is permitted if it is for the acquisition of a troubled or failing institution within the host state.

Regional Laws. These laws are the most popular and allow those banking organizations within a specified region to acquire a banking organization located in the host state. States in New England and the Southeast have laws of this type. Interstate banking is permitted only on a reciprocal basis in the region.

Several factors were responsible for the recent interest in branching across state lines. Interest rate deregulation has encouraged banks to compete for deposits on a nationwide scale, and advances in data processing and communications technology have also contributed to the competition for retail customers. Moreover, the spread of nonbanks and the nationwide development of nonbank subsidiaries by bank holding companies have encouraged states to adopt interstate banking laws. The willingness of out-of-state banking organizations to merge with failing or financially troubled institutions when no in-state organization expressed an interest to merge prompted some states to favor branching across state lines. Banking legislation is influenced by the elements of momentum and imitation, and interstate branching appears to be no exception. When bankers see banks in other states receiving new powers, they usually desire similar expansion rights and press for similar legislation. Many supporters of interstate banking argued that it would contribute to economic development of the states since additional capital would be available for credit.

Interstate branching implemented by a variety of state laws lacks uniformity and equality for all interested parties in the banking system. The greatest shortcoming of present state legislation is that there is no provision for the free entry of banking organizations; consequently, a free market from which so many benefits emerge is denied. The regional approach was designed in large part to keep money center banks from entering a state apparently because of a fear that these banks would dominate banking. To a very great extent, the patchwork we now have is a result of the inaction on the part of Congress, which has been reluctant to take the lead and provide the nation with a more desirable arrangement. Interstate banking has many advantages, but if it is to work effectively and contribute to a strong and viable banking system, uniformity and equality must be present.

The Board of Governors of the Federal Reserve System has supported the concept of interstate banking but has expressed some reservations with the recent developments in this important area and has stated that "the time has come for the Congress to review and clarify national policy toward interstate banking."[17] The board added some additional comments regarding regional laws:

> The Board recognizes that regional arrangements provide a possible transitional approach to full interstate banking. Viewed as a permanent solution, however, regional compacts would tend to balkanize banking, with a tendency toward regional concentrations. The potential weaknesses of regional compacts could be substantially ameliorated if states entering into such regional arrangements were also required, after a period of a few years, to permit reciprocal entry by banks in any state that has enacted a regional arrangement or otherwise provides for entry of banks of any other states.[18]

Some observers of interstate banking are concerned that branching across state lines may lead to the higher concentration of bank assets, which would, in turn, contribute to adverse competitive conditions and the misallocation of credit in a free enterprise society. Such economic and sociopolitical questions have been a concern of our nation for years. Witness, for example, the concern over the chartering of the Second United States Bank, the McFadden Act, and the Bank Holding Company Act of 1956. To be sure, the present interstate banking movement will probably lead to larger banks, but this within itself does not necessarily result in less competition and efficiency. Factors contributing to a more competitive environment are the substantial increase in credit-granting organizations, which include various commercial lenders and foreign bank and thrift institutions that are now permitted to make commercial and consumer loans and accept transaction accounts. Although our banking system is characterized by a plethora of small banks, it may not be as efficient as if it were made up of larger banks. How many business firms with credit needs of $5 million can be accommodated by a bank with $100 million in assets? The lending limit of a bank this size would prohibit an extension of credit of this amount. For this reason, we find business firms that need this amount of credit patronizing a much larger bank that has adequate resources. Those who fear increased concentration should note that the economies of scale are not very great in banking, as has been pointed out by bank researchers over the years. Therefore, it is unlikely that the

[17] Board of Governors of the Federal Reserve System, *Seventy-Second Annual Report* (1985), p. 160.
[18] Ibid.

present move toward interstate banking will be characterized by excessive concentration. One researcher has pointed out that

> Recent studies have begun to model financial institutions explicitly as providers of multiple products and to investigate economies of scope as well as economies of scale of operation. The eight multiproduct studies reviewed here find little evidence of economies of scale, unlike the earlier single-product studies. So there is no evidence that larger firms have a cost advantage over smaller firms. Mergers between financial firms that increase the scale of operations should not yield cost savings.[19]

The Board of Governors has considered the matter of concentration and has recommended the following:

> To forestall large concentrations of domestic banking resources, the Board has recommended that certain safeguards be included in legislation liberalizing interstate banking. The Board has suggested the following approaches: the very largest holding companies might be prohibited from merging with one another; institutions could be prohibited from obtaining by acquisition more than some fixed share of banking assets, although de novo or small acquisitions could still be permitted; and states could set limits on the percentage of banking assets within their own borders that could be acquired through acquisitions or mergers.
>
> The Board has also recommended that Congress authorize interstate branching within metropolitan areas and within neighboring areas of contiguous states."[20]

An excellent study on nationwide banking concluded with the following statement:

> The evidence to date suggests that lifting of legislation restricting interstate branching and interstate banking would improve the efficiency of the banking system. Liberalization of restrictions on interstate branching would improve convenience, increase lending activity, and create a more competitive banking system. Removal of restrictions on interstate banking would increase the number of banking alternatives, particularly in urban markets.[21]

FRANCHISING

Although not presently of major importance, franchising is another method of expanding banking services and was first introduced in the early 1980s by First Interstate Bank of California. Since that time several

---

[19] Loretta J. Meister, "Efficient Production of Financial Services: Scale and Scope Economies," *Business Review*, Federal Reserve Bank of Philadelphia (January–February 1987), p. 24.

[20] Board of Governors of the Federal Reserve System, *Seventy-Second Annual Report.*

[21] Federal Reserve Bank of Chicago, *Toward Nationwide Banking: A Guide to the Issues* (Chicago, 1986), p. 82.

other banking organizations have joined the ranks. Franchising has some favorable attributes and may become more important in the future. Franchising in banking differs from the usual concept found in the service and food industries, such as motels and fast-food restaurants. In that type of franchising, a complete start-up business is provided by the firm extending the franchise. In banking, the franchising bank accepts an existing ongoing and successful bank and provides certain services, such as name change, logo, technology and expertise in management and operations, advertising, and purchasing. The objective of this type of arrangement is to improve the product and service capabilities of the franchised bank in order to improve its prestige and competitive position. For the services performed, the bank granting the franchise charges an initial fee plus a royalty based on adjusted gross earnings of the franchised bank.

Franchised banks are not small, nor are they financially weak institutions. First Interstate limits its franchised banks to those that are profitable and with assets of $100 million or more. At year-end 1986, First Interstate had franchised 42 banks in 10 states. Two of those banks are First Interstate Bank of Wisconsin and First Interstate Bank of Golden. The franchised banks of First Interstate of California agree to offer certain services that the bank has promoted in its branch system. A very important one is the use of the bank's bank card, which serves as identification for check cashing and for ATM access. First Interstate is a founder partner in the CIRRUS network, which offers access to several thousand automatic teller machines nationwide. Another service includes a program that permits customers traveling in the bank's territory to cash checks at any franchised bank, as well as a relocation program that is designed to maintain the bank/customer relationship with present customers when they relocate from one area to another. Finally, a referral program for potential customers is provided.

The reluctance of some banks to become a part of the franchising movement is the loss of the bank's local name and the costs involved. One researcher has pointed out, however, that the franchise costs are not excessive and that the benefits are substantial. This case study of three franchised banks shows that the decline in market share of both loans and deposits was reversed and profitability increased. In a concluding paragraph, the study states

> In both Colorado and Wisconsin, the franchise banks are no longer just another "generic" local bank, but are part of a system that sets them apart from other independent competitors and gives them the look of the large downtown banks or holding companies. Yet they retain local control and the same "independent flavor" that customers have come to appreciate. They now can compete in profitability with the giants, while not exposing

themselves to the accusations from other small independent banks that they are no longer "local."[22]

QUESTIONS

1. How do you account for the trend in the assets and liabilities of the bank or banks in your community?
2. What is meant by the term "convenience and need of the community" that is so often employed in bank merger cases?
3. Do you consider commercial banking to be a "line of commerce"? Explain.
4. Bank regulatory authorities and the courts have been concerned with the degree and level of competition in banking. Has this concern been desirable?
5. Do you expect to see increased merger activity in the 1990s? Why? What factors lead you to this decision?
6. What benefits would bank customers receive from interstate banking? What benefits would accrue to bank stockholders?
7. Examine the current literature on banking and report to your class on the status of electronic banking (ATMs, ACH, in-home banking, etc.) in the area where you live.
8. Should the interstate banking issue be the responsibility of the various states or of the federal government? Why?
9. Do you agree with the position of the Board of Governors on the issue of interstate banking? Why?

SELECTED REFERENCES

ASSOCIATION OF REGISTERED BANK HOLDING COMPANIES. *The Bank Holding Company, Its History and Significance in Modern America.* Washington, D.C., 1973.

BOARD OF GOVERNORS OF THE FEDERAL RESERVE SYSTEM. *Operating Policies of Bank Holding Companies,* Staff Studies. Washington, D.C.: Federal Reserve Board, 1971.

FEDERAL RESERVE BANK OF ATLANTA. "Line of Commerce." *Economic Review* (April 1982).

———. "Positioning for Interstate Banking." *Economic Review* (September 1982).

FEDERAL RESERVE BANK OF CHICAGO. *Toward Nationwide Banking: A Guide to the Issues.* Chicago, 1986.

---

[22] William J. Carner, "Analysis of Franchising in Retail Banking," *Journal of Retail Banking*, III, no. 4 (Winter 1986–87), 65.

Loeys, Jan G. "Bank Acquisitions: The Mitigating Factors Defense." *Banking Law Journal* (September/October 1986), pp. 427–449.

Neely, Walter P. "Banking Acquisitions: Acquirer and Target Shareholder Returns." *Financial Management* (Winter 1987), pp. 66–74.

Rhodes, Stephen A. *Mergers and Acquisitions by Commercial Banks, 1980–83.* Staff Study 142. Washington, D.C.: Board of Governors of the Federal Reserve System, 1985.

Savage, Donald T. "Interstate Banking Developments." *Federal Reserve Bulletin* (February 1987), pp. 172–192.

U.S. Treasury Department. *Geographic Restrictions on Commercial Banks in the United States, The Report of the President.* Washington, D.C.: Government Printing Office, January 1981.

4

MANAGEMENT, DECISION MAKING, AND INTERNAL ORGANIZATION OF BANKS

The basic objective of commercial bank management is the same as that found in other profit-seeking organizations, namely, to maximize the wealth of the owners. Maximizing the present value of future cash flows that accrue to stockholders takes the form of increased dividends and/or capital appreciation. Fundamentally, management in banking does not differ from management in other enterprises. The basic functions of management—planning, organizing, staffing, directing, and controlling—are not foreign to bank management. Increasing the profitability of a bank is a function of a number of variables, including total revenue, overhead costs, the cost of bank liabilities, the time value of money, and capitalization. These variables are, in turn, influenced by a variety of factors such as total assets, the composition of assets, yield on assets, costs of demand, time and savings deposits, the size and composition of the capital account, dividend policy, the cost of plant and equipment, and so on.

In the search for wealth maximization there are trade-offs with which the following chapters are concerned. Is it advisable, for example, for bank management to acquire assets of low quality and increase income or to acquire high-quality assets, thus reducing risk, and realize a lower income? Should banks invest and make loans for long periods and reduce their liquidity, or should they keep maturities of assets short and realize a high degree of liquidity? These are the nagging questions with which bank management is constantly confronted.

In the attainment of basic objectives, there are restraints in banking as in every other profit-seeking enterprise. A dominant restraint and one that not only shapes the banking industry but affects its operations and thus influences its basic objectives is the multitude of laws and rules and regulations imposed by the various banking regulatory agencies.

DECISION MAKING IN COMMERCIAL BANKS

Decision making in commercial banks must be done quickly and decisively. Customers deserve and in fact demand efficient, expeditious financial services and prompt decisions on many financial requests. Banking is a labor-intensive service; consequently, for efficient operations, there are many people who must be informed and have an understanding of the policies and rules of the organization. Time does not allow for all decisions to be made at the top. Senior officials cannot from the standpoint of efficiency be concerned with many routine decisions. Even group and division managers must be spared the bulk of the repetitive routine decisions. Moreover, in branch and group banking, offices may be dispersed over wide geographic areas, the personnel of which must be kept informed of the bank's procedures.

The management cycle in every business consists of several steps or procedures such as planning, organizing, and controlling designed to accomplish a desirable end. Although there is no established point at which to start, we begin with *planning*, probably the most important procedure in the management process.

PLANNING

Planning is the activity through which a business firm charts its future course of action. The end result of planning is to develop a strategy for utilizing the resources of a business within its projected environment so as to attain its overall objectives. Many banks realize the importance of this function and have planning departments staffed with technical personnel. Others do it intermittently.

Planning is important because of the competitive environment within which banks operate and their desire to improve efficiency that will, it is hoped, result in increased growth, which in turn will result in an increase in the return on equity. Planning is an exercise; in fact, the process may be as useful as the plan itself in that it requires management to look ahead, recognize problems, and search for solutions to them.

A schematic diagram of commercial bank planning is shown in Figure 4-1. Although the five elements are usually studied, researched, discussed, and formulated simultaneously, the key step in the process is to

FIGURE 4-1 Planning Arrangement in a Commercial Bank

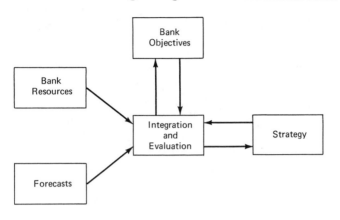

arrive at the bank objectives. This involves a substantial amount of subjective evaluation and covers many areas. Planning involves consideration and answers to three basic questions: Where are we now? Where do we want to be? How will we get there?

In the planning process, the first step is a recognition of the bank's resources—its assets, deposits, liquidity, and capital; its acceptance in the community; the expertise of its personnel; and its dominance in the marketplace. Bank management must make many assumptions about the future and project the organization into that expected environment. It is at this point that forecasting becomes important. The bank's economist, if the bank has one, will play an important role here. Assumptions must be made about many economic and financial factors that will affect the bank in the coming months. Answers must be forthcoming to such questions as the future trend of interest rates, bond yields, and the demand for credit. Will the economy be expanding or contracting? What industries will show the most progress? What will happen to wage rates, taxes, and the social and political environments? To be sure, bank officials do not have a crystal ball, but some basic assumptions must be made about the external forces that shape the banking industry in the immediate future.

After an evaluation of the external forces, bank management must turn to the internal qualities of the bank. If assumptions are made that the economic environment will indeed be bright, that there will be a high demand for credit, and that interest rates will rise, many issues are now raised. Answers are required to such questions as, Do we have sufficient personnel in certain departments to handle adequately the expected level of activity? Should we plan for additional branches or should we emphasize automated teller machines? Should we change the thrust of our advertising? Is this the year to add a leasing department or introduce a credit card program? The number of questions that can be raised as a result of planning seems to be unlimited. This is good, for it stimulates the thinking processes and management is the better because of it.

Objectives

Objectives are goals, and it is toward these end results that all activity is directed. An objective of a bank might be a return of 15 percent on equity or a capital-to-asset ratio of 7 percent. Establishing objectives is basic to the determination of the bank's policies and will affect the organizational structure of the bank as well as influence the type of personnel employed. It will also contribute to the molding of the personality of the bank. The use of policies is necessary in the work of planning a course of action. To achieve an objective, it is mandatory that sound policies be employed.

Objectives may change over time, but once formulated, they are looked upon as a firm and binding contract. Bank objectives are usually stated in short, concise terms and limited to ten to twelve items. A few items from a list of one bank's objectives follow.[1]

1. Our business is the sale of financial services in Oregon and in selected regional, national and international markets. We will extend our business into areas which provide sound expansion opportunities meeting predetermined profit criteria.
2. We will strive for stability in earnings growth, acquire investments of high quality, and pursue sound and innovative tactics. Through strategic planning and strong management, we will aggressively expand income sources while remaining in control of costs.
3. Our primary marketing objective is to increase our share of the market through superior service and appropriate products consistent with corporate strategic plans.
4. Management will provide continuity of policies and direction. Changes will be implemented quickly and in a manner that considers both individual and corporate needs.
5. Our objective is to promote people within the organization. However, expansion into new fields and the need for specialized talent may require hiring people from other sources.
6. We are sensitive to social and economic concerns and recognize our responsibilities as a corporate citizen. We support and participate in activities to improve social and economic conditions.

Policies

After the setting of objectives, the establishment of bank policies naturally follows. Policies are general statements of understandings that

[1] U.S. Bancorp, *1977 Annual Report.*

are designed to stimulate thinking and action in decision making. An example of a bank policy might involve pricing. Such a policy might state that the lending rates will be based on the market forces locally and nationally. The policy might even go farther and state that the establishment of specific loan rates shall be the responsibility of the management committee after a full discussion of the subject with the senior loan officers of the various loan departments. In this way, the officers in the consumer loan department will have had an input in the establishment of loan rates that will strengthen the bank's position. Also employee motivation has not been short-circuited.

Policies assist those people who are concerned with planning. It is difficult to conceive of the preparation of a budget without the knowledge of the overall policies. The personnel director would be unable to know how many clerks to hire without a knowledge of the policy of the bank regarding the type of loans in which the board wishes to specialize. Policies also give meaning to the objective. With definite policies, the goal becomes more concrete and comprehensible. Policies implement the delegation of authority. The employees working under the person who is directing a certain phase of bank operations know the objective; thus the supervisor's work is made easier. The person supervising this phase of work has his or her hand strengthened by the statement of policy and can use this delegated authority to accomplish the objective.

Policies also serve as an overall guide or boundaries within which the officers and committees of a bank can operate. In the event that a set of circumstances arises, the bank has a policy or a determined course of action upon which it can rely for guidance. Policy acts as a coordinating force to call forth group effort. Since each department and each employee knows the policy, there tends to be closer harmony in every phase of effort. Sound policies tend to produce decisions on the part of management that are consistent. This is important not only within the organization but outside the organization as well. There is less disgust and grumbling on the part of both employees and customers if everyone knows that each will be treated equally. The personal element is removed. There is probably nothing that causes more customer resentment than the realization that people with the same problem are treated differently. Policy also has value as far as outsiders, who may be potential customers, are concerned since it reflects the competence and capacity of the management.

Policies may appear in the minutes of the board of directors or standing committees or in the manual of organization. In smaller banks there is little written policy, but in larger banks it is almost a necessity. Policies may be established by the board of directors, by the committees, or by the officers and employees in any department of the bank.

Policies should be flexible and reviewed periodically with the idea of making improvements. Economic conditions, as well as many other factors, may make change necessary. Although there are many matters in bank management that require the establishment of policy, policy should not become a straitjacket for management.

Rules

Rules should not be confused with policies. A rule requires that specific and definitive action be taken or not taken with respect to a given situation. A bank may require that a corporation opening an account provide the bank with a resolution prepared by the firm's board of directors authorizing certain individuals to sign checks and borrow funds. This would be a rule. There are different kinds of deposits in banks—individual, sole proprietorship, partnership, joint, joint with the right of survivorship, and so on—all of which are governed by certain rules. Rules allow no deviation from a stated course of action, whereas policies are designed to guide thinking in making decisions. Rules are firm; if a deviation must be recognized, a person with a higher authority usually must approve.

Such a statement as "the bank will welcome and seek aggressively all types of deposit accounts" would be an objective. A statement that "the bank insists that each new depositor be properly identified" would be a statement of policy. For the new account officer to be required to obtain at least two items of the following pieces of identification from a new depositor—driver's license, bank credit card, retail credit card, social security number, taxpayer's identification number, employee identification card, current passport, armed forces or government agency card—would be a rule.

Strategy

Once a bank's objectives and policies are formulated, the next step is to arrive at a strategy to accomplish these goals and objectives. While objectives represent a subjective choice as to quality, direction, and pace of the enterprise, strategy is the plan by which a bank can best realize the established objectives. It is a quantification of ideas. While an objective of a bank may be to increase its market share, a strategy would deal with how this could be implemented. Strategies denote a program of action and involve the deployment of resources to attain certain objectives. It might take the form of providing the public with a new higher-yielding certificate or paying a higher rate of interest on certain certificates of deposit. The initiation of a *call program*, that is, bank personnel making personal calls on all the business firms in the community in an effort to secure commercial and industrial loans, is a strategy. The introduction of a bank credit card or home banking are examples of strategies designed to increase the customer base of a bank. An advertising program directed at certain income and/or age groups would also be a strategy.

In moving from objectives to strategy, factors that must be considered are the bank's resources and what the environment might be in the future. A bank's resources include such items as size of its assets, physical facilities, image, financial resources, and personnel. All of these would influence the kind of strategy that a bank would adopt. It would be pointless for a bank to attempt to make oil loans if it had no personnel experienced in this type of lending. A bank with assets of $25 million or less would encounter some difficulty in attracting national firms that have lines of credit in the amount of $100 million to $150 million from five to ten banks and are entitled to the prime rate. Banks operate in an economic environment; consequently, an economic forecast for the next three to five years would certainly be helpful in adopting a plan. Aggressiveness in lending is influenced by the phase of the business cycle within which the bank is operating. The level and direction of interest rates also influence the investment strategy of a commercial bank. Forecasting is not limited to economic matters alone but includes political and cultural developments as well. Local and national legislation influence banking, and population movements influence both the need for bank services and the sources of funds.

As the arrows indicate in Figure 4-1, bank objectives influence integration and evaluation; in turn, integration and evaluation influence objectives and strategy. Although there is no magical period for which a bank should plan, a five-year plan seems to be quite common. Because of many changes, it is doubtful that a plan introduced today would still be valid five years hence, but this does not lessen the value of the planning process. If major changes occur that affect the adopted plan, it should be changed. Planning is a continuous process, not a "once every five years" exercise. In a very real sense, planning is necessary because of our inability to forecast with reliability.

The planning process in banks may be administered by a management committee, a task force, or a separate department created to be concerned with planning continuously. A staff department approach to planning is found in larger banks of the nation. Although formal planning occurs more frequently in large banks than in small ones, some planning, consciously or unconsciously, is done in all banks, just as most individuals have personal budgets even though they may not be in written form.

COMMUNICATION

One of the problems in any business firm is to communicate the established objectives, policies, and rules of operation to all who have need of them, and banking is no exception. Rules of operation are very important to banking because of the many rules and regulations imposed by bank regulatory authorities. The senior officers of banks are usually in close daily contact, and the knowledge of various developments does not present a major problem. The same is true of lending officers who work closely together and are concerned with specific types of lending such as commercial and consumer loans. Communication channels must be kept open in branch and group banking organizations and among the numerous clerks, tellers, bookkeepers, computer operators, and so on who are widely dispersed throughout the organization.

The bank manual has become the major communication instrument. The manual is subdivided to cover specific areas such as tellers, commercial loan officers, computer programmers, and auditors. These manuals not only include the objectives of the bank and its policies but the rules that are to be followed by the various areas of banking activity. It is the responsibility of the department and division heads to see that the information in manuals is read and understood. The head teller, for example, is charged with the responsibility of seeing that all tellers are cognizant of the rules, and those who are in training for such positions look upon the teller's manual as the basic source of professional knowledge. If a rule is changed, a copy of a corrected page is sent to all those who possess that particular manual; and it is the supervisor's responsibility to see that all who are concerned with it are cognizant of the change and implement it immediately. This kind of communication has worked for banks and will probably long remain a fixture in the banking industry. In addition to manuals, meetings (department, divisional, etc.) are a way of dispensing information.

CONTROLLING

Of all the functions of management in banking, probably the most thoroughly executed is controlling. The reason stems from the role that commercial banks play in our society. Banks, more than any other industry, rely on public confidence. Banks hold the bulk of the cash balances of the nation and are closely regulated by bank regulatory agencies that have spawned a multitude of rules and regulations. High standards and accuracy are expected of them.

Controlling is the measurement of the performance of subordinates to ascertain whether or not they have met the objectives of the firm and have abided by its established policies and rules. The control process involves the establishment of standards, measuring performance in accordance with these standards, and correcting deviations from the established plans and programs. Many banks have employed the technique for effectuating control. When management by objectives is employed, definite objectives and standards of performance are agreed upon by the supervisor and the subordinate in every department and/or division at all levels from the chairman of the board to the lowest clerk for a definite period. During the period, frequent interviews will reveal the adherence to the established standards and the quality of work rendered.

Reports

There are many avenues for control in commercial banks. Banks are noted for the multitude of information systems made possible by the computer age and the consumption of tons of paper. There seem to be reports available on every function. The desks of senior officials and department heads are piled high with reports every morning. There are reports on every class of loan made, loans that are past due for a certain number of days, and loans that have been written off. The investment department usually has a report on its activities by the week or month that includes the kinds of securities held, the current yield, yield to maturity on tax equivalent yield, maturity of the bond portfolio, the income generated in the department, capital gains and losses, and so on. There are reports on new accounts, closed accounts, and substantial changes in the balances of various accounts. Banks do not neglect a report showing the number and amount of insufficient checks. There are many other reports, but those mentioned are sufficient evidence that banks use reports as a vehicle of control. Boards of directors receive numerous reports for the usual monthly meeting sufficient to place them in a position to judge the progress of their bank. In addition to reports, the committee system that permeates banking is an excellent means of control.

Audit

Many banks have an audit department, and those that do not normally employ an outside accounting firm to perform a periodic audit of the bank. Auditing is concerned with the review of transactions for accuracy and in determining whether or not such transactions have been recorded in conformity with acceptable accounting principles and banking regulations. Many visualize auditing in a bank as a process of searching out the would-be embezzlers of the depositors' and stockholders' funds. It is true that this is a function, but actually, the greater part of the work of an audit department is to create an environment in which it will be impossible for dishonesty and misapplication of funds to occur. The objective is to lock the door before rather than after the horse is stolen.

The activities of the audit department in a commercial bank fall into four broad categories: the verification of assets and liabilities, the proving of income and expense items, the responsibility of carrying out internal operations in accordance with established standards, and recommendation of improvements in operating procedures that will result in improved efficiency and safety. Although a bank audit may overlap a bank examination in objectives and coverage, a desirable audit goes beyond an examination. It determines the accuracy of the figures that represent the assets and liabilities and income and expenses of the bank.

To avoid any influence or suppression of unfavorable information, the bank's auditor reports directly to the board of directors of the bank. If the report reveals some activity that is not consistent with the policies or rules and regulations of the bank and/or bank regulatory authorities or prudent banking, the bank's chief executive officer is directed to make the necessary changes. Such action is entered into the minutes of the board, as is the report of the chief executive officer that the corrections had been made or were in the process of being made at a later meeting. These minutes are available to the bank examiners and are thoroughly evaluated during the course of the next bank examination.

Examination

An excellent external control is the bank examination. Federal and/or state regulatory authorities usually examine a bank once a year and those banks that are in financial difficulties more often. The objective of bank examination was presented in Chapter 2.

Bank examinations, like the call report, contain an element of surprise, since banks do not know when they will be examined. During the process of examination, which may consume considerable time, from a few days to over a month, depending on the size of the bank, the examiner and staff may have a number of conferences with various officers and employees of the bank about numerous bank matters.

If it is considered desirable by the bank examiner, a conference may be held with some of the officers of the bank, or with the board of directors, or both, at the conclusion of the examination. During this conference, suggestions for the improvement of bank operations may be made. If there has been a violation of law, it will be explained; and if there are loans or investments that are subject to criticism, they will be discussed. Shortly after the examination, a formal report will be sent to the board of directors, with a covering letter setting forth the steps that should be taken to improve bank operations, should any be necessary.

A bank examination includes four phases: the limited verification of assets and liabilities, the appraisal of the assets and liabilities, determination of violation of law, and the appraisal of management. In a bank examination, the term "verification" does not carry the same meaning as it does in auditing. In auditing, verification means the proving of the existence and ownership of various items in a balance sheet and present-ing them fairly. Bank examiners do not conduct this type of verification, because they do not have the authority or the time. They do conduct what would be termed, in the language of public accountants, a "balance sheet audit"; that is, the existence and ownership of assets and liabilities are assumed to be correct as they appear in the balance sheet.

This part of a bank examination is the most misunderstood phase by the public. Many think supervisory and regulatory authorities in the course of their examinations of banks perform a very thorough verification function, and these individuals are amazed that embezzlements and de-falcations can ever occur in banking. Examiners do verify some items that can obviously and easily be verified, such as cash, securities, some de-posits, and property held for banking purposes. Vault cash is counted, and balances carried with other banks are verified. Securities can be veri-fied if held in the bank's vault. If they are held in a Federal Reserve bank or with some other bank, they are verified by corresponding with them. Cash carried by other banks is also verified by contacting those banks. Property held by the bank can be verified by examining the records of ownership. These items, however, do not include all the assets of a bank. Loans, which are a large percentage of the assets of a bank, are merely proved to the general books. The individual deposit ledgers are proved to the general books or total deposits, just as other liability items, such as cashier's and certified checks and income and expense items, are exam-ined and analyzed.

Although a bank examination is not designed to serve as a control device, it does serve that purpose. If the bank examiner finds some viola-tion of law and other shortcomings in the operation of the bank, it is fairly obvious that the standards established by the bank were being disregarded or that this particular activity was not clearly and adequately covered by bank policy.

PLANNING AND DECISION MAKING
BY DEPARTMENTS

Once the overall planning process is completed, the various departments and divisions are in a position to implement their planning in conformity with the overall objectives, policies, and strategies of the bank. In the establishment of objectives, policies, and strategies at the department and division levels, the final plan will include many rules that are not nor-mally found at the overall level. One of the reasons for the inclusion of rules in the departmental and divisional plans is because of banking regu-lations and the various laws that govern business activity. Banking law, for example, limits the amount of credit that banks can extend to any one borrower. State law governs the mortgaging of real estate, and the Truth-in-Lending Act requires that lenders provide prospective customers with certain information about a loan. Although the establishment of plans in many well-run banks occurs in all departments and divisions, probably the most thorough planning is found in the lending and investing areas due to the amount of assets involved and the importance of income from these sources. In the lending department, policies must be established to govern such important items as maturity and quality of loans, loan commitments, and excess lines. These and other loan policies cover similar items such as the type of securities acceptable for purchase, the quality of the securities, and maturities. As in lending, the plan would include several rules, again because of banking rules and regulations.

The establishment of policies and rules makes decision making much easier, quicker, and more decisive. Moreover, it reduces the risk of making the wrong decision. Decisions are made within the parameters of policies and rules established after careful analysis of all the influencing factors. Time is not wasted, for example, in debating such an issue as to what the maturity of an automobile loan should be or whether it is advisable to take a second mortgage on some property as security. In the investment department, the officials do not have to discuss the advantages and disadvantages of a security with a 30-year maturity that has just come to market when it has been established that the maximum maturity that will be eligible for the investment portfolio is ten years or whether consideration should be given to the purchase of a Polish bond when established policy states that foreign bonds are not acceptable. Time is not consumed in making routine decisions. It should be pointed out, however, that planning should not become a straitjacket and that exceptions should not ever be made. Exceptions are acceptable and are frequently made, but this does not negate the wisdom of planning. The ability to make exceptions and the wisdom in doing so are strengthened by careful and efficient planning.

BANK ORGANIZATION

To implement strategies and attain objectives, work must be performed; consequently, someone must lead and direct. There are many types of organizational structures. They are efficient if they facilitate the accomplishment of objectives by people. Although all banks do not have the same organizational structure, there are great similarities. Part of this is due to bank regulations and part to tradition. By law, a bank must have a board of directors and certain committees and officers.

Organization charts are often helpful in explaining the structure of the firm. In this section, two hypothetical organization charts are presented for the purpose of discussion. It should not be assumed that their presentation is to imply that they are ideal. Organization charts have some limitations. They show only formal authority relationships and omit those that are informal and could be very significant. Sometimes they show what is supposed to be rather than what really exists. Finally, observers of organization charts may confuse authority relationships with status. Frequently, someone in the lower levels on the chart may really have more authority and influence in the management process than some at the higher levels. Despite these shortcomings, organization charts do have some value in explaining the lines of authority, departmentalization, and functions of commercial banks.

Banks in general are highly departmentalized. Departmentalization in banking, as in other business organizations, results from the inability of one person to perform all the tasks connected with one group of activities. It is an outgrowth of a need to assemble the specialized knowledge that develops from an increasing volume and from the complexities of bank operations and the varied services rendered to customers. Departmentalization enables improved and expanded services to customers, develops more efficient officers and employees, and reduces the costs of operation.

The degree of departmentalization varies with the size and work of the bank. The absence of one or another department does not mean that a particular function is not performed in a bank. Some banks without a consumer loan department make consumer loans; similarly, all banks purchase securities, but many do not have a bond department, and all banks have public relations even though some may not have a public relations department. Only in banks where the volume of business is sufficient to have several people concerned with a particular function do we usually find departmentalization.

The organization of banks for management purposes also varies because of differences in size, personalities, and capabilities of officers and employees; the importance of the different functions performed and services offered; and the work load of the bank. The number of employees also varies from one bank to another, ranging from as few as three or four people to thousands.

Banks utilize both the line and staff functions in their organization. Functions that are directly involved in accomplishing the objectives of the bank are line functions and include activities such as lending, investing, trust services, international banking, and the acceptance and processing of deposits. Staff functions involve assistance and advice to those in the line and include accounting, personnel, education, marketing, control, methods, and building planning and maintenance. In small banks, line and staff functions are mixed, with some officers and employees performing both types. As banks become larger, line and staff functions are more clearly separated.

For efficient management in those banks that engage in branch banking, some form of regional organization is necessary, since some branch banks may have a hundred or more branches. In branch banking we usually find the banking market, which may be statewide, divided into geographic areas with a vice president and regional manager in charge of each area. This officer would have a staff of technicians to help in the supervision of the branches in the region. The size and composition of the regional staff depend on the number of branches, the degree of decentralization approved by top management, the type of banking in the area, and the capabilities of the branch managers. A regional organization includes one or more loan supervisors. If there are several loan supervisors, they probably specialize in the areas of commercial, real estate, agricultural, and consumer loans. The staff would certainly have an operations and personnel officer, a marketing officer, and probably others. The functions performed and the number of officers and employees in a branch depend on its size and the type of clientele. The banking functions that are always present are lending and operations. If trust services and international banking are demanded, they too are provided. If the demand for these services is insufficient to warrant skilled personnel, the services would still be provided by other branch personnel, with some assistance and close supervision from the head office. Although the handling of deposits is an important function in any bank or branch, it has become less of a chore for branches since the actual preparation and posting of statements have been computerized and performed at regional centers or at the head office. This development has made possible greater accuracy at less cost, plus the release of personnel for more customer-oriented services.

Historically and traditionally, banks have been organized around two basic concepts—a strong executive and heavy reliance on committees as decision-making bodies. A strong executive, or what has been referred to by some as *rule at the top*, is probably an outgrowth of the fact that many banks started out as family enterprises. In the history of banking such names as Medici and Rothschild are well known in Europe. In America the names of Morris, Mellon, and Giannini are well known in banking circles. Many small banks in rural areas are still dominated by single families. Since the family had a great interest in the success of the bank, one of its members served as the chief executive officer and made most of the major decisions. The use of committees had its roots in the 1930s, when banking was searching for sound financial decisions in the midst of bank failures. Much was at stake then since the risks were very great. Committees, it was hoped, would come to sounder and more reliable decisions than would a single individual because of the basic philosophy that "two heads are better than one."

Organization in Small Banks

In Figure 4-2 a hypothetical organization chart for a relatively small unit bank is presented. Note that there are six departments: loans, invest-

FIGURE 4-2   Hypothetical Organization of a Unit Bank

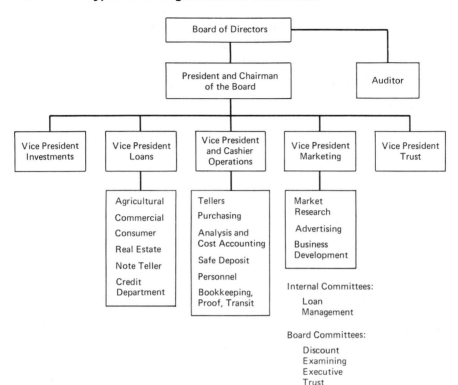

ments, operations, trust, marketing, and auditing. In our example, the investment department may not be very large or perform much work, whereas the trust department may have several officers and employees and enjoy a great deal of activity. The loan department is very important and is usually the largest in the bank. In our example, there are four areas of lending: commercial, consumer, real estate, and agricultural. The credit department is included under the officer in charge of loans, as is the note collector function. Although the investment department is important in a bank, it is normally not as large as some of the others. The reasons, of course, are that the investment department deals in relatively large units and operates in an organized and impersonal market rather than in a negotiated market, as does the loan department.

Several phases of bank operations are listed under the vice president and cashier. It would appear from the chart that the duties are numerous and that some are unrelated. To be sure, this is true; but the department would contain several officers skilled in these various areas. Many of these functions are "housekeeping" in nature and are not directly customer oriented, but they are important nevertheless. Note that the marketing department is also concerned with a wide range of activities, including advertising, market research, and business development. Business development can be quite broad and interesting. It normally includes an officer's call program, that is, visiting with customers and potential customers to increase the bank's business. It might also include contacts with national accounts and correspondent banks. Since Chapter 18 is devoted to trust services, the trust function and its organization will not be discussed here.

It may be noted that some bank services are not included in the organization chart. This does not mean necessarily that these functions are not performed. One example is international finance, which would probably be managed by the loan department in cooperation with one of the bank's city correspondents. The same may be true of issuing a bank credit card. In Figure 4-2 note that the auditor reports to the board of directors, which is the normal practice. Each of the functions in this chart is headed by a vice president. In small banks this would normally be the title used, but we might find the title of senior vice president or executive vice president. Strict uniformity does not exist in the use of titles in commercial banking; however, the larger the bank, the wider the range of titles.

In the chart the various committees are classified as board and internal. Board committees are the usual ones created by the board of directors and are dominated by the board as far as membership is concerned. Board committees would contain some bank officers who are also members of the board of directors, since their presence is necessary because of their familiarity with the subjects with which the committee is concerned. This is not necessarily true of the examining committee, which in many instances does not include any administrative officer, in the interests of objectivity. The president is usually a member of all committees, except the examination committee. In general, this is a desirable situation in a bank of this size since the president must carry out all policies and decisions of the board of directors; membership on these committees provides the president with firsthand knowledge of the decisions and thinking of the board members on the various issues.

Although internal committees are similar to the board committees, the membership does not normally include outside board members. This is due to the frequency of the meetings and the fact that they deal with day-to-day operational problems that are of no immediate concern to the board of directors. If they were, the matters would be referred to the board of directors. The management committee is made up of the top bank officers and is concerned with the coordination of all activities necessary for attainment of the bank's objectives. The loan committee is concerned with loan applications that are in excess of the lending officers' limits or that deviate in some manner from established bank policy.

The great increase in banking business has resulted in a decrease in the use of committees, since it would be physically impossible for board committees to handle the many problems that arise. In larger banks the discount or loan committee could not approve all loans, because of the time involved and the waiting that would be required of borrowers. Some borrowers might resent a period of waiting and might interpret the delay to mean that the bank considered them questionable risks.

The use of a loan committee also tends to curb the loan officer's talents. One cannot becomes a versatile and competent loan officer if all the decisions regarding loans must be made by a committee. For people to develop professionally, they must assume responsibility. This is true not only of lending but of all phases of commercial bank operations. Committees that are extremely active in management do not encourage decision making on the part of individual officers, and many functions in banking require skills that might not be possessed by committees.

In addition to the decline of committees in banking, an identifiable trend has developed toward restructuring the role of the chief executive. Since there is more to manage in a large organization, the delegation of authority to lower levels of management has increased. The extent to which this is accomplished successfully depends on the effectiveness of the bank's planning, control, and information systems. Accompanying this delegation of authority has been a more formal designation of the executive's responsibilities among those concerned with management at the top echelon. This is illustrated in Figure 4-3, an organization chart for a relatively large branch banking system.

Organization in Large Banks

As bank functions have increased, top management has been organized into groups, with several functions placed under one individual. There is a simple explanation of this development. With the increase in banking functions, it is impossible, from the standpoint of the span-of-control principle, for the chief executive to administer all of them. Consequently, different functions that are similar in nature are grouped together. The asset management group shown in Figure 4-3 is an example. For many years the loan and investment functions were separate and, to a certain degree, competed for funds. Obviously, these two functions should complement one another since the size of the investment and loan portfolios varies, depending on the stage of the business cycle. For example, in periods of expansion, loans would increase while the investment portfolio would decrease; in periods of low demand, the opposite would occur. As a result, it is logical that one person could more effectively manage the overall function, keeping in harmony with the bank's objectives.

FIGURE 4-3 Hypothetical Organization of a Branch Banking System

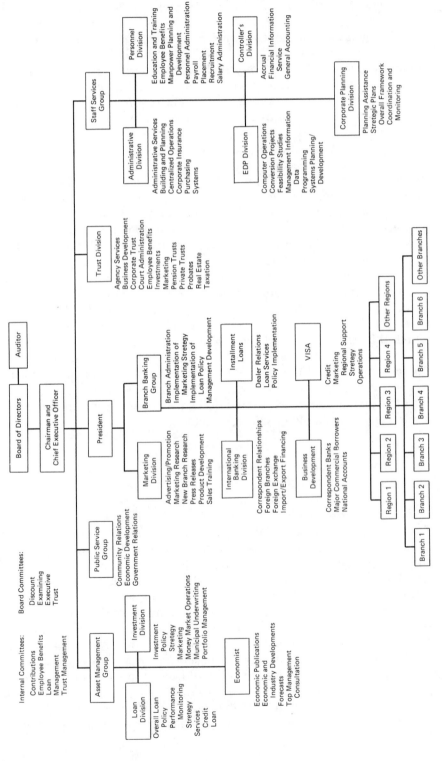

Note that a public service group has been created to handle community and government relations, a function that for years was considered an exclusive province of the chief executive. Profit planning is also a division under staff services, and this, too, was once jealously guarded by the chief executive officer. This does not mean that the officer is unfamiliar with these areas or is unconcerned with their performance. This has developed because of the increase in management duties and because the functions are of such importance that a full-time person is necessary for their performance.

A final development in recent years has been the improvement and expansion of staff capability to support a bank's line management. This trend is illustrated in the organization chart in Figure 4-3, with the cluster of functions under the staff services group. Included here are administrative services, personnel, profit planning, the comptroller function, and data processing. A lending officer cannot have available all the data that would be of value in performing his or her function. The lending officer increasingly relies on such staff services as the credit department. The computer has made it possible to assemble information of great value to a lending officer. He or she is not, however, required to write an independent program or operate the computer. Skilled technicians provide these services. Strong staff capabilities are not limited to the lending function but are found in all areas of the bank, including investments, trust services, and marketing.

The asset management group is concerned with the two most important classes of assets of the bank: investments and loans. The investment of bank funds is an operating function, whereas the loan division is a staff function concerned with overall loan policy and the quality of loans. The bank economist is a part of the asset management group since his or her expertise is of value in the allocation of bank resources. A large bank is responsible to the community, and these functions are listed under the public service group in Figure 4-3.

The president heads the branch banking group, the most important operating area of the bank, and the marketing division. The latter is included here since marketing is concerned with new services, new branches, advertising, and promotion, all of which contribute to the successful operation of the various branches. The branch banking group provides some staff services necessary for the efficient operation and administration of the branches. Installment loans and business development would probably be staff functions, but international banking and credit card would probably be operating units as well. Under the branch banking group are the various regions; under each region are the various branches.

Banks with branches differ in organization from unit banks even though the functions performed are basically the same. The major differences in organizational structure are found in the control of the various branches and in the functions performed by the senior officers at the head office. Branch banks are organized along line and staff lines, as are unit banks, although they probably place greater emphasis on staff functions. The nature of branch banking necessitates the presence of a branch administrator, through whom lines of control usually pass to the several branches of the organization.

The local branch bank organization is similar to that of a unit bank and performs those functions warranted by the amount of banking services required in the community. If the branch is located in a large community, it would probably be departmentalized similarly to the hypothetical unit bank. If it is located in a small community where the amount of business done is relatively small, it would not be departmentalized, but might take a form of organization similar to that of the small unit bank. One special advantage a small branch can offer is the service and advice of skilled personnel available to it from the head office.

Some functions of a small branch are performed at the central location, however. One of these is the investment function, which can be performed more efficiently and economically at the head office. Such concentration permits greater specialization. The correspondent banking function is also performed by personnel at the head office. Most of the personnel function is also centered in the head office, where personnel needs are known for all branches and where greater opportunities for a supervised and planned training program exist. The branch managers interview and hire local personnel at the nonofficer level, however. No mention has been made of titles in our hypothetical organization in Figure 4-3, but in a bank of this size the heads of the various groups would probably be executive vice presidents or at least senior vice presidents. It is not necessarily true that as we drop down the organization the titles follow accordingly. It is entirely possible that a branch manager would carry the title of vice president. After all, some branch banks are larger than unit banks.

Branch managers are responsible to their regional administrator. The officers located at the head office perform a staff function, and their advice usually flows through the regular chain of command to the various branches. Branch managers have a certain amount of authority; but if a problem arises that requires anything in excess of this predetermined authority, the head office is contacted for advice and counsel.

Lending is an example of this limited authority. A branch manager is usually given a certain lending limit. When requests in excess of this limit are received, the branch manager is required to contact his or her supervisor, who may have the authority to approve the request. If not, the request moves to the central office where an investigation is made by skilled people with adequate facilities at hand to determine the creditworthiness of the applicant. A decision is then reached. The argument that branch banking has more capable management than have unit banks is illustrated by this example. The skilled people at the top in every phase of banking stand ready to lend assistance to all branches at a moment's notice.

Branch managers must be skilled in two separate areas. They must possess expertise in the field of banking—lending, operations, marketing bank services, and the like; they must be managers. Branch managers are responsible for assembling the resources—human and material—at hand to attain the goals and objectives of the bank. They must be able to motivate people to accomplish their assigned tasks. In a very real sense, they weld together a team that has common goals and objectives. In addition to these important functions, the public expects a branch manager to be a financial adviser as well as a leader in the community. The branch manager is expected to serve on the local hospital board, help raise funds for the Community Chest or United Fund, attend P.T.A. meetings, and participate in chamber of commerce activities. Branch managers wear many different hats.

As already noted, small banks are not usually departmentalized, so it is not uncommon to find officers and employees performing a variety of tasks incident to the bank's operations. All officers, including the president, may be concerned with making loans of all types—business, agricultural, and consumer. However, certain officers may specialize by performing designated duties such as handling bank investments, trust services when performed, personnel, public relations, business development, and the preparation of reports required by the regulatory and supervisory agencies.

Moreover, one officer, usually the cashier, may be delegated the task of supervising such internal operations of the bank as the bookkeeping, purchasing, and deposit functions. Employees in small banks perform a variety of jobs—acting as bookkeeper, paying and receiving tellers, and note teller. It is doubtful, under these conditions, that a person can become a specialist in a particular field and that the bank's services can be as efficient as those of a more specialized bank. It is also doubtful that internal control and security attain the standards found in larger departmentalized banks. In some very small banks, the president is not an active officer, and the bank is headed, in fact, by the cashier or a vice president.

Even though a small bank may not be departmentalized, certain services are still provided. For example, if some foreign operations service were demanded by a customer, this small bank could probably perform the service by working with one of its city correspondents. A number of other demands for services could be performed in the same manner. This is one of the advantages of the present correspondent banking relationship that exists in the banking system. A small bank may not have a credit department, but this does not mean that credit analysis or the retention of credit information is not performed. Each lending officer is probably required to maintain records on the loans that he or she supervises. Too often in small banks, this information is carried mentally rather than in a written and orderly form, however. Small banks may not have an auditing department or an auditor, but the function may be performed by the officers at irregular and slack periods during the year or an examination may be performed annually by a private accounting firm under the supervision of the board of directors.

THE BOARD OF DIRECTORS

Stockholders, depositors, and regulatory authorities look to directors for policy decisions and management ability that will result in the safety of funds and profitable operations. A board of directors is not directly concerned with the day-to-day operations of its banks since it delegates authority to various officers, but the directors are ultimately responsible for the success of the bank's operation.

Requirements of Bank Directors

Federal law requires that a national bank board consist of from five to twenty-five directors. State banks that are Federal Reserve System members must conform to this provision. National bank directors are elected by the stockholders for one-year terms. State laws generally have similar provisions. A majority of national bank directors must be citizens of the United States and each must directly own shares of the capital stock in the bank he or she directs, the aggregate par value of which shall not be less than $1,000.[2]

The federal government has followed a policy of prohibiting interlocking directorates. This policy has been seen as necessary to prevent the creation of a *money trust*, the concentration of capital and credit in the hands of relatively few individuals. Apparently, this fear does not extend to interlocking directorates between banks and large businesses, since there are no national laws prohibiting such relationships. Indeed, many boards, especially in large banks, are made up of presidents and chairpersons of relatively large private corporations with which the banks have business connections. In recent years, however, regulatory authorities have not looked with favor on a bank board member serving on the board of directors of a competing financial institution such as a savings and loan association. The reason for this concern stems from the possibility of a conflict of interest.

---

[2] If the capital stock of the bank is $25,000 or less, however, the amount of stock required is only $500.

Responsibilities of Bank Directors

Bank directors have considerable authority in the performance of their duties. Although the objectives of a bank may be formulated by the officers of a bank and members of the board of directors, in the final analysis the approval of the objectives is the responsibility of the board. The board has the authority to appoint and discharge officers and employees and may require bonds of various officers or employees. It may name, appoint, and define the duties of as many committees from its membership as it desires. The board may determine the type of reports it wants from the officers of the bank.

The directors also have the power to amend the bylaws, in any legal way, as long as such amendments do not materially affect the stockholders' interest. If a change affecting their interest is thought desirable, their approval must be secured at a stockholders' meeting. The board has the authority to declare a dividend or transfer funds from the undivided profits account to surplus. In the final analysis, the board has the authority to determine the amount that will be invested in loans, bonds, and other assets.

Functions of the Board of Directors

In meeting their responsibilities to the depositors, stockholders, and supervisory agencies, the members of the board of directors perform many functions, which vary considerably among banks. Some boards of directors are more active than others, depending on the occupations of the members, the time they have to devote to the affairs of the bank, their interest in the bank's progress, and their investment in the bank. In general, however, the directors of banks would be concerned with some or all seven of the following activities.

Determination of Bank Objectives and Formulation of Bank Policies. Probably the most important functions of the board of directors of a commercial bank are the establishment of its objectives and the determination of its policies. Members of the board of directors in many banks participate in this phase of the planning process. Establishing objectives is the first task, since these are basic to the determination of the bank's policies and affect the organizational structure and influence the employment of personnel. This contributes to the molding of the bank's personality.

The development of policies is necessary in planning a course of action. Policies may appear in the minutes of the board or standing committees or in the manual of organization. Smaller banks have little written policy, but larger banks find this is almost a necessity. Policies may be established by the board of directors, by committees, or by the officers and employees in any department of the bank. Unit banks can formulate policy more easily than can branch banks because of the proximity of personnel and their smaller trade territory. Since a branch banking organization may cover larger geographic areas, its board of directors should not disregard the policy contribution made by a branch manager. A branch bank organization may have a different policy on a particular matter for each area of its operation. Areas differ in economic growth, activities, needs, and people's attitudes.

Policies should be flexible, and the board should review them periodically with the idea of making improvements. Economic conditions, among other factors, may make change necessary. Although many matters in bank management require the establishment of policy, it should not become a straitjacket for management. A few policies that need periodic reviewing are those on charge-offs, loans, investments, and insurance. These, and others, will be discussed at length later.

Selection of Bank Management. Employment of good management is an important function of the board of directors. Usually it is difficult to find skilled bankers on the board of directors, except for those members who are also officers of the bank. Nonofficer members may have good business judgment and be capable of determining the policies of the bank, but they are not trained bankers with knowledge of the actual operations of a bank. They often are busy people, operating their own businesses, who can spare only a few hours each week to the supervision of the bank's activities. Bank operations are complex and require trained personnel with a knowledge of investments, credits, operations, people, and machines; therefore, the selection of capable personnel demands careful consideration. The board selects personnel with the policies it has set in mind, since the officers of the bank will be responsible for carrying out those policies.

Creation of Committees. In addition to selecting the officers, the board of directors creates certain standing committees and elects the members. The use of committees in banking has developed for several reasons. It has been found that nonofficer directors who are local business people have a knowledge of the community and various business endeavors. The committee form of organization has been encouraged, and in some instances required, by the supervisory authorities. Since banking primarily involves the employment of depositors' funds in earning assets, a belief has developed that group decision will result in fewer bad loans and investments.

The use of committees has also developed because of their value in coordinating the various departments of the bank and serving as a medium of communication. Therefore, it is customary to set up various standing committees that may meet weekly, or more often, to handle certain matters. Special committees may be created to handle something of an exceptional nature, for example, remodeling the banking quarters or building a new building.

In general there are four principal standing committees of the board of directors:

1. *Executive Committee.* The executive committee is primarily an administrative committee handling matters that would ordinarily be taken up by the board but require attention between the regular meetings. This committee may make various studies that will be reported to the board as a whole at a future meeting.
2. *Discount Committee.* The discount committee is one of the busiest and most important committees of the board of directors. This committee may pass on all loans or loans above a certain amount, lines of credit, interest rates on loans, and the amount to be placed in the various classes of loans, such as real estate, personal, and commercial.
3. *Trust Committee.* The trust committee is concerned with the investment of funds and other matters incident to the various trust accounts.
4. *Examination Committee.* The examination committee examines the bank at unstated intervals. In a sense its work is comparable to a supervisory agency examination. The examination of the bank can be done by either the members of the examining committee or an outside agency employed by the committee.

The activities of committees vary considerably among banks. In some banks, especially small ones, committees are quite active in actual management, whereas in larger banks they are concerned primarily with matters of policy. In some small banks, for example, the loan or discount committee approves most of the loans made by the bank. In larger banks, this function is usually reserved for a committee made up of the loan officers of the bank, who are skilled in lending and who have greater knowledge of the request than do members of the board of directors.

Supervision of Loans and Investments.   Supervision of loans and investments by the board does not mean that the board actually directs these two important functions. It does mean that the board is responsible for seeing that lending and investing are carried out in accordance with sound principles, banking laws, and the regulations imposed by regulatory and supervisory authorities. Supervision of loans and investments involves a periodic review of portfolios to determine whether the bank has been following its established loan and investment policies. It also involves changing established policies to better meet the bank's objective in view of changes that may have occurred in loan demand, interest rates, and liquidity needs.

Counseling. A very important function of a board of directors is to counsel—to give advice to the officers of the bank that will aid the officers in making decisions. Their business and professional experiences give them a knowledge of the community and its people somewhat different from that of the officers of the bank, which is certainly of value in counseling with the officers. Since the directors are in contact with many people, they may be able to evaluate the actions of the bank better than people within the bank. They may also be able to predict the degree of public acceptance of some proposed change in bank policy. Bank management relies heavily on the counsel of business and professional members of the board. If a retailer is on the board, his or her advice in his or her field would be invaluable to the officers of the bank. Naturally, the same could be said about contractors, doctors, lawyers, manufacturers, and any other business or professional people who might be members.

Business Development. Well-respected leaders in the community can certainly influence many depositors and borrowers to patronize the bank of which they are directors. A bank that has an outstanding retailer, manufacturer, doctor, or lawyer on the board, who is active in his or her respective field, locally and nationally, and is a member of various civic committees is certainly in a better position to attract new business than is one with directors of lesser stature.

Review of Bank Operations. Even though bank directors are usually busy people primarily concerned with their own businesses and professions, they must maintain general supervision of the affairs of the bank. To a great extent, this is accomplished by periodic review of bank operations, usually at a monthly meeting at which various reports prepared by the executive officers are reviewed. Oral reports or visual presentations may be employed, followed by questions and a discussion of the bank's progress. In larger banks, the review must be quick because of the volume of business. Therefore, it is necessary that the reports be concise, yet adequate to give the board a picture of the month's operation.

Liabilities of Bank Directors

Bank directors cannot take their positions lightly. Both statutory law and common law impose penalties on directors for mismanagement of the bank's affairs. It is impractical to mention all the laws and situations that give rise to such responsibilities, but a few, applicable to national banks, are presented to illustrate the importance of the directors' liabilities.

Criminal Liabilities. Violation of criminal laws carries a fine of $5,000, or imprisonment of not more than five years, or both. Some of the violations that apply to directors, as well as to officers, agents, and employees of the bank are

1. False entries, false reports, and the like
2. False certification of checks
3. Theft, embezzlement, or misapplication of funds
4. False representation as to Federal Deposit Insurance coverage
5. Loans to bank examiners
6. Loans of trust funds to directors
7. Receiving fees for procuring loans
8. Making political contributions[3]

In addition to being exposed to criminal liabilities, bank directors may become liable for losses sustained by the bank as a result of some breach of statutory requirements in which they have participated, assented to, or caused because they have not exercised the due care required under common law. Issues of this kind involve both liability for statutory violations and common law liability for negligence.

The statutory liability of directors is based on the provisions of the National Bank and Federal Reserve acts. Paragraph 34 of the National Bank Act states the liability as follows:

> If the directors of any national banking association shall knowingly violate, or knowingly permit any of the officers, agents, or servants of the association to violate any of the provisions of this title (Title LXII of the U.S.R.S., consisting of the National Bank Act and related laws), all the rights, privileges, and franchises of the association shall be thereby forfeited. Such violation shall, however, be determined and adjudged by a proper circuit, district, or Territorial Court of the United States, in a suit brought for that purpose by the Comptroller of the Currency, in his own name, before the association shall be declared dissolved. And in cases of such violation, every director who participated in or assented to the same shall be held liable in his personal and individual capacity for all damages which the association, its shareholders, or any other person, shall have sustained in consequence of such violation.[4]

The courts have held that directors are personally liable for the violation of national banking statutes. Directors may become civilly liable if they knowingly authorize or acquiesce in the making of false reports to any person who is injured by relying on such published reports. In *Chesbrough* v. *Williams*, for example, the directors were held liable for falsifying the capital account of the bank, which induced the plaintiff to purchase stock in the bank.[5] In *Yates* v. *Jones National Bank*, the Court said that "an action for deceit may be maintained against the directors of a

---

[3] U.S., Treasury Department, Office of the Comptroller of the Currency, *Duties and Liabilities of Directors of National Banks* (Washington, D.C.: Government Printing Office, October 1969).

[4] 12 U.S.C., sec. 93.

[5] *Chesbrough* v. *Williams*, 244 U.S. 72 (1916).

bank by depositors induced to become such by false representations in statements of the bank's condition made by such director."[6] Directors may incur personal liability for damages sustained by the bank as a result of paying dividends contrary to law.[7]

Directors are also personally liable for losses resulting from their failure to investigate a matter that is within their power to investigate, "if bank directors deliberately refrain from investigating a matter which it is their duty to investigate, or having knowledge of facts which put them on notice of irregular or criminal acts, they deliberately refrain from utilizing available accounting methods and from employing independent auditors to determine the full extent of the loss to the bank, any resulting violation of the statute may be regarded as 'in effect intentional' or as having been committed 'knowingly.' "[8]

Thus bank directors have a duty at common law to exercise ordinary care and prudence in administering the affairs of their bank. They "cannot, in justice to those who deal with the bank, shut their eyes to what is going on around them. It is their duty to use ordinary diligence in ascertaining the condition of its business, and to exercise reasonable control and supervision of its officers."[9] Directors are also personally liable for losses resulting from *ultra vires*—acts that are beyond the power conferred upon the bank.[10] The court has been very strict in interpreting the section of federal law that prohibits national banks from making loans in excess of 15 percent of the bank's capital and surplus, with certain exceptions. "Where the directors assent to the making of loans in excess of the maximum permissible amount, they may be held liable for any losses sustained, regardless of their motives, or the financial standing of the borrowers at the time the loans were made, or the value of any security taken; and any such liability will not be limited to the portion of the loans in excess of the prescribed limit but may include the whole amount plus interest and less recovery on the loans."[11] Furthermore, liability cannot be avoided by resorting to a loan to two or more persons who are closely affiliated in a business. This same general restriction also applies to investments of commercial banks.

Common Law Liability for Negligence. Directors are subject to common law liability for negligence. As pointed out in *Gamble v. Brown*, the "National Bank Act does not relieve directors from common-law duty

---

[6] *Yates v. Jones National Bank*, 206 U.S. 158 (1906).

[7] *United States v. Britton*, 108 U.S. 199 (1883); *Dudley v. Hawkins*, 239 Fed. 386 (1917).

[8] *F.D.I.C., Receiver of the Commercial National Bank of Bradford, Pa. v. Mason*, C.C.A. 3d (1940), 115F. (2d) 548.

[9] *Martin v. Webb*, 110 U.S. 7 (1883).

[10] *Cockrill v. Abeles*, 86 Fed. 505 (1898).

[11] *Corsicana National Bank v. Johnson*, 251 U.S. 68 (1919).

to be honest and diligent, and the degree of care required in such respect is that which ordinarily prudent men would exercise under similar circumstances."[12]

Analysis of Directors' Liabilities.   The criminal and common law liabilities of bank directors are severe, but they are not as harsh as they may appear at first sight. They may be eliminated or lessened in several ways. The directors can protect themselves against these liabilities by becoming thoroughly acquainted with banking law, the regulations of supervisory authorities, and the bank's operations; by the employment of honest officers and employees, as far as this is possible; by insurance; and by internal controls. Because of the quasi-public nature of banking, dishonesty cannot be tolerated. Not only does it result in losses to depositors and stockholders, but it also erodes public confidence in the banking system. Therefore, officers and employees, as well as directors, must have a high concept and a fair code of business ethics and must respect the various banking laws and regulations imposed by the supervisory and regulatory authorities.

Directors may insure themselves and the bank against many of the statutory and common law liabilities and against various risks that may arise from the nature of the bank's operations. The Insurance and Protective Committee of the American Bankers Association has done much to improve and standardize insurance coverage for banks. This committee has from time to time published suggested amounts of minimum and maximum coverage for banks of various deposit size. Many risks are now included in one bond, commonly referred to as a blanket bond for banks. These policies cover losses from such criminal acts as embezzlement, burglary, robbery, theft, larceny, and forgery and provide for indemnity for loss of money and securities. Insurance that covers many of the risks associated with safe deposit operations can be purchased. There are policies to cover losses arising from errors and omissions in mortgages or other legal documents and from fraudulent, counterfeit, fictitious, raised, invalid, or nonexistent accounts receivable. Banks may also purchase insurance that will protect them against court costs and attorney's fees.

Directors may reduce their liability, as well as that of the bank, by the adoption of a system of audit or internal controls. This method is so important that most chartering agencies require that banks have an examination committee and, in addition, require the board of directors to examine the bank a minimum number of times each year. This examination may be done by the directors themselves, or they may hire an outside accounting firm to perform the audit. The ideal situation is for the bank to have a full-time auditor reporting directly to the board, as many large and medium-sized banks do. The auditor's function is primarily to improve

---

[12] *Gamble v. Brown,* 29F. (2d) 366 (1928).

accounting methods and systems in such a manner that they will reflect the complete record of the transactions of the bank accurately and economically and leave little, if any, room for dishonesty to be hidden.

The liabilities of bank directors are large, to be sure, but they are not of such magnitude as to prohibit the participation of capable, interested, and honest individuals in bank management, as the history of banking in this country has proved. Many ways of reducing and eliminating these liabilities exist, but none has been designed that will substitute for the basic ingredient of business and personal relations—honesty.

ADMINISTRATIVE OFFICERS

In a bank, especially a large one, several officers are responsible for the management function. The most important are the chairman of the board, president, executive vice president, vice presidents, assistant vice presidents, cashier, and comptroller. In some banks, the title of senior vice president, denoting a rank above that of vice president, is often used. In addition to these management officers, an auditor is found in larger banks.

The position of chairman of the board carries with it a great deal of dignity and respect in banking circles. The chairman is usually the chief executive officer of the bank, keeps the board of directors informed on the progress of the bank, and implements the policies established. This officer is also concerned with planning, public relations, and broad banking policies. The president is the administrative head of the bank and is responsible for administering the business affairs of the bank. It is primarily through the president that the personality of the bank emanates. A president may not be concerned with the bank's actual operations but would concentrate instead on building goodwill for the bank through personal, business, and social contacts. However, many bank presidents take part in all activities of the bank, such as interviewing customers, granting loans, and making credit investigations. Most presidents probably fall somewhere between these two extremes, as far as the nature of their activity is concerned. Officers with the title of executive vice president, senior vice president, or vice president are usually placed in charge of a major department or in charge of a branch if the bank is engaged in branch banking.

The office of the cashier is nearly as old as banking itself. Each national bank and some state banks are required by law to have a cashier. For a long time, the cashier was a person with many years of experience who had worked up the ladder from a messenger, bookkeeper, teller, or perhaps all three. Customary and traditional duties, especially in small banks, include all those incident to the internal operations of the bank and may involve personnel, records, acting as secretary to the board, insurance, and safekeeping of cash and securities. The cashier's traditional control over the money of the bank is reflected in the term *cashier's check*. The cashier is usually responsible for all reports to the regulatory agencies, such as the call report, which sets forth the assets and liabilities of the bank as of a certain date and the earnings and dividend reports.

The comptroller of a bank is its chief accounting and statistical officer. Few small banks have a comptroller, but one is often found in the larger banks. Only in recent years have the duties of the comptroller become as important as those of the other major functional officers. It is the comptroller's responsibility to gather and interpret data of value to the bank management so that wise decisions may be made regarding policy and operations. In addition to such cost accounting work, the comptroller checks on the actual operations of the bank. For example, the comptroller determines whether the note teller can skip one step of the operation and save the bank a few dollars and still maintain efficiency and accuracy of operation. The comptroller is concerned with new improvements, new machines, and new methods.

Most large banks and many small ones operate on a budget, and it is the comptroller's responsibility to draw up a tentative budget and supply the budget committee with information so that a realistic final budget can be adopted. This official is also responsible for supplying a large portion of the information included in the officers' monthly report to the board of directors.

The auditor is responsible for verifying the accounts resulting from the bank's daily operations and operating methods. The auditor's major duty is to examine the bank continually to ascertain whether the business is being conducted in accordance with acceptable accounting procedures, policies established by the board of directors, and rules imposed by regulatory authorities. The objective of this work is to safeguard the assets of the bank against manipulation, misappropriation, and waste. Through examinations of the bank's procedures the auditor is able to detect discrepancies. The auditor should be, and in many banks is, a direct representative of the board. The auditor reports, usually monthly, to the board, along with an account of any discrepancies found or any suggestions for improvement that are deemed advisable. All large banks have an auditor as, in recent years, do some smaller banks.

There are many vice presidents in banking—executive vice president, senior vice president, vice president, and assistant vice president. These titles are used primarily to differentiate levels of authority and the recognition of ability. Executive vice presidents normally are in charge of divisions or groups (see Figure 4-2). There may also be senior vice presidents who are in charge of divisions and/or departments. There might be several vice presidents in the lending area, although they might not necessarily have administrative duties. They have won this title through hard work, due diligence, and expertise. The assistant vice president title has been reserved for relatively young bankers who show great promise in a particular field of specialization. Titles in banks, as in other business firms, are in a sense rather meaningless. Functional titles might be more realistic, but the adoption of such titles would involve a break with tradition.

One of the important officers in a branch banking system is the branch manager. This person may have the title of manager or manager and vice president. This officer is very important because he or she may supervise banking assets far in excess of those in many unit banks. This person usually has had several years of experience in one or more areas of banking and has made an intensive study of the principles of management. A "full-service branch," a term that is used in the banking industry to imply that a branch provides all the services of a unit bank, requires adept management. It is for this reason that such branch managers are not only banking technicians but managers as well. About the only function not performed by such branches is that of investment. This responsibility is reserved for the home office. A full-service branch would have personnel of great expertise and experience. In a group banking system, the officers of the various banks would carry the same titles as would be found in unit banks. In some group banking systems, we may find a bank that has over one hundred branches throughout the state in which it is located.

In branch and group banking we find a level of management not found in unit banking, namely, regional administrators. As the term implies, this officer is in charge of several branches or banks in a specific geographic area. Various instructions, regulations, and policies pass through this bank official from the head office. If a branch or a bank that is a member of a group finds that it has need for advice in any area, it is the responsibility of the staff of the regional manager to pass it along or to send personnel to the particular branch office to render assistance. This is a desirable feature of branch and group banking according to the advocates of this type of banking.

QUESTIONS

1. The management of banks is regulated closely by laws and regulatory authorities. Would management be improved if there were less regulation? Why?

2. Considering the many liabilities of bank directors, would you like to serve on a bank board? Would you rather be a director of a nonfinancial corporation such as a manufacturing firm? Why?

3. From your knowledge of management, how would you evaluate the organization charts presented for hypothetical unit and branch banks? What suggestions would you make for improvement?
4. Do you think that there is too much reliance on committees in banking? Why?
5. Of all the responsibilities of the board of directors, which would you consider to be the most important? Why?
6. Do you agree that the most important function of management is planning? Why?
7. If the management of a bank came up with the idea that it should earn 12 percent on its net worth, would that be an objective or a part of its strategy? Why?

SELECTED REFERENCES

BAUGHN, WILLIAM H., AND CHARLES E. WALKER, eds. *The Bankers' Handbook*, rev. ed. Homewood, Ill.: Dow Jones-Irwin, 1978.

BRYAN, JAMES E., JR. "Changing the Internal Organization." *The Bankers Magazine*, 165, no. 3 (May–June 1982), 67–71.

THE COMPTROLLER OF THE CURRENCY. *Duties and Liabilities of Directors of National Banks.* Washington, D.C.: Government Printing Office, June 1972.

COX, EDWIN B., ET AL. *The Bank Directors' Handbook.* Boston: Auburn House, 1981.

FISHER, DAVID I. *Commercial Banking in 1975 and 1980.* Philadelphia: Robert Morris Associates, 1970.

MUELLER, ROBERT K. "What the Bank Director Needs to Know." *The Bankers Magazine*, 162, no. 5 (September–October 1979), 37–42.

5

ASSET
MANAGEMENT

Asset management is the term used to describe the allocation of funds among investment alternatives. Applied to commercial banking, the term refers to the distribution of funds among cash, security investments, loans, and other assets. Specialized areas of asset management include securities portfolio and loan management relating to the composition of securities and outstanding loans. A discussion of these specialized areas is included in later chapters. In this chapter, we are concerned with the broader aspects of the problem—that is, the conversion of deposits and capital funds into cash and earning assets.

The obvious solution to the funds allocation problem is to purchase those assets (make loans and investments) that promise the highest rate of return for the level of risk that a bank's management is prepared to assume. The management of funds in commercial banking is complicated by several factors, however. First, as banks are among the most regulated of all business enterprises, funds must be managed within the legal and regulatory framework established by statutory and supervisory authorities. Second, the relationship between a bank and its loan and deposit customers is one of trust as well as accommodation. Finally, the stockholders of a commercial bank, as is true for other investors, require a rate of return commensurate with the risk of the investment and competitive with the return available on similar investments.

The effects of legal and regulatory provisions on commercial bank asset management may be classified as those that specify how a part of a bank's assets must be invested and those that limit the use of funds in certain types of assets. An example of the first type of restriction is the provision that banks must hold a percentage of their deposits in cash or its equivalent. The second is illustrated by the prohibition on investing funds in common stocks of industrial corporations.

A great portion of commercial bank liabilities is payable on demand or with only short notice. Demand deposits are, of course, payable at the request of the depositor, and while prior notice of withdrawal may be required on time and savings deposits, banks generally regard savings deposits as payable on demand. Therefore, the first requirement of prudent bank management is to ensure the bank's ability to meet the claims of depositors. The second requirement is to make available sufficient funds to satisfy the legitimate credit needs of the bank's customers and surrounding community. The provision of such credit is the principal profit-making activity of a commercial bank. Failure to accommodate reasonable and legitimate loan requests from customers will result in immediate loss of business and, ultimately, the possible failure of the bank as a viable business organization.

Commercial banks are privately owned business firms that seek satisfactory profits subject to the constraints of liquidity and safety. At the same time, the role of banks as suppliers of most of the nation's money supply requires members of the industry to assume important public responsibilities. The public must never have reason to question the solvency, liquidity, or integrity of the banking system; and depositors must be able to maintain full confidence in the individual banking firm. The objectives of a bank's depositors and those of its stockholders are incompatible to some extent. This incompatibility is reflected in the unavoidable conflict between necessary liquidity and desired profitability that is present in virtually every financial transaction of a commercial bank.

This conflict between liquidity and profitability may be regarded as the central problem in the management of bank funds. Bank managers feel pressure from stockholders for greater profits, which may be earned by investing in longer-term securities, extending credit to borrowers with marginal creditworthiness, and reducing idle cash balances. On the other hand, the managers are acutely aware that these actions greatly reduce liquidity, which may be needed to meet deposit withdrawals and the credit demands of long-standing customers.

The risk of investing in loans and securities is defined sometimes as the dispersion of possible returns. An investment in a very short-term U.S. government security, for example, would be expected to have a virtually certain return. An investment in a low-grade corporate bond due in 20 years, on the other hand, would be subject to both credit risk and interest rate risk, and the return to be realized may vary from the loss of the entire investment to the full return promised if held to maturity. This wider dispersion of possible returns usually requires a promise of a higher interest rate to induce an investor to take the risk that the returns may be lower than promised. The trade-off between an asset's risk and expected rate of return is illustrated in Figure 5-1. As the risk increases beyond that of the safest securities, due to increased credit risk or increased time to maturity, the expected rate of return also increases. Thus a bank that takes on investments or loans that promise a higher rate of return also takes on more risk.

There is an interdependence among the management of assets and the management of liabilities, to be discussed in Chapter 6, and the management of capital funds, to be discussed in Chapter 7. Liquidity may be provided by holding cash and other liquid assets and also may be provided by an ability to attract additional deposits or to borrow from other sources. In addition, the high volatility of deposits may require larger holdings of liquid assets. It is important to relate maturities of liabilities and assets as well as their interest rate characteristics (i.e., fixed or variable rates) to maintain a profitable spread during periods when interest rates may change rapidly. Furthermore, there is a relationship between the cost of deposits and borrowed funds and the returns available from various categories of assets. A careful analysis of the marginal costs of funds relative to the marginal revenues available from loans and investments can enhance the profitability of a bank while staying within the constraints of liquidity.

FIGURE 5-1   Trade-off Between Risk and Return

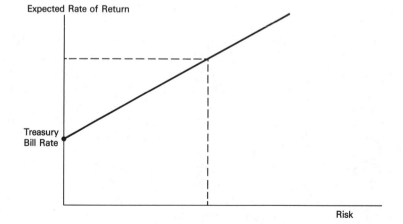

COMMERCIAL BANK ASSETS

Commercial bank assets may be divided into four basic categories: cash assets, security investments, loans, and fixed assets. The problem of asset management centers primarily on the allocation of funds among and within the first three categories; management is normally not involved on a day-to-day basis with the investment of funds in buildings and equipment. When such expenditures are planned, however, provision must be made to have sufficient cash available at the appropriate time.

Table 5-1 shows some of the complexity of the problem, presenting the asset structure of commercial banks in the United States. A considerable difference exists between the asset structure of banks and that of nonfinancial business firms. Most commercial bank assets are financial claims. Banks have relatively large cash balances and relatively small investments in land and buildings. In contrast, a typical manufacturing firm requires relatively small cash balances and has relatively large investments in inventories and fixed assets. The financial claims of a manufacturing firm are, for the most part, limited to accounts receivable and temporary investments of surplus cash.

TABLE 5-1   Assets of All Insured Commercial Banks, May 1987 (in millions of dollars)

1	Loans and securities	$2,156.2
2	Investment securities	471.5
3	U.S. government securities	296.7
4	Other	174.8
5	Trading account assets	21.4
6	Total loans	1,663.3
7	Interbank loans	128.6
8	Loans excluding interbank	1,534.7
9	Commercial and industrial	475.3
10	Real estate	520.3
11	Individual	314.5
12	All other	224.7
13	Total cash assets	213.2
14	Reserves with Federal Reserve Banks	35.9
15	Cash in vault	25.0
16	Cash items in process of collection	80.9
17	Demand balances at U.S. depository institutions	35.1
18	Other cash assets	36.2
19	Other assets	143.0
20	Total assets	$2,512.4

SOURCE: *Federal Reserve Bulletin,* August 1987.

The differences between the composition of a bank's assets and those of an industrial firm result from differences in the nature of their liabilities and the character of the profit-making activities in which the firms engage. An industrial firm derives most of its profits from the sale of goods that are manufactured from raw materials. Merchandising requires maintenance of a substantial finished goods inventory and manufacturing requires maintenance of a raw materials inventory as well as the use of expensive equipment housed in a modern plant. In contrast, bank profits are derived mostly from lending and investing and result in the bank holding notes, bonds, and other financial instruments evidencing the amounts to be repaid in the future.

CASH ASSETS

Commercial banks and other depository institutions are required by federal law to maintain a portion of their assets in the form of legal reserves consisting of cash or balances in accounts with a Federal Reserve bank or certain other financial institutions. In addition, working balances are required to make change, meet withdrawal requests, accommodate requests for loans, and provide for various operating expenses. The category "cash assets" includes balances at the Federal Reserve banks and at other depository institutions, currency and coin (vault cash), and cash items in the process of collection.

Legal Reserves

Uniform legal reserve requirements have been imposed on all depository institutions by the Depository Institutions Deregulation and Monetary Control Act of 1980 (DIDMCA). In addition to all commercial banks, the act requires other financial institutions that are federally insured or eligible for federal insurance to maintain reserves in the form of vault cash or deposit balances with a Federal Reserve bank or, in some cases, with certain other depository institutions.[1]

Legal reserve requirements are applied to all transaction accounts, nonpersonal time deposits, and certain Eurocurrency liabilities. Transaction accounts include demand deposits, NOW accounts, and other deposits "on which the account holder is permitted to make withdrawals by negotiable or transferable instruments, payment orders of withdrawal, telephone and preauthorized transfers (in excess of three per month), for the purpose of making payments to third persons or others."[2] DIDMCA

---

[1] Charles R. McNeill and Denise M. Rechter, "The Depository Institutions Deregulation and Monetary Control Act of 1980," *Federal Reserve Bulletin* (June 1980), pp. 444–453.

[2] *Federal Reserve Bulletin* (August 1987), p. A8.

specified a legal reserve requirement of 3 percent of an annually adjusted base amount—$36.7 million in 1987—of transaction accounts and authorized the Board of Governors of the Federal Reserve System to impose a requirement of between 8 and 14 percent on amounts over the base amount. The reserve requirements currently in effect are published monthly in the *Federal Reserve Bulletin*.

Reserve requirements on nonpersonal time deposits (where the depositor is not a natural person) may vary by maturity within a range of 0 to 9 percent. Requirements on such deposits were 3 percent in 1987 for those maturing within 18 months and 0 percent for larger maturities. In addition the Board of Governors may impose reserve requirements on certain Eurocurrency liabilities, and in 1987 the requirement was 3 percent.

For many nonmember state banks, reserve percentages held had been lower than the Federal Reserve requirements and generally were held in other forms than those required for member banks. The phase-in of DIDMCA reserve requirements was scheduled over an eight-year period for depository institutions other than member banks. The requirement for the first year was one-eighth of the specified amount and was scheduled to increase by one-eighth each year. The application of uniform reserve requirements for all depository institutions was designed to enhance the ability of the Federal Reserve System to control monetary policy, and brought thousands of institutions not previously subject to federal reserve requirements under such control by the Board of Governors.

Vault Cash

As the term implies, vault cash is the amount of coin and currency carried by banks in their vaults. Even though the amount is considered part of legal reserves, bank management attempts to keep it as low as possible for security reasons. Moreover, the cost of protection and insuring cash against loss is relatively high.

The amount of cash needed by individual banks varies widely. In some areas of the nation, transactions are settled in cash to a greater extent than in others where greater reliance is placed on the use of checks. Most banks experience seasonal demands for cash. Vault cash must be increased temporarily for anticipated events such as the crop harvesting season, when cash is needed for the payment of labor, and the Christmas season, when merchants and customers are accumulating larger than usual balances. Bank location is also an important factor influencing the size of cash balances. Banks situated relatively far from a Federal Reserve bank or branch or a correspondent bank are forced to carry more cash than are banks located closer to a cash supply. When a depositor requests currency or coin, it is neither good manners nor proper protocol to reply that it will arrive by courier later in the day. Country banks generally carry a larger amount of cash in relation to deposits than do city banks, partly because of their location.

Correspondent Bank Balances

The efficient collection of checks by commercial banks and the provision of services not available from the Federal Reserve banks have contributed to the continuation and growth of correspondent banking in America. Normally correspondent banks are compensated for the services they provide by investing for profit a portion of the correspondent bank account. The size of this account will vary roughly with the amount of services performed. However, the amount carried in a correspondent balance may not truly reflect the extent of the services rendered by the correspondent bank since many banks carry accounts that are seldom used. Often such accounts are maintained because of the friendship of bank executives, and much time and energy are devoted to generating and maintaining this type of account. The rising cost of providing banking services is forcing many banks to place correspondent relationships on a cost-benefit basis. This involves the pricing of individual services used by correspondent banks and asking these banks to maintain a balance sufficient to provide earnings equal to the full cost of the services provided.

SECURITY INVESTMENTS

Commercial banks purchase securities for liquidity and diversification purposes, to augment income, and to serve as collateral for deposit liabilities to federal, state, and local governments. The largest proportion of security investments is in government obligations—federal, state, or municipal. Investments in short-term U.S. government securities generally provide limited income but are highly liquid with no credit risk and little interest rate risk. Longer-term obligations normally offer greater income over extended periods of time. Often they are held until maturity or near maturity. Municipal securities have been attractive bank investments because the interest is exempt from federal income taxes and, in many cases, from state income taxes. However, the 1986 Tax Reform Act disallowed deductibility of the interest banks pay on the funds they invest in most municipal securities, so in recent years banks have increased other types of investments, such as those backed by mortgages.

The deposits of the federal government and those of many state and local governments must be secured by pledged securities to the extent they are not covered by deposit insurance. Securities pledged as collateral thus may not provide liquidity. There is evidence that there is therefore a greater demand for government securities than there would be in the absence of pledging requirements, implying reduced levels of funds for investment in other assets such as loans.[3]

Banks also hold relatively small amounts of other securities, including those held primarily to provide liquidity, such as bankers' acceptances, open-market commercial paper, brokers' loans, and Commodity Credit Corporation certificates of interest. To augment income, investments are made in the obligations of some government agencies and, on a limited basis, in high-grade corporate bonds.

Securities investments make up about 19 percent of bank assets. This is much less than in past years, due largely to the increased emphasis on lending. Also, large banks tend to have much smaller ratios of investments to total assets than small banks. Bank investments are discussed in Chapters 16 and 17.

BANK LOANS

The principal profit-making activity of commercial banks is making loans to its customers. In the allocation of funds to the loan portfolio, the primary objective of bank management is to earn income while serving the credit needs of its community. The degree of liquidity a particular loan commitment may have is of secondary importance. For example, few loans may be liquidated by sale to other institutions or individuals because of the limited secondary market in this type of financial claim. An exception has been the development of a secondary market for residential mortgage loans. Also, recent developments in "securitization" have added to the liquidity of other types of loans. Securitization results when bonds or notes are issued that are backed by a pool of loans, such as auto or commercial loans. This allows the original lender to recover indirectly funds from the loans while they are still outstanding.

The bank management must decide, too, upon the distribution of funds *within* the loan portfolio; that is, funds must be assigned to installment loans, commercial loans, real estate loans, and others. This assignment is made on the basis of the relative profitability of and demand for various classes of loans, subject to constraints required by prudence and imposed by regulation. Detailed consideration is given to loan policy and various classes of loans in Chapters 10 through 15.

PRIORITY CLASSES OF ASSETS

The assets just discussed are selected to serve various requirements, including meeting the need for operating funds and required reserves, pro-

---

[3] Ronald A. Ratti, "Pledging Requirements and Bank Asset Portfolios," *Economic Review,* Federal Reserve Bank of Kansas City (September–October 1979), pp. 13–23.

viding liquidity and generating income, and meeting the credit needs of the bank's market area. These assets are categorized below according to the priority of these various requirements.

Primary Reserves

The first priority in the allocation scheme is to establish the proportion of funds that will be allocated to primary reserves. This category of assets is a functional category that does not appear on the balance sheet of a commercial bank. Nevertheless, it is an important concept to a commercial banker and relates to those assets that can be used immediately to meet withdrawal requests and satisfy loan applicants. It is the primary source of liquidity for a commercial bank. In most instances, primary reserves are grouped under the heading "Cash and Due from Banks." Assets held as primary reserves include collected balances at the Federal Reserve banks, correspondent balances (deposits) at other commercial banks, vault cash, and cash items in the process of collection.

Note that the primary reserves include both legal reserves against deposit liabilities and the working balances that a bank's management judges to be sufficient. A common approach to establishing the proportion of funds to be allocated to the primary reserves is to use the average ratio of cash assets to deposits or total assets for all banks of similar size. Reference to Table 5-1, for example, might cause a bank with $400 million of total assets to establish a goal for primary reserves of about $34 million, or 8.5 percent of total assets.

Secondary Reserves

The second priority in the funds allocation process is providing for noncash liquid assets that contribute to the earning power of the bank. These reserves of a commercial bank consist of highly liquid earning assets that can be converted into cash with little delay and little risk of loss. The major function of these secondary reserves is to replenish and supplement the primary reserve. As does *primary reserve*, the *secondary reserve* refers to an economic concept rather than to an accounting one, so it does not appear in the balance sheet. The assets that make up this reserve are found in the securities investment portfolio usually and in the loan accounts in some instances.

Highly marketable securities have long been considered an excellent source of liquidity. Such securities can easily be converted to cash. To ensure convertibility without delay and appreciable loss, assets of the secondary reserve must meet three requirements: high quality, short maturity, and marketability. They must be free of credit and interest rate risk and be salable in the market on short notice.

No definite rule exists regarding the maturity of assets held as liquid reserves, but in general, the shorter the maturity, the better. A more realistic position is that they should be of such length that the effects of the interest rate risk encountered in buying them would be relatively insignificant. Many bankers think in terms of a maturity of one year or less before high-grade marketable securities are included in the secondary reserve.

The requirements of quality and marketability may be met by a number of different types of securities. Treasury bills are the most common security held for the second reserve. In addition, banks hold other securities issued by the federal government and its agencies. Government bonds are eligible if the maturity date is close, since interest rate risk becomes less as maturity shortens. Short-term securities of various agencies of the federal government are suitable secondary reserve instruments.

Some high-grade short-term securities from the private sector are eligible for the secondary reserve, too. Included in this category are bankers' acceptances and open-market commercial paper. A banker's acceptance is a draft that has been accepted by a bank for payment at a later date, usually 180 days or less. The use of this instrument arises primarily from the financing of international trade. Bankers' acceptances are traded in a fairly active market and are eligible for discount at the Federal Reserve banks.

Open-market commercial paper is often purchased by commercial banks for their secondary reserve portfolios. To borrow in this market, a corporation must have a very high credit rating. Commercial paper often is held by a bank until maturity, although dealers may repurchase it under prior agreement. Commercial paper may be rediscounted at a Federal Reserve bank, provided it is within 90 days of maturity and is otherwise eligible for discount.

The percentage of bank assets nationally made up of instruments qualifying for the secondary reserve can only be estimated since asset maturity is not included in aggregate reports. The average probably is 7 to 8 percent, but an individual bank may feel its needs are more or less, depending on management's willingness to trade liquidity for higher earnings opportunities and by the numerous factors that influence the variability of deposits and loans. A bank that experiences great variation in deposits and a highly erratic credit demand would need a larger secondary reserve than would a bank with stable loans and deposits.

Loan Portfolio

The third priority in the use of bank funds is the allocation of funds to the loan portfolio. After a bank has taken care of its primary and secondary reserve needs, it is free to make loans to its customers. Loans represent the most important part of total bank assets, and income from loans is the greatest contributor to bank profits. Most risks inherent in banking activities are carried in the loan portfolio.

Investment for Income

The final priority is the allocation of funds to the investment portfolio. Funds remaining after the legitimate credit needs of customers have been met may be placed in relatively long-term, high-quality securities. The functions of the investment portfolio are to provide income to the bank, diversification, tax benefits, and additions to secondary reserves as the long-term securities approach maturity.

ALLOCATION METHODS

Several approaches to allocating funds to assets have developed over the years. Three are discussed briefly in this chapter. A fourth approach, asset-liability management, has become popular since the high interest rates of the late 1970s and early 1980s and will be discussed in the next chapter. These various approaches are not totally different from one another; they overlap, as should be expected, because they all seek to provide the best returns available given the levels of risk bank managements are willing to accept. Also, as will be pointed out, all four methods have deficiencies.

The Pool of Funds Approach

The funds available to the portfolio manager of a commercial bank are derived from a number of sources, including demand deposits, savings deposits, time deposits, and capital funds. The basic idea underlying the use of the pool of funds approach is that all funds should be pooled together. Funds then should be allocated from the pool to whatever asset investment (loans, government securities, cash, and so forth) is appropriate. The source from which funds were derived to make a particular investment is immaterial to the pool of funds model as long as the investment will contribute to meeting the objectives of the bank. This idea is illustrated schematically in Figure 5-2.

This approach requires bank management to identify its liquidity and profitability requirements. Then funds are allocated to the asset categories that best satisfy those requirements. Allocation is undertaken according to several priorities, which are established to assist operating management in solving the dilemma between liquidity and profitability. These priorities have to do with the proportion of each available dollar to be placed in primary reserves, secondary reserves, loans, and security

FIGURE 5-2 The Pool of Funds Model for Asset Management

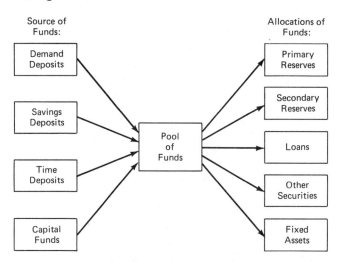

investments for income. Investments in land, buildings, and other fixed assets usually are considered separately.

The pool of funds approach to commercial bank asset management provides broad rules for a bank to follow in allocating funds to various asset categories. The approach emphasizes priorities that are stated in rather general terms. The method does not provide an explicit means for determining the proportion of funds that should be invested in each asset classification; neither does it provide a solution to the dilemma between liquidity and profitability in asset management. These problems are left to the judgment and intuition of a bank's management.

The Asset Allocation Approach

It has been contended that the pool of funds approach to bank asset management places too much emphasis on asset liquidity and fails to distinguish among the different liquidity requirements of checkable deposits, savings deposits, time deposits, and capital funds. Many bankers think that this deficiency caused an increasing amount of erosion to the profitability of commercial banks during the 1950s and 1960s. During those years time and savings deposits that required less liquidity grew more rapidly than did demand deposits. The asset allocation approach, also known as the conversion of funds approach, was developed to meet this deficiency.

The asset allocation model recognizes that the amount of liquidity needed by a bank is related to the sources from which its funds are obtained. This idea is described schematically in Figure 5-3. The model attempts to distinguish different sources of funds according to legal reserve requirements and the velocity, or turnover, of the sources. Demand deposits have a higher legal reserve requirement, for example, than do savings and time deposits and typically have a higher velocity, or turnover rate, than do the other types of deposits. Therefore, a greater proportion of each demand deposit dollar should be allocated to the primary and secondary reserves and a smaller proportion to investments such as residential mortgage loans or long-term municipal bonds.

The model establishes several liquidity-profitability centers within a bank for allocating funds obtained from different sources. These centers sometimes have been called banks within a bank because the allocation of funds from each center is made independently from the allocation of funds from other centers. Thus there may exist a demand deposit bank, a savings deposit bank, a time deposit bank, and a capital funds bank within a given commercial banking organization.

Once the liquidity-profitability centers have been identified and established, management must formulate a policy regarding the allocation of funds generated within each center. Demand deposits require the highest percentage of legal reserves and have the greatest velocity, perhaps turning over as often as 30 to 50 times per year. The demand deposit center, then, would allocate a high proportion of the funds generated in

FIGURE 5-3   The Asset Allocation Model for Asset Management

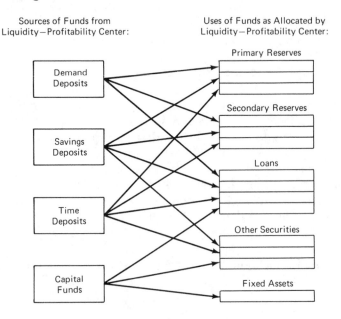

this center to primary reserves—say, 1 percent more than the required reserve percentage—then the bulk of uncommitted funds would go to secondary reserves for investment in short-term government securities. Relatively small amounts would be committed to loans—mostly in the form of short-term commercial loans. In Figure 5-3 no allocation is made from the demand deposit center to other securities or to fixed assets. The savings deposit and time deposit centers would require relatively less liquidity and so would allocate larger amounts to loans and investments. Capital funds require little liquidity and would be used to finance land and buildings, with the balance committed to long-term loans and less liquid security investments to enhance income.

The principal advantage claimed for this asset allocation approach is that it reduces liquid assets and allocates additional funds to the loan and investment accounts, thus tending to increase profitability. Advocates of this approach maintain that the improvement in profitability is obtained by eliminating excess liquidity carried against time and savings deposits and capital funds.

This model also has limitations impairing its effectiveness. While the velocity of different kinds of deposit liabilities is used as a basis for defining different liquidity-profitability centers, little relationship may exist between the velocity of a particular group of deposit accounts and the variability of the total amount of deposits within that group. A bank's demand deposits, for example, may turn over as many as 40 times per year. With some customers writing checks while others make simultaneous deposits, the sum of individual balances (or the total deposit liability of the bank) may vary by as little as 10 percent over the course of a year. As long as a bank operates, it will have a minimum deposit liability. From a practical standpoint, some funds derived from demand deposits in the aggregate may never be withdrawn and could be invested in long-term high-yielding investments prudently.

Another limitation of the model is that it assumes that sources of funds are independent of the use to which the bank puts them. This is not a realistic assumption. Practicing bankers seek to attract business deposits, for example, because business firms tend to borrow from the same bank where they maintain their checking accounts. An acceptance of new deposits, therefore, implies an obligation on the part of the bank to fulfill some of the credit requirements of the new depositors. Accordingly, a portion of the new deposits should be allocated to new loans for the same depositor group.

Other limitations apply both to the pool of funds model and the asset allocation model. Both models emphasize the liquidity of legal reserve requirements and the possible withdrawal of deposits, while giving relatively less consideration to the requirement for a bank to satisfy its customers' loan requests. It is well known that both deposits and loans tend to rise along with rising business activity. Aside from legal reserve requirements, little additional liquidity is needed to take care of withdrawal requests when this occurs, particularly if the bank's economist is able to forecast accurately when business activity and deposits are likely to taper off. In this circumstance liquidity is needed primarily to satisfy loan demand, which is likely to be rising more rapidly than deposits.

It should be noted also that there are seasonal variations for individual banks in which loan demand may be up when deposits are at a low level. Also, because of monetary policy actions, loan demand in periods of rising activity outstrips deposit growth, and, for all banks, deposit growth is more rapid in recessionary periods because of monetary policy actions, with modest growth in boom periods of high loan demand.

Both asset management models described have another shortcoming. They emphasize *average* liquidity requirements rather than *marginal* requirements. While the average ratio of cash and government securities to total deposits may be appropriate for judging the adequacy of liquidity in the banking system, it does not tell the management of an individual commercial bank how much cash it must have on hand to meet withdrawal requests and loan applications during the coming week. Only an analysis of the bank's individual customer accounts and knowledge of local business and financial activity can help in estimating immediate requirements.

The pool of funds and asset allocation models are somewhat simplistic. Rather than providing a complete set of guidelines as a basis for decision making, each model should be considered a general framework within which management might formulate policies for handling the asset management problem. Within either framework, a competent management team should be able to recognize the complex interrelationships and use the degree of sophistication in analysis and decision making appropriate to the particular bank's individual situation.

The Linear Programming Model

Linear programming is one technique used by management scientists for solving business problems. This technique will be described as an illustration of the management science approach to decision making in commercial bank asset management. It combines the asset management problem with the liability management problem and can incorporate both profitability and liquidity constraints.

A linear program is a mathematical model that expresses the relationships among various decision elements in a standard mathematical form. The model uses one of several standardized computational methods, such as the simplex algorithm, for determining the optimal combination of elements that are subject to the control of the decision maker. The mathematical and computational aspects of the model and its use are rather intricate, but it is not essential that a user master these aspects. Outside of a classroom, no one calculates a linear program manually.

The linear program model requires an explicit statement of an objective to be optimized. Optimization, for example, may consist of maximization of profits or minimization of costs. In the asset management problem, the objective is to maximize profits realized from investments in various categories of assets that may be purchased. In a simplified situation, for example, a bank's management may wish to undertake the combination of investments that would contribute most to profits. The decision variables, or alternatives available, might be short-term government securities yielding 4 percent, long-term government securities yielding 5 percent, high-grade commercial loans with an average yield of 6 percent, term loans to business firms with an average yield of 7 percent, automobile installment paper yielding 8 percent, and/or other consumer installment loans yielding 12 percent. These yields are on a net basis, after deduction of the bank's expenses of servicing the various types of assets.[4] If we let the variable x represent the amounts to be invested in the different categories of assets, the profits (P) to be derived from these investments can be described as follows:

$$P = .04x_1 + .05x_2 + .06x_3 + .07x_4 + .08x_5 + .12x_6$$

The objective of solving the linear program would be to maximize the value of P. If a banker is free to take on any risks, is not concerned with liquidity, and is not subject to any legal restrictions on investments, the solution of the equation, of course, is trivial. The answer would be to invest all the available funds in consumer installment loans (x_6) for a yield of 12 percent. This is unrealistic since banks have other customers to be cared for, and regulations and prudent banking would not permit such specialization.

The investments of commercial banks are limited by constraints imposed by law and the regulatory authorities, some of which are necessary because of the economic environment, and others desired by management to conform to good banking practices. Some constraints are more difficult than others to formulate in mathematical terms. Some constitute absolute limitations; others are a matter for the judgment of management. The amount of cash and deposits with the Federal Reserve bank, for example, must be at least equal to the minimum reserve requirements. This amount can be easily formulated as the sum of the percentages of the various categories of deposits. The maximum amount that could be invested in

---

[4] Space limitations have required many simplifications in this discussion of linear programming. One such simplification in this example is the built-in assumption that the costs of administering the various classes of assets are directly proportional to the amounts invested in those assets. Obviously, it does not cost ten times as much to manage $100 million of U.S. government bonds as it does to manage $10 million.

high-grade term loans, on the other hand, would be limited to the volume of loan applications that the bank might receive. This volume, even for the near future, is subject to some uncertainty. Management must do some forecasting and estimate the expected demand.

The constraint on high-grade term loans can be formulated mathematically when management has estimated the maximum demand for such loans. Suppose that maximum demand for such loans at a net yield of 7 percent (x_4, as shown in the illustration of the objective function) is estimated at $5 million. Then the maximum value of x_4 in the objective function would be $5 million. Stated mathematically, this is shown as $x_4 \leq \$5,000,000$. While some constraint formulations are more complex, the principle of formulation is the same.

Examples of other constraints that might be incorporated in a linear program for bank asset management would include those relating to risk, liquidity, and legal restrictions. The inclusion of a limitation on the total volume of risk assets according to the value of capital funds, or perhaps a version of the capital adequacy formula (described in Chapter 7), might be desirable to limit the risk of loss to amounts that would be considered reasonable percentages of the capital funds available to absorb the losses. To ensure sufficient liquidity, short-term government securities might be related to total deposits with a minimum percentage specified. This type of limitation should be considered by management based on likely withdrawal requests, the range of expected demands for loans in subsequent periods, and the way that investors and depositors are likely to view the liquidity position of the bank. The linear program model is flexible enough to incorporate whatever restrictions are desired by management or required by regulatory authorities.

The linear programming solution would indicate the appropriate amounts to be invested in each asset category for maximum profitability, given the set of assumptions that was included in the formulation of the model. It is likely that the program will need to be run several times with different sets of assumptions to test the sensitivity of the results to changes in the assumptions. For example, if interest rates two periods hence are subject to some uncertainty, it would be helpful to try a range of possible rates in different iterations to see what the effect would be on optimal allocation of funds to different asset categories in the current period.

The solution would also identify the opportunity costs associated with the constraints that were included in the model. Either relaxing the requirements for liquidity or actively seeking additional funds through the issue of capital notes might substantially increase the profits of a bank. The linear program solution, for example, may include *shadow prices* for each constraint that limit the value of the objective function in this type of program, that is, limit the amount of profit. A shadow price is the amount by which the objective function would increase if the constraint were relaxed by one additional unit.

Linear programming models and other management science techniques can be very valuable to banks as they consider the asset allocation question. The models have produced mixed results in practice, however, for several reasons.[5] For example, bank management may not act at all times to maximize profits, choosing instead to move at least temporarily to low-risk positions. Models based on the assumption of profit maximization will not produce useful solutions at such times. Also, difficulty in specifying constraints precisely, rapid major changes in constraints, poor quality data, and the high cost of running management science departments have all worked to limit the success of linear programming and other models.[6] The management science approach, however, has been beneficial in the development of asset-liability management programs that have come into use in recent years. These are discussed in Chapter 6.

LIQUIDITY OF ASSETS

Banks can borrow funds, as can individuals and other types of businesses, to meet immediate needs. Many banks utilize short-term borrowings extensively, on an almost continuous basis. In banking this practice is called *liability management*. It is discussed in Chapter 6. No bank, however, can take the risk of operating without a reasonable degree of liquidity embodied in its assets.

Liquidity is the quality of an asset that makes it easily convertible into cash with little or no risk of loss. Assets might be arrayed along a continuum from most to least liquid. Cash is the most liquid asset, and the ease with which other assets can be converted (through sale or collection) provides the standard of liquidity. U.S. Treasury bills provide perhaps the most liquidity of any security because they can be sold readily in an active market without substantial loss. Among the least liquid of assets are bank premises. A large portion of a bank's loan portfolio should be considered to have low liquidity as well, even though secondary markets exist for some types of loans. For many loans, there is no resale market, and the only way they can be converted to cash is to collect them. Regular amortization of the principal through monthly payments can provide considerable liquidity to a loan portfolio, but it would be difficult to liquidate the entire portfolio.

A bank is considered to be liquid when it has sufficient cash and other liquid assets, together with the ability to raise funds quickly from

---

[5] George W. McKinney, Jr., "A Perspective on the Use of Models in the Management of Bank Funds," *Journal of Bank Research* (Summer 1977), pp. 122–127.

[6] Ibid.

other sources, to enable it to meet its payment obligations and financial commitments in a timely manner. In addition, there should be a sufficient liquidity buffer to meet almost any financial emergency.

How much liquidity to hold and in what forms to hold it are constant concerns of bank management. As we have discussed, banks are required to comply with legal reserve requirements. In addition, banks need liquidity to meet seasonal and unexpected loan demands and deposit fluctuations. The majority of these transactions can be anticipated in advance and met from expected cash inflows from deposits, loan repayments, earnings, or expansion of liabilities.

It is advisable for banks to maintain a certain amount of liquidity to meet unforeseen contingencies or emergencies. Despite management's planning efforts, unexpected deposit outflows often develop. The occurrence of a prolonged labor strike, the closing of a locally important industry, or the relocation of a military installation are situations that can adversely affect bank deposits in a community. Thus, a liquid reserve to protect the integrity of the bank against such contingencies is highly desirable.

LIQUIDITY MEASUREMENT

Liquidity may be regarded as either a *stock* or *flow* concept. To measure liquidity from a stock viewpoint, one must appraise holdings of assets that may be turned into cash. To determine the adequacy of liquidity within this framework, one has to compare holdings of liquid assets with expected liquidity needs. This is a rather narrow concept of liquidity since it fails to take into consideration that liquidity may be obtained through the credit markets and revenue flows. When viewing liquidity from a flow approach, one considers not only the ability to convert liquid assets but also the ability of the economic unit to borrow and to generate cash from operations.

A standard for liquidity is difficult to determine, since future demands are not known. To obtain a realistic appraisal of a bank's liquidity position would require an accurate forecast of cash needs and the expected level of liquid assets and cash receipts over a given time period. In other words, a meaningful measure of liquidity would incorporate the flow concept in the calculation. However, the most widely used liquidity measures are gauged from the stock concept. One of these measures is the ratio of loans to deposits. When the ratio rises to a relatively high level, bankers become less inclined to lend and to invest. Moreover, they become more selective and, as standards are increased and credit is more strictly allocated, interest rates tend to rise. Although a high loan-to-deposit ratio has never been quantified, it is a force that influences lending and investment decisions. The loan-to-deposit ratio that bank management has been willing to live with has increased over the years for all banks but has been higher for the larger banks of the nation (see Figure 5-4). This higher ratio can be explained in part by the ability and willingness of large banks to solve their liquidity problems by liability management, or borrowing in the market, rather than relying solely on asset adjustments, and in part by banks' efforts to generate higher levels of income.

The use of the loan-to-deposit ratio as a measure of liquidity is based on the premise that loans are the most nonliquid of bank earning assets. Therefore, as the portion of deposits invested in loans rises, liquidity declines. The loan-to-deposit ratio as a measure of liquidity has some limitations in that it tells us nothing about the maturity or quality of the loan portfolio. Appraising the liquidity of the loan portfolio requires knowledge of the average length of maturity of loans, of whether the loans are amortized or single payment, and of the credit record of the borrowers. The ratio gives no indication of liquidity needs. A bank with a loan-to-deposit ratio of 70 percent, for example, may be relatively more liquid than one with a 50 percent ratio if the deposits of the former bank are stable while those of the latter are subject to wide variations. Finally, the loan-to-deposit ratio does not provide information concerning the nature of bank assets outside the loan portfolio. One bank might have 20 percent of its deposits invested in cash and short-term government securities while another bank might have the same percentage in bank buildings and real estate, but both banks could have the same loan-to-deposit ratio.

FIGURE 5-4 Loan-to-Deposit Ratios, Insured Commercial Banks

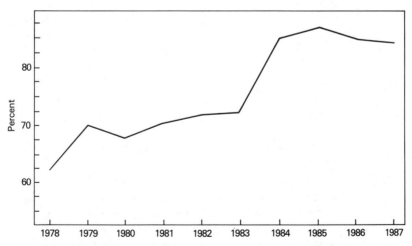

SOURCE: *Federal Deposit Insurance Corporation, annual reports, and Federal Reserve System, Federal Reserve Bulletins.*

Obviously, the banks would not have the same level of liquidity. Despite these shortcomings, the loan-to-deposit ratio does have some value in that as it rises it serves as a caution signal and stimulates bank management to make an evaluation of its overall expansion program. It is not intended to be a perfect measure of liquidity but a rough indicator.

Other liquidity measures that reflect the stock concept relate liquid assets to total deposits or to total assets. The ratio of cash assets to total deposits, for example, is superior in some ways to the loan-to-deposit ratio because this relates liquid assets directly to deposit levels rather than indirectly by considering loans, the least liquid assets, to deposits. A serious deficiency of this ratio lies in the fact that a substantial portion of cash assets are not really available to meet the liquidity needs of the bank. That portion of cash assets that is required to meet legal reserve requirements is, of course, not available to satisfy loan demand. Another deficiency of this ratio is its failure to include other liquid assets such as Treasury bills and short-term liquid securities. It gives no consideration to a bank's ability to raise funds from other sources.

DETERMINING LIQUIDITY NEEDS

Liquidity is one of the many problems with which bank management struggles constantly, and a foolproof formula for determining a bank's liquidity needs has not yet been developed. The amount of liquidity needed by an individual bank depends on the amount of variation that occurs in deposits and the demand for loans.

There are many movements in the economy—irregular, seasonal, cyclical, and secular. It is difficult to predict the occurrence or the severity of irregular movements since they do not follow established patterns. They do, however, affect the level of deposits and the demand for loans. Examples of *irregular* movements are a labor strike, the effects of some natural catastrophe such as an earthquake or a flood, a war scare, or some unusual economic or political development.

Seasonal movements, directly related to the changing seasons, differ from irregular movements by repeating themselves every year. The precise seasonal pattern may change with the passage of time. A bank located in an agricultural area might enjoy a high level of deposits in the fall after crops are harvested and experience a high loan demand in the spring. The demand for construction loans normally is higher in the summer months than in the winter. Weather is the most important factor responsible for seasonal patterns, but social custom has an influence—for example, retail sales normally rise in December because of buying practices during the Christmas season. With an expected seasonal increase in sales, retailers normally increase purchases to have sufficient goods on hand to meet seasonal demand. This, in turn, requires additional financial resources, which normally results in an increase in the demand for bank loans, perhaps secured by the larger inventories carried during the Christmas shopping season.

Cyclical movements are more difficult to predict than are seasonal movements. During the contraction period of a business cycle, loan demand declines and bank deposits may shrink. However, the monetary policy of the Federal Reserve System tends to offset the contraction of deposits in the banking system during an economic slump. During the prosperity phase, loan demand increases outstrip deposit growth, often requiring banks to sell liquid assets.

Secular movements or trends persist over a long period relative to the duration of the business cycle. Secular movements may encompass several business cycles and are a product of both short- and long-run influences such as changes in consumption, savings, investment, population, labor force, and technological developments.

As a result of these movements in the economy, forces are created that influence the level of bank deposits that makes planning for liquidity purposes highly important. In calculating requirements for a particular time period, a bank may determine the expected changes in deposits and loans from a given base period. Three things cause the changes in liquidity or excess reserves: the gain or loss in funds due to the increase or decrease in deposits, the gain or loss in funds due to the decrease or increase in loans and/or investments, and the increase or decrease in required legal reserves due to the increase or decrease in deposits. The calculation of the liquidity needs of a hypothetical commercial bank is illustrated in Table 5-2. Liquidity needs may be estimated for any time period desired by management. In the illustration, excess funds are expected to flow into the bank during the first quarter of the year, but funds will have to be obtained to meet heavy liquidity needs for the remainder of the year. These needs are reflected mainly in the anticipated growth of loan demands rather than in deposit outflows. Note that the increases in deposits toward the end of the year require additional legal reserves, thus offsetting the funds released from reserves earlier in the year.

If deposit changes and the demand for loans and investments could be forecast accurately, the problem of determining liquidity would be greatly simplified. Despite the difficulty, banks must attempt to predict loan and deposit levels. One way is to analyze the credit needs and expected deposit level of each principal customer. Forecasts constructed by this approach are usually prepared by loan officers, with each officer preparing forecasts for his or her own accounts. Responsibility for coordinating and assembling these forecasts may rest with the economics department, comptroller's department, cashier's division, or a special group of officers assigned to planning. Another method of estimating loan and

TABLE 5-2 Calculation of Liquidity Needs for a Hypothetical Commercial Bank (in thousands of dollars)

	Deposits	Change from Prior Month	Change in Required Reserves (10%)	Loans	Change from Prior Month	Liquidity Needs (−) Surplus (+)	Cumulative Needs (−) Surplus (+)
December	$10,900	—	—	$7,000	—	—	—
January	10,800	−$100	−$10	6,500	−$500	+$410	+$400
February	10,750	−50	−5	6,490	−10	−35	+375
March	10,440	−310	−31	6,400	−90	−189	+186
April	9,900	−540	−54	6,440	+40	−526	−340
May	9,840	−60	−6	6,460	+20	−74	−414
June	9,810	−30	−3	6,500	+40	−67	−481
July	9,720	−90	−9	6,530	+30	−111	−592
August	9,790	+70	+7	6,720	+190	−127	−719
September	9,840	+50	+5	6,800	+80	−35	−754
October	9,980	+140	+14	7,200	+400	−274	−1,028
November	10,500	+520	+52	7,680	+480	−12	−1,040
December	10,940	+440	+44	8,040	+360	+36	−1,004

deposit volume involves a forecast of sources and uses of investment funds for the entire economy. Estimates are made of the public and private sectors of the economy, generally employing econometric forecasting techniques. The private sector's estimated needs for funds are balanced against estimated supplies. Total bank loan volume then can be determined as the balancing item in the sources and uses of funds statement, and the individual bank can estimate its share of the total market. This method is used primarily by large banks, since small banks usually do not have the trained personnel to engage in such sophisticated forecasting. In predicting deposit and loan levels, such banks rely heavily on past experience. Records of monthly averages for several years or during the course of a business cycle are frequently used to give management an indication of expected loan and deposit fluctuations.

In forecasting bank liquidity needs, whether for a large or small bank, both local and national considerations must be taken into account. At the local level, the type, source, and stability of deposits are primary factors to consider. It is generally assumed that savings deposits are more stable than time deposits and time deposits fluctuate less than demand deposits. This is probably true for individual accounts but not necessarily true for the aggregate deposits of an individual bank. A demand deposit structure consisting of the deposits of many small- and medium-sized accounts generally is more stable than one made up of the accounts of a few business firms or large individual depositors, because the fluctuations of only a few business accounts are more likely to be correlated with each other.

Seasonal fluctuations in deposits and loans result largely from a lack of economic diversification in a bank's market area. Local economies that are heavily dependent on one or on a few industries that produce related commodities are not uncommon. Seasonal fluctuations are reflected in deposits and loans and must be recognized in planning liquidity reserves.

Although the majority of banks are primarily "small business firms" and operate in a local economy, they are influenced by factors that arise beyond their trade territory. For example, the effects of monetary and fiscal policies tend to be felt first in money market centers, but sooner or later all banks are affected. No bank, no matter how small or remote, can escape the effects of restrictive monetary policy; consequently, the management of an individual bank must keep abreast of national developments. Monetary policy is likely to be restrictive during a period of economic expansion as demand for goods and services expands more rapidly than does productive capacity. To slow down the rate of expansion of the economy, Federal Reserve officials may act to restrict the growth rate of the money supply. When this occurs, the banking system, and thus individual banks within the system, will have limited excess reserves with which to make additional loans. Liquidity can be critical for a bank at such times. Loan demand is likely to be growing more rapidly than deposits. Interest rates may rise to unusually high levels. If a bank has sufficient liquidity to meet its loan demand, it can capitalize on the high interest rates available and thereby increase its profitability. If liquidity is low, a bank may have to turn down profitable loans or sell less liquid securities at a loss to accommodate its loan customers.

THEORIES OF BANK LIQUIDITY MANAGEMENT

Theories of liquidity management have existed since the early days of commercial banking. Three are discussed here: the commercial loan, shiftability, and anticipated income theories. Chapter 6 will discuss liability management, an approach based on meeting liquidity needs by acquiring funds in the money market, and asset-liability management, which is an overall approach to structuring assets and liabilities.

The Commercial Loan Theory

The commercial loan theory was an outgrowth of English banking practices during the eighteenth century. Proponents of this theory maintained that a commercial bank's liquidity is assured as long as its assets are held in short-term loans that would be liquidated in the normal course of business; that is, banks should finance the movement of goods through the successive stages of production to consumption. Such loans today would be termed inventory or working capital loans. Throughout much of our history it was considered inappropriate for banks to make loans for the purchase of securities, real estate, or consumer goods or to make long-term agricultural loans.

The commercial loan theory was the predominant banking theory in the United States from colonial times through the 1930s. For example, the rules of the Bank of New York in 1784 provided that discounts

> will be due on Thursday in every week, and bills and notes bought for discount must be left at the bank on Wednesday morning, under a sealed cover, directed to William Seton, Cashier. The rate of discount is at present fixed at six percent *per annum*; but no discount will be made for longer than thirty days, nor will any note or bill be discounted to pay for a former one.[7]

---

[7] Bray Hammond, *Banks and Politics in America from the Revolution to the Civil War*, p. 74. Copyright © 1957 by Princeton University Press; Princeton Paperback, 1967. Reprinted by permission of Princeton University Press.

While the commercial loan theory was widely expounded by economists, regulatory authorities, and banks, it was followed rather loosely in practice. The theory's principal limitation was that it failed to take into account the credit needs of the nation's expanding economy. Rigid adherence to the theory prohibited banks from financing expansion of plant and equipment, home purchases, livestock acquisition, and land purchases. The failure of banks to meet these types of credit needs was an important factor in the development of competing financial institutions such as mutual savings banks, savings and loan associations, consumer finance companies, and credit unions.

This theory also failed to take into account the relative stability of bank deposits. Bank deposits *may* be withdrawn on demand, but all depositors are unlikely to remove their funds at the same time. This stability of deposits enables a bank to extend funds for a reasonably long period without becoming nonliquid. Further, the theory assumed that all loans would be liquidated in the normal course of business. During periods when economic activity is high, business firms have no difficulty meeting their obligations. However, in periods of economic recession, the movement of goods from cash to inventory to sales to accounts receivable to cash is interrupted, and business finds it difficult, if not impossible, to liquidate bank credit.

The Shiftability Theory

The shiftability theory is based on the proposition that a bank's liquidity is maintained if it holds assets that could be shifted or sold to other lenders or investors for cash. If loans are not repaid, the collateral from secured loans (marketable securities, for example) could be sold in the market for cash; if funds are needed, loans could be shifted to the central bank. Thus the individual commercial bank should be able to meet its liquidity needs, provided that it always has assets to sell; similarly, the banking system would be liquid, provided that the central bank stands ready to purchase assets offered for discount.

The Anticipated Income Theory

The anticipated income theory of commercial banking holds that a bank's liquidity can be planned if scheduled loan payments are based on the future income of the borrower. This theory does not deny the applicability of the commercial loan and shiftability theories. It emphasizes instead the desirability of relating loan repayment to income rather than relying heavily on collateral. Also, it holds that a bank's liquidity can be influenced by the maturity pattern of the loan and investment portfolios. Short-term business loans would have more liquidity than would term loans, and consumer installment loans would have more liquidity than would those secured by residential real estate.

The theory recognizes the development and rapid growth of certain types of loans that now constitute a major portion of the portfolios of commercial banks: business term loans, consumer installment loans, and residential real estate loans. These have one thing in common that adds to their liquidity, namely, the fact that they can be amortized. A portfolio having many loans with regular monthly or quarterly payments of principal and interest has liquidity because of the regular cash flow month in and month out that can be anticipated. When liquidity is needed, the cash can be used. Otherwise, it may be reinvested for future liquidity.

The anticipated income theory has encouraged many commercial bankers to adopt a *ladder effect* in the investment portfolio; this means a staggering of maturities so that redemptions will occur on a regular and predictable basis. The securities portfolio thus takes on the cash flow characteristics of a loan portfolio with regular amortization of principal and interest.

MANAGEMENT OF THE RESERVE POSITION

The first task in planning for the liquidity needs of a bank is to manage the money position, that is, to comply with the legal reserve requirements and have a sufficient amount of coin and currency on hand to meet customer demands. The holding of cash balances is affected constantly during banking hours as numerous transactions cause a flow of payments into and out of the bank. This task is as important as it is difficult. Cash yields no income; consequently, the objective of bank management is to hold it to a minimum.

In the management of the money position, many computations and reports are required by regulatory authorities. Banks are required to compute reserves on transaction accounts under what is termed *contemporaneous reserve accounting*. Reserve requirements are calculated as averages over 14-day periods, and banks have two days after each 14-day period to make adjustments in their reserve balances to meet required levels. The reserves required on time and savings accounts are computed on a 14-day period as well, but a lag of 17 days is allowed in meeting the requirements on these accounts. In computing legal reserves, demand deposits are adjusted so that cash items in the process of collection and demand balances due from other banks are subtracted from total demand deposits. Time deposits require no adjustment. Since day-to-day cash flow estimates cannot be absolutely accurate, an excess or deficiency in reserve requirements averaging up to 2 percent of the required reserve may be carried forward to the next reserve period. Although this leeway may make the task of managing the reserve account less difficult, it still is not easy. Banks are penalized for falling short of their required reserves, and excess reserves earn no returns. If an excess or shortage is expected to be other than temporary, banks usually make final adjustments through the federal funds market, by use of repurchase agreements, or by borrowing from the Federal Reserve. Adjustments of a longer-term nature are met by changing other asset or liability categories, as discussed in this and the next chapter.

An example of how a large bank might meet its liquidity requirements is presented in Table 5-3. Sources and uses of funds are shown for four time periods. These periods may be for a day, a week, a month, or even longer. The funds in our example are needed for increasing security holdings, meeting loan demands, and caring for a decline in deposits (listed as a minus entry under "sources of funds"). Note that demand deposits declined in the first and fourth periods, and CDs declined in every period but the second. Other time deposits were relatively stable, with the exception of the second period when there was definite disintermediation.

Our hypothetical bank used several liquidity management techniques sometime during the four periods. It borrowed from the Federal Reserve bank in two periods, then substantially entered the Eurodollar market in the third and fourth periods. It was in the federal funds market

TABLE 5-3 Example of Liquidity Management by a Hypothetical Commercial Bank (in millions of dollars)

	Periods			
	1	*2*	*3*	*4*
Uses of funds				
U.S. government securities	—	$1,000	$ 600	$ 300
Other securities	$1,000	400	1,600	1,300
Loans	1,500	2,600	3,500	2,700
Total	$2,500	$4,000	$5,700	$4,300
Sources of funds				
Demand deposits	−700	1,300	1,000	−1,200
Certificates of deposit	−2,500	200	−1,400	−500
Other time deposits	1,100	700	1,600	1,200
Borrowing from Federal Reserve bank	500	1,100	—	—
Federal funds purchased	2,100	700	1,500	1,700
Eurodollars purchased	—	—	2,000	2,100
Maturity of securities	1,000	—	—	—
Sale of securities	1,000	—	—	1,000
Sale and repurchase of securities	—	—	1,000	—
Total	$2,500	$4,000	$5,700	$4,300

every period. Some securities matured during the first period and some were sold from the secondary reserve in the first and fourth periods. A final method used was the sale of securities to a nonbank investor under agreement to repurchase for a stated length of time and at a predetermined price or yield. This might have been a large corporate customer with excess funds to invest, a government securities dealer, or a local public body with excess funds derived from a bond issue or tax collections. Although our example is unrealistic in that all these methods would not be used by a bank in a relatively short time and no consideration was given to costs, it does give us an idea of how they might be used in liquidity management. This illustration has concentrated on management of liquidity as it relates to the loan and investment portfolio and to the deposits and other liabilities of a commercial bank. In addition, the manager of the liquidity position must consider funds provided from operations as well as from the sale of other assets. Additional funds may be required for capital investments and to pay dividends to stockholders. It is appropriate to prepare a complete cash budget, including all expected cash receipts and an estimate of all cash payments that will be required.

QUESTIONS

1. How does the asset structure of a commercial bank differ from that of a manufacturing corporation? What are the reasons for the differences?

2. How would you define and quantify the risk associated with investments in loans and securities? What is an appropriate trade-off between risk and profitability for a commercial bank?

3. From which category of earning assets do banks derive most of their profits? Where does that category rank with regard to liquidity? Why?

4. Describe the pool of funds approach to bank asset management. What problems do you see in its use?

5. Differentiate between primary and secondary reserves.

6. What are the strengths and weaknesses of the asset allocation model for asset management?

7. For the linear programming example given in the text, formulate the constraint to reflect the requirements for legal reserves of member banks. Add two variables to the model: x_7 to represent vault cash and deposits with the Fed and x_8 to represent demand deposits. Assume that the bank has no time deposits. Formulate another constraint to limit the total investment in x_1 through x_7 to the total deposit funds available.

8. How does the rather strict definition of bank asset liquidity given in the text differ from a somewhat looser definition that might be used, say, by the New York Stock Exchange?

9. How would you determine the degree of liquidity of a particular commercial bank from its statement of condition? What factors might be overlooked with a ratio analysis?

10. What aspects of federal monetary policy are likely to affect bank liquidity late in a period of economic expansion? How would liquidity likely be affected?

11. How would liquidity requirements be likely to differ for a bank located in a city dependent on summer tourists as compared with a bank located in a city with diversified manufacturing for an economic base?

12. Compare and contrast the commercial loan theory of liquidity management with the shiftability theory.

13. Using the anticipated income theory of liquidity management, show how liquidity is dependent upon regular amortization of loans.

14. Obtain the annual report of a local bank. From its statement of condition for the last two years, prepare a statement of sources and uses of funds. Comment on apparent changes in the liquidity position of the bank.

SELECTED REFERENCES

BRICK, JOHN R. *Commercial Banking: Text and Readings.* Haslett, Mich.: Systems Publications, 1984.

CARGILL, THOMAS F., AND GILLIAN G. GARCIA. *Financial Deregulation and Monetary Control.* Stanford, Calif.: Hoover Institution Press, Stanford University, 1982.

COHEN, KALMAN J., AND STEN THORE. "Programming Bank Portfolios under Uncertainty." *Journal of Bank Research* (Spring 1970), pp. 42–61.

COOK, TIMOTHY Q., AND TIMOTHY D. ROWE, eds. *Instruments of the Money Market.* Federal Reserve Bank of Richmond, 1986.

CRAMER, ROBERT H., AND JAMES A. SEIFERT. "Measuring the Impact of Maturity on Expected Return and Risk." *Journal of Bank Research* (Autumn 1976), pp. 229–235.

McKINNEY, GEORGE W. "A Perspective on the Use of Models in the Management of Bank Funds." *Journal of Bank Research* (Summer 1977), pp. 122–127.

SEALY, CALVIN W., JR. "Commercial Bank Portfolio Management with Multiple Objectives." *The Journal of Commercial Bank Lending* (February 1977), pp. 39–48.

SINKEY, JOSEPH F., JR. *Commercial Bank Financial Management in the Financial Services Industry*, 2nd ed. New York: Macmillan, 1986.

STIGUM, MARCIA L., AND RENO O. BRANCH, JR. *Managing Bank Assets and Liabilities.* Homewood, Ill.: Dow Jones-Irwin, 1983.

6

LIABILITY
MANAGEMENT

Commercial banks utilize a high degree of financial leverage, with liabilities supplying about 93 percent of total funds. The use of relatively low-cost borrowed funds, including deposits, enables slim profit margins to be magnified to provide a reasonable return to the shareholders. Deposits are the chief source of borrowed funds, accounting for more than 75 percent of all commercial bank liabilities. Other sources of funds include federal funds purchased from other banks, securities sold under agreements to repurchase, bankers' acceptances outstanding, Eurodollar borrowings, and capital notes.

In a broad sense, liability management consists of the activities involved in obtaining funds from depositors and other creditors and determining the appropriate mix of funds for a particular bank. In a narrower sense, liability management has come to be known as the activities involved in supplementing liquidity needs by actively seeking borrowed funds when needed. The ability to sell certificates of deposit, to sell securities under repurchase agreements, and to borrow Eurodollars or federal funds enables a bank to rely less on low-earning secondary reserve assets for liquidity, which may enhance the earning power of a bank. These activities are not without risk. Liability management requires consideration of the extra risk as well as the difference between the cost of obtaining funds and the return that can be earned when the funds are invested in loans or securities. Thus the relationship between asset management and liability management is a critical determinant of a bank's profitability.

Commercial banks are in the business of borrowing money (mostly from depositors) and lending or investing it at higher rates. This is the business of a financial intermediary, acting as a go-between for those who have funds and those who need funds. The activities of lending money to those of high credit standing and investing in high-quality securities result in relatively low profit margins when compared with those of nonfinancial corporations (see Chapter 8). This necessitates using a high degree of financial leverage to magnify the profits for shareholders. In the United States, capital stock and retained earnings provide only about 7 percent of total bank funds. Commercial bank deposits and short-term borrowings are discussed in this chapter, together with their relationship to asset management. The management of capital funds, including long-term debt, is reserved for Chapter 7.

TRANSACTION ACCOUNTS

Transaction accounts are referred to as checkable deposits or, more commonly, as checking accounts. Withdrawals and transfers to third parties usually are made by check, although telephone transfers and transactions via automatic teller machines are common. The customer's primary reason for having a checking account is to ensure the availability of funds when needed. Ease of transfer is also important. Earning a return on funds used for transaction purposes is secondary to most customers, and that category of checking accounts known as demand deposits bears no explicit return. Demand deposits may receive indirect returns, perhaps free checks or waiver of service charges, but direct interest payments is limited to those checking accounts called NOW (negotiable order of withdrawal) accounts. Rates paid on NOW accounts generally are below those on other interest-bearing accounts, and NOWs are not available for business firms. Overall, transaction accounts make up almost one-third of bank deposits.

The reason for the popularity of checks is obvious. They are an economical and safe method of transferring a sizable amount of money, from the standpoint of transportation costs and the possibility of loss from robbery. When checks are used, the transfer is made through the clearing of checks by banks without either party, the payer or payee, giving the matter much thought. The drawer of the check worries little, even about forgery, since the bank is at fault in the event a forged check is paid. Check money also has another advantage in that canceled checks returned to the depositor serve as receipts for payments made. Even though the depositor may lose or destroy his or her canceled checks, the depositor can in most cases be furnished with a copy. A majority of banks microfilm all checks paid and keep the film for an indefinite period.

SAVINGS AND TIME DEPOSITS

Savings accounts do not have specified maturity dates or size limits. The accounts terminate when the holders choose, and additions or withdrawals are made at any time. Technically, a bank may require seven days' notice prior to withdrawal, but this restriction is not applied in normal practice. No penalties in the form of lost interest are invoked due to withdrawals.

Savings accounts are often referred to as "passbook savings" because traditionally the saver received a small book in which bank tellers recorded all withdrawals and additions, including interest, and presentation of the book was required to make a transaction. Passbooks have been eliminated by many banks, which, instead, provide the customer with a monthly statement showing all account activity. Savings accounts make up slightly more than one-fourth of bank deposits.

Time deposits make up about 40 percent of bank deposits. These accounts typically are represented by certificates of deposit (CDs) and are specified both as to maturity and amount. Early withdrawals result in penalties that may exceed the interest earned to the date of withdrawal. Interest rates on CDs may be fixed or variable, depending on the customer's choice, and additions may be allowed prior to maturity on variable rate CDs.

Special types of CDs have been developed to meet the competition for deposit funds. For example, *negotiable certificates of deposit* in large denominations are issued by many large banks. Security dealers make a secondary market for these certificates, and thus banks are able to attract funds from large investors that otherwise might place their funds in Treasury bills or other money market instruments. These negotiable CDs are generally sold to corporations, pension funds, and government bodies in $1 million or larger denominations. They are generally short-term instruments with maturities of one year or less. On average, three-month certificates yield returns 30 to 40 basis points above the bond yield equivalent on three-month Treasury bills and somewhat below the prime rate charged on loans by major banks. The CDs are negotiable instruments, being issued in bearer form, and may be traded in secondary markets before maturity.

In late 1982 for the first time since the early 1930s depository institutions were permitted by law to offer checkable deposits that are not subject to interest rate ceilings. The Garn-St Germain Depository Institutions Act enacted by Congress in October 1982 required federal regulators to authorize a new deposit for commercial banks and thrift institutions that would be equivalent to and competitive with money market mutual funds that were initiated and promoted by brokerage firms. The money market deposit account (MMDA) has become very popular. There is no interest rate ceiling, but banks cannot guarantee a fixed rate for more than one month at a time. Banks are permitted to allow as many as six transfers—including three checks—a month from the account to third parties. Should the balance in the account fall below the minimum required, the amount of interest paid reverts to the level paid on regular passbook savings accounts.

Banks also have some minor time deposit plans, including Christmas club, vacation, tax, and other so-called "savings clubs." These are offered to encourage savers to deposit in the savings department a stated sum each week that will within a stated period be a large enough amount to enable the depositor to pay Christmas or vacation bills. Banks find these savings programs desirable because they increase deposits and stimulate thrift on the part of the savers. Many people possibly would not save if banking programs of this type were not provided.

LEVEL OF DEPOSITS IN THE COMMERCIAL BANKING SYSTEM

In the commercial banking system, the level of deposits depends primarily on the amount of credit extended by banks in the form of loans and investments. If banks did not engage in lending and investing, they would have deposits equal only to the amount of currency left with them by depositors. They would be completely liquid, for the most part, and their earnings would reflect income only from their charges for performing various services. Banks are profit-seeking enterprises, however, and they attempt to loan and invest prudently as much as possible of the funds they receive from shareholders and depositors to increase operating earnings. Individual banks are normally in a position to lend or invest amounts equal to the amount of their excess funds, or what are commonly referred to as *excess reserves.*

The term "excess funds" or "reserves" as used here includes the amount of funds that are in excess of legal reserve requirements and whatever additional funds are considered necessary for liquidity purposes by commercial bankers to support the liabilities. For example, if deposits of a commercial bank are $100,000 and the reserves (including legal and liquidity reserves) necessary to back up the deposits are $25,000, the bank would be in a position to lend its excess funds of $75,000. If this were done and the $75,000 withdrawn from the lending bank and deposited in another, this second bank could in turn follow the same procedure (assuming the same reserve requirements) and lend or invest 75 percent of the newly acquired deposit, or $56,250. As these deposits were withdrawn by check and deposited in other banks, these banks in turn could do the same and the process could be repeated numerous times.

Deposit expansion is accomplished through bank lending (and investing) if there is a willingness on the part of monetary and fiscal authorities to permit such expansion by making additional reserves available. Individual banks may lure deposits away from other banks, but the total in the banking system will remain the same. Excess reserve creation is an exclusive function of the Federal Reserve System. Reserves can be increased or decreased, and hence so can deposits, by the use of open-market operations, varying reserve requirements, and supervision of the discount or borrowing function. The Federal Reserve System is continually employing these basic monetary powers to attain broad economic goals such as the promotion of economic growth, a high level of employment, and stable prices. In the attainment of these goals, the central bank influences the level of deposits of the banking system since, in a very real sense, banks serve as the conduit through which monetary policy is transmitted to the economy.

DEPOSITS AT INDIVIDUAL BANKS

Although individual banks do not have absolute control over the level of their deposits, they are in a position to influence the amount they hold. Since deposits are so important to their profitable operation, banks compete aggressively for them. Bankers burn the midnight oil thinking of ways to increase them, and advertising agencies are employed to make a bank's services more appealing to prospective customers. Progressive banks undertake sophisticated market research to identify factors that are important to their particular situations. While the monetary and fiscal policies of government are major factors that determine the level of deposits in the banking system, economic and personal factors are important to individual banks.

Competitive Interest Rates. Maintaining deposit interest rates that are competitive with those of other banks has become of overriding importance in attracting new deposits and in maintaining existing deposits. This has been particularly true when market interest rates have been at relatively high levels. Banks compete for funds not only with other banks but with other thrift institutions, money market funds, and issuers of other money market instruments. As maximum rates were removed during the process of deregulation, the maintenance of competitive rates became even more important. During periods of tight money, especially, relatively small interest rate differentials will entice savers and investors to move funds from one savings or investment instrument, or from one savings institution, to another.

Physical Features and Personnel. In general, people like to do business with a firm that has attractive quarters and is staffed by personable employees. Many banks have recognized these qualities and have made improvements in these areas. The hard marble benches and nondescript terrazzo floors have been replaced by comfortable chairs and carpets. Bank personnel are encouraged to be friendly and efficient in the performance of their tasks.

Services Offered by Banks. Banks that offer better and more diversified services usually have an advantage over those whose services are limited. Shortage of downtown parking gives those banks with ample parking facilities an advantage. The same may be said for those that have drive-in teller windows, bank-by-mail, automated payment systems, 24-hour automatic teller machines, and improved, time-saving deposit services.

Some customers are attracted to a bank that has specialized loan departments, a convenient safe deposit box department, or a trust department that has an outstanding reputation. Business firms may select a bank because of its after-hours depository service, its foreign department, and its correspondent bank relations, especially if the firm has need of loans in excess of the bank's lending limit or has business dealings in cities throughout the nation and abroad. Farmers may be attracted to a bank that has an outstanding farm representative trained in agriculture and willing to advise farmers who have production, marketing, or financial problems.

Fundamental Policies and Strength of a Bank. Bank policies regarding loans, investments, and other matters provide an important yardstick by which outsiders can judge the competence and capacity of the management. A well-disciplined and stable organization indicates to the public that banking transactions will be handled correctly and soundly. Confidence in banks lessens the possibility of "runs." This trust is a reflection of the depositors' faith in the bank management. The presence of outstanding persons of the community on the board of directors, capable officers and employees of the bank, a record of fair dealing, sound investment and loan portfolios, and a strong capital structure are reflections of good bank management.

The loan policies of one bank may be more appealing to people than those of another. A bank may enjoy increased deposits because of the installment loan, credit card, real estate, or commercial loan department. Interest rates on loans are also important to those who borrow. Some instances probably occur where one bank would permit a person to borrow on an open basis but another would insist upon security. If such is the case, borrowers would probably favor the former and carry their deposits there. Some banks specialize in certain types of loans, and people are often drawn to them because of their expertise or specialty. Banks that have a reputation of caring for their borrowing customers who need credit often are selected over those that are reluctant to lend to steady customers in periods of economic stress.

Level of Economic Activity. Deposits grow more rapidly during the prosperity phase of the business cycle than in periods of recession. During periods of prosperity, business firms build up deposits to support a higher level of sales and economic activity. A change in demand for certain products of a community leads to price increases and thus to increased deposits. An increase in crude oil prices means an increase in deposits in those banks located in the oil-producing areas. Banks in a section of the country producing lumber or wood products gain in deposits from an increase in the prices of forest products. This applies to all commodities produced, whether cotton or cars. Conversely, a decline in the price of locally produced commodities results in a decline in bank deposits.

Location. While business borrowers may be inclined to travel great distances to borrow, consumers are less inclined to do so. The individual who needs an installment loan for the purchase of a car or a television is not inclined to fight the traffic when there is an alternative. Nonborrowing customers are even more influenced by location when selecting a bank. To the average household depositor, banks are very much alike. Obviously, differences exist among banks, but when there is great similarity, accessibility becomes more important to bank customers.

Momentum of an Early Start. A bank does not differ much from any other business that enjoys a dominant position in an industry because of the momentum of an early start. Although it is not always true, an old established bank sometimes has an advantage over the newer banks. This is especially true in localities where there has not been a rapid increase in business activity and deposits. In these areas, son and daughter have a tendency to conduct their banking business where father and mother carried their account. They have been influenced by the various favors that were extended to the parents when they were just getting started. The same thing applies to local business firms. Junior executives are trained to patronize the old established bank that extended the first loans to the struggling business. Once such ties are established, they are difficult to break.

INCREASED COST OF DEPOSITS

As interest rates rose during the 1960s, bank depositors became more interest-conscious and turned to time deposits as a means of increasing income; consequently, time deposits increased at a more rapid rate than did demand deposits. Corporate treasurers began to manage their demand balances more efficiently and invest their excess funds in short-term financial assets. These assets included commercial paper, U.S. government Treasury bills, bank CDs, and, in some instances, Eurodollar balances abroad. Business concerns with several locations throughout the nation employed lock boxes to collect funds more quickly and consolidate them in central locations. Compensating balances, or minimum amounts of funds required to be maintained in checking accounts under many loan agreements, were more closely scrutinized in an effort to reduce the amount of idle funds. Increasingly, individuals have followed the lead of corporate treasurers in an attempt to hold down their demand balances. Deposits have been shifted from checking accounts to savings accounts to obtain interest income, and the introduction of NOW accounts made it possible for individuals to receive interest on checking accounts. The removal of Regulation Q ceilings on interest payments to depositors ensured that, by historic standards, the cost of deposit funds to banks would continue to be high. Maintaining rate ceilings, however, would have meant continued erosion of commercial bank deposits as depositors found higher-yielding alternatives.

CLEARING AND COLLECTION OF CHECKS

The widespread use of checks in our economy makes their clearing and collection no small task. This is done quickly and efficiently by commercial banks, however, through their own devices and in cooperation with other banks and with the Federal Reserve System. Funds are transferred from one account to another in the same bank by debiting one account and crediting another. When checks are drawn on one bank and deposited in another within a community, the banks merely exchange daily claims on each other. If a difference exists, it is ordinarily paid by a check drawn on the bank's account carried at a Federal Reserve bank or in one of its correspondent banks. In communities and cities with several banks, all or at least most, would be members of a clearinghouse that would have as its major function the clearing of checks.

When checks are drawn on banks several miles from the depositing bank, they may be cleared through the correspondent banking system or through the Federal Reserve System. Member banks carry a portion of their reserves with the Federal Reserve bank of their district, and a bank receiving a check drawn on another bank in the same district would receive credit to its account and the latter's account would be debited a like amount. Checks may be cleared between Federal Reserve districts by the use of the Interdistrict Settlement Fund in Washington, D.C. Each Federal Reserve bank maintains a balance in the fund, and daily computations are made based on reports received from each Federal Reserve bank of checks received during the day involving collections in each of the other Federal Reserve bank districts.

The completion of a nationwide *electronic funds transfer system* (EFTS) using Federal Reserve facilities was announced by the Board of Governors in late 1978. The board earlier had authorized the use of Federal Reserve facilities to provide such services to *automated clearinghouse (ACH)* associations.

The automated clearinghouse provides the basis for the electronic funds transfer systems in the United States. The function of the ACH is the same as the traditional clearinghouse except that transfers of funds are accomplished by electronic impulses stored on magnetic computer tapes instead of from paper checks. The development of automated clearinghouses has made it possible to implement a number of kinds of electronic funds transfer systems, including direct deposit of payrolls, preauthorized bill payment plans, automated teller machines, point-of-sale (POS) systems, and check truncation plans.

LIABILITY MANAGEMENT FOR LIQUIDITY

The previous chapter discussed asset management and described the roles of the primary and secondary reserves in meeting a bank's liquidity needs. Asset management to meet liquidity needs, as indicated by the three theories of liquidity management discussed in Chapter 5, historically has been the dominant approach. By the early 1960s, however, large banks in particular began to meet significant portions of their liquidity needs by borrowing rather than through conversion of assets.

Such borrowing has become known as liability management. Growth in borrowing has resulted from an increase in the demand for bank credit and the relatively slow growth in demand deposits in recent years. The rise in economic activity and the increase in the inflation rate have meant that business firms need more credit to carry on their activities. Moreover, both business firms and individuals have become more conscious of interest rates. Increasing expenses have compelled banks to employ their resources fully; this has resulted in a higher loan-to-deposit ratio and smaller secondary reserves.

The Discount Window

Borrowing from a Federal Reserve bank or a correspondent bank is one method of acquiring funds to adjust a bank's reserve position and, consequently, its liquidity position. Since passage of DIDMCA in 1980, any depository institution having transaction accounts subject to reserve requirements may borrow from the Federal Reserve bank of its district. Formerly only commercial banks who were members of the Federal Reserve System had this privilege.

Borrowing from the Federal Reserve System is seen as a privilege, not as a right that accompanies membership. The central bank cannot be considered a continuous source of funds. The length of the borrowing period depends on many factors, such as the condition of the bank that wants to borrow and the current economic environment. From recent practices it appears that if large banks wanted to borrow for more than six out of thirteen consecutive weeks, such action would be frowned upon.

Small banks have easier access to the discount window than do large banks. This has been justified on the grounds that small banks are unable to participate in all the markets available to large banks and that small banks usually experience greater seasonal movements in their loans and deposits than do large banks. In early 1973 *a seasonal borrowing privilege* was introduced by the Federal Reserve System in order to assist small- and medium-sized banks that face substantial seasonal fluctuations in the supply and demand for funds. To qualify for this type of borrowing, a bank's seasonal decline in available funds—that is, deposits minus loans—must persist for at least eight weeks and recur at about the same time each year. The length of time funds can be borrowed depends on the duration of the bank's seasonal pattern of needs.

Although borrowing from the Federal Reserve banks is never assured, a bank may reasonably expect to receive access to Federal Reserve credit when its needs are consistent with the objectives of the central bank. Funds made available by Federal Reserve banks must be fully collateralized by eligible commercial or agricultural paper, bankers' acceptances, or U.S. government securities. When bank borrowing is secured by commercial or agricultural paper, it must be evaluated by Federal Reserve officials to see that it meets established standards. Since this procedure is time consuming, most borrowing today is secured by pledging U.S. Treasury obligations; consequently, banks that borrow frequently may maintain Treasury obligations at the bank that can be pledged easily and quickly. The Federal Reserve banks closely administer the discount window to ensure that the privilege of borrowing is not abused. During periods when money market rates are above the discount rate, the Federal Reserve's task is complicated by the profit incentive of a bank to borrow.

Applications of borrowing banks are reviewed regularly, and those banks found in debt to the Federal Reserve for an excessive time are requested to find other sources of funds.

Federal Funds

The purchase of federal funds is one of the most popular methods of using credit to meet liquidity requirements. Federal funds are deposit balances held with Federal Reserve banks. A commercial bank may have excess balances because of an unexpected inflow of deposits or a decline in loans. Since these funds are nonearning assets, banks are willing to make them available to other banks for a short period of time, and those that need funds to comply with reserve requirements or to purchase assets are willing to purchase such balances. Federal funds have long been used by banks to adjust reserve positions. Prior to the early 1960s, federal funds were considered by bank management as a source of one-day funds that could be obtained at a rate no higher than the Federal Reserve discount rate. A bank that needed funds to cover a reserve deficit would purchase federal funds provided that the rate was below the discount rate. In the early 1960s, a major New York bank revolutionized the funds market by bidding for federal funds at a rate above the discount rate and was successful in attracting significant amounts of funds. Since that time, it has been common for federal funds to trade at rates above the discount rate. Today the large commercial banks view these funds as simply an alternative source that may be obtained at a price to meet liquidity and loan needs.

The use of federal funds to meet liquidity requirements has grown significantly in recent years. The volume of trading has increased as a result of the greater number of banks participating in the market. Many medium and small banks, some with deposits as low as a few million dollars, have become participants in the market in recent years.

A commercial bank wishing to purchase (borrow) or sell (lend) federal funds may deal directly with another bank or contact a federal funds broker or a correspondent bank. Many correspondent banks make a market for federal funds by standing ready to buy or sell funds without regard to their own reserve position.

Federal funds transactions usually are overnight and are basically unsecured loans. Sometimes the transactions take the form of a repurchase agreement where one bank sells U.S. government securities to another bank. These agreements usually mature in one day but may be written to mature in one week or even several weeks. The mechanics of trading in federal funds are quite simple. In the typical transaction, two banks agree on terms; the bank selling federal funds calls the Federal

Reserve bank and requests that the agreed amount be transferred from its reserve account to the reserve account of the purchasing bank. On the following day, at the opening of business, the transaction is reversed.

Repurchase Agreements

In addition to the interbank trading in federal funds, similar transactions occur between banks and U.S. government security dealers and other investors. These transactions are referred to as *repurchase agreements* or, more commonly, as *RPs* or *repos*. An RP is the sale of a financial asset with an agreement to buy it back on a specified date at a prearranged price. This financial transaction has become an important outlet for temporarily idle funds since it can be tailored to meet the needs of both parties involved. Although it can be made for periods of one day to several months, most such transactions are of a short maturity. An advantage of RPs is that little credit risk is involved since such transactions usually are based on U.S. Treasury or agency securities.

Banks supply as well as acquire funds in the RP market, just as they do in the federal funds market. Large banks operate on both sides of the market simultaneously, attempting to profit by receiving higher rates on funds supplied (the supplier of funds refers to this as a "reverse RP") than is paid for funds acquired. Although the assets most commonly involved in an RP transaction are U.S. government and U.S. agency securities, dealers may use large negotiable certificates of deposit or commercial paper as collateral. Banks must use government or agency securities as collateral to exempt the funds acquired from reserve requirements.

Eurodollar Borrowing

The Eurodollar loan is a tool of liability management available to large commercial banks in this country and used by banks that may or may not have foreign branches. The Eurodollar may best be defined in terms of the characteristics of the instrument. Eurodollars are U.S. dollar-denominated deposits with commercial banks located outside the United States, including overseas branches of U.S. banks. Eurodollars come into existence when an American or foreign owner of a deposit with a bank in the United States transfers funds to a foreign bank or to a foreign branch of an American bank. In the course of this transaction, ownership of the deposit in the United States is acquired by the financial institution abroad and is offset by that institution's assumption of a liability that is payable in U.S. dollars. In this case, the total bank deposits in the United States remain unchanged, but an additional dollar deposit liability—Eurodollars—has been created abroad. Borrowing in the Eurodollar market has

become an important way for many large banks to meet funds requirements.

Large Certificates of Deposit

Large certificates of deposit with denominations of $100,000 or more
have become the dominant instrument for liability management by large
banks. Prior to 1970, all time and savings deposits were subject to maximum interest rate regulation, and to bid actively for funds when market
rates were above the maximum rates permitted for deposits, commercial
banks had to look elsewhere. This, for example, caused a surge in the
borrowing of Eurodollars by American banks in 1969 and early 1970.
Maximum rates were suspended on CDs of $100,000 or more in June 1970
for maturities of less than 90 days and for longer maturities in May 1973.
The volume approached $90 billion by late 1974, increased again during
the tight money period in 1978 to around $100 billion, and rose dramati-
cally to more than a third of a trillion dollars during the 1981 and 1982
period of tight money.

Rates paid on certificates of deposit are either determined by direct
negotiation between the bank and potential depositor or established at a
fixed level that a depositor may either accept or reject. Banks have found
that depositors are highly sensitive to changes in rates; if a bank needs
additional funds to meet loan requests or deposits outflows, it may offer
higher rates on CDs to attract funds. It must be remembered that the rate a
bank may economically pay on CDs is determined in large part by the
earnings it can receive by investing the deposit. To attract deposits, rates
offered on CDs must be above Treasury bill yields. In addition, to improve
their market appeal, most large CDs are issued in bearer form so that
investors are not locked in until the CDs mature. A strong secondary
market in large CDs, with several dealers serving as market makers, en-
sures the liquidity of this instrument.

ASSET-LIABILITY MANAGEMENT

We have described techniques of asset management in Chapter 5 and
techniques of liability management in this chapter. For the most part the
major objectives of such techniques are to ensure liquidity of the bank, to
enable it to meet deposit withdrawal requests, to ensure sufficient funds
for legitimate loan demand, and to maintain net interest margins and
profitability. Effective management of interest margins for enhanced and
stable profits requires simultaneous consideration of both assets and liabilities, however, particularly their rate characteristics and maturities.

Asset-liability management is the approach to overall balance sheet
management that came into broad usage as a result of the high interest

rates of the late 1970s and early 1980s. It is often considered an approach designed to control interest rate risk, but more precisely it is a method of designing the makeup of assets and liabilities to ensure that their composition provides the risk-return trade-off deemed appropriate by management. A bank's asset-liability management program should be based on the degree to which management is willing to accept higher risk to pursue higher returns. The focus is net interest margin.

Net Interest Margin

Net interest margin is the difference between interest earnings and interest costs, expressed as a percentage of earning assets. In 1986 the net interest margin for all insured banks was 3.98 percent. Banks also have noninterest income from service charges, trust fees, and other sources— totaling $36 billion in 1986. Noninterest expense for personnel and other overhead costs was $90 billion in 1986. Clearly, the net interest margin must be sufficient to cover most of a bank's overhead with, hopefully, some positive remainder in the form of net income.

Net interest margin has become increasingly sensitive to changes in market interest rates because of deregulation and increased competition for funds in the financial markets. When most bank liabilities consisted of demand deposits and fixed rate savings and time deposits subject to relatively low maximum rates of interest, the net interest margin was sensitive primarily to changes in the rate that banks could earn on loans and security investments. As loan and investment rates increased, banks were able to improve their net interest margins. As loan and investment rates declined, the reverse was true. But as most liabilities were subject to low fixed rates, a minimum interest margin always was available.

With the shift of low rate savings and time deposits to short-term CDs with market-related interest rates and with the increased necessity for banks to bid for deposit liabilities and other borrowed funds, it has been necessary to emphasize variable rate earnings in the loan and investment portfolios in order to avoid reduced net interest margins as interest rates rise. For example, a large portfolio of long-term fixed rate mortgages made in the mid-1970s at rates around 8 percent became a losing proposition for a bank that was forced to bid for deposit funds to maintain them at rates around 16 percent in the early 1980s.

Gap Management

The analytical framework to relate interest rate and maturity characteristics of assets and liabilities is called *gap analysis* and the operating framework to manage these relationships is called *gap management*. The gap is the difference between interest rate–sensitive assets and interest rate–sensitive liabilities.

The interest rate sensitivity of an asset or liability is measured by how soon its earnings or costs adjust to changing interest rates. The highest degree of rate sensitivity belongs to those assets and liabilities that mature in one day, as is typical of federal funds transactions. Other examples of the most rate-sensitive assets and liabilities are repurchase agreements, Treasury bills, large money market CDs, variable rate loans, and money market deposit accounts. The lowest rate sensitivity belongs to assets and liabilities with distant maturities and fixed rates. Examples include 30-year fixed rate mortgages and bank borrowings in the form of fixed coupon notes and debentures.

A positive gap exists when rate-sensitive assets exceed rate-sensitive liabilities. A bank that deliberately maintains a positive gap of significant size is anticipating higher interest rates. If it is correct in its forecast, as rates rise its net interest margin will expand. If it is wrong, however, as rates fall the earnings on the assets composing the positive gap will decline and the cost of the liabilities that finance the gap remains static. Net interest margin will suffer.

Obviously, a basic determinant of a bank's asset-liability management program is the extent to which management wants to rely on interest rate forecasts. If management believes it can accurately forecast the direction of interest rates, it will maintain a positive gap when rates are expected to rise and a negative gap when rates are expected to decline. A management that has little confidence in interest rate forecasting will want its model to help maintain a gap closer to zero.

Asset-liability management and gap management are much more complex than suggested by this discussion. Most banks classify rate-sensitive assets and liabilities into several maturity categories, for example, 30-, 90-, 180-, and 360-day maturities. Maintaining the desired gap in each category, as well as determining the makeup of the remaining assets and liabilities, is an ongoing process that receives much attention from senior management. Large banks have asset-liability management committees continuously trying to determine the most suitable balance sheet composition, using computer models designed to the specifics of each bank. Many asset-liability management software packages are available for banks of all sizes to consider, as are the services of consultants who specialize in asset-liability management.[1]

Duration Analysis

Gap analysis is often supplemented by duration analysis, particularly by large banks. Duration is a measure of interest rate sensitivity in

---

[1] William J. Murray, "A Shopper's Guide to ALM Software," *ABA Banking Journal* (September 1987), pp. 50–56.

terms of time. More specifically, it is the weighted average life of the cash flows provided by a financial asset. Duration is a better indicator of the interest rate risk of a financial asset than is maturity date if the asset provides cash flows prior to maturity. For assets that provide no interim payments, such as Treasury bills, duration is the same as the maturity date. Assets, such as most bank loans, call for periodic payments, and for such assets duration is less than the time to the final payment.

Calculation of the duration of a 10 percent, two-year loan that requires a $1,000 payment at the end of year one and a second $1,000 payment at the end of the second year follows:

Year	Cash Flow	Present Value	Percent of Total Present Value	Multiplied by Number of Years	Product
1	$1,000.00	$ 909.09	52.38%	×1	.5238
2	1,000.00	826.45	47.62	×2	.9524
	Total (original loan)	$1,735.54	100.00%	Duration = 1.4762 years	

The duration of this loan is less than that of another loan that also matures in two years but that provides no payments prior to maturity. The duration of the second loan would be two years, and thus it carries more interest rate risk than the first loan, even though both mature in the same amount of time. Banks that employ duration analysis believe it gives a much better indication of interest rate risk when it is computed for the entire balance sheet than does gap analysis when used alone.

Asset-Liability Management Problems

Utilizing asset-liability management programs may help a bank better understand what can happen as interest rates change, but such programs do not ensure good results. First, interest rate forecasts frequently are wrong both as to magnitude of change and direction of change.[2] A bank maintaining a large positive gap expecting higher interest rates will suffer if interest rates fall, but it may experience lost earnings if rates remain unchanged for some time because rate-sensitive assets usually provide the lowest returns. Thus earnings may be lost during the long wait for higher rates.

There is some danger also that following an asset-liability management program may result in overemphasizing interest rate risk while not

[2] Michael T. Belongia, "Predicting Interest Rates: A Comparison of Professional and Market-Based Forecasts," *Review*, Federal Reserve Bank of St. Louis (March 1987), pp. 9–15.

giving credit (default) risk due concern. Bank earnings have suffered in recent years, but declines are more attributable to credit quality than to changing interest rates.

In some cases credit risk may be worsened by asset-liability management programs. To maintain the desired level of rate-sensitive assets, a bank may require many of its borrowers, in order to borrow, to accept floating rate loans. This transfers the interest rate risk of the loan to the borrower. As rates rise, the ability of some borrowers to make higher and higher payments may be impaired, and defaults may result.[3]

Banks, particularly small ones, may have some difficulty getting customers to accept loan terms or buy CDs that best fit the banks' asset-liability management programs. To some degree, this problem can be solved with attractive interest rates. In addition, financial markets provide several methods of adjusting for undesired imbalances between assets and liabilities.

Hedges, Asset Sales, and Interest Rate Swaps

Hedging with financial futures contracts or other instruments is used by some banks to protect against interest rate risk.[4] An example of a hedge using financial futures is given in Chapter 16.

Sale of loans has become very common in recent years. The secondary market in residential mortgage loans, for example, is very well developed. A bank might make long-term, fixed rate mortgage loans as desired by its customers but remove the interest rate risk of the loans by selling them to long-term investors. Sales of mortgage loans and mortgage-backed securities are discussed in Chapters 13 and 17.

Another device for dealing with interest rate risk is the interest rate swap.[5] This market has expanded dramatically in the 1980s with a network of brokers developing to bring participants together.

Interest rate swaps may be complex and involve several parties. In the basic case, one party simply trades its interest payments for those of another party. For example, a small bank may hold a $10 million long-term, fixed rate loan and would like to rid itself of the interest rate risk carried by the loan. The bank might arrange to pay a fixed rate (less than the loan rate) on $10 million for the term of the loan to a large bank active in the swap market. In return, the small bank would be paid the short-

---

[3] Paul S. Nadler, "The Perils of Gap Management," *Bankers Monthly Magazine*, February 15, 1986, pp. 22–32.

[4] David M. Moffett, "Financial Futures and Their Alternatives," *Bank Administration* (September 1986), pp. 34–35.

[5] Julian Walmsley, "Interest Rate Swaps—New Service for Smaller Banks," *Bankers Monthly Magazine*, April 15, 1985, pp. 18–20.

term CD rate, adjusted every 90 days, for the term of the loan. Then, if interest rates rise, the small bank will be receiving higher and higher payments, which will offset the rising costs of the part of its deposits required to fund the loan.

Large commercial banks are more active in the swap market than are small banks. Other participants in the market include savings and loan associations, investment banks, securities dealers, and large corporations. The total volume of activity has grown rapidly, with $189 billion of swaps taking place in 1986. Due to the size of the swap market and the large network of intermediary dealers, almost any bank can consider interest rate swaps as a means to adjust the interest rate risk in its balance sheet.[6]

QUESTIONS

1. The Depository Institutions Deregulation and Monetary Control Act required the phasing out of rate ceilings on deposits by 1986. Why?
2. Time and savings deposits at commercial banks have outstripped demand deposits in growth since 1945. What factors have contributed to this rapid growth?
3. As vice president of marketing in your commercial bank, what factors would you consider important in seeking to increase your share of the local deposit market?
4. Outline and discuss the competitive situation for deposits among commercial banks, mutual savings banks, savings and loan associations, and credit unions.
5. Describe gap management and show how it can enhance net interest margins.
6. Why do you think the market in interest rate swaps has expanded so extensively?
7. Discuss the debt instruments that large commercial banks have been using for liability management. What are the advantages and risks of liability management?
8. How do you account for the dramatic growth in volume of negotiable certificates of deposit since 1961?

SELECTED REFERENCES

BELONGIA, MICHAEL T. "Predicting Interest Rates: A Comparison of Professional and Market-Based Forecasts." *Review*, Federal Reserve Bank of St. Louis (March 1987), pp. 9–15.

[6] Steven D. Felgran, "Interest Rate Swaps: Use, Risk, and Prices," *New England Economic Review* (November/December 1987), pp. 23–31.

BICKSLER, JAMES B., AND ANDREW H. CHEN. "An Economic Analysis of Interest Rate Swaps." *Journal of Finance* (July 1986), pp. 645–655.

BIERWAG, GERALD O. *Duration Analysis: Managing Interest Rate Risk.* Cambridge, Mass.: Ballinger, 1987.

COOK, TIMOTHY Q., AND TIMOTHY D. ROWE, eds. *Instruments of the Money Market,* 6th ed. Federal Reserve Bank of Richmond, 1986.

LUCKETT, DUDLEY. "Approaches to Bank Liquidity Management." *Economic Review,* Federal Reserve Bank of Kansas City (March 1980), pp. 11–27.

NADLER, PAUL S. "The Perils of Gap Management." *Bankers Monthly Magazine,* February 15, 1986, pp. 22–32.

SCHWARZ, EDWARD W., JOANNE M. HILL, AND THOMAS SCHNEEWEIS. *Financial Futures: Fundamentals, Strategies, and Applications.* Homewood, Ill.: Dow Jones-Irwin, 1986.

SINKEY, JOSEPH F., JR. *Commercial Bank Financial Management in the Financial Services Industry,* 2nd ed. New York: Macmillan, 1986.

STIGUM, MARCIA L., AND RENE O. BRANCH. *Managing Bank Assets and Liabilities.* Homewood, Ill.: Dow Jones-Irwin, 1983.

WALMSLEY, JULIAN. "Interest Rate Swaps—New Service for Smaller Banks." *Bankers Monthly Magazine,* April 15, 1985, pp. 18–20.

7

MANAGEMENT OF CAPITAL FUNDS AND SAFETY OF BANKS

The effective management of capital funds may enhance the profitability of a bank while maintaining the traditional and necessary function of safety for depositors. Commercial banks have relied historically on asset management, rather than on liability and capital funds management, to attain their profitability and liquidity objectives. Higher profitability has been realized, for example, by shifting funds from short-term government securities to the loan portfolio. Additional liquidity requirements or increases in legal reserves have been met by shifting funds from the loan or investment portfolio to cash. Once deposits have been attracted to a bank, the emphasis of management has been placed on the means to invest or lend the funds that have been attracted, subject to whatever liquidity constraint has been imposed or was desired.

Recent years have seen a shift in the emphasis of management to include adjustments to liabilities and capital funds as ways to meet their objectives of profitability and liquidity. Many banks were able to meet their needs for additional funds during a period of tight money by short-term borrowing in the Eurodollar market instead of liquidating some of their investments. Other banks adjusted interest rates to attract (or discourage) additional funds from the sale of certificates of deposit.

Adjustments in short-term liability and deposit accounts can be used to provide liquidity and enhance the profitability of a commercial bank.

While similar adjustments in intermediate-term and long-term liabilities and capital accounts are less effective in meeting liquidity objectives, they have been found to be effective in increasing the profitability of commercial banks. Subordinated capital notes issued when interest rates are relatively low may provide low-cost funds that can be invested profitably (at higher rates) for many years. These notes may also be considered as capital funds in calculating loan limits and in providing a buffer for the protection of depositors. A dividend policy that results in a rise in the market price of a bank's stock contributes to efficient management of capital funds by making it possible to sell additional stock at higher prices. This approach may be preferable to relying on the retention of earnings to provide equity capital, except where rapid expansion of deposits and loans forces the sale of additional shares at whatever price the market may bring.

THE CAPITAL DEBATE

Few areas in banking have provoked as much debate and vacillation by regulatory authorities as has bank capital. Regulatory authorities have difficulty it seems in agreeing on a definition and the amount of capital needed by banks. At times regulatory authorities give different definitions and favor different amounts. Since there is no law that states the definition and the amount of capital required, regulatory authorities are free to adopt and enforce their criteria in this very important area. Should nonconformity occur, the wrath of regulatory authorities can be brought to bear to enforce acceptance. Banks can be denied requests for certain actions such as branching or increasing loans and investments. Moreover, special examinations can be carried out to ascertain the quality of performance.

Bankers and bank supervisors have always been at odds on the subject of bank capital. The differences arise because both consider a different set of competing objectives when arriving at the measurement and amount of capital that a bank should have. Bank management, which represents bank owners, chooses capital ratios that maximize shareholders' interests. Bank management must choose between expected return and riskiness. As risks rise so does income, and bankers realize that stockholders' welfare can be maximized by emphasizing income. This does not mean that bankers are not cognizant of risk, for they are; in fact, there are some who would say that they are too cautious. The objectives of bankers tend to cause them to favor a capital level below what is normally recommended by bank supervisors and favor subordinated debt, if there appears to be a leverage effect in doing so due to the level of interest rates. Bank management has a difficult problem in arriving at a trade-off between income and risk. No one is sure of that point—bankers or bank supervisors. History is probably as good a guide as any coupled with a knowledge about the economy and the progress of the various sectors, businesses, and governments.

Bank supervisors are agents of the public and have different objectives. These objectives include the protection of depositors, provision of a stable money supply, and the promotion of a competitive financial system that facilitates financial intermediation. Supervisors, like bankers, face a difficult trade-off among these three objectives; consequently, the first objective takes precedence since there is a belief, which had its origin in the bank panics of the past, that a bank failure may have repercussions beyond the failed bank and undermine public confidence in the banking system. Such a collapse in confidence is commonly called "runs on banks," which results in a large number of depositors demanding their money at the same time. To be sure, this has happened but has not occurred since the adoption of deposit insurance and the emphasis on loan loss reserves. The argument on the appropriate amount of bank capital and how it should be measured is a continuing one and will probably continue ad infinitum.

DEFINITION OF BANK CAPITAL

For the first time in many years regulatory authorities are in agreement on the definition of capital and in general the amount, although there is a growing desire, and rightly so, to change the method of measuring the adequacy of bank capital. Capital now consists of two elements: primary and secondary capital. Primary capital consists of common stock, perpetual preferred stock, capital surplus, undivided profits, contingency reserves, other capital reserves, mandatory convertible instruments, and reserve for loan losses. Secondary capital consists of limited-life preferred stock and subordinated notes and debentures. Secondary capital cannot amount to more than 50 percent of the amount of primary capital, and the financing instruments in secondary capital must be phased out of a bank's capital as they approach maturity.

For many years primary capital was set at a minimum of 5.5 percent. These requirements do not appear excessive, since by year-end 1986, the primary capital ratio for all banks was 7.2 percent and for total capital 7.7 percent. These average figures obscure differences among banks of various size. Banks with assets of $200 million and less, for example, have long maintained strong capital-to-asset ratios and currently average 8.8 percent. In contrast, large banks have slightly lower ratios but as a group have increased their ratios in recent years to 6.6 percent. Despite the problems banks have encountered recently in the area of lending, they now have a stronger capital base than a few years ago.

There is debate on the role that debt instruments should play in the capital base. This debate stems from the permanence of capital. Bank regulatory authorities take the position that only primary capital as now defined is permanent in the sense that it has no maturity, but once a debt instrument matures, the capital of a bank has been reduced. Debt instruments possess certain features of capital, but they lack permanence because they have maturity or redemption dates. It could be argued that once this debt matures, new debt could be issued to take its place. The FDIC would counter this argument by saying that in the event that the debt could not be rolled over, the protection offered depositors is lessened. This maturity problem has been recognized in the new definition of secondary capital by setting forth the percentage of debt that will be considered as capital based on years to maturity of the debt instruments.

Banking authorities have been inclined to favor only equity as capital, whereas the banking industry favors both equity and debt. The reason for the banking industry's position is twofold. Debt has a leverage effect and is a way of increasing the return to stockholders if the borrowed funds earn more than their cost. Moreover, debt does not dilute earnings per common share as would issuance of more shares as long as the borrowed funds earn at least as much as they cost. The use of both debt and equity instruments in providing for the capital of commercial banks adds greater flexibility to capital management. A proper mix of both contributes to lower capital costs and, consequently, to higher returns on bank equity.

FUNCTIONS AND GROWTH
OF BANK CAPITAL

Commercial banks normally utilize a much higher degree of financial leverage than do most other business corporations. For a number of years, total equity capital of insured commercial banks has funded approximately 8 percent of total assets, which means that about 92 percent is financed by debt—the funds of depositors and other creditors. In sharp contrast, a typical manufacturing firm might be expected to have only about one-third of its assets financed by borrowed funds.

Protective Function

Because such a high percentage of a bank's assets is financed by depositors—around 80 percent—the primary function of the limited amount of equity capital has been considered to be the protection of depositors. In addition to this important function, bank capital reduces the risks borne by the Federal Deposit Insurance Corporation and bank stockholders. The protective function has been viewed not only as ensur-

ing payoff of depositors in case of liquidation, but also as contributing to
the maintenance of solvency by providing a cushion of excess assets so
that a bank threatened with losses might continue in operation. However,
it is important to recognize that current earnings—not capital—actually
absorb a majority of bank losses. Also, unlike the situation in most firms,
only a portion of the capital account contributes to the maintenance of
solvency for a commercial bank. A bank is generally considered solvent
only so long as its capital stock is unimpaired, that is, as long as the value
of assets is at least equal to the value of liabilities, excluding subordinated
capital notes and debentures, *plus* capital stock.

Although the protective function of bank capital has a long history,
this role is probably less important to small depositors now because of the
protection provided by the Federal Deposit Insurance Corporation in case
of liquidation. Recovery of depositors' funds has been received or is available from the FDIC for 99.8 percent of all deposits of insured banks that
have failed since the inception of deposit insurance on a national scale.
Large depositors, with balances exceeding the maximum for FDIC insurance, have been the losers in recent bank failures when insufficient capital has been available to absorb losses in liquidation. And in deposit
assumption cases, where the liabilities of the failed bank are assumed by
another bank, even the large depositors have received full credit for their
deposits.

Regulatory authorities have emphasized the protective function of
bank capital to the highest degree. To be sure, capital does serve a protective role, but this function can be overplayed. Witness, for example, the
fact that small banks are normally more highly capitalized than large
banks, yet small banks are more prone to failure. Capital is just one of the
factors that contribute to the strength of banks and the banking system.
Such factors as the quality of management and assets, earnings, and liquidity are just as important as capital, if not more so. A final factor that
must not be overlooked is the strength of the economy. During prosperous
times banks are less likely to encounter financial problems than when
times are bad. Borrowers normally enjoy more satisfactory incomes in
good times than in periods of recession; consequently, they are in a position to repay loans. Governments, too, are able to collect taxes, pay interest, and redeem maturing obligations. Of all the desirable developments
in banking, regulatory authorities appear to place safety of banks first. Not
only are bank failures embarrassing to supervisory agencies but expensive
to the FDIC, the deposit insuring agency. One bank researcher evaluated
the role of capital correctly when she said

> The major argument against regulation of bank capital is that there is little
> evidence that capital ratios are reliably related to bank failures and, there-
> fore, bank riskiness. Most statistical studies of the causes of bank failures
> conclude that low capital ratios are not the primary cause. During the Bank-

ing Panic of 1933, for example, many banks with low capital ratios did not fail while many with high capital ratios did. Most of the banks that have failed since the 1930s failed because of embezzlement, mismanagement, and insufficient liquidity due to low earnings rather than undercapitalization.

The weakness of the link between bank capital and bank failures does not mean, however, that capital is irrelevant to bank solvency. Rather it is evident that simple capital ratios are imperfect measures of capital adequacy, as recent empirical work on bank failures has shown. Other things equal, the better capitalized a bank is, the safer and sounder it is. Moreover, simple capital ratios have the virtue of being objective measures of bank strength and being easy for bank supervisors to monitor. Because simple ratios are poor predictors of bank failures, however, other ways of controlling bank risk have received serious consideration.[1]

Operational Functions

The operational functions of bank capital have been considered secondary, in contrast to the typical nonbanking firm. Operational functions include the provision of funds for the purchase of land, buildings, machinery, and equipment and providing a buffer to absorb occasional operating losses. Total investment of insured commercial banks in buildings, furniture, fixtures, and other physical assets representing bank premises amounted to around $41 billion, approximately 20 percent of total capital funds and only 1.5 percent of total assets in 1986.

Regulatory Functions

In addition to providing a basis for operations and for protection of depositors, other functions have been attributed to the capital funds of commercial banks. These functions arise only because of the public's special interest in the successful operations of banking firms and the laws and regulations that enable public agencies to exercise some control over these operations. Regulations relating to bank capital include those that have to do with minimum requirements necessary to obtain a charter, establish branch operations, and limit a bank's loans, investments, and acquisitions. Bank capital regulations also impact bank holding companies when acquisitions are being considered. In this sense, a bank's capital helps to satisfy the supervisory authorities when they are judging a bank's condition. Moreover, to the extent that a bank's lending and investment activities are limited by the availability of capital funds to meet the requirements for such activities, a bank's capital also serves to regulate bank loans and investments.

---

[1] Karlyn Mitchell, "Capital Adequacy at Commercial Banks," *Monthly Economic Review*, Federal Reserve Bank of Kansas City (October 1984), pp. 28–29.

Growth of Bank Capital

Bank capital has shown considerable growth over the years, but has declined substantially as a proportion of total assets. Declining capital ratios are, in part, a function of the rapid increase in bank deposits and earning assets that have outstripped the growth of capital funds. Part of the deposit growth has been due to the aggressiveness of commercial banks in competing with other financial institutions and part has been due to an expansionary monetary policy to provide for the credit needs of the economy. It is important to note that a monetary policy that results in expansion of the money supply is accomplished by encouraging growth of deposits and loans. Growth of capital is subject to different forces from growth in deposits. Traditionally, *equity capital*—preferred and common stock, surplus, undivided profits, and certain contingency reserves—has been the major component of commercial banks' capital accounts. However, reserves for loan losses and capital notes and debentures have increased in recent years (see Figure 7-1). Although primary capital has increased sharply, total capital has increased at a slightly more rapid rate due to the greater increase in capital notes and debentures.

FIGURE 7-1   Capital of Insured Commercial Banks

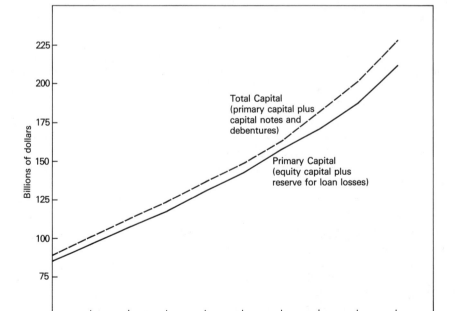

SOURCE: Federal Deposit Insurance Corporation, annual reports.

SOURCES OF BANK CAPITAL

The most important source of bank capital in the past decade has come from retained earnings; in fact, approximately 70 percent of the increase in capital was from this source. Reserves for loan losses and the sale of common stock provided about 22 percent, and the remainder was derived from the sale of debt securities.

Common Stock

The bulk of the new equity funds was provided by retention of earnings, for several reasons. Some relate to the costs of marketing new issues and the difficulty in finding buyers. Others relate to the likely dilution of earnings and control for existing stockholders. The retention of earnings is often the easiest and least expensive way to provide additional equity capital. Some banks have found, however, that bank stock prices are influenced by the level of dividend payments; consequently, a higher dividend payment ratio leads to higher stock prices. Thus paying more dividends performs a dual function: increasing the wealth of existing stockholders and making it easier to sell additional stock to provide needed increases in capital. Furthermore, many dividend-conscious stockholders may prefer their current dividends in the short run to possible future gains, thus making the buildup of capital by earnings retention more difficult.

For most small banks, as for small business in general, no ready market exists for the sale of common stock. Only a few of the largest banks have listed their stock on a national exchange. The stock of many other large banks is readily traded in the over-the-counter market. For most of the country's banks, however, the relatively small number of stockholders and shares outstanding preclude the existence of an active market for their stock. Even where a ready market exists, the cost of distributing relatively small issues of common stock in the over-the-counter market may be substantial.

For a small bank whose stock is closely held, issuing new shares of stock to outsiders may dilute the ability of the existing stockholders to control the bank's operations. In many instances, this factor would cause existing stockholders to veto a sale of new shares of stock.

In a nonfinancial corporation, the bulk of equity funds typically is invested in productive physical assets that enhance the earning power of the firm. This is seldom true for commercial banks, and issuing new shares of stock may not increase their earning power materially. A greater possibility exists that it may affect existing stockholders adversely. When a bank issues new stock, it usually means that earnings per share will be diluted. While total earnings may be slightly higher, earnings per share may be somewhat less because more shares would be outstanding.

The major way in which additional capital can increase the earning ability of commercial banks substantially is by influencing the lending and investing policies. With an increase in capital, banks can make larger loans to a single borrower and possibly adopt a more liberal lending policy. Banks could also adopt a more aggressive investment policy by increasing the amount invested in longer maturities or lower-rated issues.

Sometimes the retention of earnings is considered to be an inexpensive source of funds, but retained earnings must result in enhanced prices if stockholders are to be as well off as if dividends had been paid. This is because dividends paid to shareholders can be spent or reinvested to earn additional returns. If the funds are retained by the bank, the only justification for doing so is that management believes that the added capital will allow it to pursue policies that will increase those values and thus provide more benefit to stockholders than they would have experienced from dividends.

Reserves for Loan Losses

Lending involves risk, and losses do occur; consequently, most banks maintain a reserve for loan losses. This practice has been encouraged by bank regulatory authorities and the Internal Revenue Service. Until 1969, increases in reserves for loan losses contributed substantially to the growth of bank capital. Prior to 1969, banks were permitted to make additions to reserves for loan losses out of pretax income until these reserves reached a maximum of 2.4 percent of the eligible loans. This maximum was reduced in steps over the years, and now all banks must use the *experience method;* that is, banks are permitted to establish reserves only up to the average of actual losses experienced over the most recent six-year period. Since reserves for loan losses serve to protect depositors, these reserves have been included as an important source of bank capital over the years.

PREFERRED STOCK, CAPITAL NOTES, AND DEBENTURES

Preferred stock and subordinated capital debt instruments share some characteristics of common equity capital and some characteristics of savings-type debt instruments, such as promissory notes and certificates of deposit with longer maturities. They provide long-term or permanent additions to a bank's capital structure.

While debt must be repaid at maturity, it often is desirable to refund a long-term issue of capital notes or debentures. A typical issue may provide for a lump-sum repayment at maturity. A growing bank will have continuing needs for long-term capital to finance growth and may prefer to keep debt capital as a permanent part of the capital structure. This can be accomplished by refunding or paying off a maturing debt issue with the proceeds of a new issue of capital notes or debentures.

Many issues of long-term debt have been convertible into common stock. The debenture agreement may provide, for example, that debentures may be exchanged by the holder for a given number of shares of the bank's common stock. The conversion feature would permit the holder to share in the good fortunes of the bank if its stock grew in value and would permit the bank to obtain funds in effect from issuing common stock at a price somewhat above the market price at the time the debentures were issued. Convertible debentures and capital notes usually carry a lower interest rate than does straight debt because the lenders have an opportunity for a capital gain by converting to common stock.

Senior securities enable a commercial bank to use capital funds to provide additional financial leverage. When the proceeds of a debenture or preferred stock issue can be loaned or invested to earn more than the rate that must be paid to the security holder, the difference will accrue to the benefit of common stockholders. Where such opportunities exist, the earnings on common equity may be increased at the same time as additional protection is made available to depositors. In cases where prudent banking practices dictate obtaining additional capital funds even though the earnings rate may not justify the sale of securities, there still may be an advantage to using senior securities. The use of debt or preferred stock usually will not dilute earnings on common equity as much as will the sale of additional common stock.

The comparative effect on earnings of issuing common stock or long-term debt is illustrated in Table 7-1. In this hypothetical example, it is assumed that an additional $1 million of capital should be raised to support the rapid growth of deposits and assets. The existing position of the bank is shown in the first column, with earnings per share of $24 on 50,000 shares. The additional capital funds could be raised by the sale of an additional 6,667 shares at $150 each or by the sale of 8 percent subordinated debentures. The after-tax interest cost on these debentures would be 4.8 percent, assuming a marginal income tax rate of 40 percent federal and state. It is assumed that the capital funds are invested in short-term government securities earning 5 percent to provide additional liquidity. No immediate additional deposit growth is realized. In this illustration, the earnings per share would be diluted by 9 percent if common stock were sold and only 1.5 percent if subordinated debentures were issued. The earnings rate on total assets remains about the same, but use of low-cost debt capital instead of selling stock limits the dilution of earnings per share of common equity.

TABLE 7-1 Effect of Alternative Methods of Raising Capital on Earnings per Share

	Existing Position	Expand Capital by Issuing	
		Common Stock	*8% Debentures*
Total assets	$100,000,000	$101,000,000	$101,000,000
Deposits	92,500,000	92,500,000	92,500,000
Debentures	0	0	1,000,000
Common equity	7,500,000	8,500,000	7,500,000
Earnings before interest	$ 2,000,000	$ 2,050,000	$ 2,050,000
Interest on debentures (8%)	0	0	80,000
Earnings before taxes	$ 2,000,000	$ 2,050,000	$ 1,970,000
Less income tax (40%)	800,000	820,000	788,000
Earnings after taxes	$1,200,000	$1,230,000	$1,182,000
No. of shares outstanding	50,000	56,667	50,000
Earnings per share	24.00	21.71	23.64
Earnings dilution		9.0%	1.5%

Preferred Stock

Preferred stock is considered a component of primary capital, whereas limited-life preferred stock is considered a part of secondary capital. The restrictions imposed on these securities are similar to those applicable to capital notes and debentures and are discussed in the paragraphs that follow. Although preferred stock accounts for less than 1 percent of the total equity capital of all banks, there has been considerable interest in this type of financing by large banks and bank holding companies in recent years. Banks have been reluctant to issue preferred stock because of the stigma attached to it as a result of its use in bank financing during the Great Depression. In the 1930s the Reconstruction Finance Corporation made financial infusions to a large number of commercial banks that were in financial distress by purchasing preferred shares in these banks. Consequently, investors and others looked upon the issuance of preferred stock as an indication that banks were in financial trouble.

The continued association of preferred stock with distress financing in the minds of many bankers and investors is unfortunate. Even though features of the income tax laws make the after-tax cost of preferred shares a higher-cost financing instrument than debt (because of the deductibility of interest for tax purposes), preferred stock has a legitimate place in the financial structure of a corporation. It may be considered an appropriate alternative to common stock for raising capital funds (rather than a substitute for debt) when equity capital is desired. The existence of fixed dividend payments may provide additional financial leverage (though at a somewhat higher cost than debt), and dilution of voting rights for common stockholders may be avoided. If the market price of common stock is depressed when the funds are needed, the convertible feature may permit later conversion of preferred securities to common stock when the market price is at a higher level.

Capital Notes and Debentures

Although the issuance of capital notes and debentures by commercial banks also was associated with the need for so-called "distress financing" in earlier years, bankers' and supervisory authorities' attitudes have changed as to the desirability of long-term instruments in the capital structure of commercial banks. In late 1961, the Comptroller of the Currency ruled that subordinated debentures and capital notes were appropriate financing instruments for national banks and that they could be considered as a portion of unimpaired capital for purposes of calculating lending limits on unsecured loans to any one borrower. State member banks are more limited in their use of debt as a portion of capital funds. State member banks may not include capital notes and debentures as a part of capital, capital stock, or surplus for purposes of calculating limits on various lending, borrowing, and investment activities according to a ruling by the Board of Governors of the Federal Reserve System. Most states now permit the issue of capital debt by commercial banks, but only about 50 percent of them permit its use when calculating lending limits. Federal Deposit Insurance Corporation approval is required by insured banks prior to repayment of capital debt issues.

Generally such securities must have a minimum of seven years to maturity at the time of issue if they are not to be considered subject to legal reserve requirements. Subordination of capital debt to the claims of depositors generally is required by supervisory authorities when commercial banks issue such debt. Subordination causes debt to serve the same protective function as equity from the viewpoint of depositors. The other functions of bank capital are served by debt as well as by equity. Therefore, subordinated debt, subject to legal requirements and supervisory authority approval, is appropriately considered a portion of the capital funds of a commercial bank. The interest cost of capital notes and subordinated debentures for a large commercial bank is similar to the cost of long-term unsecured debt for a nonfinancial corporation of high credit standing. Smaller banks generally pay higher rates. Although large amounts of subordinated notes and debentures have been issued in recent years, the bulk of new bank capital has been derived from the issuance of new stock and from retained earnings.

Capital notes and debentures, just as limited-life preferred stock, are considered as a part of secondary capital. These instruments must meet certain conditions to qualify, however. They must have an original maturity of at least seven years. If the instruments have a serial or installment repayment program, the payments must be made annually and once started, the amount paid must be the same each year. As mentioned previously, the amount of limited-life preferred stock and subordinated debt may not exceed 50 percent of the amount of primary capital of a bank. Finally, as these secondary capital components approach maturity, redemption, or payment, the amount considered to be capital declines in accordance with the schedule set forth earlier.

VARIATIONS IN THE SOURCES OF BANK CAPITAL

The sources of external capital have varied over the years. Investors' interests change. At times one type of security is more attractive than another, and securities of one industry may take precedence over another. The economic as well as the political climate are major factors influencing investors' decisions. As a result of these many variations, the cost of raising capital varies with the type of security offered in the marketplace as well as the performance of the industry and the firm. Bank management is very much concerned with the cost of raising external capital and hopes for the best price consistent with the bank's needs, its ability to service the newly acquired capital, the financial impact on present stockholders, and the guidelines established by regulatory authorities.

Convertible securities have been used frequently in recent years. The purchaser of a convertible bond receives a fixed rate of interest plus the right to exchange the bond for common shares as set forth in the bond indenture. As interest rates rise or when there is a desire not to dilute stockholders' equity, banks are inclined to sell convertibles. Convertible securities are attractive to investors who want a steady income but yet want to be in a position to share in the growth of the institutions if and when the price of the stock rises. They are a "have your cake and eat it too" kind of investment vehicle.

Because of depressed price-earnings multiples from common stocks, banks are sometimes encouraged to sell preferred stock. Prior to 1975, preferred stock was seldom used by bank holding companies because of the stigma attached to it, but in recent years due to its favorable cost, it is receiving increased consideration. Preferred stock may be issued with a fixed or a floating rate. One of the major advantages of preferred stock with a ceiling on rates is that the dividend cost remains constant. In financing with common stock, this is not the case since each new share of common is required to earn an increasing amount in subsequent years to avoid dilution.

There have been distinct waves of common stock financing. When interest rates are high, investors tend not to be attracted to common stock; but when rates subside, investors purchase common stock because of its relative stability and constant dividends. The heavy reliance on common stock is due in large part to the insistence of regulatory authorities on this type of external capital.

Small banks in most instances are forced to rely on local markets for external capital; consequently, their stock is not widely traded. Frequently, the stock of small banks is sold by one or more persons associated with the bank or a local bond broker by spreading the word in the community that the bank plans to issue some stock. It is not unusual to find a situation in which potential stockholders in a small community place their names on a list with the president of the bank or some other bank official as potential buyers the next time any stock is available. In this manner a crude market is maintained that benefits both the buyer and seller. It is not uncommon for the stockholders of a small bank to take the entire issue through a rights offering. If a small bank decides to issue some form of debt, it probably would not be done through an underwriter since the size of the issue would very likely not warrant the cost. It would in all likelihood be placed directly with an institutional investor or sold locally as would a common stock offering. It might also be sold to a correspondent bank that buys debentures of smaller banks.

COMPOSITION OF BANK CAPITAL

Table 7-2 presents the composition of bank capital. Note that earnings of commercial banks in the form of surplus, undivided profits, and reserves

TABLE 7-2 Composition of Capital of Commercial Banks (in millions of dollars)

	1980	1986	Percent Increase
Primary capital		$129,685		$211,585	63
Common stock	$23,557	$29,579	26
Surplus	40,327	63,944	59
Undivided profits	54,186	87,700	62
Perpetual preferred stock	171	1,425	733
Loan loss reserves	11,444	28,937	153
Secondary capital		6,465		16,993	163
Limited-life preferred stock	NA	81	—
Subordinated notes and debentures	$ 6,465	$16,912	162
Total capital		$136,150		$228,578	68

SOURCE: Federal Deposit Insurance Corporation, annual reports.

for loan losses accounted for nearly 80 percent of total capital. Banks in general traditionally rely on earnings as a source of capital and have reluctantly issued common stock, primarily because of a fear that earnings of present stockholders would be diluted. This has especially been true of small banks. Moreover, the market for the stock of small banks is limited, consequently the heavy reliance on retained earnings. Large and regional banks that enjoy a relatively broad market frequently issue common stock. It is obvious from the information in Table 7-2 that two sources of bank capital have been increasing substantially in recent years, namely, perpetual preferred stock and subordinated notes and debentures. As pointed out previously, the level of interest rates has played a role in this decision. In general, debt instruments and preferred stock have been employed by the larger banks. Secondary capital has shown the greatest increase recently, but primary capital is still the major component of bank capital and accounts for over 90 percent of the total.

ADEQUACY OF BANK CAPITAL

Although the capital of commercial banks has increased over the years, the more rapid increase in total assets and deposits continues to focus attention on the adequacy (or inadequacy) of bank capital. Regulatory authorities are especially concerned with this matter since they have been charged with the responsibility of bank safety.

Even though the number of failures has been relatively small, the greater incidence of failure in the mid-1980s has focused attention on the reasons for bank failures and the role that adequate capital funds has in preventing failures. While it may be difficult to determine precisely the amount of capital that a bank or the banking system should have, the capital should be sufficient to fulfill the basic functions we have discussed: financing the organization and operation of a bank, providing protection to depositors and other creditors, and inspiring confidence in depositors and supervisory authorities. In this context the protective function is most important, of course. Sufficient capital funds to absorb losses and to assure depositors of the safety of their funds often may prevent the failure of a particular bank.

The safety of deposits has been guaranteed by deposit insurance held in most banks through the Federal Deposit Insurance Corporation. Public knowledge that insured deposits will be paid in full (up to $100,000) undoubtedly has prevented mass withdrawals from banks that may have had temporary financial problems. Such runs in the early 1930s forced closure of many banks that otherwise would have survived.

The amount of capital funds a bank needs is related to the risks it assumes. If a bank assumes great risk in its loan portfolio, for example, it should have more capital funds than if it were more conservative in its lending policy. Basically, a bank has two choices when establishing the size of its capital account. It can increase its capital as the risks it assumes increase, or it can invest in assets that are relatively free of risk. This is not to say that banks, to be on the safe side, should follow an ultraconservative loan and investment policy. This, too, has its pitfalls. Such a policy might not result in a bank serving its trade area properly and thus would be openly inviting competition from a new bank, other established banks, or other financial institutions. Determining the size of a bank's capital is not easy, but it is important. And if a bank is to grow, with increased deposits and earning assets, it must expand its capital base but at the same time keep the risk level constant.

Capital Ratios

Many interested parties have wished to establish a set of standards that can be employed to test the adequacy of capital funds of a particular bank or of the banking system, and this has been done. Although a ratio may be helpful as a starting point in analyzing the capital adequacy of an individual bank, it should not be considered an end in itself. A bank does not have adequate capital just because it conforms to some statistical average. Is it beyond criticism just because it meets some ratio? Ratio analysis of capital adequacy differs very little, if any, from the use of ratio analysis in credit analysis of a bank borrower's financial statement. The inquiry must go beyond the ratio to an examination of the bank's operations and the risks it assumes in its loan and investment portfolio.

Capital funds have been measured in relation to various balance sheet items such as total deposits, total assets, or risk assets. The ratio of a bank's capital funds to these balance sheet items has been thought to indicate the extent to which a bank could suffer losses of one kind or another and still have enough capital to assure the safety of depositors' funds. Various levels of these ratios have been used by supervisory authorities and others as standards of capital adequacy; the bank whose capital ratios were not at least equal to then current standards has often been considered under-capitalized for the volume of business it was doing or for the volume of assets or deposits it held.

The ratio of capital funds to total deposits has enjoyed the longest use of any ratio devised to measure and determine capital adequacy. The Comptroller of the Currency recommended its use in 1914 when he stated in his annual report that national banks should be required by law to maintain at least one dollar of capital funds for each ten dollars of deposits. Earlier, several states had made use of this ratio, and it was widely used as a standard for capital adequacy until World War II.

The ratio of capital funds to total assets came into use by some supervisory authorities in the late 1940s. It was argued that the amount of capital a bank needs is not related to deposits, but to assets. Because a measure of capital adequacy purports to indicate the extent that a bank's capital can absorb loss and still protect the interest of depositors, a valid measure would have to be related to all items in the balance sheet that might be subject to loss. Losses are reflected in the bank's balance sheet by reduced values of assets; therefore, a measure of capital adequacy should logically relate capital funds to those assets and not to deposits.

In 1948, the Comptroller of the Currency announced abandonment of the use of the relationship between capital structure and deposits in determining capital adequacy. At that time he adopted the ratio of capital funds to loans and investments other than U.S. government securities as a rule of thumb for preliminary screening. The ratio of capital funds to total assets, less cash and U.S. government securities, came into use later under the name of *risk-asset ratio*.

Until very recently, the ratio of capital to total assets was in vogue. It is a ratio that is quite simple, easily understood, and based on considerable logic. Although all of the ratios we have discussed reached a low point in the late 1970s, this trend has been reversed. The primary capital-to-asset ratio increased noticeably in the 1980s (see Figure 7-2). In 1980, for example, this ratio was 6.3 percent compared to 7.2 percent six years later. It should be noted that the capital-to-asset ratio for the period in Figure 7-2 was above the minimum of 5.5 percent established by the three regulatory agencies. When secondary capital is added, the ratio becomes

FIGURE 7-2   Primary Capital-to-Asset Ratios, Commercial Banks

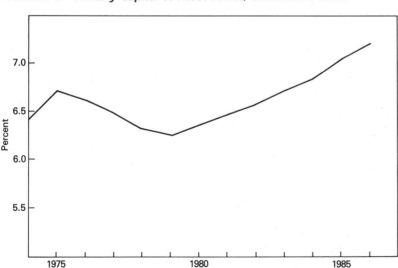

SOURCE: Federal Reserve Bank of Philadelphia, *Business Review* (July/August 1987).

even higher, approximately 7.7 percent. Banks in the aggregate have, therefore, improved their capital position in recent years.

Bank regulatory agencies are not completely satisfied with the present capital adequacy guidelines, and for that reason the three federal agencies have proposed a revision that takes into account the risks of a bank's assets. In early 1986 the three agencies submitted for public comment what might be termed a "risk-adjusted ratio" that would create five categories of bank assets that have certain common characteristics and assign a certain weight to each in arriving at a bank's capital adequacy. This would mean that banks with a high proportion of risky assets would be required to maintain more capital than if assets possessed a lower risk.

The risk-adjusted ratio calls for five weighted categories: 0 percent, 10 percent, 20 percent, 50 percent, and 100 percent, each of which is determined by the quality of the obligor. Cash, for example, would have a weight of 0 percent, as would U.S. government securities with a maturity of less than 90 days. This is another way of saying that these assets are considered to be risk free; consequently, no capital would be required to support them. U.S. government securities with maturities in excess of 90 days would have a weight of 10 percent. The reason for this increased weight, of course, is that longer maturities have greater interest rate risk than shorter maturities. General obligation bonds of states and municipalities would fall into the 20 percent category. Public purpose general revenue bonds will be weighted at 50 percent and loans at 100 percent. A hypothetical example of the classification of a bank's assets might be as follows:

	Amount in Millions of Dollars	Percent Weight	Weighted Assets in Millions of Dollars
Classification of assets:			
1. Cash and U.S. government securities with a maturity of less than 90 days	100 ×	0 =	0
2. U.S. government securities with maturities in excess of 90 days	100 ×	10 =	10
3. General obligation bonds of states and municipalities	200 ×	20 =	40
4. Revenue bonds of municipalities	200 ×	50 =	100
5. Loans	400 ×	100 =	400
Total	1,000		550
Amount of capital required, assuming a requirement of 7 percent			$38,500,000

Although this is a simple explanation, it does illustrate the mechanics of arriving at the risk-adjusted ratio of a bank. There are several items in the portfolio of a bank that would require close scrutiny and evaluation, such as off–balance sheet items. A two-step procedure would be required in evaluating such an asset. It would first involve arriving at the credit risk of each instrument and then assigning a credit equivalent. This credit equivalent would then be included in the risk-asset framework. The implementation of the risk-adjusted ratio involves considerable subjective evaluation, and of course both the weighted categories as well as the established ratio applicable to the weighted assets are subject to change.

The new risk-based capital requirement is now being implemented, but the capital rule will not take effect until the end of 1992. This is when banks would have to maintain an 8 percent capital-to-asset ratio of which half, or 4 percent, would have to consist of common equity (i.e., common stock, surplus, undivided profits, and capital reserves). For the 1990–92 period it is expected that the ratio would be 7.25 percent of which 3.25 would be common equity. Until the end of 1990 the ratio would be 6 percent. The reason for this gradual introduction of the capital ratios is that the objective is quite challenging and some of the banking organizations may be placed in a position of having to issue common stock, make provision for an increase in retained earnings, or restructure their risk portfolios.

A variety of reasons prompted the introduction of the risk-adjusted ratio, including the growth of off–balance sheet items and the decline in the quality of loan portfolios of many banks, including loans to Third World countries. Off–balance sheet items, such as letters of credit, loan commitments, and promises to guarantee loans, are not considered to be assets; consequently, they do not presently require capital backing. Off–balance sheet items have grown sharply in recent years. For the ten largest banks such activity increased from about $23 billion in 1980 to $1.7 trillion six years later. Meanwhile, the most liquid asset of banks, cash and short government securities, declined from 29 percent of assets in 1976 to 17 percent ten years later. The objective of the risk-adjusted ratio is to alter a bank's asset mix and thus contribute to a safer banking system.

This risk-adjusted capital ratio was developed in conjunction with the Bank of England. This involvement with a foreign bank indicates that the regulatory agencies would like to influence the quality of foreign loans that proved to be troublesome in the mid-1980s. (Foreign lending will be discussed in a later chapter.) One of the features in the risk-based plan is the exclusion of reserve for loan losses when calculating the primary capital of a bank. The suggestion of a risk-adjusted capital ratio for a measure of capital adequacy is reminiscent of the risk-asset ratio adopted in the late 1940s when the deposit-to-capital ratio was abandoned. Regulatory agencies frequently restructure the measure of capital adequacy as the composition of assets changes and risks are increased. We will undoubtedly be introduced to others as the asset mix of banks changes and bank risks rise in the future.

BANK CAPITAL AND BANK SIZE

Our discussion of capital and capital ratios has centered on banks in the aggregate. It should be pointed out that the size of the capital account of banks varies. In general, small banks are more highly capitalized than large banks, primarily because of the requirements imposed by regulatory authorities.

According to regulatory authorities, there are several reasons for what appear to be glaring disparities in capital requirements. These can be categorized into three basic areas, namely, management, diversification of assets, and operations. Small banks in general have less management depth, salaries are usually lower, and opportunities for advancement are often fewer than in large banks. Small banks have always had these problems. They normally have less diversification in both the loan and investment portfolios than do large banks. The loan territory of large banks covers a much greater area. The larger banks make loans in regional markets and even nationally and internationally, whereas small banks are restricted primarily to one community frequently dominated by one industry. Obviously, this limited diversification contributes to increased risks. Sometimes the investment portfolio is less diversified in small banks. They often find themselves in a position of being forced to purchase municipal bonds of the city and/or county in which they are located. The attitude prevails that the deposits of the bank are derived locally; therefore, the funds should be invested locally.

One reason for these purchases is that the municipal issues are not rated, which limits their marketability; consequently, they are not in demand by investors in other areas. Moreover, many of the assets of small banks are not sensitive to the movement of interest rates, which influences the bank's liquidity. The internal controls of small banks unfortunately are not of the quality found in larger banks. The expertise and professionalism are not always present. Small banks are not generally as liquid as large banks because of the type of assets held and in some instances because of lower reserve requirements. Another factor that contributes to small banks having more risk than large banks is that the market for their stock is generally limited. This places them at a disadvantage if and when a decision is made to raise capital externally. Finally, a larger portion of the deposits of small banks is covered by deposit insurance, which increases the need for more bank capital.

It should not be assumed from the foregoing that large banks present no risk, for they do as is evidenced by the failure of some large banks in recent years. Some observers point out that large banks should have more equity capital because of the risks associated with the large amount of international loans held that are subject to country and currency risk. Moreover, large banks have more uninsured depositors than do small banks and rely more heavily on potentially volatile purchase money.

Criticisms of Ratios and Formulas

Those who have attempted to develop standards of capital adequacy have not been without their critics. All these ratios and formulas have been judged, at one time or another, to fall short of the requirements necessary for a valid standard of the adequacy of a bank's capital funds. To the extent that adequate capital means enough to absorb losses and prevent failure, all have been poor predictors of bank failures and thus poor measures of capital adequacy.

The *Comptroller's Manual,* until its 1971 revision, provided official guidelines for the determination of capital adequacy that specifically denied reliance on capital ratios. Instead, the following eight factors were listed by the Comptroller as those to be considered in assessing the adequacy of capital:

1. The quality of management
2. The liquidity of assets
3. The history of earnings and the retention thereof
4. The quality and character of ownership
5. The burden of meeting occupancy expenses
6. The potential volatility of deposit structure
7. The quality of operating procedures
8. The bank's capacity to meet present and future financial needs of its trade area, considering the competition it faces

Each of these factors relates in some way to the various kinds of risk that a commercial bank faces. Most have been mentioned before as being related to the amount of capital funds a bank should have. In addition to these qualitative factors, the regulatory agencies assess the growth rate in earnings and assets when attempting to judge the adequacy of bank capital. If a bank is not growing in earnings and assets, it obviously has more risk than does one that is enjoying a healthy growth. The existence of more risk indicates a need for more capital, other things being equal, than is necessary for a bank with less risk.

Some shift has been noted in regulatory authorities' attempts to identify banks that appear to be vulnerable to financial deterioration and possible failure. Statistical tests have been used to compare a number of financial ratios of individual banks with those same ratios in other banks in an attempt to find disparities that would provide an early warning to banks likely to be subject to criticism and classification later as problem banks by examiners. Korobow, Stuhr, and Martin have reported, for example, that five ratios have proved to be most useful for this purpose, based on tests of member banks in the Second Federal Reserve District and on limited tests in other districts. These are

1. Total loans and leases to total sources of funds
2. Equity capital to adjusted risk assets
3. Operating expenses to operating revenues
4. Gross charge-offs to net income plus provision for loan losses
5. Commercial and industrial loans to total loans

The ratio of operating expenses to operating revenues has been found to be a particularly good indicator of management ability and predictor of classification of problem banks in conjunction with other ratios.[2] This seems to indicate that adequate capital, by itself, does not prevent bank failure. Operating and investment losses must be absorbed from profits if a bank is to be viable, and narrow profit margins will not indefinitely postpone problems when adverse circumstances occur.

The Federal Deposit Insurance Corporation implemented an integrated monitoring system (IMS) in 1977 to monitor bank performance between examinations. This computerized system was designed to identify banks that merit closer supervisory attention. The IMS utilizes eight factors that "measure a bank's capital adequacy, liquidity, profitability, and asset and liability mix and growth against a predetermined standard."[3] The results of the IMS tests are used as a basis for follow-up activity such as early examination or visitation of the bank.

The ratio of capital funds to deposits continues to show a surprising degree of popularity after having been denounced as a measure of capital adequacy for more than a third of a century. The continued use of this and other ratios for analysis of capital suggests that one of the failures of later formula approaches and of methods of analysis that depend on a great deal of subjective determination of relative factors is their lack of simplicity. It is fairly easy to compute a simple ratio and to compare such a ratio computed for an individual bank with comparable figures for other banks. This is a decided advantage for a banker, so that he or she can easily

---

[2] L. Korobow, D. P. Stuhr, and D. Martin, "A Nationwide Test of Early Warning Research in Banking," *Quarterly Review*, Federal Reserve Bank of New York (Autumn 1977), pp. 37–51. See also J. F. Sinkey, Jr., "A Multivariate Statistical Analysis of the Characteristics of Problem Banks," *Journal of Finance* (March 1975), pp. 21–38.

[3] Federal Deposit Insurance Corporation, *1977 Annual Report of Operations*, p. 9.

compare his or her position with that of others. It is an obvious advantage, too, for a bank supervisor to be able to make such simple computations.

Simplicity can be a virtue in a measure of capital adequacy, but simplicity is not an adequate guide. Bank management owes to itself, to the depositors, and to the economy as a whole a careful appraisal of all the risks facing the bank when ascertaining the adequacy of bank capital. Bank management should not be lulled into a sense of false security by good times. Bank failures result in losses to depositors and stockholders, the inability to meet the legitimate demands of borrowers, and shake the public's confidence in the financial structure of the nation. The depression of the 1930s was the last period in which our commercial banking system suffered great losses. Losses on loans approached $2 billion during the 1930–36 period, an amount equal to 22 percent of the capital of all operating commercial banks in 1929, and an average loss of 1.76 percent on loans. Losses on securities for the 1931–34 period were a little in excess of $800 million.

SAFETY OF COMMERCIAL BANKS

The safety of commercial banks has always been of concern to stockholders, depositors, and supervisory and regulatory authorities, since bank failures probably have a more adverse effect on the economy than do failures in any other type of business. Safety is important to stockholders because bank losses, if of serious proportions, may involve a loss of their investment. Losses in deposits represent the life savings of many depositors and the working capital of many business firms. Bank losses have a detrimental effect on public confidence, which is transferred to other segments of the economy.

Bank suspensions and failures have been a serious problem in several periods of our history, all of which were characterized by serious recessions, such as 1837, 1873–79, and 1929–33. Since the insurance of deposits in 1934, the number of bank failures has not been large until recently. In fact, from 1943 to 1981 the number of bank failures averaged around six each year, and the amount of deposits, with the exception of three years, never exceeded $350 million. Most of the failed banks were small banks with deposits of less than $50 million. Figure 7-3 shows the number of bank failures and the amount of assets involved in troubled banks since 1960. It may be noted that for years, the number of failures was minimal. Since 1981 through 1987, however, 611 banks have failed, nearly two and a half times the number for the period 1943–81. The amount of assets of troubled banks was also not sizable until the sharp increase in the mid-1980s.

Although it is difficult to identify exactly the causes of bank failures, the history of failures certainly indicates that economic conditions are an important contributing cause. For example, the recession of the early 1920s was quite sharp and especially serious in agricultural areas of the nation. Although bank suspensions occurred throughout the nation, the rate was unusually high in rural areas and small towns. The Great Depression of the 1930s was no respecter of any area or economic sector of the nation. Gross national product (in constant dollars) plummeted nearly 31 percent from 1929 to 1933, the largest drop ever experienced; unemployment rose from 3.2 percent to 24.9 percent during the same period. Obviously, banks as well as all other financial institutions encountered difficulties in remaining solvent in an economic environment of this kind.

In the most recent period of bank suspensions, it appears that failures were caused by poor quality agricultural, energy, and real estate loans. Banks in agricultural states were adversely affected by the decline in foreign sales of agricultural products and a drop in farm prices. With lower export sales and income, many farmers could not generate sufficient cash flow to service their debt. As farm prices declined, so did farm land values, which made it impossible for farmers to pay off their debts by selling land. Many agricultural loans became delinquent and nonperforming, which placed the financial condition of many banks in jeopardy. Evidence of this situation is that in the years 1984 through 1986 about half of the 240 banks that failed were agricultural banks, those with ratios of agricultural loans above the unweighted national average. Similarly, the decline in oil prices placed many loans of banks financing oil drilling, production, and distribution on the nonperforming list. These developments were transferred to the real estate industry, especially to the com-

FIGURE 7-3   Bank Failures, FDIC-Insured Banks

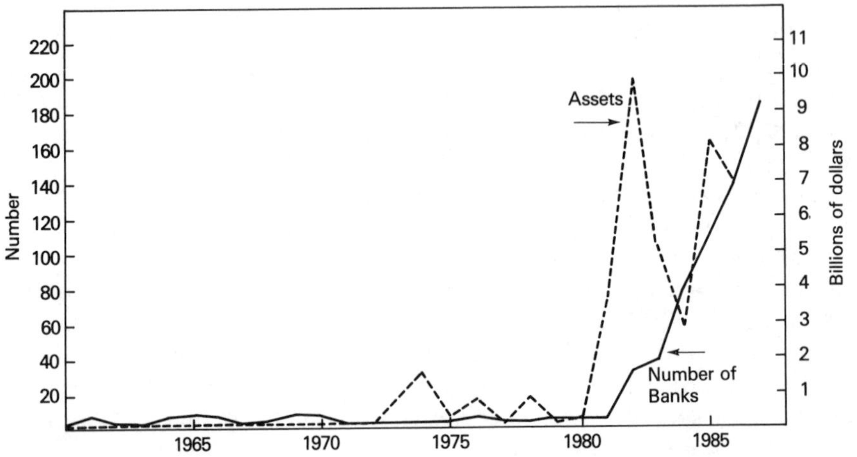

SOURCE: Federal Deposit Insurance Corporation, annual reports.

mercial real estate sector where it soon became obvious that a considerable amount of overbuilding had occurred.

The economic plight of some banks was prompted by management's inability to adapt to the deregulation of deposit interest rates in the early 1980s. Small banks, especially, were placed in a more competitive environment for funds and suffered a decline in income and liquidity. Research on bank failures points to the fact that bank risks increase as the quality of assets deteriorates, liquidity is impaired, earnings decline, and capital accumulates slowly or is reduced. A weak economy places banks in just such an environment and failures become prevalent.

In addition to unfavorable economic conditions, other causes of bank failures include managerial weakness and illegal practices. Fraud, embezzlement, kiting, and other manipulations, unfortunately, are further causes.

The present federal deposit insurance plan, which became effective January 1, 1934, at first provided for the insurance of each account up to $2,500. The maximum insurance coverage has been increased several times and now amounts to $100,000. The insurance plan was adopted for three basic reasons: to restore public confidence in our banking system that had been ravaged by bank suspensions and failures, to provide protection to depositors who were not in a position to judge the quality of a bank, and to provide for improved supervision and examination of banks that were not members of the Federal Reserve System. At mid-1987, the deposit insurance fund, which is derived from an annual assessment on insured banks and from earnings on the investments of the fund, amounted to $18.3 billion. Although a relatively large sum, it was only equal to 1.12 percent of insured deposits. Approximately 75 percent of total bank deposits are covered with insurance because of the $100,000 limit on each account. In addition to the insurance fund, the FDIC has the authority to borrow up to $3 billion from the U.S. Treasury. This amount could be increased by the Congress should conditions warrant such a move.

In protecting depositors' funds, the Federal Deposit Insurance Corporation may follow one of three avenues in case of a bank failure: (1) it may act as a receiver and provide direct payoff to insured depositors, (2) it may provide aid in facilitating the merger or consolidation of a bank in financial difficulties with another stronger bank, or (3) it may organize a Deposit Insurance National Bank to operate for a period of two years. Under the deposit payoff method, the FDIC makes payments to each depositor, up to the insurance limit, as soon as the records of the deposits are verified. Those depositors with accounts in excess of the insurance limit become general creditors of the failed bank for that portion of their account that exceeds the limit. Whether or not such large depositors receive full payment on their uninsured deposit depends on the liquidation value of the failed bank's assets. There are two important disadvantages in handling a failed bank in this manner. First, there is a disruption in the banking services of the community. Second, the assets of failed banks normally are of more value to another bank than to the FDIC, especially if another bank could operate the failed bank as a going concern.

The FDIC prefers to handle a failed bank in accordance with the second method, frequently referred to as purchase and assumption, or P&A. Under this method, the FDIC solicits bids for the failed bank from other banks in the community for the purchase of assets and the assumption of deposit liabilities. Although the deposits are known, the value of some of the assets is not. The market value of the investment account can ordinarily be determined, but the value of the collateral that supports the loans and the ability of borrowers to service their debt may be questionable. It is here that the interested banks must make some subjective judgments. These value judgments are contained in the offering prices for the failed bank. If the assets are determined not to be worth their book value, the FDIC would have to advance some cash to the purchasing bank. The amount of cash advanced by the FDIC is an amount equal to the liabilities of the failed bank minus the value of the assets of the failed bank.

Which method is used by the FDIC depends on the estimated cost under both methods based on the bid of the highest purchase premium. It is fairly obvious that the second method of handling a failed bank has certain advantages over the payoff method in that banking services are not interrupted and the confidence of depositors is not undermined. Of course, this method cannot be used when fraud is present or if there is virtually no interest by other banks in acquiring the failed bank.

In addition to the handling of failed banks, the FDIC has considerable latitude in rendering assistance to financially troubled banks. This assistance may be in the form of making loans, encouraging other banks to extend loans to the bank in trouble, suggesting a merger with another bank, demanding management changes, purchasing loans from the troubled bank, infusing capital in exchange for preferred stock callable at the option of the corporation, or purchasing subordinated notes. The most celebrated case involving all of these items was Continental National Bank of Chicago, which had assets of approximately $47 billion when financial problems were encountered. This bank required approximately $4.5 billion in financial aid to avert failure, including loans from the Federal Reserve Bank of Chicago and private banks, and the purchase of subordinated notes by the FDIC. Another large banking organization that encountered financial problems—First Republic Bank Corp. of Dallas, with assets of $33 billion—was handled in a similar manner. There has been some criticism of this method of financial assistance on the grounds that we have a "double standard" for aiding banks in financial trouble. The press has used the term "bailout" to describe this type of action by the Federal Reserve System and the FDIC. Although there is some truth in this contention, it should be pointed out that there is also some logic to this method of handling large banks since failure would result in a huge depletion of the FDIC insurance reserve. Moreover, the confidence in large banking organizations would be adversely affected.

The FDIC has had an enviable record in handling bank failures. During the 1934–86 period there had been 1,149 bank failures; of this number approximately 60 percent were payoff cases and the remainder deposit assumption. Deposits of failed banks totaled nearly $42 billion. The FDIC disbursed nearly $27 billion, but recoveries and estimated recoveries have been placed at approximately $17 billion for a net loss of only $8.8 billion.

The safety of commercial banks has been greatly improved by external controls that arise outside the banking system and are the responsibility of the various regulatory and supervisory agencies. These agencies exercise their controls by requiring periodic reports that reflect a bank's condition and operation and by the examination of banks. The objectives of these examinations are its soundness and solvency, whether banking laws are being violated, the competence and integrity of bank management, and whether any unsafe and unsound banking practices and policies are being followed, so that corrections may be made.

Internal controls, too, are important in maintaining efficiency and safety. In the structural organization of relatively large commercial banks, the responsibility of the audit function rests with the auditor or the audit department. Their job is improving accounting methods and systems to produce accurate and complete records of bank transactions in an efficient and economical manner and in conformity with the various regulations applicable to the bank.

Although the consensus at times seems to be that our knowledge of depressions, our so-called "built-in" stabilizers, and our antidepression monetary and fiscal powers and other techniques are of such quality and abundance that a serious recession accompanied by bank failures cannot recur, this is extremely doubtful, and few people, if any, are willing to believe it. Even though the commercial banking system is strong, stronger in fact than it was in the past, the citizenry must not become complacent or procrastinate in making improvements that would result in greater strength.

Bank capital should be increased in those banks that have capital weaknesses; bank management must continue to increase its alertness in regard to the management of bank funds; capable and educated personnel must be attracted to banking; bank auditing should become more widespread and efficient; and regulatory and supervisory authorities must continue to secure and train capable people to examine and supervise banks. Inefficient banks must go by the way, and banks should not rely on the deposit insurance fund to furnish protection to depositors.

ISSUE OF FDIC ASSESSMENT

Although the insurance of deposits has worked well, there are some who question the method of determining the insurance premiums imposed on banks. Some observers take the position that the premiums should be determined by the amount of risks possessed by a particular bank. At the present time, a flat rate system is used, that is, the assessment rate on insured deposits in all banks is the same. This method of assessment has not distributed the burden on deposit insurance appropriately among insured banks of the nation. Banks that have low risks are, in effect, subsidizing those with high risks. In fact, some observers contend that the flat rate system encourages banks to invest in riskier activities.

The flat rate system of assessment was introduced in 1934, when Congress was concerned with runs on banks. It was held that if funds were readily available to financially troubled banks to meet demands there would be no runs and, hence, no financial collapse of the banking system. To be sure, this is a worthy objective and was of great value in restoring confidence in the banking system and, in fact, the entire financial system of the nation. There have, however, been some changes in the economy that have reduced the emphasis on this approach. First, we have not had runs on banks as have occurred in the past or as envisioned by the Congress in 1934. Second, the financial system has undergone changes since the concept was introduced and the dominant role of banks in the financial system has declined. There are other financial institutions, should they fail, that would have an adverse effect on the financial environment just as banks do. Third, the bank failures that have occurred since the introduction of deposit insurance have not been due to the collapse of the economy as in the 1930s but because of individual financial problems and local and/or regional economic problems. Because of these facts the present method of assessment should be reexamined, and a greater part of the cost of maintaining the insurance reserve assigned to individual banks based on their riskiness. This is another way of saying that the insurance of deposits should be more closely related to the principles employed by insurance companies in the private sector such as life and casualty companies.

Our present program of deposit insurance was designed primarily for small banks, yet the large banks pay most of the assessment. Moreover, it is highly unlikely that deposit insurance will ever be used in the case of financially troubled large banks. This is true because the insurance fund is not sufficiently large to pay off depositors of relatively large banks. The near collapse, for example, of Continental Bank did not involve the disbursement of funds to depositors, for the bank did not fail. As mentioned, it was a bailout by the FDIC, which was the practice followed in solving the financial problems of some other large banks. In 1986 there were 138 bank failures, 58 percent of which involved state nonmember banks with average deposits of less than $41 million. Ten banks had deposits in excess of $100 million, two in excess of $500 million, and only one in excess of $1 billion. Of the 138 banks, 21 were payoff cases, and the remainder were handled on a purchase and assumption basis.

In discussing the causes of bank failures in 1986, the FDIC had the following to say:

> While economic factors were major contributors to bank failures weak management, poor lending practices, insider abuse and fraud continued to play a significant role. Some 32 percent of bank failures in 1986 involved insider abuse or fraud to at least some degree.[4]

This statement about the causes of bank failures is not much different from those enumerated in previous annual reports of the FDIC. Thus, it seems that the causes of bank failures are not those that were envisioned by Congress in 1934 but are brought about by factors that can be attributed to inefficient management. The FDIC is correct in stating that economic factors were a major contributor to bank failures, but this alone does not exonerate bank management from responsibility. Recognition and evaluation of economic conditions are the responsibility of bank management, as well as proper diversification and investing in high-quality assets.

An ideal premium structure would relate each bank's deposit insurance assessment to the risk that the bank possesses. This suggestion would be consistent with the proposal of the three supervisory agencies to relate capital adequacy to bank risk. The FDIC has made various proposals designed to account for bank risk. The most recent one is based on the assumption that risks can be identified from bank examinations and on operating characteristics that differentiate problem from nonproblem situations;[5] in fact, in early 1986 such a proposal was released for public comment. This issue will probably be debated for some time, but it appears that we may move away, and rightly so, from the long-established flat rate assessment.

QUESTIONS

1. What are the functions of bank capital? How do they differ from the capital functions in a manufacturing firm?
2. Usually one thinks of regulation being accomplished by people who are regulators. How does bank capital serve to perform a regulatory function?
3. How can a small bank increase its capital to support deposit growth if there is no active market for its shares?

[4] Federal Deposit Insurance Corporation, *Annual Report 1986.*

[5] Federal Deposit Insurance Corporation, *Deposit Insurance in a Changing Environment* (Washington, D.C., 1983), chap. 11.

4. How can an increase in reserves for loan losses be considered an addition to equity capital? A reduction in assets?

5. Do you agree with the proposition that bank capital should be related to risks? Why?

6. If bank capital is related to risks, why not the deposit insurance premium? Comment on the wisdom of this question.

7. Table 7-1 provides an illustration of how issuing debentures can minimize the dilution effect on earnings of new capital funds. Under what conditions could the sale of debentures or capital notes make a positive contribution to bank earnings?

8. Support the argument that capital ratios have little value in judging the capital adequacy of commercial banks.

9. What statistical techniques would you use to isolate ratios that might be good predictors of "problem bank" status? Review the studies referred to in the text and evaluate their statistical methodology.

10. It has been said that the existence of deposit insurance serves in itself to reduce the frequency of loss by depositors. Develop arguments to support this position.

11. How would you justify requiring small banks and banking organizations to have more capital than large ones?

SELECTED REFERENCES

ANDERSON, R. N., W. C. HANDORFF, AND M. P. MCCARTHY. "Bank Size and the Management of Capital Ratios." *The Bankers Magazine* (January–February 1982), 64–69.

BUDD, GEORGE A. "Convertible Securities: Something for Everybody—Or Nobody?" *The Bankers Magazine* (May–June 1982), 85–91.

BUSER, STEPHEN, ANDREW H. CHEN, AND EDWARD J. KANE. "Federal Deposit Insurance, Regulatory Policy, and Optimal Bank Capital." *Journal of Finance* (March 1981), 51–60.

FEDERAL DEPOSIT INSURANCE CORPORATION. *Deposit Insurance in a Changing Environment.* Washington, D.C., 1983.

KEELEY, MICHAEL C. "Bank Capital Regulation in the 1980s: Effective or Ineffective?" *Economic Review,* Federal Reserve Bank of San Francisco, no. 1 (Winter 1987), 3–20.

PETTWAY, RICHARD H., AND JOSEPH F. SINKEY, JR. "Establishing On-Site Bank Examination Priorities: An Early-Warning System Using Accounting and Market Information." *Journal of Finance* (March 1980), 137–150.

SINKEY, J. F., JR. "Identifying Large Problem/Failed Banks: The Case of Franklin National Bank of New York." *Journal of Financial and Quantitative Analysis* (December 1977), 779–800.

VOJTA, G. J. *Bank Capital Adequacy.* New York: First National City Bank, 1973.

8

PROFITABILITY
OF BANKS

Gross income of commercial banks is determined by the rate of return on loans and investments, by the level of various fees and charges imposed for the performance of services, and by the size and composition of assets. Bank assets, as we have learned, have increased substantially in recent years and so has gross income. Although service fees have increased and will probably do so in the future, interest on earning assets, from loans and investments, provides almost 90 percent of bank income.

Banking is a highly personalized service industry; consequently, the expenses of commercial banks are to a great extent fixed, especially in the short run. Banks, like public utilities, bear a certain degree of public interest, and the capacity to serve the public must be available at all times. Banks are not in a position to produce for inventory, suspend operations, or reduce their labor force appreciably as are some industries; therefore, expenses in the short run are not closely correlated with the volume of business conducted. This is not to say that bank management has no control over expenses in the long run. Over the years, banks have improved their organizational structures, expanded their services, and automated many activities in an effort to reduce their cost of operation.

INCOME FROM BANK LOANS

The lending function is the single most important source of gross income for commercial banks (see Table 8-1). In recent years, approximately two-

TABLE 8-1 Income, Expense, and Profits, All Insured Commercial Banks, 1981–86 (in millions of dollars)

Item	1981	1982	1983	1984	1985	1986
Operating income, total	**$247,577**	**$257,293**	**$239,264**	**$274,273**	**$273,461**	**$269,292**
Interest, total	230,148	237,193	216,059	245,640	239,952	230,702
Loans	164,715	168,619	153,323	181,873	175,679	168,429
Balances with banks	23,905	23,867	16,739	16,557	13,590	11,132
Gross federal funds sold and reverse						
repurchase agreements	12,183	11,309	9,198	10,464	9,352	8,922
Securities (excluding trading accounts)	29,345	33,398	36,799	36,746	41,331	42,219
State and local government	9,704	10,648	10,620	11,817	12,820	14,956
Other	19,641	22,749	26,179	24,929	28,511	27,263
Service charges on deposits	3,892	4,584	5,399	6,512	7,280	7,902
Other operating income[1]	13,538	15,517	17,806	22,121	26,229	30,689
Operating expense, total	**227,490**	**238,274**	**220,236**	**254,273**	**252,057**	**250,399**
Interest, total	169,078	168,651	143,215	167,335	154,094	140,467
Deposits	138,830	141,185	119,843	139,331	128,837	115,889
Large certificates of deposit	38,896	37,366	22,523	25,761	22,472	19,257
Deposits in foreign offices	46,696	41,754	29,021	35,781	30,013	24,440
Other deposits	53,238	62,065	68,299	77,789	76,352	72,192

Gross federal funds purchased and repurchase agreements	23,752	20,628	16,438	19,323	16,236	15,766
Other borrowed money[2]	6,496	6,838	6,934	8,682	9,020	8,812
Salaries, wages, and employee benefits	27,901	31,244	33,637	36,463	39,338	42,258
Occupancy expense[3]	8,558	9,975	11,101	12,092	13,407	14,551
Loss provision	5,080	8,429	10,621	13,690	16,965	21,194
Other operating expense	16,873	19,975	21,662	24,694	28,254	31,929
Securities gains or losses (−)	−1,595	−1,282	−30	−142	1,504	3,773
Income before tax	18,491	17,737	18,998	19,858	22,908	22,665
Taxes	3,859	2,976	4,076	4,665	5,369	5,261
Extraordinary items	57	64	70	217	318	271
Net income	14,689	14,826	14,992	15,409	17,858	17,674
Cash dividends declared	5,841	6,542	7,338	7,585	8,402	9,135

[1] Includes income from assets held in trading accounts.
[2] Includes interest paid on U.S. Treasury tax and loan account balances and on subordinated notes and debentures.
[3] Occupancy expense for bank premises net of any rental income plus furniture and equipment expenses.

SOURCE: Board of Governors of the Federal Reserve System, *Federal Reserve Bulletin* (July 1987).

thirds of bank operating income has been composed of interest on loans. There has been a decline in this source recently, however, due primarily to a decline in commercial and industrial loans as a result of business firms' reliance to an increasing extent on the issuance of commercial paper.

Interest earned on "balances with banks" comes primarily from Eurodollar redeposits and is most significant to large banks that have foreign operations. Although not classified as such by the Federal Reserve, interest on balances with banks is essentially interest on loans.

Another item of income that is in reality interest on loans is "income on federal funds sold and securities purchased under resale agreement." Although bankers use the terms "buy" and "sell" when discussing federal funds transactions and repurchase agreements, these are, in fact, loans. A bank earns interest when it lends (sells) some of its excess balances in a Federal Reserve bank to another bank. It also earns interest when it buys securities from another bank or a bond dealer whereby the seller has agreed to buy the securities back at the same price plus interest for the period. Since none of the risks of investment goes with either transaction, both are technically loans.

Factors Affecting Bank Loan Rates

Interest rates on bank loans differ from rates on money market instruments, such as Treasury bills and commercial paper, in that they are negotiated between borrower and bank rather than determined in an organized market. As a result of this negotiated method of establishing the price for credit, interest rates on bank loans are not uniform. They reflect both the characteristics of the individual loan and supply of and demand for credit in the money and capital markets. Rates vary also with the degree of credit risk associated with the loan, its maturity, the size of the loan, the cost of making and supervising the loan, the deposit balances of the borrower, and security. In addition, rates are influenced by habit and custom, competition between banks and other sources of funds, legal maximum rates, and the attitudes that bankers and borrowers may have regarding future economic conditions.

In general, the ability of banks to lend is dependent on the level of excess reserves in the banking system. If the demand for bank credit remains relatively stable and excess reserves increase, interest rates on loans fall as banks search for earning assets. However, if a strong demand exists for bank credit and excess reserves remain constant or rise more slowly than the demand for credit, interest rates rise. Attitudes also influence bank interest rates. If the economic outlook is pessimistic, bankers may not lower the rate as much as the supply of loanable funds might warrant. If the attitude is optimistic, that is, officials feel that the Federal

Reserve System will make additional funds available, rates may not be raised appreciably even though the level of excess reserves is relatively low.

INCOME FROM SECURITIES

Although interest on securities is the second most important source of income for commercial banks, it has declined as a percentage of total income in recent years as banks have changed their asset mix in an effort to increase earnings. The amount of income from this source depends on the size and composition of the investment portfolio and the rates of return on the various classes of securities. Yields on all classes and maturities of securities have increased substantially.

The considerations in choosing the various investment securities are discussed in Chapters 16 and 17. Banks continuously balance the income possibilities offered by securities against their own periodic liquidity needs. Funds for securities investments usually are made available only after the liquidity needs of the bank are met. This subordinated position of the investment account adds to the complexity of bank securities management and to the variations in income from securities from year to year. Even greater complications result from the fact that securities income is in two forms: interest income and capital gains (with, of course, frequent capital losses as well).

Securities Gains and Losses

Gains and losses on securities do not appear as items of operating income on the income statement as does interest on securities. The reason is that gains and losses are considered as not arising from normal operations but as occurring at irregular intervals, resulting from forces not entirely within the control of bank management. Therefore, gains and losses appear as a separate item after "Other operating expense" in Table 8-1. With a sharp rise in interest rates, losses can be great, and with a drop in rates, gains can be equally sizable. During the 1978–82 period, when interest rates rose to unprecedented heights, security losses occurred every year. Security losses became minimal in 1983–84, and then gains became sizable, especially in 1986, when market interest rates dropped appreciably.

Large losses on securities might give the feeling that banks do a poor job of investing. One must be aware, however, that banks tend to have more funds to invest when interest rates are low and securities prices are high, but are frequently forced to sell securities to raise funds to meet loan demands when interest rates are high and securities prices are down.

Securities losses are somewhat illusory. True enough, showing the loss recognizes the decline in the value of an asset; but such a loss was taken usually to switch from bonds to higher-yielding loans during a high interest rate, tight money period. The loss is thus partially offset by higher earnings. Bank management should be alert to the movement of interest rates and be willing to take losses and gains to meet credit demands of the community and to increase earnings.

OTHER SOURCES OF INCOME

Although other sources of bank income are important, they are not large when compared with the income from loans and investments. Other sources include trust department income, direct lease financing, service charges on deposit accounts, other charges and fees, and other operating income (see Table 8-1).

Trust Department Income

Although trust income has increased over the years, the increase has lagged that of total operating income. Trust departments vary from extremely profitable to extremely unprofitable. Trust departments provide services and do not utilize bank funds. The assets with which they work belong to trust customers. Therefore, if a trust department has a good list of profitable accounts, its earnings relative to expenses can be very high. However, many trust departments, particularly small ones, do not have sufficient numbers of profitable accounts to be profitable themselves. Much of what these trust departments do is the result of the desire to be *full-service banks*, that is, to provide services to customers who are valued for their commercial business (for example, taking the small trust of a business owner for the benefit of a grandchild when the trust department would prefer to refuse such small accounts).

Service Charges on Deposit Accounts

To help cover the cost of handling demand deposit accounts, most banks impose a service charge. Service charges normally are not imposed on time deposit accounts since the interest paid on such accounts takes into consideration the cost of handling the account. The income derived from service charges on deposit accounts has declined in recent years as a percentage of operating income.

With the removal of Regulation Q, banks introduced a multitude of deposit accounts designed for every conceivable preference of customers. This was done during a period of rising interest rates that provided an environment conducive to increasing service charges on deposits. Within this environment, accompanied by a cost-conscious attitude, banks increased service charges to a more realistic level; and as a result, this source of income more than doubled in the past five years. In 1986 service charges on deposits accounted for nearly 3 percent of total income compared to half that amount five years earlier. Some banks have eliminated service charges on demand deposit accounts if balances do not drop below some established minimums such as $300 or $500. A few banks do not have any service charge on checking accounts. These practices do not necessarily mean that it is becoming less expensive for banks to maintain checking accounts; instead, it is a way of competing for deposits. These banks are assuming that the extra income generated by the use of new deposit funds will more than offset the cost of maintaining the accounts. This assumption may prove false. If all banks eliminated service charges, the competitive edge would no longer exist, and bank income would be reduced.

Other Operating Income

This category includes a multitude of items, for example, commissions on the sale of insurance policies; charges for the collection of domestic checks, notes, and bills of exchange; the sale of bank drafts; the acceptance of bills of exchange in domestic trade; servicing real estate mortgages or other loans held by others; equipment leasing and rental fees; data processing services; gross rentals from other real estate and safe deposit boxes; net trading account profits; any recoveries on securities previously charged off when no securities reserve exists; and loan commitment fees. This final item is a charge that banks frequently make in return for the commitment to have loan funds available at some later date, for example, the permanent financing on a building to be constructed. To have such funds available may mean keeping a higher proportion of assets in liquid form than would otherwise be necessary. Since liquid assets usually produce low returns, the commitment fee is charged to offset the income lost as a result of the commitment.

Established fees for various bank services have been raised by many banks in recent years, and new ones added in an effort to offset rising costs and to increase income. Of all the items of income listed in Table 8-1 "Other operating income" has shown the largest percentage increase and accounted for nearly 14 percent of total income.

BANK EXPENSES

In the long run, all costs are variable, and this is as true of banking as it is of any other industry. Thus, bank management has been able to reduce many costs in recent years, most notably by the automation of various functions and services. This automation program has, in part, offset the tremendous increase in the expenses that would have occurred as bank assets increased and services were expanded.

Salaries, Wages, and Employee Benefits

Salaries, wages, and fringe benefits composed nearly 17 percent of operating expenses; this compares with 28 percent in 1970 and 41 percent in 1962. These figures show that a relatively declining salary expense has at least partially offset the rise in the interest expense of time and savings accounts. The reduced salary expense is due largely to the fact that the number of employees has increased less rapidly than have assets. In the last ten years, total assets have doubled, while total employees rose by only one-third. One important reason for the number of employees in the banking industry not increasing rapidly has been the breakthrough in electronic technology. This has been especially true in the processing of checks and other paper transactions. The number of paper transactions that occur in banks has been increasing at a 5 to 7 percent annual rate in recent years. At mid-1980 it was estimated that more than 20 billion checks were written and that this volume was expected to increase at a compounded annual rate of 5 percent in the next decade. Without the electronic technology now possessed by banks, clerical workers would increase at a rate proportional to the number of paper transactions handled by banks.[1]

Interest on Time and Savings Deposits

The largest expense item by far is interest on time and savings deposits. This item of expense accounted for over 50 percent of total expenses in 1986, down slightly from earlier years only because of the decline in interest rates. This item will probably continue to be the largest expense of banks in the future and will vary as interest rates fluctuate.

Federal Funds

The most variable operating expense item is the interest paid on federal funds and repurchase agreements. The size of this item reflects the tightness of the money market during a portion of the period and the need on the part of banks for borrowed funds in the management of assets.

[1] Gregory M. Solomon, "Strategic Implications of ATMs: Why Haven't All Tellers Gone?" *Journal of Retail Banking* (Fall 1986), pp. 43–52.

Although this item is relatively large, it should be remembered that banks also earn from lending (selling) federal funds and securities sold under repurchase agreements. The category "Other borrowed money" includes interest paid on U.S. Treasury tax and loan account balances and on capital notes and debentures. Although this is not a large item of expense, it is a significant outlay for some banks that have issued debt securities.

Occupancy Expense

Occupancy expenses include the salaries of officers and employees concerned with the management and operation of bank buildings, depreciation, maintenance and repairs, fire and other insurance, parking lots, leasehold improvements, and taxes on bank premises. This item of expense is net of any rental income. Occupancy expenses have increased in large part because of the addition of branch offices.

Provision for Loan Losses

Since lending involves risk, banks normally maintain a reserve for loan losses. The amount that can be transferred from income for this purpose is closely regulated by the Internal Revenue Service. The amount transferred to loan losses has increased substantially in the last few years. From 1981 to 1986 this item increased fivefold. Because of the unusually large loan losses since 1980, banks have increased their loan loss reserves, which for all banks rose to nearly $29 billion at the end of 1986. Loan loss provisions in recent years have increased with net charge-offs but have exceeded them and thus allowed expansion in this reserve account. In 1986 net charge-offs were equal to 1 percent of total loans, with small and medium-sized banks experiencing higher than usual losses. In early 1987 many banks that engaged in foreign lending transferred substantial amounts to their loan loss reserves. This has proved to be a wise decision by bank management.

Other Operating Expenses

Other operating expenses include all those not classified previously but that nonetheless are necessary for the successful operation of commercial banks. Some major expenses included in this classification are the assessment for federal deposit insurance, insurance coverage for a variety of risks and bonding, advertising, supplies, cost of examination by supervisory authorities, retainers' fees, expenses related to the use of automobiles for bank business, and some minor taxes. Other operating expenses is one of the largest expense categories in Table 8-1.

One of the major items in this classification is the assessment made by the Federal Deposit Insurance Corporation for the insurance of deposits. The annual rate of assessment, which has been in effect since 1935, is one-twelfth of 1 percent of assessable deposits. The FDIC returns up to 60 percent of the assessment to banks in the year following the assessment, the amount depending on the FDIC's need to maintain its insurance fund.

Premiums for insurance other than on deposits is a relatively important expenditure made by commercial banks. An adequate insurance program is important to banks, since probably no other business is exposed to as many risks. In addition to the usual risks associated with the ownership of property such as fire, flood, windstorm, riot, and civil commotion, banks are subject to additional risks inherent in the nature of banking. Since banks deal in a medium of exchange, the possibility of embezzlement and defalcation is ever present. Other important banking risks include burglary, robbery, and the loss of notes, checks, drafts, securities, and other important documents carried by messengers or in transit. Many risks are associated with the safe deposit function. Losses also occur from forged checks and other documents.

Banks usually carry insurance that protects them from losses arising from the loss of securities. Protection against errors and omissions in various documents is needed also. Commercial banks follow a policy of eternal vigilance as a means of protecting themselves against such risks, but the risks are so great that the sharing of them through insurance is a necessity. The American Bankers Association, in cooperation with insurance representatives, has studied the risks of banking and has made recommendations, which many banks have followed, regarding the type, kind, and amount of insurance that banks of various sizes should carry. As a result, it is probably correct to say that commercial banks are relatively well insured.

Advertising has become a sizable expense item in commercial banking, especially in areas where considerable competition exists among banks and between banks and competing financial institutions. As banks have attempted to reach lower economic levels of income receivers who need banking services, advertising expenditures have tended to increase.

Another major expense is for printing and office supplies. Commercial banks and their customers use large amounts of printed forms and documents—checks, drafts, notes, deposit books and slips, mortgage forms, loan applications, and the like.

Income Taxes

Banks are subject to the usual taxes imposed on other business firms—federal and state income, local property, and all other levies at the local level. In recent years taxes on banks have accounted for about 20 to

25 percent of the item "Income before tax" in Table 8-1. Banks have endeavored to reduce their tax liability by investing heavily in tax-exempt municipal bonds and by leasing certain assets. Investing in municipal bonds is discussed in detail in Chapter 17. Banks lease a variety of items, such as bank premises, buildings, parking lots, and such equipment as automobiles, computers, and other business machines. One of the reasons for leasing is that lease payments are considered expense items in determining income tax liability. Leasing also frees capital for other purposes. Although the top federal corporation tax rate was reduced in a major revision of the federal income tax in 1987, banks lost some of the benefits they had long enjoyed.

COMMERCIAL BANK PROFITS

Although the net income of banks has varied over the years, the trend has generally been upward (see Figure 8-1). However, the growth of net income has slowed when compared to the profitability of banks in the 1970s. In fact, in 1986, there was a slight decline in net income for the first time in three decades. There were many reasons for the slowing in the rapid growth of net income, namely, the level and movement of interest rates, increased competition from other financial institutions, an increase in loan losses especially in recent years, and a deterioration of the econ-

FIGURE 8-1   Profits and Dividends of All Insured Banks

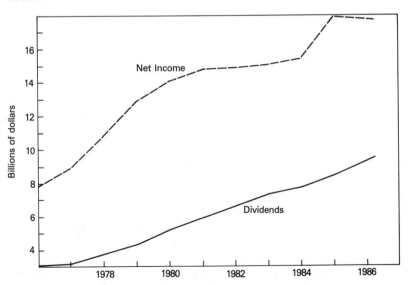

SOURCE: Board of Governors of the Federal Reserve System, *Federal Reserve Bulletins.*

omy in the areas of agriculture and energy. Bank profits generally reflect the health of the economy. Economic expansion, rising interest rates, and a high proportion of resources in high-yielding assets contribute to bank profitability, whereas declining interest rates and economic stagnation are not conducive to a high level of profits.

Measurement of Bank Profits

Bank regulatory authorities and bank analysts use three popular profitability measures: return on assets (ROA), return on equity (ROE), and net interest margin. The ROA ratio is obtained by dividing a bank's net income by its average assets. It is a gauge of how well a bank's management is employing its assets. The rate of return on assets is a valuable measure when comparing the profitability of one bank with another or with the commercial banking system. A low rate might be the result of conservative lending and investment policies or excessive operating expenses. If time and savings accounts are an unusually large proportion of total deposits, interest expense may be higher than average. Banks could, of course, attempt to offset this by adopting more aggressive lending and investment policies to generate more income. A high rate of return on assets may be the result of efficient operations, of a low ratio of time and savings deposits to total deposits, or of high yields earned on the assets. If the last case is true, the bank may be assuming a high level of risk, for the higher the returns yielded by assets, the more likely they are to embody higher degrees of risk. This is not necessarily bad, for the bank may be doing a good job of managing its assets, although it may be subjecting itself to large potential losses.

The ROE ratio is calculated by dividing a bank's net income by its average total equity—that is, common and preferred stock, surplus, undivided profits, and capital reserves. This measure of profitability is the most important for a bank's stockholders, since it reflects what the bank is earning on their investment. The capital of some banks consists entirely of stockholders' equity and in others may consist in part of capital notes and debentures.

For a given bank, the rate of return on total assets may be relatively low, yet the rate of return on equity may be very high. If this is the case, such a bank would be heavily leveraged; that is, its equity would be small relative to its assets. A heavily leveraged bank may be risking the safety of deposits and may also be criticized by the regulatory authorities, although from the owners' standpoint it appears to be performing well because of the high rate of return on equity. A financial arrangement of this kind highlights a shortcoming of the return on equity method of measuring bank profitability.

Net interest margin is roughly analogous to the profit margin of a business. It measures the spread between a bank's interest income and its interest expense. Net interest margin is calculated by subtracting a bank's interest expense from its interest revenue net of loan losses and dividing that result by its net interest earning assets. Net interest margin is watched closely by bank management, for it signals the profitability of the bank. If the spread between net interest expense and income narrows, it is obvious that if a certain level of profitability is desired steps should be taken either to increase income by whatever means available or to reduce expenses.

A final measurement of bank profits that is especially appealing to owners of bank stock is earnings per share. It is an excellent indicator of how well a bank has done compared with previous years or to management's expectations. It is calculated by dividing net earnings by the number of shares held by shareholders. Despite its acceptance by shareholders as a measure of profitability, it is difficult to use this measure to compare banks because dividend ratios may differ.

If one bank has a high payout ratio and another a low payout ratio, the percentage growth in earnings for the first, all else remaining equal, would not be as great as for the second because of the smaller increase in the first bank's capital base in the previous year. A second weakness of the earnings per share method of comparing banks is evident in the case of a rapidly growing bank that must add outside equity capital to maintain an adequate equity base. The new shares will dilute earnings per share so that for two or three years after the new issue is sold, earnings per share will not be a fair indicator of the bank's performance.

Each method of measuring profitability has its good and bad points, but the earnings per share method has no applicability to measuring the profitability of the banking system. Either of the other methods is appropriate, depending on the answers sought. Returns on assets and equity for the past decade are presented in Figures 8-2 and 8-3. Note that both the return on assets and equity rose during the latter part of the 1970s and then showed a sharp decline in the 1980s because of some special problems in the banking industry (to be discussed later). The net interest margin for all banks followed the same patterns for similar reasons.

Profitability of Banks

Several factors influence the profitability of banks, including the following:

1. Management
2. Economic conditions
3. Size
4. Interest rates

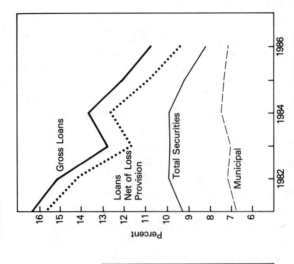

FIGURE 8-4 Rates of Return on Selected Assets

SOURCE: Board of Governors of the Federal Reserve System, *Federal Reserve Bulletin* (July 1987).

FIGURE 8-3 Return on Equity, All Insured Banks

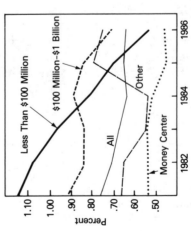

SOURCE: Board of Governors of the Federal Reserve System, *Federal Reserve Bulletin* (July 1987).

FIGURE 8-2 Return on Assets, All Insured Banks

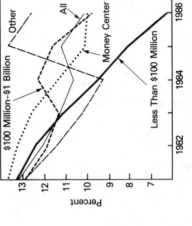

SOURCE: Board of Governors of the Federal Reserve System, *Federal Reserve Bulletin* (July 1987).

5. Competitive conditions
6. Percent of resources employed
7. Securities gains and losses
8. Loan losses and recoveries

As pointed out in Chapter 4, management includes such factors as planning, organizing, staffing, directing, and controlling. Banks that have expertise in these areas are more likely to experience profitability than those that do not. Some banks, because of limited resources, unfortunately are at a disadvantage in securing the services of personnel experienced in these important areas.

The profitability of banks depends to a very great extent on the economic health of the community that it serves. This fact has been well demonstrated during the 1980–86 period when certain sectors of the economy were depressed, namely, agriculture and energy, and banks dependent on those economic markets were adversely affected. Moreover, the larger the economic base of a bank, the less likely it is to experience profitability problems. As indicated in Figures 8-2 and 8-3, the drop in profitability was less pronounced in the larger banks than in smaller banks.

It has been pointed out that small banks are less profitable than larger banks. This fact has become more and more evident since the deregulation of banks in 1980. Bank researchers have found that banks with assets below $25 million are too small for maximum efficiency. Before interest rate regulation, small banks could cover their inefficiencies with greater interest margins, but deregulation has forced smaller banks to pay higher rates on deposits and these rates have not been fully offset with greater loan charges. This is another way of saying that small banks secure their funds in a national market and invest in a relatively small local market.

Obviously, the return on assets is a very important factor in determining bank profitability. Normally, as lending rates and the return on securities rise so does the profitability, since there is a slight lag in rates paid on deposits. However, because of increased competition for deposits, this lag is becoming less and less. During the 1981–86 period, rates on loans and securities declined. As can be seen in Figure 8-4, loan rates show more variation than return on securities and dropped more sharply during the period. Because of the rise in loan losses, the return on loans net of loss provision declined more than the return on loans.

The competitive position of banks influences profitability by reducing the amount of resources available to banks and by forcing up rates that must be paid on these resources; consequently, a bank's net interest margin is lessened. The degree of competitiveness that exists in the marketplace varies with the breadth of a bank's market. In general, since the introduction of DIDMCA in 1980, banks have been in a much more competitive market than they have ever experienced. Mutual savings, savings and loan associations, and money market funds provided by the securities industries have all limited the resources available to commercial banks. The reduced growth of commercial banks, because of increased competition, is reflected in the growth of bank assets, which rose at a compounded annual growth rate of 12.6 percent during the 1970s but dropped to 8.4 percent during the 1980s.

The amount of bank resources invested in earning assets contribute to increased income and profitability. The amount to be allocated to loans and investments is an important management decision and depends on many factors, including the liquidity needs of a bank. In recent years the percentage of resources invested in earning assets has varied from 80 to 90 percent, with money center banks averaging in the low 80s and banks below $100 million in assets in the 90s.

Security gains and losses have an important impact on bank profitability. Banks hold securities for income and liquidity purposes. Securities are fixed income assets, and the market price varies with the level and movement of interest rates. When securities are sold, normally there is a gain or a loss. For the 1980–84 period, banks experienced losses on securities (see Table 8-1). However, with the decline in interest rates in 1985 and 1986, gains were realized. In fact, the gains realized in 1986 were the largest in many years and came at a good time in that funds were available to absorb huge loan losses.

Portfolio appreciation acts as a form of hidden reserves for banks and provides a cushion against future declines in operating profitability. During 1986, for example, nearly 20 percent of the return on assets came from the income from the sale of securities.

The downturn in overall profitability of commercial banks in the 1980s was primarily an asset-quality phenomenon. As pointed out in Chapter 7, loan loss reserves more than tripled during the 1980–86 period and in 1986 were equal to 0.7 percent of assets. Provision for loan losses increased from approximately $5 billion to slightly over $21 billion six years later (see Table 8-1). These large transfers from current earnings to reserves for loan losses have had a severe impact on bank profitability.

Profitability and Bank Size

Profitability of banks has varied by bank size (see Figures 8-2 and 8-3). Although the return on assets and equity declined in all banks during the 1981–86 period, the most noticeable decline occurred in banks with assets of less than $100 million. In fact, the decline in return on assets was 54 percent compared to a decline of only 16 percent for all banks. The decline in return on equity was also 54 percent compared to a decline of 22 percent for all banks. The decline in return on assets and equity for money center banks was less than for most other classes of banks. From a comparative standpoint, the two measures of profitability for money center banks were less than for the other classes of banks. "Other" banks, which had $1 billion or more in assets and were composed primarily of what has been termed regional banks, turned in the best performance when compared to all banks and all classes of banks. This classification showed the largest increase in any year during the period.

Many banks were unprofitable in 1986. In fact, 2,741 banks, or about 20 percent of all banks, failed to show a profit. This was a postdepression high and was up from 17 percent in 1985, 8 percent in 1984, and 4 percent in 1979, which was a relatively high profitability year. Profitability declines were most prominent in the smaller size groups of banks, a performance that has been evident for several years.

Banks that are classified as agricultural banks[2] have shown the poorest profitability performance in recent years and for the obvious reason that the agriculture sector of the nation has been depressed. Banks that had a large proportion of their loan portfolio in energy loans also experienced profitability problems in the last few years due to the economic problems that have beset the energy sector of the nation.[3]

Future Prospects for Bank Profits

Although bank profits declined during the 1980s, what will happen in the future is problematic. There are forces at work that will affect the bank profitability scene, some of which have already been discussed— increased competition, the decline in commercial and industrial loans, and securitization.

For nearly a half-century commercial banks and thrift institutions had a virtual monopoly of the market for consumer liquid savings at interest rates held down by regulatory fiat in the form of Regulation Q. Moreover, banks have lost their monopoly in the provision of transaction accounts (demand deposits). Most thrifts can now offer such accounts. Banks must compete for what proved to be, for many years, low-cost funds. With the removal of Regulation Q and the availability of transaction accounts made possible by DIDMCA to other financial institutions, this monopoly no longer exists. These changes have forced banks and other financial institutions to pay market rates of interest established by competitive forces; consequently, the cost of funds has risen and will

[2] Agricultural banks are those banks that have 25 percent or more of their loan portfolios in agricultural loans.

[3] Energy banks are those banks that have 25 percent or more of their loan portfolios in energy related loans.

continue to be determined in a free market. Moreover, the amount of funds that are attracted by banks has declined and with the aggressive growth of competing institutions, this situation may very well continue and even intensify.

One of the traditional functions and sources of income of commercial banks has been lending to business firms. Although this is still an important function, some business firms, especially those that are large and financially sound, have turned to the issuance of commercial paper as a source of credit. This trend will probably continue and, obviously, affect the earnings of some banks.

Recently the introduction of securitization by many financial institutions, even including some banks, will probably affect the profitability of commercial banks. Under securitization, financial institutions assemble packages of loans and sell securities that represent a claim against the loan package. Under this type of arrangement the securities market supplants the banks in their purely intermediary role by funding the underlying loans; consequently, the banks' overall position in credit flows shrinks and so does bank income and profitability.

These developments will ultimately bring about some changes in the structure and operation of the industry, as now constituted. Reduced profitability of some banks will force them to adjust to the new financial environment. Those firms that do not provide a sufficient return to present stockholders and to attract capital in sufficient amounts to meet regulatory standards will pass from the scene either by liquidation or merger with other firms. This is not an unusual development. It is a common occurrence in a capitalistic and profit-oriented economy such as ours. It is your authors' opinion that we will probably see many more mergers in the future and that the number of banks—not banking offices—will decline in the future. It is interesting to point out that the United States has more banking organizations than any other country in the world. The reasons for this situation have already been discussed in previous chapters. Of the largest banks in the world, the United States has only two—Citibank and Bank of America—that are listed in the top 25. Our discussion of future profitability of the banking industry does not take into consideration the changes that may occur in government regulations that might provide for banks to expand into other financial services and, in so doing, increase income and profitability. Should the Glass-Steagall Act be rescinded in some manner, for example, a new activity would be available to the banking industry.

DIVIDEND POLICY

Until very recently, banks have followed a policy of retaining a relatively large portion of their profits after taxes. During the past six years the payout ratio of all banks was nearly 47 percent (see Table 8-1 and Figure 8-1).

The dividend payout ratio varies from bank to bank, but almost any profitable, growing bank strongly prefers to build equity capital through retained earnings rather than through the issuance of new shares. This is because of the dilution effect on earnings per share that results when new shares are issued. This dilution effect is much greater for banks than for corporations in most other industries because such a small proportion of bank assets is financed with equity capital. As of the end of 1986, equity capital of insured banks composed only 6.2 percent of "total liabilities and equity capital." Since net income as a percentage of total assets is much less for a profitable bank than net income as a percentage of equity capital, the assets financed with the proceeds of a new stock issue cannot produce net income sufficiently high to sustain the rate of return on equity capital that existed prior to the new stock issue. The precise impact of the dilution depends on a number of factors, including the price received for the new shares in relation to book value of the previously outstanding shares and any actions the management might take to cushion the impact. Nonetheless, bank stockholders usually view the announcement of a new stock issue as a negative event. Of course, the main function of equity capital in a bank is to provide a cushion of safety for depositors and not to finance assets, so if a new stock issue allows more rapid growth of assets than would have otherwise been expected, the dilution effect may decline in importance.

A low payout is a result of three factors. First, the stock of many small banks is very closely held. A majority of the stock may be family owned or held by a small group of investors. Since most of these stockholders are more interested in appreciation of the stock than in income, they are satisfied with the low payout. This action reduces their personal income tax liability. Because the stock of many small banks is not widely held or traded, retained earnings may be the only reliable source of common equity. There is a belief among some bankers that the most economical method of raising equity capital is to retain earnings.

Banks whose stock is widely held generally have a larger payout than do smaller banks, although the payout is usually not as large as that found in public utilities and most industrial companies. A low payout may not in the long run be the correct policy for all commercial banks. Retained earnings may not always be a sufficient and reliable source of equity capital. There have been instances of regulatory authorities forcing banks to sell common stock. If a bank is forced to seek equity capital from the public, it might not be forthcoming, or if it is, it might be at a relatively high price since there appears to be an increasing number of potential stockholders who desire larger returns on their investment than banks pay. It might be desirable for bank management to adopt a more liberal policy regarding dividend payments and in so doing improve its position in the equity market. Some observers have noted that a desirable dividend policy for banks is one that makes it possible for them to raise funds from any source—retained earnings, debt, or equity—when it is needed. Few banks accept this premise, however. Bank management takes the position that retained earnings are preferable to a large payout.

VARIATIONS IN BANK PROFITABILITY

Within the banking industry, as in any other, profits vary. Some banks are more profitable than others. Although the environment within which banks operate influences profitability, some of the variations stem from management decisions. An excellent insight into the profitability of banks comes from a study of high-performance banks. The study traced the fortunes of 1,000 high-performance banks through a five-year period (1972–76) that included a complete interest rate cycle and what has been recognized as a serious economic recession.[4] The banks selected were required to have a very high rate of return for the period and be in the top 50 percent in profitability for the year 1976. These high-performance banks had a slightly higher yield on assets and lower expenses than did the other 13,000 banks. On average, they earned 20 percent more per year on their equity during the entire period. In fact, the return on equity was 69 percent greater than that of the rest of the industry, at 20.8 percent compared with 12.3 percent for the remaining banks. The reasons for this enviable record were that

1. The group deployed less of their assets in Treasury and other U.S. government securities—11.80 percent versus 13.15 percent.
2. The high-performance banks invested more of their assets in tax-exempt securities—15.50 percent versus 11.60 percent. Moreover, the banks attained higher yields on such securities than did other banks—a tax equivalent yield of 10.24 percent versus 9.86 percent for a difference of 58 basis points.
3. The banks in the study were less "loaned up" than were other banks. This finding runs counter to the common belief that the most profitable banks have a high loan volume.
4. In the area of loan pricing the high-performance banks achieved higher yields by 18 basis points. The quality of their loan portfolios was also better than average.
5. The high-performance banks invested nearly 25 percent less of their funds in fixed assets than did all other banks—1.35 percent versus 1.80 percent of funds.
6. Because of lower loan losses, the high-performance banks transferred 35.6 percent less to loan loss reserves than did other banks.

---

[4] William F. Ford and Dennis A. Olsen, "How 1,000 High-Performance Banks Weathered the Recent Recession," *Banking* (April 1978), 36 ff.

7. Since the high-performance banks maintained a better than average quality in their loan portfolios, experienced fewer losses, and transferred less to loan loss reserves, they were in a position to operate with slightly less capital than were other banks; consequently, their return on equity was higher.

8. The payroll costs were about 15 percent less for the high-performance banks than for all other banks. In terms of $100 of assets, the outlay for wages, salaries, and benefits was $1.30 for high-performance banks compared with $1.52 for all other banks. Because of the importance of the payroll to the banking industry, this was very significant.

9. The productivity of employees was greater in the high-performance banks than in all others. In terms of assets, the employees in the first group managed 16.5 percent more assets per employee than in all other banks. They also employed fewer people but paid them better. As a result of this management technique, the high-performance banks experienced 90.6 percent more net income per person than did all other banks.

10. Although not highly significant, high-performance banks were more successful in controlling some minor expenses than were other banks, including occupancy and other operating expenses such as the telephone and electrical bills, postage, travel and entertainment, and so on.

11. The success of high-performance banks was not due to sacrificing growth. In fact, the growth of assets, loans capital, and net income for the period under review was slightly higher than that for other banks.

It is fairly obvious that high profitability is a result of the asset mix, the quality of assets, and the control of expense items. Only consistent good management can guarantee these results.

FUNCTIONAL COST ANALYSIS

To ensure continued profitability, it is necessary for bank management to have knowledge not only of the cost of funds but of the cost of providing the various services that are and might be offered to bank customers. Such knowledge places management in a better competitive position and is absolutely necessary for proper planning. Services that are not profitable should be discontinued or steps should be taken to make them profitable. It is for this reason that many banks have a section or department that is concerned with the determination of the cost of such services as demand deposits, savings and time deposits, the sale of traveler's checks, the various loans, and the cost of capital. Determining the cost of the multitude of services offered is not an easy task in commercial banking since practically all the costs are joint. Employees, for example, work at various functions, and many of the costs are those termed "overhead costs," such as the president's salary, insurance, the cost of the banking office, and so on.

Cost analysis involves the allocation of costs to various bank func-

TABLE 8-2 Installment Loan Function, Selected Banks

	161 Banks with Deposits Up to $50 Million		259 Banks with Deposits of $50 Million to $200 Million		81 Banks with Deposits of over $200 Million	
1 Number of loans outstanding	1,277		3,973		20,469	
Volume						
2 Consumer installment loans	$3,790,059	83.98%	$12,559,639	83.95%	$66,099,128	78.73%
3 Check credit loans	48,066	1.06	363,589	2.43	2,913,111	3.47
4 Consumer loans, subtotal	$3,838,126	85.05%	$12,923,229	86.38%	$69,012,240	82.20%
5 Commercial, equipment, and other loans	669,874	14.84	1,517,645	10.14	9,834,960	11.71
6 Floor plan	4,613	.10	519,745	3.47	5,105,225	6.08
7 Commercial loans, subtotal	674,488	14.94%	2,037,391	13.61%	14,940,185	17.79%
8 Total installment loans	$4,512,615	100.00%	$14,960,620	100.00%	$83,952,425	100.00%
Income						
9 Consumer installment loans	$ 539,686	14.240%*	$ 1,699,670	13.533%*	$ 8,700,996	13.164%*
10 Check credit loans	7,981	16.605*	54,477	14.983*	449,152	15.418*
11 Commercial, equipment, and other loans	82,969	12.386*	188,808	12.441*	1,192,383	12.124*
12 Floor plan	522	11.335	57,349	11.034	575,195	11.267
13 Interest and discount, subtotal	$ 631,159	13.987%	$ 2,000,305	13.370%	$10,917,728	13.005%
14 Other income	31,511	.698	78,079	.522	340,207	.405
15 TOTAL INCOME	$ 662,671	14.685%	$ 2,078,385	13.892%	$11,257,936	13.410%
Expense						
16 Officer salaries	$ 46,456	1.029%	$ 119,458	.798%	$ 504,960	.601%
17 Employee salaries	24,734	.548	82,154	.549	518,077	.617

18 Fringe benefits	14,205	.315	45,806	.306	250,175	.298
19 Salaries and fringe, subtotal	$ 85,396	1.892%	$ 247,418	1.654%	$ 1,273,213	1.517%
20 Data services	13,196	.292	36,572	.244	197,069	.235
21 Furniture and equipment	9,853	.218	24,828	.166	110,749	.132
22 Occupancy	13,642	.302	35,022	.234	198,652	.237
23 Publicity and advertising	5,731	.127	18,491	.124	91,337	.109
24 Other operating expenses	38,432	.852	105,254	.704	527,436	.628
25 Total operating expense	$ 166,252	3.684%	$ 467,588	3.125%	$ 2,398,459	2.857%
Earnings						
26 Net earnings before losses	$ 496,419	11.001%	$ 1,610,796	10.767%	$ 8,859,477	10.553%
27 Net losses	39,215	.869	95,031	.635	329,717	.393
28 Net earnings	$ 457,203	10.132%	$ 1,515,765	10.132%	$ 8,529,759	10.160%
Memoranda						
29 Cost of money	349,594	7.747	1,128,324	7.542	6,231,527	7.423
30 Net earnings after cost of money	$ 107,609	2.385%	$ 387,441	2.590%	$ 2,298,232	2.738%

MISCELLANEOUS DATA

Number of installment loan personnel						
31 Officers	1.62		4.15		17.24	
32 Employees	1.96		6.59		39.34	
33 Total personnel	3.58		10.74		56.58	
34 Number of tellers (included in employees)	1		1		6	
35 Number of banking offices			4		20	
36 3-Year average loan losses	$ 36,130	.80%	$ 71,730	.47%	$ 251,094	.29%

* Gross yield.

SOURCE: Board of Governors of the Federal Reserve System, *Functional Cost Analysis, 1985, Average Banks* (Washington, D.C., 1986), p. 27.

tions. Any method of allocation of indirect overhead costs is a matter of judgment and is subject to criticism. It must, however, be done with the recognition that it is impossible to attain perfection. Some costs, such as those for labor, can be allocated to various functions through efficient time and motion studies, but others, such as supplies, are more difficult since the maintenance of detailed and accurate records of such may not warrant the time and effort. This is especially true of small banks. In general, cost analysis is more accurate in large than in small banks for the simple reason that large banks have available to them a wider range of resources and expertise. Small banks, however, recognize the importance of cost analysis and are making great strides in this area. With increased competition in the financial sector, we will undoubtedly see increased interest in cost analysis.

Banks can receive considerable help from the Federal Reserve banks in the area of cost analysis by participating in a program introduced by the Federal Reserve Bank of Boston over 20 years ago and now supported nationwide. Over the years the scope of the program has been expanded and improved to include the major bank functions. Participating banks provide the raw data to their respective Federal Reserve bank. Data on costs are reported by the banks in accordance with standards established by the Federal Reserve banks and on worksheets provided by them. These data are then analyzed, assembled, and reported in a standardized format to the participating banks. The reporting bank can then compare its performance with that of other banks that are approximately the same size and structure. These data provide the basis for a host of management tools and techniques that can be implemented in the future in an effort to achieve greater operating efficiency and increased profitability. The data are of great value in the areas of profit planning, work measurement, and work simplification and system analysis.

Some idea of the coverage of functional cost analysis and the value of participating banks are presented in Table 8-2. These data cover the installment loan function. The data are broken down by volume of the installment loan portfolio and the composition of this volume. Also presented are the income and costs associated with the installment loan function. A participating bank can compare its performance with that of the average banks in its district. It may discover, for example, that its expenses are high for computer services fees. If so, this is an area that would bear close examination. It might have larger losses than the other banks, which might prompt a program of upgrading the quality of installment loans. If losses were extremely low, it might mean that the loan quality could be reduced in an effort to increase volume and profitability. If the average cost of making a loan by the participating bank is very high compared with that of other banks, it would probably encourage management to evaluate all costs that are incurred in making a loan. One of the values of the functional cost analysis program is that it causes bank management to think about its performance.

The Need for Adequate Profits

It is essential that commercial banks earn adequate profits. Bank profits are necessary to attract new capital to make possible the expansion and improvement of banking services. If the return on existing capital is not comparable to the returns on other investments, capital will be attracted to other more profitable pursuits. An important function of profits in banking is to provide reserves for contingencies and losses that may occur incident to the business of banking. Finally, profits in banking, just as in other businesses, act as a stimulant to management to expand and improve the business, reduce costs, and improve services.

Bank profits are important to every group in the economy. Stockholders are interested in profits since they represent their return on invested capital. Bank profits result in benefits to depositors by producing a stronger, safer, and more efficient banking system through the increase in reserves and improvements in services. Borrowers also have an indirect interest in adequate bank profits since the lending ability of a bank depends on the size and structure of the bank's capital accounts, and bank profits constitute the major source of equity capital. Even economic groups that may not directly use the services of commercial banks are benefited indirectly by adequate bank profits, inasmuch as a strong banking system, in part the result of bank profits, results in the safety of deposits and the availability of credit to the economy on which business firms and consumers depend.

In Figure 8-5 is presented the rate of return on stockholders' equity for durable and nondurable manufacturing and for commercial banks. Although there may be differences in accounting practices as to both profits and capital funds between business firms in these industries, the comparison is of some value in evaluating the trend in bank profits. Note that the rate of return on equity in nondurable manufacturing exceeded that of banks and that durable manufacturing was slightly below banks. Commercial banks showed greater stability than found in the other areas. Although bank profits are influenced by the business cycle, the impact is less than that found in manufacturing. Banks have the ability to invest in loans when loan demand is high and in securities when loan demand is low, which reduces the variability of profits. Tax swapping also results in an increase in profits when money rates are relatively low and security prices are relatively high.

The profitability of many banks exceeds the averages presented in Figure 8-5. In general those banks that have a higher return are located in growth areas, are relatively large, enjoy the economies of scale, are inno-

FIGURE 8-5   Rate of Return on Stockholders' Equity, Durable and
Nondurable Manufacturing Corporations, and All Insured Commercial
Banks

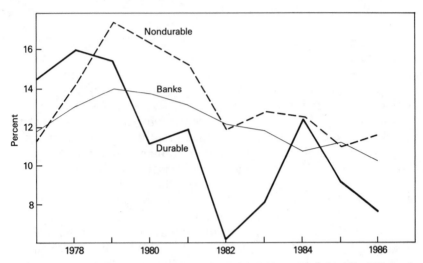

SOURCE: Federal Deposit Insurance Corporation, annual reports, and Council of Economic
Advisers, Economic Reports of the President.

vative, and are excellently managed. Bank management is constantly concerned with bank profitability, as are all business firms, for the simple
reason that banks are competing in the marketplace for capital, and a high
rate of return is the key to attracting bank investors as well as keeping
present stockholders happy. As pointed out, there have been many
changes in banking in the last few years, and there are indications that
there will undoubtedly be more in the decade of the 1990s due to the
likelihood of interstate banking, further deregulation, and the broadening
of banking powers. As the financial structure changes, it will likely result
in larger, more efficient, and more profitable banks and banking organizations.

QUESTIONS

1. How do you account for the fact that in the recession of 1980–82, when
   interest rates were relatively high, the profits of commercial banks held
   up much better than did those of savings and loan associations?
2. What are some of the characteristics of bank profits? Why?
3. If you were investing in common stock, would you give consideration
   to bank stock? Why?

4. It is not unusual for the return on assets of large banks to be less than that for small banks, yet the large banks may have a higher return of equity than do small banks. Why? What does the smaller spread of equity returns versus total assets returns indicate about the relative equity capital positions of large and small banks? Why would the return on assets be so much lower for the large banks?

5. If a bank has a higher than average rate of return on capital but a lower than average rate of return on total assets, what is indicated about the bank's capital position?

6. In what ways did the risk character of banking change in the 1970s?

7. Assume that a bank that has $100 million of total assets and $7 million of equity capital and is earning 0.7 percent on total assets issues new shares that increase the total shares outstanding by 10 percent. Assume further that the sale of the new shares nets the bank $700,000, which, on a per share basis, is the same as the book value of the previously outstanding shares. What would be the rate of return on equity capital in the year after the new shares are issued if all else remained constant? How much would issuing the new shares dilute earnings per share?

SELECTED REFERENCES

BAUGHN, WILLIAM H., AND CHARLES E. WALKER, eds. *The Bankers' Handbook*, rev. ed. Homewood, Ill.: Dow Jones-Irwin, 1978, chaps. 23, 24, 25.

BOARD OF GOVERNORS OF THE FEDERAL RESERVE SYSTEM. *Federal Reserve Bulletin*. Washington, D.C., August 1981, pp. 453–465, and subsequent August issues.

BRICK, JOHN R. *Bank Management: Concepts and Issues*. Richmond, Va.: Robert F. Dame, 1980, sec. V.

FEDERAL RESERVE BANK OF CHICAGO. "Crosscurrents in 1986 Bank Performance." *Economic Prospectives* (May/June 1986), pp. 23–35.

FEDERAL RESERVE BANK OF NEW YORK. *Recent Trends in Commercial Bank Profitability*. New York, 1986.

FORD, WILLIAM F., AND DENNIS A. OLSEN. "How 1,000 High-Performance Banks Weathered the Recent Recession." *Banking* (April 1978), pp. 36 ff.

KOLASI, JAMES, AND ASGHAR ZARDKOOHI. *Bank Cost, Structure, and Performance*. Lexington, Mass.: D. C. Heath, 1987.

PAYNE, C. MEYRICK. "Profitability Management: Banking's Next Generation." *The Bankers Magazine* (Spring 1977), pp. 51–57.

9

CREDIT ANALYSIS

The numerous and varied risks in lending stem from the many factors that can lead to the nonpayment of obligations when they come due. Losses sometimes result from "acts of God" such as storms, droughts, fires, earthquakes, and floods. Changes in consumer demand or in the technology of an industry may alter drastically the fortunes of a business firm and place a once profitable borrower in a loss position. A prolonged strike, competitive price cutting, or loss of key management personnel can seriously impair a borrower's ability to make loan payments. The swings of the business cycle affect the profits of many who borrow from banks and influence the optimism and pessimism of business people as well as consumers. Some risks arise from personal factors that are difficult to explain. In determining whether or not to grant a loan a banker must attempt to measure the risk of nonpayment. This risk is estimated through a process referred to as *credit analysis*.

OBJECTIVES OF CREDIT ANALYSIS

The principal purpose of credit analysis is to determine the ability and willingness of a borrower to repay a requested loan in accordance with the terms of the loan contract. A bank must determine the degree of risk it is willing to assume in each case and the amount of credit that can be prudently extended in view of the risks involved. Moreover, if a loan is to be made, it is necessary to determine the conditions and terms under which it will be granted. Some of the factors that affect the ability of a borrower to repay a loan are very difficult to evaluate, but they must be dealt with as realistically as possible in preparing financial projections. This involves looking into the past record of the borrower as well as engaging in economic forecasting. Thus, the bank lending officer attempts to project the borrower and the environment, including all possible hazards that may affect them, into the future to determine whether the loan will be repaid in the ordinary course of business. Loans should not be based entirely on a borrower's history and reputation—they may be contracted today, but they are paid in the future.

The work of credit analysis is basically the same in all banks, but certain functions may be emphasized to a greater extent in some banks than in others. In general, they include the collection of information that will have a bearing on credit evaluation, the preparation and analysis of the information collected, and the assembling and retention of information for future use. In some banks the credit department may make recommendations regarding a credit application, but the final decision regarding a loan is left to the lending officer and/or the loan committee. In addition to these important functions, the credit department serves as a training ground for future loan officers. In small banks the loan officers typically perform their own credit analysis.

FACTORS CONSIDERED IN CREDIT ANALYSIS

Many factors are considered by bank credit people in analyzing a loan request. They are the ingredients that determine the lending officer's faith in the debtor's ability and willingness to pay the obligation in accordance with the terms of the loan agreement. For years credit people referred to the *three C's of credit*—*capacity, character,* and *capital.* Over the years numerous other credit analysis factors have been specified as worthy of consideration, and, with a little imagination, each of these can be labeled with a word beginning with "C."[1] The most important of these are *collateral* and *conditions.* For purposes of discussion, we shall classify the essential factors in credit analysis as *capacity, character, ability to create income, ownership of assets,* and *economic conditions.*

Capacity to Borrow

Banks are interested not only in the borrower's ability to repay but also in his or her legal capacity to borrow. Banks make few loans to

---

[1] Jack R. Crigger, "An Ocean of 'Cs,' " *The Journal of Commercial Bank Lending* (December 1975), pp. 2–8.

minors, since they can disaffirm at a later date unless the proceeds of the loan are used for essential purposes. When a loan is made to a minor, a parent, guardian, or other person of legal age is usually asked to cosign the note.

In lending to a partnership, it may be advisable to require that all members of the partnership sign for the loan. If that is not feasible, the lending officer should determine whether the signing partners have authority to borrow for the partnership. A verified copy of the partnership agreement or power of attorney may be used for this purpose. When such evidence of authority is not received, the lender may find it difficult to collect from nonsigning partners if they establish that the borrowed funds were not used to further the business of the partnership. In general, every partner has authority to execute instruments for the partnership, but if the nonsigning partners can show that the partner(s) who purportedly acted on behalf of the partnership did not have such authority and that the lender knew this or, in some cases, should have known it, they may avoid any responsibility for the loan.

In lending to a corporation, it is advisable to examine the charter and bylaws to ascertain who has authority to borrow in its behalf. In many cases, banks also follow the practice of requiring a corporate resolution signed by the members of the board of directors setting forth the borrowing authority and designating the person or persons who have the authority to negotiate for loans and to execute borrowing instruments. Banks may also require a resolution to borrow from cooperatives and other organizations such as churches and other nonprofit associations.

Banks sometimes find it inadvisable to lend unless certain other creditors of the borrower agree to subordinate their claims to that of the bank. This occurs frequently in lending to small corporations, where the corporation has borrowed sizable amounts from its major stockholders. In such cases the bank may be willing to lend to the corporation only on the condition that the lending stockholders, and perhaps other creditors as well, agree to permit the corporation to pay the bank first in the event of liquidation of the business. Through this process of subordination the bank becomes a preferred creditor and is assured a prior claim on the assets of the business over those who have agreed to subordinate their claims.

Character

The concept of character, as it relates to credit transactions, means not only the willingness to repay debts but also a strong desire to settle all obligations within the terms of the contract. A person of character usually possesses attributes such as honesty, integrity, industry, and morality, but character is a difficult thing to evaluate. It is entirely possible for a person not to have all of these qualities but to still wish to repay financial obligations. The Mississippi River gambler may have paid his debts as agreed even though he was unacceptable as a whole to society because of certain socially undesirable traits. Character worthy of credit is largely a function of a person's honesty and integrity, and is just as important in lending to business firms as to individuals. The past record of a borrower in meeting his or her obligations is usually weighed heavily in evaluating his or her character for credit purposes. Sometimes, however, assessment of character is largely a matter of judgment, unsupported by extensive factual information.

Ability to Create Income

If a loan is to be repaid from earnings, it is essential to evaluate the borrower's ability to earn a sufficient amount to repay the loan. Some loans are made with the expectation that repayment will come from the sale of assets, from other borrowings, or from the issuance of common stock in the case of corporations. The primary source of repayment of most loans, however, is the revenue-generating capacity of the borrowers.

An individual's power to generate income depends on such factors as education, health and energy, skill, age, stability of employment, and resourcefulness. For a business firm, generating income depends on all factors that affect sales volume, selling prices, costs, and expenses. These include the location of the firm, the quality of its goods and services, the effectiveness of its advertising, the amount of competition, the quality and morale of its labor force, the availability and cost of raw materials, and the quality of its management. Many credit people rank the quality of management as the chief factor in deciding whether to extend credit. They refer to it as the *management factor*—the ability of a firm's managers to assemble personnel, raw materials, and capital assets to produce a satisfactory flow of goods, services, and profits. Some businesses rise while others fall, and the difference is often attributable to management. Effective management sees and takes advantage of new opportunities, makes timely adjustments in production in response to changes in demand for the firm's products, replaces inefficiency with efficiency, and provides products and services with strong customer appeal because of their quality and/or pricing. It is difficult to evaluate the managers of a firm, particularly when they have not been on the job very long, but it is nevertheless important.

Ownership of Assets

Ownership of assets is similar to capital and collateral in the C's of credit. Manufacturers must have modern machinery and equipment if they are to be competitive producers. Retailers must have a stock of merchandise and attractive buildings and fixtures if they are to attract customers. Credit will not be supplied to business concerns unless capital has been supplied by the owners to support the debt. The net worth of a firm (the capital supplied by the owners) is one measure of its financial strength. It is often one of the principal determinants of the amount of credit a bank is willing to make available to a business borrower. The amount and quality of the assets held by a firm reflect the prudence and resourcefulness of its management. Some or all of these assets may serve as security for a loan and thus as insurance that the loan will be repaid should the borrower's ability to create income not be sufficient to retire the loan. It should be emphasized, however, that while security does reduce the risk, banks prefer that borrowed funds be repaid out of income.

Consumer loans are frequently secured by assets of the borrower. Most cars, for example, are purchased on credit, and the automobile serves as collateral for the loan. The same is true for houses and, to a lesser extent, for household furnishings and appliances. If the value of the pledged assets has not depreciated below the unpaid balance of the loan, the borrower has a strong incentive to continue the payments.

Economic Conditions

Economic conditions affect the ability of the borrower to repay financial obligations but are beyond the control of the borrower and the lender. Economic conditions make up the environment within which business units and individuals operate. Borrowers may have good character, an apparent ability to create income, and sufficient assets, but economic conditions may render the extension of credit unwise. It is here that the loan officer must become an economic forecaster. The longer the maturity of the loan, the more important economic forecasting becomes, since there is a greater possibility of an economic downturn before the loan has been fully repaid. The economy is subject to short- and long-run fluctuations that vary in intensity and duration. These movements are never the same, conform to no definite pattern, and may affect different industries and areas of the country differently.

Many borrowers fare well in periods of prosperity, but in periods of recession capital may be dissipated, income may decline, and even character may diminish. These factors give rise to the nonpayment of debts. A bank lending officer must, therefore, keep informed as to the economic pulse of the nation, the community, and the industry or industries in which he or she makes loans.

In extending credit to business borrowers, a bank is interested in the economic function performed by the business and its importance in the industry. A knowledge of what is happening in the industry is very important—changes in competitive conditions, technology, the demand for products, and distribution methods. If a loan applicant is not performing a function basic to the operation of the economy, the lender will be less likely to act favorably on the credit application than if the opposite situation prevails.

Relative Importance of the Credit Factors

Although all the factors mentioned earlier are important in credit analysis, most bankers agree that the collateral available for a loan is generally the least important. Credit is granted with the expectation that the funds will be repaid as agreed, not that the pledged assets will have to be sold to provide the funds needed for repayment. Security is taken in most instances to strengthen a weakness found in one or more of the credit factors, such as the ability to create income.

Every loan application is unique. One credit factor may be most important in one situation while another one is in a second situation. Over the entire spectrum of credit analysis, however, character emerges as the most important factor. If a borrower is of poor character, the probability is high that at some time he or she will not comply with the terms of a loan agreement.

SCOPE OF CREDIT INVESTIGATION

The scope of a credit investigation will vary, depending on such determinants as the size and maturity of the loan, the operating record of the business, the security offered, and previous relations with the borrower. No definite routine is followed since each applicant for credit may have some peculiar features that should be investigated more thoroughly than others. The objective is to accumulate information that can be used to evaluate the applicant's character, assets, ability to create income, and the probable economic environment. In the investigation of a business loan application, banks like to know something about the history of the business—the firm's operating record, labor relations, experience in the development and marketing of new products, and sources of growth in sales and earnings. Since management is of great importance, information about the executives of a firm is a necessity. Information about their experience, background, outside affiliations, and interests is of value, as are the opinions of others concerning their integrity and capabilities. It is also important to know whether adequate provision has been made for management succession in the firm.

Banks should know about the nature and operation of the business:

what types of products are handled or produced, what types of services are rendered. Whether the goods are staple or styled, consumer or capital, luxury or necessity would be worthwhile information. The source and stability of raw materials and labor as well as the proximity to market are important. Buying and selling terms, distribution methods, extent of fabrication, hazards in the business, and the importance of the business in the economy are important facts that will place the business in proper perspective.

The bank would certainly want information on the concern's financial condition. This necessitates reviewing financial statements, investigating the possibility of contingent liabilities, and examining the insurance coverage. Since the condition and efficiency of the firm's physical facilities are very important, the lending officer may wish to examine them personally. It may also be helpful to contact other banks with which the firm has done business, as well as suppliers and customers of the firm. Information about competitive conditions in the industry and the trends of sales and profits may be of considerable importance also in evaluating the firm's future.

SOURCES OF CREDIT INFORMATION

The many sources of credit information include interviews with loan applicants, the bank's own records, a variety of external sources, inspection of applicants' places of business, and applicants' financial statements.

Interview of Loan Applicant

In the interview with the applicant, the lending officer learns the reason for the loan and whether the loan request meets various requirements established in the loan policies of the bank. Even if the loan request is not in harmony with bank policy or violates some regulation established by law or a bank regulatory agency, the lending officer may offer the applicant advice regarding other possible sources of funds. From the interview, the lending officer can also get some idea as to an applicant's honesty and ability and may form an opinion as to whether security will be necessary. Information about the history and growth of the business, the backgrounds of key personnel, the nature of the products and services, sources of raw materials, competitive position, and plans for the future can be obtained through the interview and, if desired, checked later against other sources. In the interview, the lending officer will also advise the applicant as to what additional financial information will be needed for evaluating the proposed loan.

Bank's Own Records

A bank may maintain a central file of all its depositors and borrowers from which credit information can be obtained. For example, it will show the payment record on previous loans, the balances carried in checking and savings accounts, and whether the applicant has a habit of overdrawing his or her account. Even if the applicant has never been a customer of the bank, the central file may contain some information if the applicant has been solicited by the new business department.

External Sources
of Credit Information

Dun & Bradstreet, the most widely known credit reporting agency, collects information on several million businesses in the United States and Canada and makes it available on a subscription basis. Brief information and credit ratings on each firm are published in national and regional reference books. More detailed information on individual firms is supplied in the form of credit reports (see Figure 9-1).

The first of the six sections in the report is a summary showing the name and address of the firm; the Standard Industrial Classification Number and the DUNS (Data Universal Numbering System) number; the type of business; composite credit rating; year of the firm's origination; promptness with which payments are made by the firm; sales, net worth, and number of employees; and the general condition of the firm and the trend of the business. The composite credit rating for a firm consists of two parts—two letters (or a number and a letter) followed by a number. The first part indicates the firm's estimated financial strength, and the second its composite credit appraisal. The rating of CC2 for Rettinger Paint Corporation, for example, indicates that the firm's estimated net worth is $75,000 to $124,999 and its credit rating is good. A "1" would be high, "3" fair, and "4" limited.

The second section of the report contains information from the firm's suppliers as to how promptly it has been paying its bills and the highest credit granted during the year. The third section contains a recent balance sheet and information as to the firm's sales and profits, if available. This section may also include information regarding insurance coverages, leases, trends of sales and profits, and important recent developments such as major asset acquisitions and new financing. The fourth section provides information as to the usual size of the firm's deposit balances and its payment record under loan agreements. The fifth section contains significant biographical information about the principals or owners of the business, including their previous experience, outside business affiliations, and past financial difficulties, if any. The final section of the report

FIGURE 9-1 Dun & Bradstreet Credit Report

CONSOLIDATED REPORT		{FULL REVISION}

DUNS: 06-647-3261
RETTINGER PAINT CORP.

727 WHITMAN WAY
BENSON, MI 48232
  TEL 313 961-0720

CARL RETTINGER, PRES.

DATE PRINTED
AUG 13, 197—

WHOL PAINTS &
VARNISHES

SIC NO.
51 98

	SUMMARY
RATING	CC2
STARTED	1950
PAYMENTS	DISC-PPT
SALES	$ 424,612
WORTH	$ 101,867
EMPLOYS	5
HISTORY	CLEAR
CONDITION	GOOD
TREND	STEADY

SPECIAL EVENTS   Business burglarized July 3 but $18,000 loss is fully insured.

PAYMENTS   {Amounts may be rounded to nearest figure in prescribed ranges}

REPORTED	PAYING RECORD	HIGH CREDIT	NOW OWES	PAST DUE	SELLING TERMS	LAST SALE WITHIN
07/7—	Disc	30000	17000	-0-	2 10 30	1-2 mos.
	Disc	27000	14000	-0-	1 10 30	2-3 mos.
	Disc-Ppt	12000	4400	200	2 10 30	1 mo.
	Ppt	9000	8000	-0-	30	1 mo.
06/7—	Disc	16000	7500	-0-	2 10 30	2-3 mos.
05/7—	Disc	9000	3800	-0-	2 10 30	1 mo.
	Ppt	1500	-0-	-0-	30	1-2 mos.

FINANCE
06/22/7—   Fiscal statement dated May 31, 197—:

Cash	$ 20,623	Accts Payable	$ 47,246
Accts Rec	55,777	Owing Bank	34,000
Merchandise	92,103	Notes Pay {Trucks}	7,020
	---------		--------
Current	168,503	Current	88,266
Fixts. & Equip.	13,630	Common Stock	35,000
Trucks	8,000	Earned Surplus	66,867
	-------		--------
Total Assets	190,133	Total	190,133

SALES {Yr}: $424,612. Net profit $17,105. Fire ins. mdse $95,000;
equipt $20,000. Mo. rent: $3500. Prepared by Steige Co., CPAs, Detroit, MI.

--0--

06/22/7—Laswon defined monthly payments: $3000 to bank, $400 on notes.
Admitted collections slow but losses insignificant. Said inventory will drop
to $60,000 by December. Expects 5% sales increase this year.

PUBLIC FILINGS
03/25/7—   March 17, 197— financing statement H741170 named subject as debtor and
NCR Corp., Dayton, O. as secured party. Collateral: equipment.
05/28/7—   May 21, 197— suit for $200 entered by Henry Assoc., Atlanta, Ga. Docket
A27519. Involves merchandise which Lawson says was defective.

BANKING
06/25/7—   Account, long maintained, carries average balances low to moderate five
figures. Unsecured loans to moderate five extended and now open.

HISTORY
06/22/7—   CARL RETTINGER, PRES.   JOHN J. LAWSON, V PRES.
DIRECTORS: The Officers
Incorporated Michigan February 2, 1950. Authorized capital 3500 shares,
no par common. Paid in capital $35,000, officers sharing equally.
RETTINGER, born 1920, married. Employed by E-Z Paints, Detroit 12 yrs,
five as manager until starting subject early 1950.
LAWSON, born 1925, married. Obtained accounting degree 1946 and then
employed by Union Carbide, Chicago until joining Rettinger at inception.

OPERATION
06/22/7—   Wholesales paints and varnishes {85%}, wallpaper and supplies. 500
local accounts include retailers {75%} and contractors. Terms: 2 10 30. Peak
season spring thru summer. EMPLOYEES: Officers active with three others.
LOCATION: Rents 7500 sq ft. one-story block structure, good repair.

SOURCE: By permission of Dun & Bradstreet Credit Services, a company of the Dun & Bradstreet
Corporation.

describes in some detail the nature of the firm's business, the kinds of customers to whom it sells, and its physical facilities. It may also give the approximate number of customers served by the firm and the numbers and types of its employees.

Dun & Bradstreet issues several kinds of reports in addition to that shown in Figure 9-1. One of the most useful of these is the Key Account Report, which contains considerably more detailed information about a firm.

Several credit agencies in addition to Dun & Bradstreet are generally classified as special mercantile or trade agencies. These agencies usually limit their coverage to a single trade or industry or to a limited number of allied trades or industries, in contrast to the comprehensive coverage of Dun & Bradstreet. An example is the Lyon Furniture Mercantile Agency, which limits its services to the fields of furniture, home appliances, department and general stores, funeral parlors, and interior decorators.

Banks sometimes check with other banks that have had relationships with the loan applicant. They may also check with various suppliers and customers of the firm. Suppliers can give information on how the firm's bills have been paid, whether discounts have been taken, the high and low credit outstanding, and whether unjust claims are made and discounts deducted to which the firm is not entitled. Checking with the firm's customers can provide information as to the quality of its products, the reliability of its service, and the amount of merchandise that has been returned. Such checking with the trade and with other banks may also reveal something about the character and ability of the firm applying for the loan, or its managers.

Another source of information is the Credit Interchange Service of the National Association of Credit Management, an organization that provides information about the credit experience of the suppliers of a firm on a nationwide basis. This organization provides its members with an answer to the question, How well does the firm pay? However, it only presents the facts and does not provide an analysis or interpretation or offer any recommendations. Other sources of information on business firms, especially large ones, include trade journals, newspapers, directories, public records, and statistical reporting services such as Standard & Poor's. Some banks even check with the competitors of a business firm. Such information must be used with great discretion, but it can be very helpful.

Sources of consumer credit information changed in several important ways with the passage of the Fair Credit Reporting Act in 1970. For many years banks and other lenders relied heavily on retail credit bureaus that specialize in gathering credit information on consumers. These agencies are either privately owned or are owned and operated mutually by the firms that they serve in the community, including the banks. Information on an individual's employment, income, number of dependents, indebtedness, paying habits, and other facts that have a bearing on his or her credit is gathered and made available to members or customers, either by telephone or written report.

The basic objectives of the Fair Credit Reporting Act are to protect consumers from inaccurate and obsolete information in credit reports about them and to safeguard their privacy. The act places heavy responsibilities on consumer reporting agencies and users of consumer credit information. Consumer reporting agencies, as defined in the legislation, include any person or business firm that, for profit or on a cooperative nonprofit basis, regularly engages in the practice of assembling and disseminating consumer credit information in written or oral form.

A consumer has several rights under the act. With a few exceptions, the law gives the consumer the right to know the nature, substance, and sources of the information collected by a consumer reporting agency. Also, the consumer has a right to be told who has received a consumer report containing this information and to have the agency correct any incorrect information relating to the consumer and to notify those to whom the incorrect information has been distributed. Should a dispute develop between the consumer and the credit reporting agency, the consumer has the right to request that his or her version of the dispute be placed in the file and included in subsequent reports. The act also provides that a consumer is entitled to be notified when a party is seeking information from a credit reporting agency of such a nature that it would constitute an "investigative report" and has a right to request that additional information about him or her be disclosed. An investigative credit report pertains to a consumer's character, general reputation, personal characteristics, or mode of living and is obtained generally through personal interviews with friends, neighbors, and associates.

The act is not concerned with the practices of persons and firms other than credit reporting agencies who give reports based solely on transactions between consumers and themselves. This is known as *direct checking*. If a consumer has been delinquent in payments on a personal loan, for example, it is perfectly all right for the lender to report this information to a bank or retail firm where the consumer has asked for an extension of credit. It is not acceptable, however, for the lender to report the financial relationship as "unsatisfactory" or "poor" or use some other similar description. Direct checking is much more expensive than obtaining similar information from a credit bureau. Therefore, the cost of consumer credit information can be quite high relative to the average size of consumer loans and is a factor in determining the cost of such loans.

Inspection of Applicants' Places of Business

Businesses applying for loans should be willing to allow a loan officer to visit and tour their places of business. An experienced loan officer will learn a significant amount about how productive and well managed a business is from a tour of the facilities. The loan officer should note how well the business is organized and whether or not employees seem to be performing effectively. A neat and orderly appearance is usually a positive indication about a business as is "balance" in the work being performed. Are some workers excessively busy while others seem to have little to do? Are delivery vehicles standing idle because production in the plant is slowed by bottlenecks? Does inventory seem excessive? Is some of the inventory old or partially deteriorated?

If a firm is a retailer, a visit during a normally busy period may indicate the strength of the firm's business as well as the proficiency of the sales staff. In the case of visiting a manufacturing firm, particular note should be made of the equipment and the production layout. Equipment should be well maintained and, if not modern, at least of sufficient efficiency to avoid creation of production bottlenecks.

Financial Statements

Financial statements are required of most borrowers, especially if the amount involved is relatively large. Even in consumer credit, where loans are usually quite small, an applicant may be asked to list what he or she owns and owes, income and expenses, current bills outstanding, dependents, and other information that will reflect his or her financial condition. The proper evaluation of information contained in financial statements is of great importance in the credit analysis process. The remainder of this chapter is devoted to the discussion of methods of financial statement analysis.

ANALYSIS OF FINANCIAL STATEMENTS

Financial statements of borrowers and prospective borrowers are among the most important sources of credit information available to bank lending officers. In dealing with business borrowers in particular, banks find that historical financial statements, pro forma statements, and cash budgets provide not only a good basis for evaluating a loan applicant's financial condition and profitability but also the applicant's ability to generate cash flows for operating purposes and making loan payments. The usefulness of historical financial statements in making credit decisions depends, of course, on the timeliness and quality of the statements. The extent to which lending officers use financial reports and projections in evaluating loan proposals depends on such factors as the size, purpose, and maturity of the loan, and the amount of security being furnished.

Lenders use financial statements and budgets to estimate the extent of the borrower's need for funds, evaluate the probability of loan repayment, estimate the potential loss if the borrower does not pay, and decide on the terms of the financing if a loan is to be made. Loan officers must avoid placing too much reliance on historical balance sheet information, since a firm's financial condition can deteriorate rapidly if it begins to incur operating losses. Information provided by prior income statements must also be used with discretion in view of the fact that past profits are often a poor indicator of future earnings. This is not to deny the importance of evaluating as accurately as possible the borrower's current financial condition and examining the level and trend of past earnings; nevertheless, lending officers should also examine pro forma financial statements and cash budgets that show what the borrower's financial condition, profitability, and cash requirements are expected to be in the future. A major value of historical financial statements is the help they provide in appraising the soundness of the borrower's cash and profit projections. For example, if a borrower's pretax profit margin had averaged 5 percent in recent years and never exceeded 6 percent, a projection showing a margin of, say, 8 percent, should be questioned.

The validity of any conclusions drawn from financial statements can be no better than the information contained in the statements. The financial statements of many small companies are not audited and thus must be evaluated with great care and a degree of skepticism. Often it is necessary to work with audited statements many months old, supplemented by unaudited interim statements. In that case, the loan officer should consider carefully the quality of the interim statements even if they have been prepared by persons who appear competent. Even audited statements must be used with discretion. Many judgments are required in determining the book values of a firm's assets and the amount of its earnings. Lenders are interested in the degree of conservatism with which these judgments have been made. It is not enough that the firm has been following generally accepted accounting principles, since those principles often permit a great deal of latitude in the recognition of income and expenses. If reliance is to be placed on a borrower's cash forecasts and pro forma financial statements, the loan officer must examine critically the underlying assumptions that have been made with respect to important profit determinants such as sales volumes, selling prices, wage rates, and selling and administrative expenses. Many of the same techniques used in analyzing historical statements can also be used in analyzing profit projections and pro forma financial statements.

EVALUATION OF ITEMS
ON THE FINANCIAL STATEMENTS

One method of analyzing financial statements is to evaluate each significant item to determine its accuracy and reasonableness. This method often involves trimming down various items to more reasonable and conservative figures. A thorough analysis is made of each item that appears in the financial statement in an effort to appraise its fair value, but no reference is made to proportions, relationships, or ratios. Obviously, a bank credit analyst must have some knowledge of the business and statement items in order to appraise them properly.

Evaluation of Asset Items

Accounts receivable should be analyzed carefully because they represent the nearest thing to cash and may be the principal source of repayment of short-term loans. Information about the size, age, and sources of the accounts is important. If receivables are concentrated in a few large accounts, the inherent risk of nonpayment may be greater than if they are distributed over many accounts. In some cases an investigation into the financial strength and paying habits of the debtors is in order. The bank credit analyst should require an aging schedule of accounts receivable to allow identification of receivables that may be of doubtful value. If many accounts are past due, they must be evaluated accordingly, and an adequate reserve for bad debts must be established. In the investigation of accounts receivable, it is also important to determine whether any accounts have been factored or assigned to others; usually the better accounts are disposed of in this manner. Also, the possibility exists of a contingent liability if the accounts were assigned with recourse, that is, the assignee promises to pay in the event the accounts receivable are not paid.

In many instances notes receivable arise because customers of the business are not paying their accounts according to the credit terms, and notes are obtained in an effort to strengthen the firm's position. If notes receivable appear large in relation to accounts receivable, a thorough investigation should be made to determine the soundness and liquidity of the notes. If notes receivable have been discounted with a lending institution, there is the possibility of a contingent liability, as in the case of accounts receivable. When notes receivable have been discounted with recourse, they should remain on the balance sheet as an asset item, and the amount of the loan should appear as a liability.

A bank credit analyst is interested in the age, liquidity, and price stability of the inventories, the degree to which they are free of risks of obsolescence and deterioration, the adequacy of insurance coverage, and the firm's method of inventory accounting. One must also know whether the inventories are based on a physical count, whether the firm uses the first-in, first-out (FIFO) or the last-in, first-out (LIFO) method of valuation, and whether the quantities on hand are excessive. If one is thinking in terms of the probable liquidation value of the firm, then goods in process and supply inventories should be largely discounted because of their limited marketability. Since raw materials usually have a broader market than finished goods, they are more likely to maintain their value. And if one is looking to inventories as security for a loan, some control procedures must be maintained.

Normally, banks do not look to the sale of fixed assets as a source of funds for repayment of a loan. However, if the debt is intermediate or long term, fixed assets are likely to take on more significance. This is especially true when fixed assets are taken as security for the loan. Usually, however, the principal importance of fixed assets in credit analysis is their role in generating income. The credit analyst should be certain that the firm is taking adequate depreciation, is maintaining the properties in good condition, and has adequate insurance coverage. With respect to liquidation values, the analyst would consider whether the properties are general purpose or special purpose, since this would affect their marketability.

Intangible assets such as goodwill, trademarks, copyrights, patents, leaseholds, and franchises are usually accorded little value by bankers. Patents, copyrights, franchises, and leaseholds that have substantial value are occasional exceptions. However, as a general rule, bank credit analysts are interested principally in tangible assets and tangible net worth.

When the balance sheet shows that the firm owns stock in one or more companies, the analyst is interested not only in the value of the investment but also in any interrelationships between the companies. The financial relationships or commitments that may affect the debt-paying ability of the borrowing firm are of particular interest. If the assets of the firm include amounts due from officers and employees or affiliates and subsidiaries, these will be investigated very closely. Bankers take a dim view of amounts due from officers and employees of a firm. And, in the case of accounts receivable from affiliates and subsidiaries, a careful evaluation must be made of their ability to pay. If any sinking funds appear on the borrower's balance sheet, the banker is concerned with their adequacy. Sinking funds for repaying other obligations are not available for repayment of bank loans of course, but the banker wants to be certain that all sinking fund provisions have been complied with.

Evaluation of Liabilities and Net Worth

There are three types of creditors—secured, preferred, and general— and the amount owed to each may influence the amount of credit a business can obtain from a commercial bank. *Secured creditors* hold a lien on specific property, such as a mortgage on plants and equipment. *Preferred creditors* have preference over all others by operation of law. Preferred claims include taxes owed to governmental bodies and wages due employees. *General creditors* have been provided with no security and have no preference in the event of liquidation. They usually share proportionately in any assets remaining after the preferred and secured creditors have been paid.

Commercial banks are quite interested in the amounts and maturities of all liabilities for which a loan applicant is responsible. If a firm's accounts payable are large relative to its scale of operations, it may need additional equity capital or borrowed funds. Careful investigation is usually made if there are notes payable to suppliers, since this may indicate that the firm has been slow in paying its trade obligations and has been asked or compelled to give notes to evidence the indebtedness. If the firm has obligations under conditional sales contracts, an investigation may be made to determine if any payments are past due, and if so, the penalties that are likely to be involved. If the firm owes a significant amount to its shareholders or officers on notes payable, the bank may ask that such liabilities be subordinated as a condition to granting the firm a loan. In many cases the analyst will want to review the amounts accrued for taxes and other expenses to evaluate their adequacy.

Long-term liabilities consist of mortgage loans, debentures (senior and subordinated), notes, term loans, and all other forms of indebtedness that do not mature within one year. The credit analyst is concerned with the nature and maturity of these obligations and the provisions that have been made for meeting the required payments. The default provisions of the various agreements and whether the loan applicant is in full compliance are of interest also. For example, failure to pay interest on bonds or term loans can cause the entire unpaid balance to become due and payable immediately.

The owners' equity, or net worth, is an item on which bankers place great value in extending credit. In the case of proprietorships and partnerships, where the owners are individually responsible for the debts of the firm as well as for any debts they have contracted outside the business, it is important to consider not only the income and net worth of the firm itself but also the owners' earnings, assets, liabilities, and net worth outside of the business.

The possibility of contingent or undisclosed liabilities is always a matter of concern. Such liabilities may arise, for example, from borrowing on the security of notes and accounts receivable, endorsing or guaranteeing the obligations of others, guaranteeing products or services, injuring third parties or damaging their property, and underreporting taxable income. Liabilities of this nature may arise without any warning and can easily impair the debt-paying ability of the firm; to the extent possible, they should be insured against. However, the banker will want to be certain insofar as possible that the exposure to noninsurable potential liabilities is not very great.

Evaluation of the Income Statement

A firm's earnings tell us something about the quality of the assets reported on the balance sheet as well as the effectiveness of the management. The importance of income statement analysis increases with the maturity of the loan. Bankers may place more emphasis on balance sheet items in negotiation of short-term loans, but with longer maturities the income statement takes on a greater significance. Analysis of the firm's income statements will reveal the degree of stability in its operations and the efficiency with which it is being managed. The firm's accounting practices should be examined carefully to see that no changes have been made that would cause the figures to be noncomparable from year to year.

Income statement analysis is facilitated by developing a common-size statement in which all items are expressed as a percentage of sales. The percentage figures are easily compared then with similar figures for previous periods and with the percentages of other firms in the same type of business. For example, if an analyst were to find that the selling expenses of a firm had been increasing steadily as a percentage of sales over a period of years and that the percentage figure for the latest year was considerably above that of other firms, reasons for this apparently unfavorable situation must be determined. The fact that certain expenses appear to be out of line in comparison with those of other firms does not necessarily mean that they are too large. But if the firm is spending either too much or too little in a particular category, the banker should review the situation with the borrower to help find ways of improving operations.

Extraordinary income and expenses are given particular attention if they are substantial items. Extraordinary expenses might include losses on the sale of fixed assets, uninsured losses from natural causes, inventory shortages, and abandonment losses. Extraordinary income often consists of profits on the sale of operating assets or land. Such profits are likely to be nonrecurring.

Evaluation of the Statement
of Changes in Financial Position

Along with the balance sheet and income statement, firms should prepare a statement of changes in financial position covering the reporting period. This statement often is referred to as the sources and uses statement. Its purpose is to reflect changes in the firm's liquidity—usually in terms of working capital—during the year or other reporting period.

The statement shows additions or reductions of working capital from operations, from changes in asset accounts, and from changes in liability and net worth accounts. The statement is important to the credit analyst in assessing the impact of operations and certain management decisions on the firm's liquidity. For example, a firm's sales may have expanded significantly during the last year, and net income may be sharply higher. However, the increased level of operations was possible only because assets were expanded. Not only did the higher sales levels require more inventory, but accounts receivable grew and certain fixed asset investments were made.

If the firm financed the growth in assets with additions of equity and longer-term debt capital as well as with increased short-term borrowings, it may have not experienced a deterioration of its liquidity. However, it is not uncommon for a rapidly growing firm to delay acquiring long-term financing. If the statement of changes in financial position shows that the major sources of funds during the year were increases in accounts and notes payable, then the credit analyst must be aware that the firm's liquidity has suffered during the year in spite of its profitability. A priority item in the discussion of a possible loan to this firm should be to ask what it expects to do to improve its liquidity.

RATIO ANALYSIS

Figures on a firm's balance sheet and income statement are often much more informative when related to other figures on those statements or to averages for comparable firms in the same industry. While it may be interesting to know that a firm's profits were $5 million last year, it may be considerably more helpful to know that those profits were earned on sales of $500 million, assets of $400 million, and net worth of $200 million. Lending officers are interested in relationships that shed light on the direction in which a firm appears to be moving as well as on its current financial condition and recent profitability. In analyzing trends, the lending officer is concerned not only with the year-to-year and possibly month-to-month changes in aggregate quantities such as sales and profits, but also with the trends of such important ratios as net income to sales, current assets to current liabilities, and total debt to total assets.

The ratios that could be computed with the figures in a firm's financial statements are almost limitless, but logic and experience tell us that only a handful are really useful. In general, ratios based on historical statements are used in searching for answers to questions such as the following:

1. Will the firm be able to continue to meet its obligations as they come due?
2. Are the firm's accounts receivable and inventories reasonably current and liquid?
3. Is the firm achieving a satisfactory volume of sales in relation to its investment in current and fixed assets?
4. Is the firm earning a reasonable rate of return on sales, assets, and net worth?
5. How much could the firm's profits decline before it would be unable to meet fixed charges such as interest, rentals, and principal payments?
6. If the firm were to fail, how much could the assets shrink in value from the balance sheet figures before unsecured creditors would sustain any losses?
7. Is the firm's financial condition generally strong, weak, or something in between?

The reader will note that none of these questions relates directly to the firm's future profitability—a matter of great importance to a lender, particularly a lender of intermediate- or long-term money. In one way or another, it is necessary to estimate the probability that the borrower's profits will decline to levels that would make it impossible to comply with the repayment schedule of the proposed loan. The probable duration of any such periods of low profitability or losses should also be considered. This kind of forecasting usually requires a study of the competitive conditions, demand and supply conditions, and future prospects of the borrower's industry or industries. It also requires a careful analysis of the strengths and weaknesses of the borrowing firm itself: the quality of its management, the efficiency of its production organization, the effectiveness of its marketing, the health of its employee relations, the condition of its physical facilities, the availability and cost of labor and raw materials, the value of any intangibles such as patent rights and licensing agreements, and the possibility of contingent liabilities.

We will examine the ratios customarily found most useful in financial analysis to gain an appreciation of the insights ratio analysis can provide as well as an awareness of its limitations. Basically, there are four types of ratios: *liquidity, activity* (or *turnover*), *financial leverage,* and *profitability* (see Table 9-1). Each of these four aspects of a firm's financial health can be measured in more than one way by the use of ratios, and it is often useful to consider more than one measurement. In some instances, two similar ratios provide essentially the same information in different form, as in the case of the ratios of debt to total assets and debt to net worth, both of which are measures of the proportion of the firm's total financing that has been supplied by creditors. In other instances, two ratios of a given type provide essentially different information, as in the case of the current ratio and the acid-test or quick ratio, both of which are measures of liquidity. If the firm has a significant amount of inventories, the acid-test ratio is a far more stringent test of liquidity than is the current ratio, since inventories are included in the numerator of the current ratio but not in the acid-test ratio.

In working with financial ratios, it is important to keep in mind that proportionate increases in the numerator and denominator leave the ratio

TABLE 9-1 Commonly Used Financial Ratios

Type of Ratio	Name	Numerator	Denominator
1. Liquidity	Current ratio	Current assets	Current liabilities
2. Liquidity	Acid test	Current assets minus inventories	Current liabilities
3. Activity	Turnover of total assets	Net sales	Total assets
4. Activity	Turnover of fixed assets	Net sales	Net fixed assets
5. Activity	Collection period	Accounts receivable	Daily credit sales
5.*Activity	Turnover of receivables	Credit sales	Accounts receivable
6. Activity	Inventory turnover	Cost of sales	Inventories
7. Financial leverage	Debt/asset ratio	Total debt	Total assets
7.*Financial leverage	Debt/net worth ratio	Total debt	Net worth
8. Financial leverage	Fixed charges coverage	Earnings before fixed charges and taxes	Fixed charges
9. Profitability	Operating profit rate of return	Earnings before interest and taxes	Total tangible assets
10. Profitability	Net profit margin	Net profit	Net sales
11. Profitability	Return on assets	Net profit	Total assets
12. Profitability	Return on common equity	Net profit minus preferred dividends	Common stock equity

NOTE: Ratios 5* and 7* are alternatives to 5 and 7.

unchanged. For example, if the current assets of a firm increase from $400,000 to $600,000 and current liabilities from $200,000 to $300,000, the current ratio remains unchanged at 2 to 1. In this case, if one were to consider the current ratio alone, one would conclude that the firm's financial condition had not changed. But this conclusion could be very much in error. A more thorough investigation might reveal that current assets and current liabilities had both increased to levels that were too high in relation to the firm's sales, and that some of the firm's current assets were becoming quite illiquid. In this case the current ratio is misleading. Generally, it is unwise to consider a single financial ratio by itself without reference to other aspects of the firm's financial condition and profitability.

The use of ratios in financial analysis will be illustrated by comparing two business firms assumed to be operating in the same industry (see Tables 9-2 and 9-3). Company A is about twice as large as company B in terms of assets and sales. The 1989 financial statements and ratios for the two firms in the tables reveal a number of differences and highlight certain areas that seem to merit further investigation.

TABLE 9-2   Balance Sheets, December 31, 1989 (in thousands of dollars)

	Company A	Company B
Assets		
Cash	$ 200	$ 25
Accounts receivable	400	125
Inventories	600	500
Total current assets	$1,200	$ 650
Fixed assets (net)	2,100	750
Other assets	100	100
Total assets	$3,400	$1,500
Liabilities and net worth		
Accounts payable	$ 400	$ 175
Notes payable	100	10
Accrued liabilities	100	15
Total current liabilities	$ 600	$ 200
Deferred income taxes	400	50
Long-term debt	1,000	100
Common stock	400	300
Retained earnings	1,000	850
Total liabilities and net worth	$3,400	$1,500

TABLE 9-3 Income Statements, Year 1989 (in thousands of dollars)

	Company A	Company B
Sales	$4,200	$2,000
Cost of goods sold:		
Cash costs	2,470	1,280
Depreciation	200	125
Total	$2,670	$1,405
Gross profit	1,530	595
Selling and administrative expense	800	355
Operating profit	730	240
Interest expense	100	10
Earnings before taxes	630	230
Income taxes (40%)	252	92
Earnings after taxes	$ 378	$ 138

NOTE: State and federal income taxes combined are assumed to total 40 percent.

Liquidity and Activity Ratios

Looking at the liquidity ratios for companies A and B (Table 9-4), we see that A is less liquid than B in terms of the current ratio but more liquid in terms of the acid-test ratio. This reflects the substantial differences in the proportions of cash, accounts receivable, and inventories in the current assets of the two firms. Cash and accounts receivable are 50 percent of

TABLE 9-4 Liquidity, Activity, and Leverage Ratios

	Company A	Company B
Current ratio	2 : 1	3.25 : 1
Acid-test ratio	1 : 1	.75 : 1
Turnover of total assets	1.24	1.33
Turnover of fixed assets	2.00	2.67
Accounts receivable turnover	10.50	16.00
Collection period (360-day year)	34.3 days	22.5 days
Inventory turnover	4.45	2.81
Debt/asset ratio	.59 : 1	.23 : 1
Debt/net worth ratio	1.43 : 1	.30 : 1

NOTE: Deferred income taxes have been considered as debt in computing the leverage ratios.

total current assets for company A but only 23 percent of current assets for company B. In that respect, company A appears to be more liquid than B. However, we must also consider the quality of the receivables and inventories of the two firms, and neither the current ratio nor the acid-test ratio provides any information on that. One indicator of asset quality is the speed with which the asset appears to be turning over as measured by its relationship to sales in the case of accounts receivable, or cost of sales in the case of inventories.

In considering activity ratios, we will assume that operations for both firms were essentially level throughout the year, exhibiting little in the way of seasonal influences. With that assumption, it is appropriate to relate year-end accounts receivable to sales for the year and year-end inventories to cost of sales for the year. Otherwise, it might be more appropriate to relate receivables and inventories to sales and cost of sales for the last few months of the year. When inventories vary widely from month to month, analysts sometimes relate the average month-end inventories for the year to cost of sales for the year to get an average turnover figure. However, this computation obviously does not indicate whether inventories at year end were at a reasonable level. If it is the level of year-end inventories with which we are concerned, then it is the year-end inventories that should be related to a cost of sales figure. Such a turnover figure can then be compared with similar figures for other firms and with prior years' figures for the same firm.

The turnover figures for accounts receivable and inventories show that here, too, are significant differences between the two companies (Table 9-4). The turnover rate for the accounts receivable of company A is only about two-thirds that of company B. Or, in terms of collection periods, the 34.3 days for A is about 50 percent longer than the collection period of 22.5 days for B. With respect to inventories, the turnover rate of 4.45 for A is considerably faster than B's rate of 2.81. These differences in turnover rates appear large for two firms in the same industry.

A number of things could cause A's collection period to be 50 percent longer than B's. For example, A's credit and collection policies may simply not be as tight as B's, and this could mean that A's receivables are inferior in quality to B's. To determine whether a quality difference exists in the receivables, it would be a good idea to compare the credit terms of the two companies and to examine aging schedules of their accounts receivable to see the amounts that are past due and for what periods. It might be found that A has different credit terms from B. Another possibility is that the two firms sell largely to different types of customers. Or it could be that company B sells a substantial part of its receivables to a factoring firm, in which case the receivables remaining on B's books might actually be lower quality than A's, even though the reverse appears true at first glance.

The large difference in inventory turnover for the two firms (A's turnover being more than 50 percent greater than B's) would also seem to merit investigation. The turnover figures may indicate that A's inventory management is considerably better than B's, but there are a number of other possible explanations. It may be that A carries very "thin" inventories and loses some sales as a result. The two firms may sell to different classes of customers and use different channels of distribution, or have a different product mix. Or perhaps company B sells a substantial part of its total output on a consignment basis and finds itself with large inventories held by its consignees. Another possibility is that B is carrying large safety stocks in anticipation of interrupted shipments from one or more of its suppliers. These are examples of the many things that could account for the difference in the turnover ratios. Ratio analysis is useful principally in locating areas of possible difficulty or weakness. Once such areas have been discovered, it is necessary to investigate further to determine why the firm's ratios are out of line with those of other firms or with its own past norms.

Looking next at the total asset and fixed asset turnover ratios (Table 9-4), we find the first of these about equal for both companies, but the turnover of fixed assets is higher for B than for A. This could be due to B's having a more modern and efficient manufacturing facility than A. It could also be the result of B's utilizing its plant for more hours during the year by working crews at night or on weekends. The difference between the two might be of little significance if other ratios are considered acceptable.

Financial Leverage

The financial ratios in Table 9-4 show A's greater dependence on borrowed capital. It should be noted that in computing these ratios deferred income taxes have been treated as debt, even though it is possible that such taxes will not have to be paid for a very long time, if ever.

A third measure of financial leverage, in addition to the debt/asset and debt/net worth ratios, is the ratio of earnings before taxes and fixed charges to fixed charges, known as the fixed charges coverage. Although we will use the 1989 figures to compute the coverage of fixed charges, it should be recognized that a bank lending officer's real concern is with the extent to which the future fixed charges of a firm, including those associated with any loan the bank is considering for the firm, will be covered by future earnings. In computing the fixed charges coverage, we will assume that the annual principal payments are $100,000 for A and $10,000 for B. Fixed charges include rentals, interest expense, and principal payments. Principal payments must be converted to a before-tax basis (since they are not deductible for tax purposes), and this is done by dividing the payments by 1 minus the income tax rate. With an income tax rate of 40 percent, the principal payments are divided by .60. So we find that A must earn approximately $167,000 before taxes, and B, $17,000, to make their principal payments of $100,000 and $10,000. As shown in Table 9-5, the coverages of fixed charges for the two firms are very different.

Assuming that all of the earnings are available to pay fixed charges, the earnings of company A would still cover fixed charges if a decline of 63 percent were experienced, but B would still be able to cover fixed charges if its earnings dropped 89 percent. Although coverage of fixed charges is widely used as a measure of financial condition, it is important to recognize the limitations of this ratio. The numerator of the ratio (earnings before taxes and fixed charges) is a very crude measure of a firm's capacity to make required payments, and the denominator does not include all payments that a firm may be required to make. Nevertheless, the ratio is useful because cash inflows do depend to a considerable extent on earnings, and because payments under loan agreements and noncancelable leases do in many cases represent a firm's most significant financial obligations. A projection of the coverage of fixed charges, however, is not an adequate substitute for detailed forecasts of cash inflows and outflows. The fixed charges coverage ratio is not in terms of cash flows and does not take into account, for example, the cash required to finance an increase in net working capital or an increase in net fixed assets. To evaluate properly a firm's ability to make future loan payments, cash forecasts should be prepared using various plausible assumptions as to sales volumes, selling prices, and costs. In this way it is possible to estimate the probability that the borrower will be able to comply with the repayment provisions of the proposed loan.

Profitability

The profitability ratios of the two firms are set forth in Table 9-6. Company A emerges as the most profitable under all profitability ratios. It is performing particularly well for its stockholders in comparison with B.

TABLE 9-5   Fixed Charges Coverage, Year 1989 (in thousands of dollars)

	Company A	Company B
Operating profit	$730	$240
Interest expense	100	10
Principal payments (before-tax basis)	167	17
Total fixed charges	$267	$ 27
Fixed charges coverage	2.7X	9.0X

TABLE 9-6   Profitability Ratios and Fixed Charges Coverage

	Company A	Company B
Operating profit rate of return	21.5%	16.0%
Net profit margin	9.0	6.9
Return on assets	11.1	9.2
Return on common equity	27.0	12.0
Fixed charges coverage	2.7X	9.0X

NOTE: Computation of the fixed charges coverage is based on the assumption that annual principal payments for A and B (in thousands) are $100 and $10, respectively. See details in Table 9-5.

In addition to looking at these ratios, the analyst will want to determine whether there are any significant differences in the accounting practices of the two firms that affect the profit comparisons. If so, it might be wise to explore the possibility of adjusting the earnings so as to place them on the same basis. The analyst will also want to examine the profit trends of the two firms over a period of years.

While company A is clearly more profitable, company B is much less dependent on debt, as is shown by its strong leverage ratios and high fixed charges coverage. Which is the preferred loan applicant? This depends on the answers to a number of questions, including the purposes of the requested loans and each firm's potential within its market. However, A has demonstrated its ability to earn high rates of profit while B has maintained a strong liquidity position. Profitability is often more important in judging the desirability of making a long-term loan, whereas short-term loan decisions may rest more on the strength of a firm's liquidity.

Ratio Trends

Significant developments often come to light through an examination of the trends of a firm's financial ratios over a period of years. Just as it is helpful to compare the ratios for one firm with those of other firms or with industry averages, it may also be helpful to see whether a firm's financial condition or profitability is improving or deteriorating and, if so, in what respects. Based on the 1989 figures, company A appears to be more profitable than B, but if A's return on assets has been declining steadily for the last few years and B's has been improving, an investigation of the reasons for the profit trends might indicate that B's return will soon be as high or higher than A's. In any event, the directions in which a firm's financial condition and profitability have been moving are matters of great interest, since they may provide an indication as to what the future will be. Of course, sales and profit trends often change direction, sometimes quite abruptly, so it is never wise to forecast earnings by simply extrapolating from past trends. Often it is desirable to examine in depth the strengths and weaknesses not only of the loan applicant but also of the industry in which the firm is operating. This involves a study of the demand and supply conditions in the industry. In the final analysis, a bank lending officer wants to know where the firm's sales and profits have come from in the past and where they can be expected to come from in the future.

SOURCES OF COMPARATIVE FINANCIAL INFORMATION

Financial ratios for various industries can be found in a number of places, one of which is *Annual Statement Studies* published by Robert Morris Associates. This volume contains composite financial data for over 340 different lines of business, based on the financial statements of approximately 67,000 different firms. The figures are presented for four size groups of companies within each industry and for the industry as a whole. The number of business firms in each group is shown along with the financial data, which consist principally of 16 financial ratios and a common-size balance sheet and income statement for each group. In the common-size statements, each balance sheet item is shown as a percentage of total assets and each income statement item as a percentage of sales. Three values are reported for each of the ratios for each group of firms: the upper quartile, the median, and the lower quartile. This method of reporting the ratios avoids distortions that could be caused by a few extreme ratios if an arithmetic mean were used, and it gives a good indication as to the dispersion of the ratios within each group of companies. For example, if a credit analyst finds that some ratios for a particular firm are either substantially above the upper quartile or below the lower quartile, it can readily be seen that they are unusual. The editors of *Annual Statement Studies* point out to the reader that the figures contain inconsistencies. First, the sample of companies is not selected in a scientific manner. Second, many companies operate in more than one industry, yet they are placed in the industry of their primary product line. The editors recommend, therefore, that the figures be used as general guidelines rather than as absolute norms for a given industry.

Dun & Bradstreet also is a source of financial ratios covering approximately 800 lines of business. Fourteen ratios are published annually for these firms in Dun & Bradstreet's *Key Business Ratios*. Another source of ratios is the *Almanac of Business and Industrial Ratios* published by Prentice Hall. Still another is the Federal Trade Commission's *Quarterly Financial Report for Manufacturing Corporations*.

Financial analysis software is available from numerous companies that incorporate ratios from Robert Morris Associates or other sources. A properly selected program can be of great benefit to credit analysts in making calculations, organizing data, and making comparisons, but such a program is not a replacement for the skills of the analyst. Rather, the increasing sophistication of computerized financial analysis systems calls for commensurately skilled credit analysts to make the best use of the systems.

CASH BUDGETS AND PRO FORMA FINANCIAL STATEMENTS

In evaluating a proposed business loan, it is not only important to consider how funds will be obtained for repayment of the loan but also to forecast what the borrower's financial condition will be at various times over the life of the loan. Information of this kind is developed in cash budgets and pro forma financial statements. Although such statements will often be quite wide of the mark, their preparation and use are necessary when planning for the future. The accuracy of pro forma statements depends heavily on the assumptions made about future developments, so bank lending officers are interested in the reasonableness of such assumptions. A forecast of a substantial increase in income, for example, based on an unprecedented rise in sales or a sharp decline in unit costs, would certainly be questioned. All borrowers do not provide lending officers with pro forma financial statements. Many are not accustomed to making such projections, and in some cases they are not necessary. If the maturity is short and the loan well secured, elaborate statements are not required. The longer the maturity, the greater the need for pro forma statements in making a proper analysis of a loan request.

Cash budgets for larger firms are typically prepared for the most part from the information contained in projected income statements and balance sheets. A satisfactory analysis of the projected sources and uses of cash can usually be prepared from the income statement and comparative balance sheet information. Sources of cash include decreases in assets and increases in the liabilities and net worth of the firm. Uses of cash include increases in assets and decreases in liabilities and net worth. Reference to projected income statement figures makes it possible to show some of the more important details underlying the balance sheet changes. Net profit and noncash charges (principally depreciation) are shown as sources of cash, while dividends and the net addition to gross fixed assets are shown as uses of cash.

Besides serving as a source of information from which cash budgets can be prepared, pro forma financial statements can be used directly in appraising the level of risk in a proposed loan. For this purpose they can be subjected to ratio analysis in the same way as historical statements. The usefulness of cash budgets and pro forma statements does not end with the approval of the loan. The borrower's actual performance and financial condition in future periods can be compared with the earlier projections. Such comparisons may give an indication as to why the borrower's profits and financial condition are either better or worse than expected, and this may be helpful in deciding whether any action should be taken to protect the interests of the bank.

QUESTIONS

1. Why does analysis of the balance sheet receive relatively more emphasis than analysis of the income statement in the case of short-term loans, while the reverse is true in the case of long-term loans?
2. The credit analysis performed by your bank shows that a potential business borrower does not quite qualify for a loan from your bank. You are the loan officer who must tell the applicant that his firm does not qualify for a loan. How do you tell him?
3. What does it mean if the current ratio is rising and the quick ratio is falling?
4. What would it mean if the return on assets was declining but the return on equity was rising?
5. Certain ratios vary widely from industry to industry. For example, in comparing the retail grocery industry with most other industries, would you expect the current ratio to appear high or low? Why? What about turnover of total assets and net profit margin?
6. A high inventory turnover ratio would normally be considered to indicate efficient inventory management. However, an exceptionally high ratio could carry negative implications. Why?
7. Which of the C's of credit would you consider to be the most difficult to evaluate? Why?

SELECTED REFERENCES

ALTMAN, EDWARD I. Financial Handbook, 5th ed. New York: John Wiley, 1981, pt. 4.

HELFERT, ERICH A. Techniques of Financial Analysis, 6th ed. Homewood, Ill.: Richard D. Irwin, 1986.

LEVINE, SUMNER, ed. Financial Analysts Handbook. Homewood, Ill.: Richard D. Irwin, 1975, sec. 4.

MORRIS, (ROBERT) ASSOCIATES. *Annual Statement Studies.* Philadelphia: Robert Morris Associates, annual.

NORDGREN, ROGER K. "Understanding Cash Flow: A Key Step in Financial Analysis." *The Journal of Commercial Bank Lending* (May 1986), pp. 2–17.

O'MALIA, THOMAS J. *Banker's Guide to Financial Statements,* 2nd ed. Boston: Bankers Publishing Co., 1982.

SIHLER, WILLIAM W., ed. *Classics in Commercial Bank Lending.* Philadelphia: Robert Morris Associates, 1981.

STRISCHEK, DEV. "Return of the Leveraged Debtor: ROA vs ROE." *The Journal of Commercial Bank Lending* (May 1987), pp. 2–12.

10

LENDING PRACTICES AND POLICIES

Lending is the most important activity of commercial banks. Table 10-1 shows that loans were 59 percent of bank assets at the end of 1986. Typically, 65 to 70 percent of bank income is generated by the lending activity. The success of a bank is heavily dependent on its lending programs, and successful lending emanates from well-formulated lending policy.

CLASSIFICATION OF LOANS

Bank loans can be classified in a variety of ways, including purpose, the type of security if any, maturity, method of repayment, and origin. Other classifications exist, but these are sufficient to give us an understanding of the lending activities of commercial banks.

Purpose

A common classification of loans is by purpose or use of the borrowed funds. The broad categories of loans are shown in Table 10-1. Loans to individuals are primarily for autos and other consumer goods. The category "Other loans and leases" consists largely of loans to other financial institutions, to state and local governments, and for the purpose of buying and carrying securities.

TABLE 10-1   Loans of FDIC-Insured Commercial Banks, December 31, 1986 (in millions of dollars)

Total Assets	$2,940,940
Real estate loans	515,214
Commercial and industrial loans	600,860
Loans to individuals	335,741
Farm loans	31,694
Other loans and leases	272,972
Total loans and leases	1,756,481
Less: Reserve for losses	28,786
Net loans and leases	$1,727,695

SOURCE: Federal Deposit Insurance Corporation, *Quarterly Banking Profile*, First Quarter, 1987.

Secured and Unsecured Loans

Secured loans involve the pledge of specific collateral. An example is a loan that is secured by a chattel mortgage on an automobile or some other form of personal property. Pledged collateral for secured loans may consist of a variety of assets such as real estate, warehouse receipts, accounts receivable, plants and equipment, trust receipts, negotiable bills of lading, oil runs, corporate stocks, and bonds. The basic requirement of such assets is marketability. The main reason for requesting that a loan be secured is to reduce the bank's risk of loss in the event that the borrower is unwilling or unable to repay the loan at maturity. Security does not assure that the loan will be repaid; however, it does reduce the risk, since the bank becomes a preferred creditor in the event of liquidation, and takes precedence over general creditors in the liquidation of any assets pledged to the bank as collateral.

The value of the assets securing a loan may deteriorate, and this deterioration, coupled with a forced sale, may not furnish sufficient funds to cover the indebtedness. In arranging security for a loan, it is imperative that the bank obtain the primary claim to the collateral and that its value be as great as, or greater than, the amount of the loan. Should the value of the collateral exceed the amount of the loan, and the bank be forced to liquidate it because of default on the part of the borrower, the excess is returned to the borrower. In the event that the security is not sufficient to cover the loan, the bank can in some instances obtain, through court proceedings, a deficiency judgment for the difference. This entitles the bank to a claim on additional property or income, should the borrower have any. In recent years some states have enacted legislation limiting the use of deficiency judgments in the area of consumer lending. In most instances this has taken the form of eliminating the deficiency judgment when the loan is reduced below a certain level. The objective of limiting deficiency judgments was to reduce overcharging on consumer durable goods at the retail level. The limitation was later extended to lenders as well. Limiting the use of the deficiency judgment increased the risk of lending and probably reduced the availability of credit to certain borrowers.

Security is required on loans for several reasons. One of the most common is the borrower's financial weakness. Such weakness may be indicated by several factors, including heavy obligations to creditors, poor management, and insufficient income. Borrowers in this financial condition can strengthen their credit by pledging certain assets. Having a secured loan may also be a psychological advantage for a bank. As long as the borrower has greater equity in the pledged assets than does the bank and the bank is in a preferred position and can foreclose in the event the loan agreement is broken, the borrower has a strong incentive to repay the obligation. The length of a loan also has a bearing on whether it will be secured. As the term of the loan lengthens, the risk of nonrepayment increases. Loans for purchasing real estate are nearly always secured, especially if the funds are borrowed for long periods of time, because of risk of nonrepayment.

Several federal agencies have been created by Congress since the 1930s that, as one of their functions, guarantee loans granted by commercial banks and certain other lenders. Such agencies include the Federal Housing Administration and the Small Business Administration.

Unsecured loans are based on the borrower's integrity and financial condition, expected future income, and past record of repayment. Contrary to popular belief, the largest loans and the greatest dollar volume of loans made by some banks are granted on an unsecured basis. The largest commercial borrowers are able to borrow on an unsecured basis. Some companies are considered by banks to be prime borrowers, and in many cases they receive the most favorable interest rate. Such companies have competent management, products and services that are well accepted in the marketplace, relatively stable profits, and a strong financial condition. They provide their banks with financial statements from which it is relatively easy to determine their financial condition and keep track of their progress.

Business firms are not the only ones who borrow on an unsecured basis—many individuals enjoy this privilege. Persons who own their own homes, have steady jobs, and have records of prompt payment often borrow on an unsecured basis.

Maturity

Bank loans can be classified according to the maturity of the loan contract as short, intermediate, or long term. Short-term loans are usually defined as those with maturities of one year or less, intermediate loans mature in more than one year and up to seven or eight years, and long-term loans have still longer maturities. Short-term loans may be made for a specific period of time—up to a year—or on a demand basis. A demand loan is one that has no stated maturity, and, since it is payable on demand, repayment can be requested at any time. The granting of a demand loan often implies that the borrower is in a relatively liquid position and that the assets in which the borrowed funds have been invested can be liquidated in a very short time.

A great deal of vagueness surrounds the definition of an intermediate loan. It is not uncommon to find a loan made for a period of ten years considered an intermediate loan. Many consumer loans may be classified as intermediate. Business term loans, which have increased greatly in recent years, usually have maturities of ten years or less. Real estate loans for the purchase of houses and for the financing of industrial and commercial buildings are the most common type of long-term loans.

Method of Repayment

Bank loans may be repaid in one lump sum or on an installment basis. Lump-sum loans are usually referred to as *straight loans*, which means that the contract calls for repayment of the entire principal on one final maturity date. Some loans are payable on demand or, if demand is not made, on a specified maturity date. Interest payments, however, might be due at various intervals or when the loan matures. Installment loans require periodic payments of principal. Payments may be monthly, quarterly, semiannually, or annually. Installment lending recognizes the principle of amortization, whereby the principal amount is amortized over the life of the contract. In this manner repayments do not become as great a burden on the borrower as if the total loan were due at one time. For example, in real estate lending the repayment schedule is comparable to the rent a person would pay if he or she were renting rather than buying a house. Installment loans serve as a budgeting instrument for many people. Repayment of loans on an installment basis is not reserved exclusively for consumer and real estate loans. Many term loans to businesses are made on this basis, with payments closely tied to the amount of income generated by the borrower.

Origin

The loan portfolio of commercial banks is derived principally from four major sources: directly from borrowers, by the purchase of notes from dealers of automobiles and other consumer goods, by purchasing "participations" in loans originated by other banks, and by purchasing notes from commercial paper dealers. By far the largest number of loans are made directly to borrowers who apply for loans at the banking office. Included in this category would be loans resulting from credit card purchases, since cardholders originally made application for their cards at the bank.

Many banks derive a large portion of their loan portfolio by purchasing notes from dealers of various products. A final source of loans, less important than those already discussed, is the purchase of commercial paper and bankers' acceptances.

REGULATION OF BANK LENDING

Bank lending is highly regulated for a number of reasons. One is to protect the safety of banks, an example of which is a limitation placed on the amount of credit that can be extended to a single borrower. The objective of such a rule is to avoid undue concentration and reduce risk. In recent years Congress has enacted several statutes designed to protect borrowers that are applicable to all lenders including commercial banks. These include the Truth-in-Lending Act (1968), which is intended to ensure that prospective borrowers will be advised of the effective costs of the credit for which they are applying; the Fair Credit Reporting Act (1971), one of whose principal purposes is to protect borrowers from being denied credit because of erroneous information in their credit files; and the Equal Credit Opportunity Act (1974), which prohibits lenders from discriminating on the basis of sex, marital status, race, color, religion, national origin, or the receipt of public assistance benefits.

Another reason for regulating bank lending is to encourage or limit particular kinds of lending because of the expected impact on the economy. The Community Reinvestment Act (1977), for example, is intended to ensure that banks meet the credit needs of their market areas, consistent with sound lending practices, and including the needs of low and moderate income neighborhoods. Regulation U of the Federal Reserve Board, issued pursuant to the Securities Exchange Act of 1934, limits the amount that can be loaned to purchase or hold securities and is designed to reduce speculation.

In the past, banks generally were limited in the amount that could be loaned to one borrower to 10 percent of capital and surplus. The passage of the Garn-St Germain Depository Institutions Act in late 1982 expanded the loan limit to 15 percent of capital and surplus for loans "not fully secured." Additional amounts fully secured by marketable collateral can be loaned up to an additional 10 percent of capital and surplus. Thus a loan to one borrower, if 10 percent is fully secured, can equal 25 percent of unimpaired capital and surplus.

The act also set forth several exceptions to these limitations where no limits apply. One of these pertains to loans secured by obligations of, or guaranteed by, the United States. Another pertains to loans to the

Student Loan Marketing Association. Yet another applies to loans secured by deposits in the lending bank. Several other partial exceptions provide a straight 25 percent limitation.

The 15 percent restriction is designed to limit the amount of risk concentrated in credit extended to any one borrower. Exceptions to the rule are justified on the grounds that the loans are well secured or are secured by collateral that will maintain its value and marketability during the life of the loan. The rule limits the small bank in making loans to relatively large borrowers and, as a result, encourages them to seek larger banks to participate in loans that exceed the small bank's legal limit. It also encourages banks to increase their capital stock and surplus accounts so that they will be in a position to make larger loans. The lending limit in the past has encouraged the merger of banks for the same reason.

Real estate lending has been closely regulated since the adoption of the National Bank Act of 1864, but over the years the regulations have been liberalized. Both the amount of loans that a bank can make and the maturity of individual residential loans have been increased. These limitations are discussed more fully in the chapter on real estate lending.

Loans to executive officers are closely regulated in amount and purpose, and loans to bank examiners are prohibited. In general, banks are prohibited from making loans secured by their own stock. If lending on this type of security were permitted, it would be possible for bank owners to borrow from the bank the equity that is necessary for the protection of the depositors. The reason for this law is obvious—the practice would be contrary to the public interest. However, national banks are permitted to make loans secured by the bank's own stock in cases where it is necessary to prevent loss on a debt previously contracted in good faith. If such a loan is made and defaulted, the stock must be sold at public or private sale within six months.

Loans to affiliates and bank holding companies are closely regulated. In general, a bank cannot invest in or purchase the securities of these organizations. However, it can lend to them under certain conditions. The securities pledged for such loans must have a market value of at least 20 percent more than the amount of credit extended unless they are securities of governments, in which case the margin may be less. These provisions do not apply to affiliates such as those engaged in holding bank premises or conducting a safe deposit business.

Secured bank loans must meet various requirements established by regulatory and supervisory authorities to ensure that the bank has a valid and enforceable claim. Real estate loans made by national banks, for example, must be secured by a mortgage, trust deed, or other instrument that constitutes a lien in fee simple. If warehouse receipts are taken as security, the commodities they represent must be in the exclusive possession and control of a genuine independent public warehouse operator. Loans secured by the cash value of an insurance policy must be recognized by the life insurance company.

LOAN POLICY

The restrictions imposed by statutory law and administrative regulations do not provide answers to many questions regarding safe, sound, and profitable bank lending. Questions regarding the size of the loan portfolio, desirable maturities, and the types of loans to be made are left unanswered. These questions and many others about lending must be answered by each individual bank. Thus, it is desirable to have explicit lending policies to establish the direction and use of the funds from stockholders, depositors, and others; to control the composition and size of the loan portfolio; and to determine the general circumstances under which it is appropriate to make a loan. More and more banks have developed formal, written lending policies in recent years. The Comptroller of the Currency insists that national banks have such policies. Although written lending policies serve a number of purposes, the most important is that they provide guidance for lending officers and thereby establish a greater degree of uniformity in lending practices.

FACTORS THAT INFLUENCE A BANK'S LOAN POLICIES

Since lending is important both to the bank and to the community it serves, loan policies must be worked out carefully after considering many factors. For the most part, these same factors determine the size and composition of the secondary reserve and the investment account of a bank. Many of these factors have been discussed elsewhere and are mentioned here only briefly. The most important are

1. Capital position
2. Risk and profitability of various types of loans
3. Stability of deposits
4. Economic conditions
5. Influence of monetary and fiscal policy
6. Ability and experience of bank personnel
7. Credit needs of the area served

The capital of a bank serves as a cushion for the protection of the depositor's funds. The size of capital in relation to deposits influences the amount of risk that a bank can afford to take. Banks with a relatively large capital structure can make loans of longer maturities and greater credit risk.

Since earnings are necessary for the successful operation of a bank, all banks consider this important factor in formulating loan policy. Some banks may emphasize earnings more than others. Banks with greater need for earnings might adopt more aggressive lending polices than those that do not consider earnings to be paramount. An aggressive policy might call for making a relatively large amount of term or consumer loans, which normally are made at higher rates of interest than short-term business loans.

The fluctuation and types of deposits must be considered by a bank in formulating its loan policy. After adequate provisions have been made for the primary and secondary reserves, banks can then engage in lending. Even though these two reserves are designed to take care of predictable deposit fluctuations and loan demands, unpredictable demands force banks to give consideration to the stability of deposits in formulating loan policy.

The economic conditions of the area served by a bank are influential in determining its loan policy. A stable economy is more conducive to a liberal loan policy than is one that is subject to seasonal and cyclical movements. Deposits of feast or famine economies fluctuate more violently than do deposits in an economy noted for its stability. Consideration must also be given to the national economy. Factors that adversely affect the nation as a whole may, if they are of serious magnitude, eventually affect local conditions.

The lending ability of banks is influenced by monetary and fiscal policies. If monetary and fiscal policies are expansive and additional reserves are made available to the commercial banking system, the lending ability of banks is increased. Under these conditions banks can have a more liberal loan policy than if the opposite situation exists.

The expertise of lending personnel is not insignificant in the establishment of bank loan policy. For example, officers may have considerable ability and experience in business lending but practically none in making real estate loans, while in other banks their specialty may be consumer lending. One of the probable reasons that banks were slow in entering the consumer lending field was the lack of skilled personnel. Some banks may be so specialized in certain fields of lending that their presence may influence the loan policy of other banks.

An obvious factor influencing a commercial bank's loan policy is the area it serves. The major reason banks are chartered is to serve the credit needs of their communities. If this cannot be done, there is little justification for their existence. Banks are morally bound to extend credit to borrowers who present logical and economically sound loan requests. Banks in areas where the economy is predominantly one of cattle raising, for example, cannot turn their back on this type of lending, but must tailor policy to fit the needs of this economic activity.

ITEMS INCLUDED IN A LOAN POLICY

Written loan policies differ greatly from bank to bank, both as to the items included and the extent to which policy items are explained. The following items, however, should be common to most loan policies.

Loan Territory

The territory to be served by a bank will depend on many factors, including the amount of its resources, competition, the demand for loans, and the bank's ability to supervise or keep in close contact with the borrowers. Banks may have no territorial limitations for certain classes of loans. For example, very large banks make loans to large national business firms no matter where their principal offices may be located.

Types of Loans to Be Made

Bank management must decide what types of loans would be best for the bank. Some of the more important considerations in making this decision are the risks associated with various kinds of loans, the need for diversification to spread the risk, the need for liquidity, the types of customers the bank wants to serve, the capabilities of bank personnel, and, certainly, the relative profitability of various kinds of loans. To the extent that it is practicable, banks diversify their loan portfolios among the various broad categories of loans such as business, consumer, and agricultural and strive also for considerable diversification within each of these broad categories.

Acceptable Security and Creditworthiness

To facilitate lending, reduce risks, and maintain standard practices, a bank's loan policy should deal with the question of what is considered acceptable security and creditworthiness. If certain loans are to be secured, the lending officers should have some indication of what is acceptable security. For example, some banks may not want to accept accounts receivable as security, except on a notification basis, or may frown on accepting consumer loans that are endorsed by the borrower's friends or relatives. Banks may not wish to make real estate loans on single-purpose buildings. Construction loans may be made only in cases where the work is being supervised by a competent architect and the contractor has provided a completion bond and acceptable security. Banks may not want to lend more than a certain percentage of the fair market value of farm chattels or a certain percentage of the retail price of automobiles. Some collateral may not be acceptable at all, such as cars over five years old or highly perishable commodities. Banks may wish to limit the amount of individual consumer loans to a certain percentage of a borrower's annual disposable income. For acceptable collateral, an indication should be given as to the amount of funds that will be advanced on such security.

Banks receive many requests for loans from applicants who do not have acceptable creditworthiness. To save the time of the credit department and lending officers, policy should outline what is considered acceptable. Consumer loans might be restricted to persons who are presently employed and have been for a minimum period and who have an assured income and a satisfactory credit record. Loans to business people may be restricted to those who have been in business for a certain length of time and have demonstrated an ability to produce a commodity or render a service profitably.

Credit analysis was discussed in detail in the last chapter. While all the specific procedures of credit analysis need not be inserted in the loan policy, the policy should make clear what the results of the analysis should mean in the lending process. For example, how strong financially must an applicant be to justify receiving an unsecured loan or, at the other extreme, what should the analysis show to justify rejecting a loan application? Policy should also indicate how credit analysis should be applied on an ongoing basis as long as credit is outstanding.

Maturities

Loan policy should cover the extent to which a bank will make and hold intermediate- and long-term loans so that a consistent approach to protecting against the interest rate risk of such loans can be followed. The maturity of a bank's loan portfolio will affect bank liquidity as well as its risk exposure. Term loans to businesses are less liquid than 30-, 60-, or 90-day business loans, and the 20-year real estate loan lacks the liquidity of one made for a period of 10 years. As loan maturities increase, credit risks also have a tendency to increase. Some banks may not wish to make loans on real estate for exceptionally long periods, and some may not want to make many business loans on a term basis. Moreover, some banks may wish to limit loans for the purchase of new automobiles to 36 months, while others may consider 48 months appropriate. To serve as a guide for the loan officer, the policy regarding maturities should be definite.

Excess Lines

One problem confronting many banks is that of loan requests exceeding their legal lending limit. The applicant may be a customer of the bank who is entitled to the credit requested, and the loan would be satisfactory from the standpoint of security and maturity. The bank is then faced with the choice of either working out a satisfactory arrangement with a correspondent bank to carry the excess portion of the loan or of refusing the request and running the risk of losing the applicant's account, which may be valued highly. Some banks may not handle such requests or even lend up to their limit. Others may have a policy of arranging for a correspondent bank to carry the excess loan.

Loan Liquidation

To maintain an acceptable degree of loan quality and liquidity, a bank must have an adequate policy of loan liquidation. Numerous renewals of a loan impair the liquidity of the loan portfolio and increase the risk. Moreover, a *slow* loan becomes subject to an unfavorable classification by bank examiners. Some banks may want all business borrowers to liquidate their loans, other than term loans and revolving credit, once each year and to stay out of debt to the bank for a reasonable period of time. Missed payments are frowned upon, and after a few occur, corrective steps—even legal action—may be taken.

Problem Loans

Steps that may be taken after a creditor falls behind in making loan payments or some other act of default occurs are the subject of Chapter 15. Loan policy should describe warning signs that indicate problems with a borrower may be developing and what steps the bank should take as these appear. One question policy should resolve is whether a loan, once it becomes a problem loan, should be administered by the officer previously responsible or whether the bank should employ one or more officers who specialize in handling problem loans.

Compensating Balances

Banks require borrowers to carry a deposit balance with them; after all, borrowers must carry a deposit somewhere, and the most logical place is with the lending institution. Moreover, loans cannot be made unless banks have deposits. The term *compensating balance* is used to describe a deposit balance primarily of a business firm that is required and is part of the consideration for the extension of credit. If the balance thus required is greater than the borrower otherwise would have carried, the effective rate on a loan is increased. Compensating balances may also be used as a protective device for a lending bank. If the borrower experiences financial difficulties and it appears that default is imminent, the bank may be able to apply the borrower's deposit to the balance of the loan.

Compensating balance requirements vary among banks and are influenced by conditions in the money market. A common requirement is referred to as "10 plus 10," meaning that the deposit balance required is 10 percent of the unused portion of a loan and another 10 percent once the loan is made for a total of 20 percent of the unpaid balance. Under such an arrangement, a borrower who has a commitment for $1,000,000 would carry a deposit of $100,000 during the time the loan was committed until it was used, and once the funds were drawn down would carry an average deposit of $200,000.

Although compensating balances are looked upon with favor by commercial banks, they have lost some popularity in recent years. The growing emphasis on commercial bank profitability analysis has caused banks to become increasingly aware of all the costs and benefits associated with a borrower's account. Two disadvantages in requiring a compensating balance rather than a higher lending rate are that legal reserves must be carried against the balance and an FDIC assessment must be paid. Because of these factors, the benefits received by the bank from the borrower's balances are apt to be less than their cost to the borrower. Thus, in some cases it is better to charge a higher lending rate than to require a compensating balance.

Loan Commitments

Many bank customers, especially large business borrowers, plan their borrowing needs with the bank in advance of the time the funds will be needed. Therefore, banks adopt policies regarding the types of commitments that will be made, the types of enterprises to which they will be made, the amounts that will be made available, and the charge for such commitments. Such planning is of value to the bank in that it gives some indication as to the demand for credit during certain periods of the year, and plans can be made regarding the maturity of other loans and secondary reserve securities.

A commitment is an agreement, oral or written, between a bank and a borrower whereby the bank stands ready to extend an agreed amount of credit for a specified period of time. A commitment may have no restrictions attached or may be subject to a number of conditions such as compensating balances, security, fixed asset limitations, officer salary limitations, and so on. Normally, loan commitments do not exceed one year and may take several forms. Probably the simplest form is an oral commitment that a certain amount of credit will be available at a certain time in the future. Many loan commitments take this informal arrangement and are referred to as open lines of credit. It is not uncommon for such a statement to be in written form, however. An even more formal commitment would be what is commonly referred to as a *standby commitment*.

A standby commitment is usually a more binding and exacting financial arrangement than is a line of credit. The bank and the borrower enter into a formal contract in which the bank agrees to lend a certain amount to the borrower. The agreement includes a statement regarding the time the funds will be available and such lending terms as security, interest rate, and liquidation of the loan. The borrower pays a fee for this commitment that is usually based on the unborrowed amount of the commitment.

A revolving credit is usually of longer maturity than is a line of credit. It firmly obligates the bank to lend a certain amount to a borrower for a stated period. The terms of the agreement are written out in detail since the agreement usually runs from one to three or more years. Under a revolving credit, the borrower agrees to borrow in accordance with the terms set forth and to pay a fee that is usually computed on the unborrowed portion of the established maximum. A revolving credit agreement can become quite detailed and can include such items as the use of the borrowed funds, the rate of interest, the maturities of the notes, submission of financial statements and other financial and production data, security, and, in case of default, provisions regarding termination of the agreement and repayment of the loans outstanding.

Size of the Loan Portfolio

What proportion of a bank's assets should consist of loans is a matter of overall bank policy and, by extension, a guiding element in the loan policy. Since loans are generally the most profitable assets held by banks, there is constant pressure to increase the relative size of the loan portfolio. However, loans generally are less liquid and carry more credit risk than most of the securities banks buy, so the size of the loan portfolio must be limited.

No categorical answer exists as to what is the optimum size of a bank's loan portfolio. Every bank operates within an environment of its own. The credit demands of the community, the depositor's demands for funds, capital funds, the abilities of bank personnel, and the liquidity needs are all different for different banks. The size of a loan portfolio must be computed by analysis of the various needs or priorities for bank funds. Since priorities vary, it is impossible to establish hard and fast rules regarding the size of the loan portfolio of an individual bank or the banking system as a whole.

Bank loan portfolios have increased over the years as measured by the loan-to-deposit ratio. In general, large money center banks have higher loan-to-deposit ratios than do smaller rural banks. Several factors have contributed to these higher ratios. In addition to the desire to increase income, the ability to maintain liquidity has contributed greatly to this trend. The federal funds market and improvements in both asset and liability management have contributed greatly to a rise in the loan-to-deposit ratio as well as an improvement in credit analysis and the evaluation of credit risk. Finally, an expanding economy without many serious downturns has also contributed to a favorable lending market.

LOAN PRICING

The pricing of bank loans involves the setting of interest rates, the establishment of a compensating balance requirement—especially for business firms—and in many cases, the imposition of loan fees. Interest rates may be either fixed or variable. As the term implies, a *fixed rate* is one that remains the same during the loan contract. A *variable rate* is one that may change during the term of the loan due to changes in the reference rate or index to which it is tied. Until recent years the reference rate used for most variable rate loans was the *prime rate*, the rate charged the most creditworthy business borrowers. The prime continues to be the reference rate for most small and intermediate-sized business loans and is generally understood to be a bank's base lending rate. In recent years, however, many large, short-term business loans have been pegged to a money market rate, and these rates typically are below the prime. This change has come about due to competition from the commercial paper market and foreign lenders.[1] Also, many residential real estate loans are made on a floating rate basis. The rates on these *adjustable rate mortgages* (ARMs) usually are adjusted, every six months, due to changes on U.S. Treasury securities of certain maturities or an index of open market interest rates. Assuming a loan is tied to the prime, it might be made at a rate of one or two percentage points above the prime rate. For example, if the prime rate were 8 percent and the rate were set at 10 percent, the interest would change automatically as the prime rate increased or decreased. The reason for this type of arrangement is the belief on the part of both borrowers and bankers that it is more equitable than negotiated rates, and it helps the bank to reduce the interest rate risk inherent in fixed rate loans.

Fees are charged on many loans. Commitment and loan origination fees have become much more common in recent years as interest margins

---

[1] Thomas F. Brady, "Changes in Loan Pricing and Business Lending at Commercial Banks," *Federal Reserve Bulletin* (January 1985), pp. 1–13.

on loans have deteriorated. Fees are found especially in the granting of term loans and in real estate lending. Commitment fees are charged in many cases in connection with credit lines, revolving credit agreements, and commercial real estate loans.

The numerous factors that are considered in pricing loans include

1. The direct interest cost of funds.
2. Bank overhead expense.
3. The costs of originating and administering the loan. These costs, as a percentage of the loan, are a function of the size of the loan, the amount of credit investigation required, the cost of acquiring and maintaining control of the collateral, and the expense of collecting the loan.
4. The credit (default) risk of the loan.
5. The maturity (interest rate) risk of the loan.
6. Rates available to the borrower from competitive sources of funds, including other lenders and the commercial paper and bond markets.
7. The overall relationship between the bank and the borrower. This includes income earned on the borrower's deposit balances as well as expenses incurred in performing services such as paying checks and collecting deposited items for the borrower.
8. The rates of return that can be earned on alternative investments.
9. The desired return on stockholders' equity.

Loan pricing cannot be taken lightly by bank management since loans produce the largest share of bank earnings. Loan policy should contain complete, written guidelines covering the setting of interest rates for all categories of loans. The loan officer should be able to rely on policy and not be forced to negotiate the rate on every loan "from the ground up." It may not be desirable to have a rate schedule that is fixed to the last basis point, but when the loan officer enters into discussion with the loan applicant, he or she should know within a small range what rate will apply if the loan is granted.

Many banks have installed systems for loan pricing, profitability analysis, and documentation.[2] Pricing systems are available from commercial sources if a bank does not wish to, or does not have the resources to, develop its own. Such a system would incorporate the nine factors just listed plus any others bank management considers appropriate.

Rates on Business Loans

Rates charged to businesses generally are the lowest of all bank lending rates, particularly those on large, short-term loans. As stated earlier,

---

[2] Andrew Heytow, "Technology Update . . . Microcomputer Systems for Loan Pricing and Documentation," *The Journal of Commercial Bank Lending* (December 1986), pp. 42–47.

FIGURE 10-1   Short-Term Interest Rates

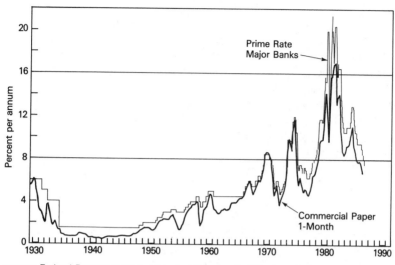

SOURCE: *Federal Reserve System, Historical Chartbook, 1986* (1987).

such loans are often made at rates below the prime rate. But even for those financially strong firms that do borrow at or somewhat above the prime, the rates typically are only slightly above money market rates (see Figure 10-1).

There is a strong tendency for the prime to be the same at all banks. Changes are usually initiated by large money center banks, and other banks follow suit. If a bank tried to maintain a prime higher than that of the competition, it would lose business rapidly. If its prime was below the prevailing prime, it would be inundated with loan requests.

It has been suggested that the prime has become "sticky" in recent years, at least at some major banks. As a result of volatile, and generally rising, interest rates in the past decade, most banks have increased sharply the proportion of loans made on a floating basis, particularly in the case of business loans. Thus in periods when credit market conditions and the need to expand lending both would suggest that a drop in the prime is called for, the potential for lost revenue from existing floating rate loans may make this a sluggish process.[3]

---

[3] Randall C. Merris, "Business Loans at Large Commercial Banks: Policies and Practices," *Economic Perspectives*, Federal Reserve Bank of Chicago (November–December 1979), pp. 15–23.

Interest Rates on Farm Loans

Rates on farm loans are usually higher than those on business loans primarily because of their greater risk and smaller size. Farming is a risky enterprise because of such factors as weather, disease, infestation, over-supply, and changes in consuming patterns. Farm loans also have a long maturity. Most operating loans, which are considered the shortest of all farm loans, have a maturity of six months to one year normally. The extension of farm loans for another season or year is not uncommon as a result of some unforeseen development that adversely affects production or harvesting.

In addition to being higher, interest rates on farm loans are less variable than those on business loans. The difference in rates for small and large loans reflects the cost of making and supervising loans and the bargaining power of the borrower. Although large farm borrowers may not have as many sources of credit available to them as do large business borrowers, some alternative sources are the Federal Land Bank, Interme-diate Credit Bank, individuals, and life insurance companies. This fact is recognized by commercial banks; if the loan is desired, competitive rates must be met.

Interest Rates on Consumer Loans

Interest rates on consumer loans are higher than are those on most other bank loans because of their small size and the risk involved. Banks have costs to meet just as do other businesses, and in consumer lending, the costs are greater per dollar of loan than are those in any other type of lending. The major reason for this is that a large number of people are required in the process. The break-even point on consumer loans varies from bank to bank, but many bankers discourage small installment loans. The cost of making small loans has prompted many banks to avoid loans for household items such as televisions, radios, refrigerators, and other appliances. Those banks with credit card programs have encouraged cus-tomers to use them for such purchases.

Consumer lending involves risks that contribute to the relatively high cost of consumer credit. The borrower's ability to pay may be inter-rupted by unemployment, sickness, accident, or some other unforeseen development. Unfortunately, in some instances the borrower's intention to repay may deteriorate after the loan is made, and a loss is then incurred by the bank. Maturity also influences the level of consumer loan rates, just as it does in other types of lending. All these factors contribute to a relatively high and sticky rate when compared with other types of bank loans.

Residential Real Estate Interest Rates

Interest rates on residential real estate loans are influenced particularly by the maturity of the loan, the loan-to-value ratio, the availability of loanable funds, the need for liquidity, and whether the loan is guaranteed or insured by an agency of the federal government. In general, the higher the loan-to-value ratio, the higher the rate of interest, since the credit risk is obviously greater. This is especially true of conventional loans and, to some extent, of those underwritten by the various government agencies. The maturity of the loan is a very important factor since the longer the maturity, the greater the money rate risk to the bank. The guarantee and insurance of real estate mortgages provided by various government agencies influence rates in that the credit risk involved in such loans is reduced. Since commercial banks have a greater need for liquidity than do other major lenders of real estate funds, their liquidity needs influence the interest rate that they will charge. As liquidity needs increase, interest rates usually increase; if not, banks at least become less eager to make real estate loans. This condition developed at many banks in the late 1970s. Real estate loan rates are discussed further in Chapter 14.

Usury

A factor that has been important in loan pricing in the past, and may be again, especially in some areas of lending, is the usury laws of the various states. Usury laws limit the amount of interest that can be charged on loans and are found in all states, except Massachusetts and New Hampshire. The ceilings imposed by such laws are of ancient origin and stem from the belief that loans are unproductive and, in fact, immoral. Although this view does not prevail today, most legislators adhere to the belief that charging "excessive" interest on a loan should be prohibited.

DIDMCA preempted state usury ceilings on business and agricultural loans in excess of $25,000 unless a state reimposes the ceiling. It also eliminated ceilings on residential mortgage rates unless a state reimposed the ceiling within three years. The extent of the constraint imposed by usury rates in the future thus depends on whether or not they are permanently displaced by federal legislation as well as on market levels of interest rates.

ADMINISTRATION OF THE LOAN POLICY

After the loan policy of a bank has been formulated, provision for its proper execution must be made. Certain individuals must carry out the loan policy, and some provisions should be made for its periodic review and evaluation to make any necessary changes. It should be remembered that a loan policy serves as a guide to lending, not as a straitjacket. Economic conditions change and so should a loan policy. Periodically, the loan portfolio and lending practices should be compared with the loan policy to determine whether it is being followed and if changes should be made.

The person in charge of the overall lending organization should be in charge of supervising the bank's loan policy. In small banks this may be the president or one of the vice presidents. In banks that rely to a great extent on a loan or discount committee to supervise lending, this body would be responsible for effecting the lending policies of the bank. In larger banks the responsibility would probably be assigned to the senior vice president in charge of lending, who would explain the provisions of the loan policy to the lending officers and secure their cooperation in carrying it out, which is necessary for a loan policy to be successful. Lending officers cannot consider what is desirable to them; they must consider what is good for the bank. The purpose of a lending policy is to promote the objectives of the lending function, not to serve as an end within itself.

ORGANIZATION OF BANK LENDING

The organization of the lending function depends on numerous factors, including the character and quality of the lending officers, the size of the bank, the size of the loan portfolio, the type of loans made, and the board of directors' attitude toward the amount of authority delegated. The legal responsibility for bank lending rests with the board of directors, and some boards play a more important role in lending than do others. In general, larger banks delegate lending authority and specialize in lending more than do smaller ones.

The lending officer usually makes personal contact with the borrower, receives applications for loans, interviews the applicants, decides whether the applications are worthy of consideration, and may obtain all the necessary information about the applicant, or part of it may be obtained by the credit department. The lending officer may make the decision to grant the loan request, or this may rest with a committee or the board of directors, depending on the size of the request. Once the loan has been made, the lending officer usually supervises the loan, that is, keeps in close contact with the borrower during the life of the loan. This may include plant visits, occasional visits with the borrower in the bank, and requests for financial and other credit information from the borrower and from other sources. In the event of difficulty with the loan, the lending officer will exert every effort to collect the amount outstanding. If renewals or additional funds are requested, the lending officer handles these requests.

In small unit banks, all the officers may perform lending functions along with their other activities. Each officer may handle all types of loan requests, whether they are for consumer, business, or real estate purposes. Little formal specialization prevails. However, one officer may specialize in some type or types of loans because of special interest or experience. Each officer must secure the necessary credit information and maintain the credit files, since few small banks have a separate credit department. Each officer may have a lending limit within which decisions can be made regarding loan requests. Loans above a certain amount may be submitted to a loan or discount committee that will make the decision or, in smaller banks, refer the request to the board of directors for further consideration if the loan is extremely large or in any way unusual.

In medium-sized unit banks, there is more delegation of authority and specialization regarding lending. Many medium-sized banks have credit departments. Each officer may have an established lending limit, which is usually higher than that in the small bank. Sometimes a loan committee composed of senior loan officers may exist within the bank to handle loan requests above the lending officer's limit. Members of the board of directors may be on this committee. If this is the case, only those requests requiring special attention would be referred to the discount committee and the board of directors. As in the small bank, supervision of the loans would be the responsibility of the lending officers.

The lending organization in large unit banks differs considerably from that in small banks and, to some degree, in medium-sized banks, in the departmentalization and specialization of lending activities. Large banks may have such lending departments as real estate, business or commercial, consumer, and agricultural. Some of these departments are broken down further. Business loans, for example, can be divided according to industry, with a lending officer in charge of each industry or related industries. One large bank, for example, may have separate loan divisions for iron and steel, automobiles, machinery, agricultural implements, electrical products, energy, and manufacturing sundries. Many banks divide their lending activities on a territorial basis.

Lending officers in large banks have lending limits, but they are usually higher than those in smaller banks. Larger banks make greater use of officer loan committees than do small and medium-sized banks. They may be organized on a formal or informal basis according to departments. For example, a request for a real estate loan larger than the lending officer's established limit would be referred to an officers' loan committee composed of real estate lending officers rather than of officers from several departments. With an organization of that kind, only the very large requests are referred to a loan or discount committee, and probably few, if any, requests are referred to the board of directors for action.

In larger banks, the credit department plays a much more important role in the lending process than it does in smaller banks. The lending officer turns over to the credit department all the information received from the applicant that would be used in the preparation of a formal loan request. Additional credit information on the applicant would be secured from many sources and assembled in one folder for the use of the lending officer, who in turn may discuss it with some colleagues or the officers' loan committee. The report of the credit department may include such items as financial statements (with balance sheets and profit and loss statements for a period of years arranged on one sheet so they can be evaluated at a glance), various financial statement ratios that have been calculated by the credit department, credit agency reports, pictures of the applicant's place of business, budgets, analysis of the industry's prospects as well as the applicant's, and many other details of value in making a decision on whether to grant the credit request.

The lending organization in branch banks varies considerably. Branch managers and officers may have limited loan authority, just as in a unit bank. Loan requests above this limit might be referred to the head office where consideration would be given to the request by the regional supervisor of that particular branch and a decision reached. The regional supervisor may also have a lending limit. Loans exceeding this limit would be referred to a loan or discount committee. In very small branches, the lending organization may be very similar to a small unit bank, but in large branches, it may be more like the lending organization found in large unit banks, with a great deal of specialization and departmentalization. From a practical standpoint, it is not desirable to have a great deal of centralization of lending authority in the head office. Borrowers do not like to wait for credit decisions, and much of the personal touch important in credit evaluation is lost if many requests must be directed to the head office. When there are many branches, the head office usually performs general policy supervision and permits branch managers considerable discretion in lending. This, in fact, is about the only way branches can be operated efficiently.

QUESTIONS

1. What are the reasons for the regulation of bank lending? What is the purpose of the legal lending limit?
2. Why have banks increased the portion of loans made with floating rates in recent years?

3. What are the advantages of having formal, written lending policies? What variables influence bank lending policies?

4. What considerations are involved in determining the appropriate size for a bank's loan portfolio?

5. How is an open line of credit similar to yet different from a revolving credit?

6. How do rates in the money and capital markets influence bank lending rates? Discuss the importance of the prime rate in bank lending.

7. Why are rates on consumer installment loans generally more stable than money market rates?

8. What variables influence lending rates for commercial and industrial loans?

9. What should comprise the cost of funds to a bank in setting the interest rate on a loan?

SELECTED REFERENCES

BARROW, CHARLES H., GROVER ELLIS, WILLARD ALEXANDER, AND GLENHALL E. TAYLOR, JR. "Credit Policy Administration and Some Considerations for the 1980s." *The Journal of Commercial Bank Lending* (February 1981), pp. 12–22.

BRADY, THOMAS F. "Changes in Loan Pricing and Business Lending at Commercial Banks." *Federal Reserve Bulletin* (January 1985), pp. 1–13.

BRICK, JOHN R. *Commercial Banking: Text and Readings.* Haslett, Mich.: Systems Publications, 1984.

GILL, EDWARD K. *Commercial Lending Basics.* Reston, Va.: Reston, 1983.

HAYES, DOUGLAS A. "Commercial Loan-Pricing Policies." *The Bankers Magazine* (January–February 1977), pp. 2–9.

———. *Banking Lending Policies,* 2nd ed. Ann Arbor: University of Michigan Press, 1977.

MOTT, HUBERT C. "Establishing Criteria and Concepts for a Written Credit Policy." *The Journal of Commercial Bank Lending* (April 1977), pp. 2–16.

MUELLER, P. HENRY. "The Most Challenging Issues Facing Bank Lending." *The Journal of Commercial Bank Lending* (March 1977), pp. 16–24.

PROCHNOW, HERBERT V., ed. *Bank Credit.* New York: Harper & Row, 1981.

SINKEY, JOSEPH F., JR. *Commercial Bank Financial Management in the Financial Services Industry,* 2nd ed. New York: Macmillan, 1986.

SLATER, JOHN, JR. "New Tools to Make Commercial Loan Pricing More Effective." *The Journal of Commercial Bank Lending* (September 1986), pp. 2–12.

11

SHORT-TERM BUSINESS AND FARM LOANS

Commercial banks are major suppliers of short-term loans to businesses. In addition, commercial banks do a substantial amount of short-term lending to farmers, securities dealers, and nonbank financial institutions. Loans of this kind are highly regarded by commercial bankers. They have less credit and interest rate risk than do longer maturities and, in general, have more liquidity than do many other types of loans.

Short-term loans are widely used in financing seasonal increases in current assets and in the temporary financing of capital expenditures and other long-term commitments pending negotiation of long-term loans or the flotation of stock or bond issues. Commercial banks also commonly grant short-term loans with the understanding that if the borrower's financial condition and profitability continue to be satisfactory, the loans will be renewed at maturity and thus become a source of longer-term debt capital.

BUSINESSES THAT BORROW ON A SHORT-TERM BASIS

Retail firms, food processors, and manufacturers with seasonal operations are among the most important users of short-term bank loans. Many retail firms borrow heavily during Christmas and Easter seasons to carry increased inventories and accounts receivable. Food processors often require short-term funds when crops are brought in for processing. Manufacturing firms may require short-term financing when seasonal factors impact either their production or their sales, For example, firms in the forest products industry find it necessary to build up large inventories of logs to keep their manufacturing plants supplied with raw materials during seasons when logging operations cannot be carried on. Manufacturers of items such as lawn mowers and lawn furniture may produce in anticipation of a seasonal increase in demand and rely on short-term loans to finance a temporary increase in inventories. Steel mills located on the Great Lakes usually accumulate inventories of iron ore during the summer to supply their needs during the winter when lake freighters are unable to operate. Fish canneries must do their processing as the fish are caught, which often results in the accumulation of substantial inventories. Building contractors achieve higher levels of production when the weather is favorable. These industries and many others look to commercial banks for funds during their busy seasons.

Commercial banks are major suppliers of funds for home builders and mortgage companies. Most home builders must borrow at least part of the funds required for carrying inventories of materials and houses. Short-term construction loans granted to home builders are usually repaid, as the homes are sold, with funds obtained by the home buyers from long-term lenders. Mortgage companies often serve as connecting links between the home buyer and the supplier of the long-term funds. They originate the loans with home buyers and arrange with investors for the long-term financing. In performing these functions, they sometimes find it necessary to carry loans on inventory for a short period of time before turning them over to a permanent investor such as a life insurance company. A bank loan obtained to finance such an inventory of mortgage loans is known as a *mortgage warehousing loan*. The security for a mortgage warehousing loan includes the mortgage loans themselves plus the forward commitment of the permanent investor to take over the loans.

Securities firms, many of which perform three major functions—investment banking, commission brokerage, and security trading—are large borrowers of short-term funds from commercial banks. As investment bankers, they need short-term funds for the underwriting and distribution processes since it is often necessary to make payment to the company issuing the securities before the entire issue has been sold and the proceeds received by the underwriters. If a firm elects to operate as a dealer in securities, it must be prepared to carry inventories, which often require bank financing. Securities held by the dealer are provided as collateral for such loans. In performing as a broker, a securities firm makes loans to customers who buy and hold securities on margin. The investments of the customer can serve as collateral not only for the broker's loan to the customer but also for a loan obtained by the securities firm from a commercial bank. Typically, loans to brokers and dealers for the purpose of financing margin accounts and dealer inventories are "callable" by the bank, or repayable by the borrower, at any time on one day's notice and so are known as *call loans*. The rates on call loans are among the lowest granted by commercial banks and are announced daily by the major money market banks in New York City.

When borrowers need long-term financing, banks may provide them with temporary financing with the understanding that the loans will soon be repaid with funds from other prearranged sources. For example, when a corporation has a commitment from an investment banking firm to purchase a certain amount of its securities, it may borrow from a commercial bank on a short-term basis, use the funds to pay for fixed assets or increase working capital, and repay the loan when its securities have been sold. This is referred to as a *bridge loan*, and it may involve a high degree of risk if the borrower does not have a firm commitment from a substantial investment banking firm to buy its securities. In the absence of such a commitment, the commercial bank will want to evaluate the loan as it would any other, recognizing that it may turn into an intermediate- or longer-term credit. Businesses may borrow from banks on a short-term basis to construct manufacturing plants, warehouses, and office buildings, having arranged for permanent financing with some investor such as an insurance company or a pension fund. The agreement of the long-term investor to take over the loan after the facility has been constructed is known as a *take-out commitment*.

Finance companies borrow short-term funds from commercial banks, although large finance companies may meet most of their short-term needs in the commercial paper market. Such commercial paper borrowings generally must be backed by open lines of credit at commercial banks. This gives investors added assurance that the commercial paper can be retired at maturity. The largest finance companies may have open lines at several hundred banks. Banks require compensating balances in payment for maintaining the open lines. How much, if any, is borrowed under the lines depends in part on comparative rates and availability of funds. Typically the cost of borrowing through the issuance of commercial paper is a fraction of a percentage point less than the cost of a bank loan, even before taking into account compensating balances. However, in times of extreme credit tightness, the commercial paper market can be an uncertain source of funds.

CREDIT LINES

Short-term lending to businesses is often accomplished through line of credit arrangements. Establishing the line requires that both borrower and banker plan well ahead to the time when funds will be needed. The borrower can order merchandise or begin production knowing that funds can be drawn under the line when needed. However, a line of credit arrangement normally is not considered legally binding on the bank. If developments in the borrower's business after establishment of the line create sufficient feeling at the bank that extending funds under the line would be excessively risky, the line may be canceled.

A line of credit frequently is drawn down in various amounts and may be repaid in the same manner. For example, a swimsuit manufacturer may begin producing swimsuits in the fall of the year to distribute to retailers the following spring. During the manufacturing period, inventories would build up, payrolls would be met, and other costs incurred that required funds. These funds would be supplied by gradually drawing down the line of credit arranged before manufacturing commenced. In the spring, as swimsuits were sold and proceeds received, the line would be reduced and eventually retired. After a two- or three-month period, the process would begin again.

The method of determining interest charges on the line is established at the time the line is arranged. The rate on a line of less than $1 million probably will float with the prime rate. It might be set at, say, two percentage points above the prime, or it might be set at some percentage of the prime, perhaps 115 percent. Thus if the prime is at 10 percent, the loan rate will be 11.5 percent. A compensating balance of perhaps 10 percent of the line may be required before any funds are drawn down, with an additional 10 percent of funds drawn.

Due to competition from the commercial paper market and foreign banks in recent years, large banks have moved more and more into money market pricing of large loans, including lines of credit. The rates on such loans float with a reference rate from the money market, say, the rate on large certificates of deposit, to which an appropriate spread is added. These loan rates almost always are below the prime.[1]

UNSECURED SHORT-TERM BUSINESS LOANS

Firms that borrow on an unsecured basis are those that are properly financed and have adequate capital and net worth, competent management, stable earnings, a record of prompt payment of obligations, and a bright future. A business firm that meets these criteria would have little trouble obtaining an unsecured loan for 90 days. Business firms that borrow on an unsecured basis are the prime borrowers of the business community—the elite from the standpoint of creditworthiness. The mechanics of making

---

[1] Thomas F. Brady, "Changes in Loan Pricing and Business Lending at Commercial Banks," *Federal Reserve Bulletin* (January 1985), pp. 1–13.

an unsecured loan are quite simple. In deciding to make an unsecured loan, the banker relies heavily on the borrower's financial statements. If they are satisfactory, the most important document involved in the extension of this type of credit is the promissory note.

The chance that a bank will be willing to make a loan without requiring security is enhanced if the funds are to be invested in current assets that are likely to be converted into cash within a reasonably short period of time. Such loans are termed *self- liquidating*. If the principal purpose of the loan is to permit the borrower to accumulate inventories, the salability of those inventories becomes an important factor. In some cases the cost and inconvenience of providing security for a loan are so great as to make it prohibitive. The banker must then decide whether it would be wise to make the loan on an unsecured basis.

SECURED SHORT-TERM BUSINESS LOANS

Most businesses are small, and most of these are not financially strong enough to borrow a significant part of their short-term needs on an unsecured basis. Also, many firms have not established records of stable earnings, have unseasoned managements, or have not secured adequate shares of the markets in which they operate. Thus security is required for their borrowings. Sometimes when security is not required, the borrower provides it in order to receive a lower rate of interest. When security is needed, it is necessary to decide what type of security would be acceptable and how much margin would be required. In making such judgments, the bank must consider the financial condition and profitability of the firm and the marketability and probable liquidation value of the various assets. Staple commodities, for which there is a relatively steady demand, can be sold more promptly in the event of liquidation than can specialized machinery, for which the demand is quite limited. Many types of collateral serve as security for short-term business loans.

Endorsed or Comaker Loans

Many short-term business loans are secured by the endorsement or guarantee of parties other than the borrower. When the borrower is a corporation, the principal shareholders may be required to endorse or guarantee the loan so as to commit, to some degree, their personal assets outside the business to repayment of the loan. The lender should consider not only the amount of assets outside the firm (present as well as probable future) held by the shareholders but also the extent to which the shareholders have given, or can be expected to give, similar guarantees to others. A loan may be endorsed or guaranteed by a corporation as well as by an individual. For example, a corporation may guarantee a loan to one of its subsidiaries or to a firm that supplies it with essential materials or serves as an important outlet for its product.

When a loan is guaranteed, the lender can usually assume that the guarantor will attempt to use his or her influence to see that the borrowing firm is operated in such a manner that the loan will be repaid. It is sometimes said that the best collector is the endorser or guarantor of a loan. In making such loans, banks try to satisfy themselves that those who are offering to be secondarily liable on the loan would be willing to make payment and have sufficient funds to do so if necessary. An assessment of the guarantor's willingness to make payment, if need be, is important since banks do not like to be in the position of having to force payment. Experience has shown that guarantors are sometimes reluctant to pay a loan on behalf of the borrower even though they were quite willing to issue the guarantee in the first place. Bankers evaluate requests for loans of this kind very carefully, not only to see that the security is adequate but also to advise the guarantor or endorser of the risks associated with the loan.

Assignment of Contracts

Construction companies and firms that supply materials under contract often find it necessary to borrow for their operations pending the receipt of payments under their contracts. In such a case a firm may assign its contract to the lending bank as security for a short-term loan. Then, as it performs under the contract, payments are made directly to the bank by the other contracting party. Sometimes the borrowing firm is a subcontractor, in which event payments may be made to the bank by the prime contractor. It is not unusual for both the prime contractor and the subcontractors to be borrowing from commercial banks to finance their particular activities.

Assigned contracts can be attractive collateral, but they are not without hazards. The value of an assigned contract as security for a loan depends on the ability and willingness of the other contracting party to make payments as well as the ability and willingness of the borrower to perform under the contract so that he or she will be entitled to payment. For example, if the borrower is supplying a product under the contract that is inferior and not up to specifications, payment will probably not be forthcoming and the contract may be canceled. Prior to making the loan, the lending banker must know the terms of the contract and be assured that the borrower will perform according to the conditions set forth. The banker must also evaluate the financial capacity of the party for whom the work is being performed or the products supplied, since that party is the ultimate source of the funds with which the loan will be repaid.

Assignment of Accounts Receivable

Accounts receivable financing by commercial banks has grown sub-stantially in the past three decades, particularly at larger banks. Receiv-ables are frequently used as collateral for both short-term seasonal loans and revolving credits. When a loan is secured by receivables, the amount of credit available to the borrower tends to increase as the need for credit grows. Typically, a seasonal loan is paid off as inventories and receivables are reduced following a period of high production and sales. With revolv-ing credit, on the other hand, the lending may be more or less continuous; if the borrower is a growing firm, the size of the credit may continue to grow over a considerable period of time.

When commercial banks lend on the security of accounts receivable, it is usually—but not always—on a nonnotification basis, with the cus-tomers of the borrower not being advised that their accounts are being pledged as security for a loan. Borrowers often prefer this because of a feeling that borrowing on the security of receivables may be viewed as a sign of financial weakness. With nonnotification financing, the borrower agrees to forward directly to the bank all payments received from cus-tomers whose accounts have been assigned. On the other hand, when financing is on a notification basis, the borrower's customers are advised to make all payments directly to the bank instead of to the borrower. The bank notifies the borrower of their receipt and applies the payments to the loan. Some bankers who prefer nonnotification financing contend that if a borrower cannot be trusted to abide by an agreement on a nonnotification basis, credit should not be extended at all.

The decision to make an accounts receivable loan, and if so, the amount of funds that will be advanced on a given amount of receivables, rests not only on the creditworthiness and integrity of the borrower but also on the nature and quality of the receivables. The credit standing of the borrower's customers is another important factor. The size of the individual accounts, the type and quality of the borrower's merchandise, the number of merchandise returns, and the age of the receivables are also important considerations. The sales and credit policies of the borrower should be considered: if the borrowing firm sells to nearly everyone who applies for credit to achieve high sales volume, troubles may develop. However, if the borrower has a policy of selling only to firms that pay their bills promptly and have good management and a high credit rating, the lender will be exposed to little risk.

The type and quality of the merchandise sold by the borrowing firm are factors to consider in deciding whether to lend on accounts receivable. The higher the quality of the goods, the fewer the returns and refusals to pay. Banks review carefully the amount of merchandise returns in rela-tion to sales before agreeing to loan on a firm's accounts receivable, and they continue to watch the returns closely after a lending relationship has been established. They also investigate the age of the borrower's accounts receivable to evaluate the paying habits of its customers.

The maximum that a bank will loan on a given amount of accounts receivable usually ranges from 50 to 90 percent of the face value of the accounts. If the borrower's bad-debt losses have been large, the bank may decide not to grant any loan at all, or the amount of the loan may be limited to a relatively small percentage of the total accounts. The sizes of individual accounts and the degree to which the borrower's receivables are concentrated in a relatively few accounts are also considered. Banks favor lending on larger accounts because it involves less paperwork and may involve fewer returns and disputed items. On the other hand, banks do not like to see receivables heavily concentrated in a few accounts unless they are with customers having high credit ratings. Typically, the maximum loan is 75 to 80 percent of the total receivables pledged.

Some important items usually covered by a loan agreement for accounts receivable financing follow:

1. The duration of the lending arrangement.
2. The right of the bank to screen the accounts presented to it by the borrower to determine which are acceptable as security.
3. The procedure by which accounts held by the bank are to be replaced or the loan reduced, if they become past due.
4. The percentage that the bank will loan against the face amount of the receivables.
5. The maximum dollar amount of the loan.
6. The evidence required from the borrower to show the amount owed by each customer. As additional sales are made, the borrower may be required to submit copies of invoices or other evidence of shipment.
7. The responsibility of the borrower to forward directly to the bank payments received on assigned accounts.
8. Authorization for the bank to inspect the borrower's books and to verify, through confirmation by a public accounting firm or other agency, the accounts receivable.
9. The frequency with which the borrower can submit evidence of additional sales and must deliver to the bank any payments received from customers. Often this is done on a daily basis, with daily adjustment of the security base and the loan balance.

When a firm is borrowing on accounts receivable, it can quickly fall into serious difficulty if some of the pledged receivables become delinquent. The problem is apt to be serious if previously pledged receivables are rejected at a time when the borrower has no surplus funds and no other means of raising money. Instead of supplying the borrower with additional funds as new sales are made, the banker may substitute the new receivables for those no longer acceptable as collateral until the deficiency has been eliminated. If the amount of delinquent receivables is large, the borrower may be faced with the prospect of having to operate for a considerable period of time without receiving any cash from either its customers or its bank. Sometimes this is an impossibility.

The cost of borrowing on the security of accounts receivable is higher than the cost of an unsecured loan. There are two reasons for this: firms that borrow against receivables tend to be weaker financially than firms that can borrow without security, and accounts receivable financing requires a great deal of clerical work for the bank as well as careful supervision. In addition to charging an interest rate that is usually two or three percentage points above the prime bank rate, it is customary to impose a service charge amounting to 1 or 2 percent of the borrower's average loan balance.

Factoring

The *factoring* or buying of accounts receivable is more than a method of financing. Typically, the factor buys the accounts of his or her clients on a nonrecourse basis and performs a number of services in addition to the advancement of funds before the accounts have been collected. These services include credit analysis, bookkeeping, the collection of accounts, and the assumption of the credit risk. The factor evaluates the credit of the client's present and prospective customers and establishes credit limits in advance. The client's customers are instructed to remit directly to the factor, who receives copies of the invoices. The client's drawings against uncollected receivables are usually limited to 80 or 90 percent of the invoice value, net of discounts and the factor's commission. The 10 to 20 percent reserve is retained by the factor for protection against merchandise returns, shortages, and other claims by the client's customers. Usually at the end of each month the factor calculates the fees earned and the amount of the holdback on uncollected receivables and makes any excess funds available to the client.

The factor's compensation is in the form of a commission (for credit analysis, bookkeeping, collection of accounts, and assumption of the credit risk) plus an interest charge on the daily balance of drawings against uncollected receivables. Interest is earned from the date of the advance to the due date of the receivables. The commission usually runs from 1 to 2 percent of the gross amount of the accounts factored, depending on the client's volume of business, the level of risk, and the amount of work required of the factor in relation to the volume of business. The amount of risk assumed by the factor depends largely on the credit standing of the client's customers, while the amount of work required for a given volume of business depends primarily on the average size of the invoices. The commissions tend to be a considerably larger source of income for the factor than is the interest on advances. If the rate is 1.5 percent, for example, and the accounts turn over in 30 days, the commission amounts to 18 percent of the receivables on an annual basis.

A few major banks have been factoring for many years. However, it was not until 1963, when the Comptroller of the Currency ruled that factoring was a legitimate banking activity, that banks began to move strongly into this field. A number of major banks have entered the factoring business in recent years, mostly by acquiring factoring companies rather than by starting up factoring departments de novo. A few banks have set up factoring operations on a joint venture basis with large finance companies.

Factoring has been used mostly in the textile and furniture industries, but in recent years, it has spread to other industries. With factoring operations, major banks find it possible to expand their customer relationships in a number of industries. Moreover, they are able to perform a service for correspondent banks whose customers need factoring services.

Assignment of Oil Runs

Commercial banks make two major types of oil loans: production loans and oil payment loans. Production loans are made to oil operators for purchasing machinery and for other purposes that will improve operations; they are usually payable out of the monthly proceeds of the operator's share of the production. The collateral for a production loan is the operator's interest in the oil produced, often together with a security interest in some of the operator's other assets.

Lending on oil and gas in the ground is quite technical and requires the specialized services of a petroleum engineer. The value of the collateral must be determined before the loan is consummated and the funds are released. Many banks in oil and gas areas have petroleum engineers on their staffs to perform this very important function. Others rely on the appraisals of independent engineers.

An oil payment loan is secured by a contractual arrangement providing for payments at designated intervals and arises from the sale of an economic interest in oil and gas properties. The payment is assigned to the bank, and the loan is paid off as the oil payments are received. Although some oil loans are for one year, many are for longer periods.

Loans Secured by Inventories

The desirability of inventories as security for bank loans depends on the nature of the inventories as well as on the effectiveness with which they can be controlled or policed by the lender or an independent third party. In general, to be acceptable as security, inventories must be readily marketable, nonperishable, and insurable. A reasonable degree of price stability is also desirable. The amount that a bank will loan against inventories depends in large measure on these characteristics. Commodities and products such as grain, cotton, wool, coffee, sugar, logs, lumber, canned foods, baled wood pulp, automobiles, and major appliances tend to be very acceptable as collateral. Not as attractive, for obvious reasons, are such items as special purpose machinery, fresh produce, and advertising materials. One of the requirements for inventory financing is that the inventory be insured at all times, with a loss-payable clause in favor of the bank.

When a loan is made on the security of inventories, the lender is concerned that the inventories will actually be there to satisfy the loan if the borrower should default in the payments. When pledged inventories are left in control of the borrower, there is a definite risk that they will be liquidated before the loan is repaid if the borrower gets into serious financial difficulties. Operating losses often lead to a shortage of cash, which in turn leads to slowness in the payment of suppliers and a problem in keeping adequate inventories on hand. Inventories that may seem to provide ample security when a loan is made can disappear rapidly. Sometimes the disappearance results from fraudulent acts on the part of the borrower. Banks find it advisable, therefore, either to remove the inventories from the borrower's control or to police them very carefully if they are to be accepted and relied on as collateral.

Warehouse Receipts. For the lender's protection, inventories are best controlled by placing them in the custody of a warehouse company. When this practice is followed, warehouse receipts are issued and serve as security for a loan. Warehouse receipts may be negotiable or nonnegotiable. Negotiable warehouse receipts are used to finance inventories in which trading is active, such as corn, cotton, and wheat. The major disadvantage of negotiable warehouse receipts is that they are easily transferred, are usually in large denominations, and must be presented to the warehouse operator each time a withdrawal is made. Banks therefore prefer the use of nonnegotiable receipts issued in the name of the bank, which provides better control of the pledged inventory. The bank is thus in a position to permit the borrower to withdraw inventory only as it is sold, and apply the funds derived from the sale to the loan. When nonnegotiable receipts are used, withdrawals can be made with a prepared form known as an *order for warehouse release* or simply by writing a letter.

In a situation where the use of a public warehouse would be too costly or too inconvenient for the borrower because of the space required or the need to move goods in and out at frequent intervals, a field warehousing arrangement may be used. In field warehousing, the goods are stored on the premises of the borrower but are under the control of a person employed by the warehouse company. Sometimes that person is an employee of the borrower who is engaged by the warehouse company on a part-time basis to take custody of the inventories. The storage facility can be a building; a portion of a building; an oil tank; a log pond; an outside area where products such as lumber, coal, or wood pulp can be stored; or almost any other kind of space or container that can be kept under control. Signs are posted around the storage area to show that the goods located there are in the custody of the warehouse company, and the custodian is instructed to keep the inventories under lock and key. Except for the fact that storage is on the premises of the borrower, a field warehousing arrangement operates the same as does a public warehouse—receipts are issued by the warehouse company to the lender and goods are released only at the direction of the lender. Field warehousing is widely used to provide security for business loans. Warehoused inventories range from small, high-valued items such as jewelry to large and bulky items such as logs, lumber, wood pulp, and coal. Food canners were among the first to use field warehousing, and their products generally make very good security.

When a loan is made on the security of warehouse receipts, the lender places great reliance on the competence and integrity of the warehouse company, assumes that the company will issue receipts only against actual physical inventories, and will not release inventories without authorization. Usually it operates that way, but notable exceptions have occurred. In certain instances lenders have sustained large losses when the warehouses failed to contain the property for which warehouse receipts had been issued, and the warehouse companies were incapable of making good the deficiencies. By far the largest and most notorious case of this kind was the great salad oil swindle of the early 1960s. Total losses in the salad oil case were over $100 million, and among the losers were a dozen of the country's leading banks, two brokerage houses that were bankrupted, and the American Express Field Warehousing Company—the company that issued warehouse receipts against well over $100 million of nonexistent salad oil inventories. It was found that many of the storage tanks existed only on paper, and others, which were real, contained mostly water. The deception occurred primarily because both the warehouse company and the lenders disregarded some very basic principles of credit evaluation and loan administration. Thorough inspections of warehouse facilities did not take place, and apparently a weak link developed in the issuance of warehouse receipts.

In making loans secured by warehouse receipts, banks are concerned perhaps above all with the honesty and integrity of the borrower, particularly if field warehousing is used and the custodian is an employee or former employee of the borrower. Banks are also interested in the suitability of the warehouse. Goods that must be kept refrigerated require a warehouse that will maintain the desired temperature. If the goods must be kept dry, the warehouse must be constructed to keep dampness out. Warehouses do not guarantee the quality of the goods that are warehoused unless the grade is definitely stated in the warehouse receipt. If the bank has agreed to loan funds only on goods that meet a certain standard of quality, a certificate of quality or grade may be required from the borrower. Such a certificate would be issued by a qualified third party. Generally, loans secured by warehouse receipts should not exceed 85 percent of the market value of the collateral.

Warehouse receipt financing is relatively expensive to the borrower. In addition to the interest charge, there is the cost of warehousing, typically from 1.5 to 2 percent of the amount of the loan. Costs tend to be higher when inventories are small or the number of deposits and withdrawals from the inventory is large. In field warehousing there may be an additional charge for establishing the warehouse.

Trust Receipts. Retail firms seldom find it practical to use warehouse receipt financing because of the need to display products for sale and have them available for immediate delivery. The same is true for most wholesalers. Thus, in lending to retailers and wholesalers, it is generally feasible to use inventories as security only if they are left in the possession of the borrower. If inventories consist of items that can be specifically identified by description and serial number, trust receipt financing, commonly known as *floor planning*, is appropriate. When trust receipts are used, the lender buys the items from the firm that supplies them to the borrower. Delivery is made to the borrower, who agrees to hold the inventories in trust for the lender. The lender holds legal title to each item financed until it is sold, at which time the borrower is obligated to remit the amount loaned against it. The borrower's obligation is normally in the form of a demand note, that is, a note that the lender can ask the borrower to repay any time. Trust receipts are used extensively in financing the inventories of automobile dealers, heavy equipment dealers, and retailers of major appliances.

From a lender's standpoint, one advantage of trust receipt financing over unsecured lending is that the lender owns the property and can reclaim it if the borrower becomes bankrupt or for any other reason defaults the agreement. In addition, if the property has been sold and the proceeds are still held by the borrower, they are deemed to be held in trust for the lender. However, the lender's protection is far from perfect—he or she does not have the right to recover the property from someone who has purchased it from the borrower in good faith. Thus it is important to use trust receipt financing only with borrowers who are deemed trustworthy. In any case, it is good policy to make periodic checks of the borrower's inventories to see that all items for which the lender has not yet received payment are still on hand. These checks, called *flooring inspections,* normally consist of surprise visits by bank officers during which they check the serial number and description of each financed item against the trust receipts held by the bank.

Uniform Commercial Code and Floating Liens

Prior to the Uniform Commercial Code, which has now been adopted in all states except Louisiana, a lender could obtain a security interest in the inventories of a borrower by such legal devices as chattel mortgages, conditional sales contracts, trust receipts, and factor's liens. Under the Uniform Commercial Code these devices have been merged, technically, into one called a *security interest,* which is created through a security agreement. However, the names of the old security devices are still used to a considerable extent in agreements between borrowers and lenders even though they may no longer be mentioned in the statutes.

A *floating lien* applies to the borrower's more or less constantly shifting stock of inventories and/or receivables. This security agreement gives the lender a security interest in after-acquired assets of the borrower as well as in those existing at the time the agreement is made. The floating lien may also provide security for future advances of money and may cover proceeds from the sale of inventories, as well as the inventories themselves. When the agreement covers the proceeds of sales, the lender has a security interest in any accounts receivable arising from sale of inventories. Proceeds also include cash received from sale of inventories, so long as such cash can be separately identified.

There are various ways by which a lender can obtain a security interest in at least a portion of the borrower's current assets if another creditor has already obtained an interest in them by means of a security agreement. For example, if a lender wants to extend accounts receivable financing to the firm, the first creditor can be asked to subordinate its interest in the receivables to the lender. Or if the lender wants to obtain a security interest in certain new items to be purchased by the borrower with funds advanced by the lender, he or she can arrange to become a purchase money financier. This can be accomplished by perfecting a security interest in new items before they are delivered to the borrower. The floating lien holder must be notified by registered mail that these particular new items are being financed by the lender. Perfecting a security interest means taking the necessary steps so that the lender's security interest in the collateral is enforceable against third parties.

Under the Uniform Commercial Code, as before, the lender must decide what controls over the collateral and proceeds from the sale of the collateral are needed for proper protection. It is important to recognize that the lender does not exercise control over the borrower's inventories with a floating lien; for that reason, it is likely to be inferior to either trust receipt financing or warehouse receipt financing in the protection it affords. Some believe that a floating lien should be viewed only as a secondary or supplemental source of protection. It is also thought that little, if any, reliance should be placed on the value of a floating lien unless the management of the borrowing firm is of high integrity and the outlook for the firm is good; it is not good policy to rely heavily on the protection of a floating lien in any situation where the degree of risk indicates that security is important.

Loan Secured by Plants and Other Real Estate

By offering a mortgage on plants and other real estate, business firms are sometimes able to borrow larger amounts for short-term purposes than they could otherwise obtain, especially if their earnings have been low. The amount that banks will lend on land, buildings, and equipment varies considerably, depending on such factors as location, type of construction, marketability, and the debt-paying ability of the borrower. Legal restrictions may also come into play. The type of construction and location are extremely important since they influence the marketability of the property. Single-purpose buildings have a more limited market and are generally less attractive as security than are buildings with more versatile potential uses. If a factory building, for example, can be remodeled inexpensively and adapted to another use, its marketability will be improved.

In lending money on the security of plants, equipment, and other real estate, banks are interested in more than just the marketability of the property and the probability that it can be sold at a price equal to or greater than the loan. No banker or appraiser can be sure that the property will sell for its estimated market value or how long a time will be required to sell it. Primarily, banks are concerned that the firm has the ability to generate sufficient cash flow to repay the loan, so it will not be necessary to sell the security. Collateral does not turn a bad loan into a good loan.

Loans on Securities

Many firms hold substantial amounts of securities that can be pledged to secure business loans. Several factors are considered before making a loan secured by stocks or bonds. One of the most important is marketability. The credit rating of the governmental unit or corporation that issued the securities is also important. Securities issued by business concerns and governments with a record of prompt payment of principal and interest or a record of stable dividends have greater price stability and broader acceptance in the market than do those that fail to meet these qualifications. If there is an indication that the issuer of bonds will be unable to meet the interest payments or retire the securities when they mature, or that an issuer of stock will be unable to maintain a stable dividend, the securities probably will not be acceptable as collateral for a commercial bank loan.

The amount that a bank will loan on securities also depends largely on credit risk and marketability. U.S. government securities, which have no credit risk and are easily sold, are highly acceptable for bank loans; it is not unusual for banks to loan from 90 to 95 percent of the market value of such securities pledged. On stable, marketable securities of large and financially strong corporations a bank may advance funds equal to 80 to 85 percent of the market value. In general, more will be advanced on bonds than on stocks. Stocks of small, closely held companies do not make attractive security, and a bank should not lend money to a stockholder of a small business firm on the security of that company's stock if the bank already has a loan outstanding to the company.

When the collateral for a bank loan consists of securities, periodic checks are made to ascertain their marketability, the financial soundness of the issuer, and the market price of the collateral. Banks prefer securities that are listed on an exchange or are traded actively in the over-the-counter market. Stocks closely held and not traded actively may be difficult to sell, so the price received for a large block may be substantially less than the latest published quotations.

In making business loans secured by stocks and bonds, banks must take precautions that the funds will be used for business purposes, not for the purchase of additional stock. If the latter is the purpose, the loan must comply with Regulation U of the Federal Reserve Board relating to margin requirements. Banks must also be sure that the securities are assignable. U.S. savings bonds, for example, are nonmarketable and therefore cannot be assigned or transferred to another person. Another important factor is ownership: if the securities are owned jointly, both owners must jointly pledge them. Bonds may be in either bearer or registered form. When the securities are bearer bonds (as distinguished from registered bonds, where the owner's name appears on the face of the security), banks must take reasonable precautions to establish that the person pledging the bonds is the legal owner.

When registered bonds or stocks are accepted as collateral, a *stock* or *bond power* is usually obtained for each separate issue assigned by the owner. Stock and bond powers are *powers of attorney* that authorize the bank to sell the pledged securities in the event of default on the loan. Instead of executing powers, the owners could endorse the certificates if they wished, but this is not the most desirable procedure since the endorsement remains on the certificate after the loan is repaid. Also, if a certificate is endorsed in blank, a financial loss may be sustained if the certificate is either lost or stolen. Stock certificates are sometimes carried in the name of the broker through whom the owner purchased the stock, and, if so, are referred to as being in *street name*. When that is the case, the bank requests that the stock be transferred to the name of the borrower.

Loans Secured by Life Insurance

Loans to small business firms are sometimes secured, in whole or in part, by the assignment of the cash surrender value of life insurance policies. Generally speaking, this is a very desirable type of security because of its liquidity, definite value, and ease of handling. However, certain precautions should be taken when accepting the assignment of a life insurance policy as security for a loan. It is important to determine whether the insurance company is strong financially and can be depended on to pay the cash surrender value if necessary. The bank must ascertain whether the insurance policy is assignable. If the insured has irrevocably designated a beneficiary, he or she cannot assign the policy without the beneficiary's consent. For that reason, some banks have a standard practice of requiring the beneficiary to join in the assignment. The bank must also verify that the policy has not already been assigned to a third party. Finally, a loan should not be made on the security of a policy until the insurance company has been given a copy of the assignment and the bank has received written communication from the insurance company acknowledging receipt of the assignment.

LOANS TO FARMERS

Although farm loans are considered separate and distinct from business loans, they are similar in nature. The same fundamental principles of credit analysis are employed in making such loans. Banks are major providers of credit to farmers. Table 11–1 shows that banks held 36 percent of the non–real estate debt of farmers at the end of 1985. Most of this debt can be considered short term.

Farm lending is of negligible importance to most urban and money center banks, but to many others it is a major activity. The Federal Reserve, in 1986, considered 4,847 banks—34 percent of all U.S. banks—to be agricultural banks. As a group, farm loans averaged 35.7 percent of the loan portfolios of these banks, compared to 3.4 percent for the total banking system.[2]

---

[2] Emanuel Melichar, "Agricultural Banks under Stress," *Federal Reserve Bulletin* (July 1986), pp. 437–448.

TABLE 11-1   Farm Debt Outstanding, December 31, 1985

Type of Debt and Lender Group	MEMO: Amount Outstanding, December 31, 1985 (billions of dollars)
1 Total debt	205.02
2 Commodity Credit Corporation	17.3
3 Total debt excluding CCC	187.8
4 Banks	46.9
5 Farm Credit System	59.2
6 Life insurance companies	11.8
7 Farmers Home Administration	27.3
8 Individuals and others	42.6
9 Real estate debt	105.6
10 Banks	11.4
11 Federal Land Banks	44.6
12 Life insurance companies	11.8
13 Farmers Home Administration	10.6
14 Individuals and others	27.2
15 Non–real estate debt	99.6
16 Commodity Credit Corporation	17.3
17 Non–real estate debt, excluding CCC	82.2
18 Banks	35.5
19 Production credit associations	14.1
20 Federal Intermediate Credit Banks	.5
21 Farmers Home Administration	16.8
22 Individuals and others	15.4

SOURCE: Emanuel Melichar, "Agricultural Banks under Stress," *Federal Reserve Bulletin* (July 1986), p. 448.

Farm loans for current expenses include loans made by commercial banks for financing recurring seasonal expenses of crop and livestock production, such as seed, fertilizer, labor, and fuel; for family living outlays; and to purchase feeder livestock. These loans are comparable to short-term business loans. Most current expense loans to farmers are secured, and most have been relatively small in the past. However, with inflation and the continuing growth in the size of the average farm, these loans have become larger. A security interest may be taken therefore in growing and harvested crops, machinery, and livestock. For operators who have a limited net worth, real estate and endorsements are also relied on as security.

Farm loans for intermediate-term purposes include loans to purchase assets that will last several years, such as livestock (other than
feeder livestock), machinery, and property improvements. In most cases
security consists of chattel mortgages on the items purchased with the
funds. Farm real estate is commonly used as security for loans, especially
if the funds are used to improve land and buildings. A large percentage of
intermediate-term farm loans is repayable in installments.

The risk in farm lending has been increasing as debt/asset ratios have
risen, operating costs have risen, and prices of farm products have remained relatively low. Prices for farm products are extremely volatile,
and falling prices can drastically reduce the value of the lender's collateral. To reduce their risk in agricultural lending, bankers sometimes encourage their customers to diversify operations and produce more than
one crop, thereby reducing the risk of losses from price declines in one
commodity. Bankers may also urge farmers to sell their products three or
four times a year, instead of when the crop comes in or instead of waiting
for a higher price, to avoid the risk of selling at the bottom of the market.

In periods of declining prices, bankers often find that farmers do not
wish to sell at reduced prices to pay off the loans. However, if the loans
are renewed, which is often the case, the borrowers may need additional
credit to cover operating and storage costs. Periods of low prices or poor
crops, or both, are characterized by decreased rates of loan repayment,
large numbers of loan renewals, and refinancings. As an alternative to a
loan extension or refinancing, borrowers may be urged to sell commodities, land, or equipment, even at depressed prices, to raise funds for making repayment. Sometimes hard-pressed borrowers can refinance through
one of the emergency plans of the Farmers Home Administration (FmHA);
in some cases they are able to take advantage of appreciation in land
values and convert short- or intermediate-term debt into long-term real
estate debt.

In periods of poor crops or low prices, loan demands by farmers are
especially heavy, and loan-to-deposit ratios of rural banks are apt to rise
sharply, in some cases to well over 80 percent. Banks respond to these
conditions in a number of ways: by raising their credit standards and
turning down more loan requests; by requiring larger down payments on
equipment loans; by sharing their loans through participation with larger
correspondent banks; by encouraging borrowers to take advantage of one
or more of the Farmers Home Administration programs or a loan guaranteed by the Small Business Administration; and by selling loans.

Much of the farm sector in the United States has been depressed in
recent years, and this has created loan portfolio problems for many banks,
even causing numerous failures. The FDIC reported that 62 of the 118
bank failures in 1985 were considered agricultural banks by that agency.
Melichar estimated that at the start of 1985, one-sixth of the nation's

farmers, who owed two-fifths of the farm debt to banks, faced "a current or intermediate-term threat of default."[3]

A majority of agricultural banks have avoided major problems with their farm loans, and many have had excellent experience with agricultural lending for many years. To ensure continuance of this favorable experience, banks have become more insistent on good financial planning by their borrowers, requiring their borrowers to supply historical financial statements as well as detailed plans for their future operations along with budgets, cash flow projections, and pro forma financial statements showing the expected results of those operations.

Indirect Lending

Indirect lending to farmers is done by purchasing notes of dealers in agricultural machinery and equipment and by purchasing the bonds of various federal agricultural lending agencies. Arrangements between commercial banks and implement dealers are similar to the arrangements with automobile dealers in consumer financing. In general, indirect financing through dealers involves less risk for the bank, since the dealer usually endorses the paper purchased by the bank.

QUESTIONS

1. Comment on precautions that should be taken when lending on the security of an endorsement or guarantee.
2. What precautions should be taken when lending on the security of accounts receivable?
3. Under what circumstances are inventories satisfactory collateral for a business loan?
4. Explain how a field warehousing arrangement operates.
5. Explain how trust receipt financing operates. Compare the lender's protection in trust receipt financing with the protection in warehouse receipt financing.
6. What is a floating lien? How good is the protection it affords?
7. What precautions should be taken in lending with pledged securities as collateral?
8. What precautions should be taken in lending on the security of pledged life insurance policies?
9. Comment on the risks involved in non–real estate farm loans.

---

[3] Ibid., p. 444.

SELECTED REFERENCES

BARUCH, H. "Risks in Loans Collateralized by Securities." *The Journal of Commercial Bank Lending* (June 1977), pp. 29–40.

BRADY, THOMAS F. "Changes in Loan Pricing and Business Lending at Commercial Banks." *Federal Reserve Bulletin* (January 1985), pp. 1–13.

GILL, EDWARD K. *Commercial Lending Basics.* Reston, Va.: Reston, 1983.

HAYES, DOUGLAS A. *Bank Lending Policies*, 2nd ed. Ann Arbor: University of Michigan Press, 1977.

LOGAN, JOHN B. "Clearing Up the Confusion about Asset-Based Lending." *The Journal of Commercial Bank Lending* (May 1982), pp. 11–17.

MARSMAN, EDGAR M., JR. "Commercial Loan Structuring." *The Journal of Commercial Bank Lending* (June 1986), pp. 2–20.

MELICHAR, EMANUEL. "Agricultural Banks under Stress." *Federal Reserve Bulletin* (July 1986), pp. 437–448.

PROCHNOW, HERBERT V., ed. *Bank Credit.* New York: Harper & Row, 1981.

QUILL, G. D., J. C. CRESCI, AND F. D. SHUTER. "Some Considerations about Secured Lending." *The Journal of Commercial Bank Lending* (April 1977), pp. 41–56.

SIHLER, WILLIAM W., ed. *Classics in Commercial Bank Lending.* Philadelphia: Robert Morris Associates, 1981.

TUFARO, RICHARD C. "Issues in Lending . . . Adequate Protection for Undersecured Creditors." *The Journal of Commercial Bank Lending* (April 1987), pp. 33–37.

12

INTERMEDIATE-TERM
BUSINESS LOANS

Banks are important suppliers of intermediate-term credit to businesses. Long-term credit, for periods of, say, ten years and longer, generally must be acquired in the bond and mortgage markets.

TERM LOANS

The term loan is of major significance in the extension of intermediate-term credit. It is defined by the Federal Reserve as "a commercial and industrial loan with an original maturity of more than one year or a loan granted under a formal agreement—revolving credit or standby—on which the original maturity of the commitment was in excess of one year."

Real estate mortgage loans to business firms are not considered term loans even though they are of relatively long maturity. Although not considered term loans by most bankers, installment equipment loans are similar to term loans. An installment equipment loan is similar to a conventional term loan in that both are usually amortized over a period of years, but it differs from a term loan in certain significant respects. First, the loan agreement for an installment loan typically is much less elaborate than that for a term loan and does not place similar obligations and restrictions on the borrower. Second, the effective interest rate on an installment equipment loan tends to be higher than the rate on a term loan. And, third, installment equipment loans are for the purchase of specific items of equipment, whereas the proceeds of term loans are often used for general corporate purposes, including, for example, working capital and the acquisition of land and buildings.

REASONS FOR THE GROWTH
OF TERM LOANS

A business may find a term loan preferable to other forms of external financing for several reasons. Normally a term loan is much easier to arrange than is the flotation of a bond issue where the borrower is a corporation. The maturities of term loans are easily adapted to the duration of the borrower's need for funds. For example, firms that can pay for fixed assets in a short period of time may find term loans more advantageous than long-term bonds or equity capital. With a term loan, they can reap the benefits of financial leverage without surrendering control of the firm or being faced with the problem of calling bonds or preferred stock when the funds are no longer needed. Also, with a term loan, in contrast to a renewable short-term loan, the firm does not face the possibility of having to pay the total loan at one time; instead, payments are made according to a schedule that is based on a projection of the firm's cash flows at the time the loan is made.

Another reason for the growth in term lending has been the borrowers' increased demand for longer-term loans. Among the users of term loans are business firms too small to secure funds economically from the capital markets. In many cases, large corporations also find substantial benefits in term loan financing. For example, they may turn to their banks for funds rather than float new securities when conditions in the securities markets are unfavorable for new issues. However, as conditions in the capital market improve, they may issue securities to the public and use the proceeds, or a portion of them, to repay term loans negotiated at an earlier date.

Banks have discovered through experience that term loans are desirable earning assets when properly made and supervised. Banks have been encouraged to make term loans to smaller firms by the activities of the Small Business Administration. Many banks now make many term loans to small business firms, with and without SBA participation.

BUSINESSES USING TERM LOANS

Although term loans are made to all classes of business, they are most prevalent in certain industrial classifications characterized by heavy fixed capital requirements, such as durable goods manufacturing, chemicals and rubber, petroleum refining, mining, transportation, and public utilities. However, a significant portion of the total term lending is to firms in industries such as trade and services where the demand for funds is primarily for working capital.

The loan size varies considerably among industries, with larger loans being made, as one would expect, to firms with heavy investments in plants and equipment. A greater part of the total dollar amount of term lending is to large business firms. However, most term loans are made to small businesses that rely on such loans partly because of their limited access to the capital markets.

Large firms use term loans for the flexibility they provide, among other reasons. By negotiating directly with the lender, the borrower may obtain terms better suited to his or her needs than those available with a public bond issue. Also, with a term loan, some terms may be renegotiated with the lender at a later date if need be. Bank term loans are more flexible than a public bond issue in another respect: they can usually be prepaid without penalty, except where the funds used for prepaying are obtained by borrowing at a lower interest rate from another commercial bank. The shorter maturity of a term loan, as compared with the usual public bond issue, may in itself be considered an advantage in a period of high interest rates. The borrower may use a term loan with a view to replacing it in a few years with proceeds from a public bond issue at a lower interest rate. Another advantage of term borrowing over the issuance of bonds is that the costs of arranging for the financing are almost sure to be less, and the interest rate may be lower. With a term loan, the borrower avoids the costs of registration, underwriting, and selling that are usually incurred with a public issue of securities.

USE OF TERM LOAN FUNDS

Funds derived from term loans are used for a number of purposes. One of the most important is the purchase of buildings and equipment needed by the borrower to maintain a competitive position and keep pace with the demand for the firm's products. In addition, increased sales usually call for increased working capital, which may be financed through term borrowing. Term loans are used to finance new ventures, as when a firm adds a new product or integrates vertically to produce some portion of the raw materials needed in its operations. Term borrowing is also used to refinance existing obligations.

Frequently, the borrower needs to draw down the funds over a period of many months, as in the case of a major plant expansion or the acquisition of a fleet of aircraft. In such cases it is common practice to

combine the term loan agreement with a commitment agreement or revolving credit. The lender agrees to make funds available to the borrower
as they are needed over a period of, say, two years up to a specified total
amount. The agreement also provides that at the end of the commitment
period the entire amount borrowed to that date shall be incorporated in a
term loan. For an arrangement of this kind, the borrower is normally
required to pay a commitment fee of from one-fourth to one-half of 1
percent on unborrowed amounts during the period of the bank's commitment.

MATURITY, SECURITY, AND METHOD
OF PAYMENT OF TERM LOANS

The maturities of term loans vary considerably, but they usually range
from two to six years. Although some are for longer periods, few are for
more than ten years. The maturity of a term loan is in part a function of the
purpose for which the funds are being borrowed. For example, if the
funds are to be used to purchase short-lived assets, the maturity would
also be short. It is not unusual for term loans to be repaid before their
maturity date. Since an early repayment usually means that the customer
has fared well and is in a strong financial condition, banks are generally
not averse to early payments if the funds are derived from the firm's
operations. However, they do not look with favor on repayments made
with funds borrowed elsewhere at a lower rate of interest and may impose
a penalty for this kind of prepayment. In general, commercial banks require security on a larger proportion of term loans than short-term loans.
This, of course, is because of the greater risk associated with longer-term
loans. Also, term loans to small firms are secured more often than are
loans to larger businesses.

Most term loans are amortized, which means that installment payments are required on a monthly, quarterly, semiannual, or annual basis.
Repayment provisions sometimes provide for a larger, balloon payment at
the end, in which case a new loan may be negotiated prior to the final
payment date for some portion of the balloon payment. Some lenders
favor this type of arrangement when the borrower's needs are for a longer
period than the lender would like to grant. It is believed that the balloon
provision gives the bank an opportunity to take a fresh look at the credit
when the balloon payment is due. In some cases, however, the purpose of
a balloon payment is simply to give the borrower more flexibility during
the early years of the loan, and both parties fully expect that the borrower
will be able to make the payment when it is due.

INTEREST RATES

Interest rates on term loans depend on the general level of interest rates, the amount and maturity of the loan, and the credit standing of the borrower. The rate for a term loan is generally higher than the rate the same borrower would pay on a short-term loan, because it is less liquid and involves more risk. Rates on large term loans are generally lower than are those on small loans because the costs of originating and administering a loan do not increase proportionately with an increase in the amount of the loan, and because larger loans are usually made to larger business firms. It is generally assumed that larger borrowers have less risk of failure. The borrower's financial condition and profit prospects also have an important influence on the interest rate. It can be expected, for example, that firms with high debt/asset ratios will be required to pay higher rates than firms with low debt/asset ratios because of a greater risk of failure and a smaller equity cushion for the creditors in the event of failure.

Given the prime bank rate, the range of interest rates on term loans tends to be quite small. Typically, the rates on loans granted during a period when the prime rate remains unchanged will fall within a range of about .25 to 2.5 percentage points above the prime rate. This rather narrow spread confirms that banks generally are willing to make term loans only to borrowers whose credit ratings are quite high. The differences in risk among term loans are generally not very great.

The rates on many small term loans are fixed for the life of the loan. Large loans, on the other hand, often have provision for a variable rate—that is, a rate that is adjusted upward or downward with changes in the prime bank rate or, in the case of some very large loans, some other reference rate. For example, loans to large corporations with access to international financial markets may float with the London Interbank Offer Rate (LIBOR). LIBOR is discussed in Chapter 19.

Variable rate provisions often include a ceiling and a floor (sometimes referred to as a *collar*) so that the rate cannot move outside a specified range. For example, if a loan were made when the prime rate was 12 percent, the initial rate might be 12.5 percent with provision for subsequent adjustments to keep the rate half a percentage point above the prime rate, but never above 14.5 percent or below 10.5 percent.

Borrowers of term loans are sometimes required, either by the loan agreement itself or by informal understanding with the lender, to maintain a compensating balance. When that is the case, the effective cost to the borrower will exceed the stated rate if the required balance exceeds the amount the borrower would otherwise have on deposit. In some cases it is required that the compensating balance be carried as a time deposit, which may or may not draw interest. Small borrowers are seldom required to carry compensating balances, but they are usually expected to deal exclusively with the lending bank and not maintain deposits elsewhere.

LOAN PARTICIPATIONS
AND GUARANTEED LOANS

Commercial banks sometimes participate with insurance companies, pension funds, and other long-term lenders in making term loans. Participations with insurance companies are usually in the form of large loans, and the banks take the shorter maturities. On a 15-year loan, the banks might take the amount repayable in the first 5 to 7 years, and the insurance companies would take the rest because of their relatively slight need for liquidity. Because of their preference for long-term lending, insurance companies usually impose more severe prepayment penalties on the borrower than are normally imposed by commercial banks.

Two government agencies, the Small Business Administration and the Farmers Home Administration, have important programs for promoting term loans to small and, in the case of the FmHA, moderate-sized business firms. The SBA works closely with commercial banks in administering several lending programs, including regular business loans, minority business loans, economic opportunity loans, real estate development company loans, revolving lines of credit for small contractors, and loans to displaced businesses. The law intends that the proceeds of such loans be used for productive purposes—to create employment and increase the flow of goods and services within the economy. The SBA guarantees 90 percent of a loan deemed appropriate, but only if the borrower has been unable to obtain the funds without a guarantee.

SBA-guaranteed loans can be very attractive to commercial banks, partly because of the ease with which the guaranteed portion of the loan can be sold in the secondary market. Broad secondary market has been developed in which investment banking firms arrange for the sale of SBA-guaranteed loans to insurance companies, pension funds, trust funds, credit unions, and others. By selling the guaranteed portion of a loan, the lending bank recovers most of the funds it has loaned out; yet it continues to service the loan and receives a fee for doing so.

The Farmers Home Administration's lending program for business firms provides up to a 90 percent guarantee on loans obtained by corporations for investment in rural cities of less than 50,000 population. The objective is to maintain and create employment in rural areas. As with SBA-guaranteed loans, the lender has the privilege of selling the guaranteed portion of the loan. In contrast to the SBA program, however, FmHA-guaranteed loans can be made to larger firms, and the borrowing corporation is not required to demonstrate that it would be unable to borrow the funds at a reasonable rate without the guarantee.

SOURCES OF REPAYMENT FOR TERM LOANS

Term loans are ordinarily repaid from different sources than are short-term bank loans. A common purpose of short-term borrowing is to obtain funds for seasonal increases in accounts receivable and inventories. After inventories have been sold and receivables collected, the loan is repaid. Thus the inventories and receivables for which financing was required provide the funds for repayment when they are liquidated. Conversely, term loans are used primarily to acquire fixed assets and working capital that will be needed for relatively long periods; the usual source of funds for repayment is cash generated by profitable operations over an extended period. The use of funds derived from profitable operations to repay loans means that a business firm substitutes equity funds for debt funds in its capital structure. This relative increase in equity may make it easier to borrow additional funds at a later date. Banks therefore look on term loans and short-term loans quite differently.

It is sometimes said that in making term loans a bank can look to the borrower's total cash flows (earnings plus noncash charges) as a source of funds for loan repayment. However, this is often not true, especially in the case of a growing business where a portion of the cash flows must be used to finance increases in net working capital and fixed assets. The borrower's future growth must be taken into consideration in planning repayment schedules. And, even where little if any growth is involved, business firms are often compelled to make large capital expenditures to keep up with new technological developments and maintain their position in the market. For example, many manufacturing firms find it necessary to make annual investments in fixed assets that exceed their provision for depreciation. In addition, firms may find it necessary to carry increased inventories and allow longer credit terms to their customers. Such possibilities should be considered in reviewing a borrower's term loan proposal.

FACTORS CONSIDERED BY BANKS IN TERM LENDING

Since term lending involves greater risk than does short-term lending because of the need for profitable operations by the borrower over a relatively long period, banks take added precautions when committing themselves to term loans. Economic conditions can change drastically from the time a loan is made until its final maturity. The borrowing firm's position within the industry is also subject to change during the term of the loan.

Internal Factors

A commercial bank making term loans must appraise its own present and future financial condition. Such a self-evaluation includes an appraisal of the nature and fluctuation of deposits; the type, quality, liquidity, and diversification of earning assets; and an analysis of the capital account. Much has already been said about the importance of deposits in influencing the decisions of bank management, but it should be emphasized again that the type and fluctuation of deposits have much to do with the extension of term loans.

The type, quality, liquidity, and diversification of a bank's assets influence the extent to which it will engage in term lending. A bank that has a relatively large amount of assets in the form of long-term real estate loans is not in as favorable a position to engage in term lending as one that has few long-term real estate loans and a large proportion of short-term commitments. Banks whose loan portfolios consist largely of loans to high-quality borrowers can engage in term lending to a greater extent than can those with a larger number of marginal borrowers who may be slow in meeting their obligations and may request extension of their loans when they come due.

Banks often request other banks to participate in some of their term loans, either because the loan exceeds their legal limit or because they desire to spread the risk. This means that banks find it advantageous to have correspondent bank relations that are favorable to participation and pool arrangements in lending. Finally, it is important to have loan personnel and legal counsel trained in term lending. This kind of lending requires skills that are not necessarily acquired through experience with short-term lending or the making of real estate and consumer loans. Term loan agreements frequently require the services of attorneys, engineers, and people who have extensive knowledge about the industry in which the borrower is operating.

The proportion of a bank's loan portfolio that may appropriately consist of term loans is influenced by many factors that vary considerably from bank to bank. A few banks have adopted policies limiting their total term lending in relation to their time deposits or their capital or the sum of the two. In such cases the limitations are usually placed on the total of term loans and real estate loans combined. A review of the bank's liquidity needs and the condition of the term loan portfolio, in terms of both quality and liquidity, must be a continuous process for sound and profitable term lending.

Creditworthiness of the Borrower

Credit analysis for term lending is similar to that for short-term lending, but because of the longer maturities involved, considerably more emphasis must be placed on the borrower's profitability. In term lending the bank is, in a sense, becoming a partner of the borrower and may remain one for several years. There must be no doubt as to the character and management ability of the principals involved in the business. There is no place for those who must be watched and doubted continuously for the duration of the loan.

The success or failure of a business is largely dependent on the abilities of those who direct its affairs, so banks must have confidence that the firm has good management before a term loan is granted. Economic conditions, competition, and technological factors may change after a term loan is established, making it imperative that basic changes be made in the borrower's operations. Determining what those changes should be and putting them into effect are functions of management. Banks want to be assured that the term loan applicant has a management that can adapt to a changing environment, accept new ideas, and adopt new practices. Businesses dominated by one person that have no new managers "coming up the ladder" are not favored as candidates for term loans.

In evaluating an application for a term loan, banks place great emphasis on conditions in the industry and the applicant's competitive position and relative stability. Businesses that are very cycle sensitive or that operate in a feast or famine industry are not good candidates for a term loan. The bank should make a study of the trends in the industry, including technological changes, new processes, and changes in customer demands. Technological change, for example, might completely alter the economic importance of an industry.

If the applicant's management is capable of meeting the changes that occur, chances of survival and continued success are certainly enhanced. If a firm's past growth and financial success have been the result of a monopolistic position based, for example, on patents or control of the supply of raw materials, which may change with the passage of time, these factors must be considered before entering into a term loan agreement. A firm that has sound labor policies, an effective research and development program, and an ability to keep in touch with changes in consumer demand has a greater chance of survival and success than does one that neither projects its position into the future nor plans for improvements to meet the competitive challenge from other business firms. Political considerations and potential governmental controls and taxes must also be taken into account. Bankers are primarily interested in the borrower's ability to repay the loan as agreed. Estimating this involves investigating the firm's past record carefully as well as projecting its cash flows into the future.

THE TERM LOAN AGREEMENT

Loan agreements have been designed to offer a considerable amount of protection for banks involved in term lending. Sometimes the agreement is incorporated in the note, but usually it is prepared as a separate document that is referenced to the note. The loan agreement is normally prepared by the bank's legal counsel and is reviewed by the borrower's attorney. The provisions of term loan agreements are tailored to each specific situation but usually contain provisions under each of the following headings:

1. Preamble
2. Amount and term of the loan
3. Representations and warranties
4. Conditions of lending
5. Description of collateral
6. Covenants of the borrower
7. Restrictive clauses
8. Events of default
9. Miscellaneous

Preamble

The preamble sometimes does nothing more than name the parties and state that they are entering into an agreement; however, it may also contain a statement of the purpose of the loan.

Amount and Term of the Loan

This portion of the agreement sets forth the amount of the loan, the manner in which the borrower may take down the funds, the interest rate, the maturity dates, the amount of fees, if any, and the provisions relating to prepayments. The usual arrangement is for equal periodic installment payments. As mentioned previously, provision is sometimes made for a balloon payment at maturity. In this case, a provision is sometimes included in the loan agreement to the effect that if additional income above a certain amount is derived from operations or from the sale of assets, a certain portion will be applied to the reduction of the balloon portion of the note.

Banks do not generally impose a fee for prepayment of an installment or for early retirement of the entire loan if the funds are derived from current operations, from funding the debt, or from the sale of assets. However, if the early payments are made possible by borrowing from another bank, a penalty is imposed.

As mentioned previously, a commitment fee may be charged if the loan is a revolving credit with provision for converting the credit into a term loan. The bank is justified in imposing a fee for unused but committed funds since they must be readily available for the borrower's use. The bank will not feel free to invest these funds in high-earning assets such as other loans of intermediate maturities.

Representations and Warranties

It is here that the borrower represents and warrants that the financial statements on which the credit decision was based are correct and truly reflect the borrower's financial condition. Other representations commonly made by the borrower include the following:

1. The company is duly incorporated and in good standing.
2. The company has the power to make the agreement and execute the notes and to perform thereunder.
3. The properties of the company are free and clear of all liens and encumbrances other than those set out in the agreement.
4. No actions or suits are pending or threatened against the company other than those described in the agreement.
5. The company possesses adequate licenses, patents, copyrights, trademarks, and trade names to conduct its business substantially as now conducted.
6. The consummation of the transaction and performance of the agreement will not result in the breach of, or constitute a default under, any other agreement of the company.
7. The business and properties of the company have not been materially affected in an adverse way since the date of the latest audited financial statements.
8. The company has no federal income tax liability in excess of the amount shown on its balance sheet.

Conditions of Lending

This article, like the previous one, is legalistic in that it is concerned with the conditions that must exist, the representations that must be made, and the documents that must be delivered to the lender before the loan is made. Here, a legal opinion is in order. Before disbursing any monies under the loan, the legal counsel for the bank must be satisfied with the documents submitted by the borrower. If the agreement provides for a revolving credit followed by a term loan, it is further provided that before each disbursement an officer of the borrower shall provide the bank with a certificate stating that all previously made representations and warranties are still accurate and that no event has occurred that would constitute default under the loan agreement.

Description of Collateral

When the loan is a secured loan, the agreement sets forth a detailed description of the collateral and how it is to be handled. If the collateral consists of securities, the agreement normally specifies who is to receive the interest or dividends, who is to have the right to vote the stock, under what conditions the securities are to be sold, and if sold, who is to receive the proceeds from the sale.

Covenants of the Borrower

This is a very important part of the loan agreement. The number and detail of the covenants will depend somewhat on the financial strength of the borrower and the quality of management. If the borrower is strong financially and has excellent management, the number of covenants will be less than if the borrower's financial condition and management are only moderately strong.

Affirmative Covenants. The affirmative covenants are obligations imposed on management. One of the most common is the requirement that the bank be furnished with financial statements at periodic intervals and with such other relevant information as may be reasonably requested. In this manner, the bank is kept informed of the borrower's financial condition; if trouble appears to be developing, steps may be taken to prevent it. It is common practice to require unaudited statements for the first three quarters of the borrower's fiscal year, in addition to audited statements at year end. Term loan agreements generally require, also, that the borrower carry insurance satisfactory to the bank to reduce those risks that are insurable.

Many term loan agreements require the borrower to maintain working capital above some stated minimum amount. Some bankers consider this to be one of the most important provisions of the loan agreement since its purpose is to have the borrower maintain a certain amount of liquidity. However, this provision may not provide much protection if the composition and quality of a borrower's current assets change to the lender's detriment. It would be possible for a business to maintain the requirements established in the term loan agreement but not be very liquid simply because of having too much invested in slow-moving inventories or inferior receivables. Therefore, a close check should be kept on the quality of items that make up the working capital. Nevertheless, the working capital requirement is a potent force, since it gives the bank the right to declare the borrower in default should the working capital drop below the agreed minimum.

An affirmative covenant that is sometimes incorporated in term loan agreements requires the borrower to maintain management satisfactory to the bank. This is another important provision since the management is closely tied to the success of a business firm. This provision means that if the management should change due to resignation, death, or other causes, the bank must give its blessing before new personnel can be employed. Banks often require, also, that key person insurance be carried on those people in responsible positions who cannot be readily replaced.

Negative Covenants. Negative covenants are the actions a borrower agrees not to take during the life of the loan unless prior consent is obtained from the lending bank, usually by an amendment to the term loan agreement or by letter. The objectives of negative covenants are to prevent a dissipation of assets that would weaken the firm's financial strength and the assumption of obligations (definite or contingent) that might reduce the borrower's ability to repay the loan. A common negative covenant is the *negative pledge clause,* usually found in unsecured loans, by which the borrower agrees not to pledge any assets as security to other lenders and not to sell receivables. Even though this clause may be included if the loan is secured, its importance is probably lessened since other lenders would be reluctant to loan sizable amounts to a firm that has already pledged most of its assets. Such a covenant assures the bank that other lenders will not be placed in a more favorable position than it occupies.

Prohibitions regarding merger and consolidation, except with the approval of the bank, are also generally included for the bank's protection. To assure that the productive ability of the concern remains intact, a prohibition is usually included against the sale or lease of substantially all the borrower's assets. Term loan borrowers also usually agree not to make loans to others or to guarantee, endorse, or become surety for others. Such a prohibition reduces the possibility of cash withdrawals, a weakened financial position, and the assumption of contingent liabilities.

Restrictive Clauses

Restrictive clauses seem similar to negative covenants but are basically different. Negative covenants prohibit certain acts of management in general; restrictive clauses permit certain acts but restrict their latitude. For example, a negative covenant may prohibit a term loan borrower from mortgaging plant and equipment during the life of the loan, whereas a restrictive clause may limit the amount of dividends that the borrower is permitted to pay. The bank recognizes that the borrower must have some latitude in management but that certain acts must be limited or restricted if the bank is to be protected.

To assure that the borrowing firm will retain a portion of its earnings in the business so as to strengthen its financial condition, restrictions are usually placed on the amount of dividends that may be paid. Limitations may also be placed on salaries, bonuses, and advances to officers and employees, as well as to others. The objectives of such restrictions are to encourage, if not force, the borrower to be less dependent on borrowed funds and to increase the amount of equity in the business. The limitation on salaries and bonuses is a way of forcing a borrower to conserve funds until adequate capital is available. The restriction on dividends may be in terms of a certain percentage of earnings, or it may be specified that dividends not be allowed to reduce earned surplus below a certain level.

Banks realize that the borrowing firm may need short-term funds to take care of seasonal needs. Such borrowings are permitted, but usually a limit is placed on total borrowings, both long and short term. The amount that will be permitted varies, of course, with the nature and needs of the business.

A restriction may be placed on the amount of funds that a term loan borrower can invest in fixed assets such as plant and equipment. The purpose of this limitation is to prevent the firm from overextending itself. The amount that can be invested may vary considerably and may be limited to the company's annual depreciation charges. To prevent a weakening of the firm's financial strength, a restriction may also be placed on the amount of funds that can be used for the purchase of its capital stock.

If a borrower owes long-term debts to others, a limitation may be placed on the amount that may be retired annually without also retiring a portion of the term debt owed to the bank. The purpose of such a provision is to prevent the bank from being the last to be repaid. It also prevents the firm from using the bank's funds to pay off some other lender. Finally, a restriction may be imposed on the purchase of securities, with the usual exception of U.S. government obligations. This limitation is designed to prohibit speculation in securities.

Events of Default

All term loans have default provisions to make the entire loan immediately due and payable under certain conditions. This is done through an *acceleration clause*, which provides that if certain conditions are not met, the total loan is immediately due. If such a clause were not included in the agreement, the bank would be forced to wait until each installment was due before legal action could be taken against the borrower. This would certainly be more expensive, troublesome, and risky than suing for the entire amount at one time. Usually when default is in the offing, the liquidation value of the firm declines rapidly, and it is desirable to act immediately.

Several default provisions are ordinarily included in term loan agreements. Probably the most important act of default is failure to pay principal or interest according to the terms agreed on. When this happens, the firm is not necessarily in a serious financial condition, but it is at least a signal that trouble may be developing. If such is the case, steps can be taken to collect the loan. Another act of default is the misrepresentation of information presented in financial statements. This is an indication not only of financial trouble but also of management's lack of integrity. Since financial statements provide means by which management can be evaluated, misrepresentation is a clear indication that the borrower is not of high moral character and that it would be best for the bank to dissolve the relationship. Failure to perform or observe any of the terms of the agreement is also a default. This is indeed a broad provision. Evidence of insolvency or bankruptcy is also included as an act or event of default.

Term loan agreements may appear burdensome and strict, but the terms and conditions express sound financial principles. True, they are designed to protect the bank, but they also have as their objective the continued financial health of the borrower. One of the difficulties in drawing up a term loan agreement is that conditions change after the loan is consummated, and some may become obsolete and too restrictive. This is recognized, of course, and it is not uncommon for the parties to negotiate a change in some terms after the agreement is in effect.

REVOLVING CREDIT

Revolving credit was defined in Chapter 10 and compared to lines of credit in Chapter 11. The revolving credit agreement may, at the outset, extend one to three years, thus qualifying it as intermediate-term credit. This form of credit is flexible from the borrower's standpoint in that funds can be drawn as needed and repaid as available over the period of the agreement.

A revolving credit may be converted to a term loan at the end of the agreement period, depending on how the borrower has performed under the agreement and the borrower's financial condition. Many times this is the intent when the revolving credit is established. In other cases the revolving credit is paid off as the borrower gradually increases its equity capital through retained earnings. Other revolving credits may, however, go on for many years, with the agreement being extended over and over as

long as pledged collateral—usually inventory or receivables—has sufficient liquidating value to secure the debt. This is often termed *asset-based
lending*. It also has been called *permanent capital lending* since it is
essentially a substitute for owner's equity.[1] Such borrowers usually do not
have the financial strength to borrow long term and cannot or choose not
to increase owner's equity.

LEASING

Many business firms meet some or all of their intermediate-term credit
needs by leasing fixed assets. They "borrow" the assets rather than borrow
money to buy the assets. There are legal and tax differences that may make
either leasing or borrowing appear advantageous, depending on the circumstances, but the purpose—having assets to use in the business—is the
same. Thus it is appropriate to consider the leasing of assets by banks as a
form of intermediate-term credit.

In recent years, lease financing has become one of the most dynamic
areas in commercial banking. Direct participation of commercial banks in
lease financing began in the early 1960s, and in 1971 the Federal Reserve
Board ruled that bank holding companies could establish subsidiaries to
lease personal property and equipment. In 1974 the authority of bank
holding company subsidiaries was broadened to include the leasing of
real property under certain conditions. The finance leasing of equipment
ranges from small items of office equipment to commercial aircraft and
oceangoing tankers. Banks and bank-affiliated companies are limited in
their leasing authority to *full-payout net leases*, also known as finance
leases, financial leases, or capital leases. A full-payout lease is one from
which the lessor expects to realize the return of its full investment in the
leased property plus the estimated cost of financing during the base term
of the lease. The lessor's expected return is derived from rentals, plus
estimated tax benefits, plus either the estimated residual value of the
property at the expiration of the base term of the lease or a guarantee of the
residual value by the lessee or a third party. In finance leasing, the leased
asset is purchased by the lessor at the request of the lessee, and the lessee
assumes virtually all the responsibilities of ownership, including maintenance of the property and payment of all property taxes and insurance.

Leveraged Leasing

It is estimated that over 85 percent of all full-payout leasing is in the
form of *leveraged leases*, also known as *third-party equity leases* or *inves-*

---

[1] Edgar M. Morsman, Jr., "Commercial Loan Structuring," *The Journal of Commercial
Bank Lending* (June 1986), pp. 2–20.

tor leases. A leveraged lease is one where the lessor borrows up to 80 percent of the cost of the leased property from one or more long-term lenders. In a typical leveraged lease transaction, the lessor receives a fee for originating the financing, in addition to interest income and rapid recovery of the investment by virtue of heavy tax deductions for depreciation and interest expense in the early years. The long-term money is usually borrowed by the lessor on a nonrecourse basis, with the rentals and equipment pledged as collateral for the loan. For tax purposes, the lessor reports the rentals as gross income and is allowed to deduct accelerated depreciation on the leased equipment as well as interest on the long-term borrowing. As a consequence, the lessor has substantial tax losses and large cash inflows in the early years of the lease period, followed by cash outflows in the later years. In the final year of the lease, cash may come in from the residual value of the equipment and from the tax benefit that results from disposing of the asset at a loss, if that is the case.

Leveraged leasing is often used on large transactions with lessees who are unable to take advantage of the investment tax credit or accelerated depreciation. This may be because they have inadequate profits or their income is largely or entirely tax exempt, as in the case of producer cooperatives. By leasing instead of buying, the lessee is able to transfer valuable tax benefits to the lessor in return for financing at interest rates often substantially below the lessee's ordinary borrowing rate.

Tax Advantages

It is often stated that leasing is advantageous to lessees because rental payments are fully tax deductible as an operating expense, and the lessee thus pays for the use of the equipment out of current, untaxed income. This ignores the fact that a finance lease is a substitute for conventional borrowing and that if the asset is purchased by a business firm with borrowed funds, it can deduct interest expense as well as depreciation. If the firm uses accelerated depreciation, the present value of the tax benefits may actually be greater with borrowing and buying than with leasing.

Leasing may have a tax advantage in two situations, one of which occurs when the lessee would be unable to take full advantage of the depreciation if the asset were purchased instead of leased. The other occurs when some of the leased property consists of land. By leasing land instead of buying it, the lessee may, in effect, be able to deduct the cost of the land over a period of years. For this privilege the lessee gives up the possibility of building up an equity, however. Furthermore, since the lessor cannot depreciate the land, the rentals (other things equal) will be higher than on depreciable property.

Since banks involved in leasing own the leased assets, they take the depreciation charges against their own income. The 1986 Tax Reform Act reduced accelerated depreciation rates and corporate tax rates, however, so the appeal of leasing programs to banks probably has declined.

ORGANIZING AND ADMINISTERING A LEASING PROGRAM

The size and nature of the staff required to operate a leasing program depend on the volume of business, the size and complexity of the leases granted, and the extent to which assistance is obtained from leasing experts in other organizations. It is one thing to handle leases of short duration on equipment costing no more than a few thousand dollars, for which standard leasing agreements can often be used with little or no modification, and quite another to grant leases with maturities of eight to twenty years on airliners, ocean tankers, nuclear cores, railroad cars, or the principal equipment of a major manufacturing plant. Large leases of this kind typically involve the participation of outside investors, stiff competition from other lenders, and an elaborate agreement tailored to the specific circumstances of the transaction.

One way in which to participate directly in finance leasing without setting up an extensive organization is to employ another bank or leasing company to handle all lease negotiations, arrange the necessary documentation, and provide administrative services. For example, the United States Leasing Company handles the leasing operations for a number of important regional banks whose assets average close to $1 billion. In this program, the bank originates the lease and provides all the funds, while United States Leasing or one of its subsidiaries is the lessor and holds title to the equipment. The lease is made only with the bank's approval, and the bank receives an assignment of the lease receivable and a security interest in the equipment. Another way of participating in lease financing without having a special leasing staff is to buy participations in leases originated or underwritten by others. Typically this occurs only with large leases negotiated by major banks, investment banking firms, or leasing companies. Of course the underwriter must structure the lease so that it will be attractive both to the investors and the lessee. The underwriter's compensation is principally in the form of front-end fees for arranging the transaction and sometimes an additional fee for disposing of the equipment at the end of the lease. When the lease is handled through a trust arrangement, the underwriter may also receive a small fee for trustee services.

QUESTIONS

1. Why is it unwise to assume that a borrower's total cash flows will be available to repay a term loan?

2. What aspects of a bank's financial condition determine the amount of term lending it should do?
3. How would you evaluate the creditworthiness of a term borrower?
4. List eight representations and warranties commonly found in term loan agreements. How do representations and warranties differ from affirmative covenants, negative covenants, and restrictive clauses?
5. List five affirmative covenants that may be found in a term loan agreement. Which of these are not likely to be found in an agreement with a major corporation? Why?
6. List four negative covenants and five restrictive clauses often found in term loan agreements. How do restrictive clauses differ from negative covenants?
7. What are the usual acts or events of default under a term loan agreement? What is an acceleration clause and why is it important?
8. What is a leveraged lease? Why are such leases attractive to banks and bank leasing companies?
9. What is the difference between a line of credit and a revolving credit?

SELECTED REFERENCES

See Chapter 11.

13

REAL ESTATE LENDING

Real estate loans make up almost one-third of the loans and one-fifth of the assets held by commercial banks. Although the total value of real estate loans held by banks exceeds one-half trillion dollars, it does not fully depict bank activity in real estate lending. Banks sell many of the real estate loans they make, so the dollar amount of real estate credit extended by banks far exceeds the balance sheet total.

The largest category of real estate loans made by banks is one- to four-family residential. This category is almost 60 percent of real estate loans held by banks. Most of the balance consists of construction and development loans and loans on commercial properties.

Because of regulations and the fact that real estate loans are not as liquid as some other types of loans, commercial banks have not always been important real estate lenders. Prior to amendments to the National Bank Act in 1916, national banks were not permitted to make urban (residential) real estate loans. Although state banks generally were not restricted by regulations from making such loans, they simply chose not to participate heavily in real estate lending. For several years the amount of real estate loans a national bank could make was limited to an amount equal to the capital and surplus of a bank or to 70 percent of the time deposits, whichever was greater. With the insurance of residential real estate loans, their improved liquidity, and the creation of a secondary market, real estate loans became much more popular, and the rules and regulations applied to this area of lending were relaxed or eliminated.

RESIDENTIAL REAL ESTATE LOANS

There are numerous reasons banks have favored extending residential mortgage credit. Borrowers tend to keep their deposits and meet their other banking needs at the institutions where they finance their properties. Banks generally prefer to lend in ways that are socially beneficial, and few if any types of credit meet that criterion more so than residential real estate lending. Also, once made, most loans on residential properties require very little administration over the long periods during which they generate revenues. However, the long maturities of the traditional, fixed rate mortgages carry high levels of interest rate risk, and that generally has caused banks to limit their holdings.

The unprecedented interest rate levels of the late 1970s and early 1980s proved the prudence of banking's somewhat cautious approach to making and holding long-term mortgage loans. Banks and other real estate lenders found themselves holding mortgage loans producing 7, 8, or 9 percent, for example, as the cost of funds soared. For example, rates on large (over $100,000) CDs were as high as 18 percent at times in 1981.

Higher and higher mortgage rates eventually eliminated most consumers from the residential mortgage market, at least in the traditional sense. Conventional mortgage rates reached 18.5 percent in 1981. Innovative financing techniques were replacing the old fixed rate mortgage to a small degree (these methods are discussed later in the chapter), and home buyers and sellers also developed many "creative financing" approaches; as a result, some activity continued in residential lending even when interest rates were at their highest.

Commercial banks did not withdraw completely from mortgage lending, including residential lending, during those years, even though the risk of making and holding mortgage loans seemed to be intensifying. Banks provided $24.1 billion to the home mortgage market in 1978, $20.0 billion in 1979, $11.3 billion in 1980, and $12.2 billion in 1981.[1]

The activities of several agencies of the federal government have contributed to the growth of residential real estate lending. Because homeownership is regarded as a desirable aspect of American life, the federal government has fostered several programs to promote the flow of funds into housing and to ease the terms under which mortgages are made. The Federal Housing Administration (FHA) was created in 1934 and charged with the responsibility of insuring residential real estate mortgages to encourage housing and homeownership.

FHA insurance is provided for loans on homes and apartments based on specific criteria concerning the nature of the property and the qualifi-

---

[1] Charles Luckett, "Recent Developments in the Mortgage and Consumer Credit Markets," *Federal Reserve Bulletin* (May 1982), pp. 281–290.

cations of the borrower. The maximum amount of the loan, the required down payment, the maturity limits of the loan, the amount charged for mortgage insurance, monthly prepayment of taxes, appraisal, inspection, and maximum interest rate are stipulated by FHA. In general, the conditions of an FHA mortgage are similar to those of conventional loans except that the rate of interest tends to be lower than rates on comparable conventional loans. The Veterans Administration (VA) guarantees loans to veterans and operates under stipulations similar to those of FHA. Other agencies, mentioned below, have facilitated residential real estate lending by fostering the secondary market for mortgage loans.

Secondary Mortgage Market

The secondary market in residential mortgage loans has expanded dramatically in the last two decades. This development has facilitated the flow of funds from investors to home buyers and has made possible the adjustment of mortgage portfolios of mortgage holders. Two types of transactions take place in the secondary mortgage market. One involves the buying and selling of mortgages; another involves what is commonly referred to as *mortgage pools*. The mortgages bought and sold in the secondary market may be either federally insured or conventional loans. A mortgage lender, such as a bank or mortgage company owned by a one-bank holding company, might sell as many as a hundred or more mortgages with a value of several million dollars to an insurance company or other long-term investor. In many cases the bank or mortgage company will continue to service the loans, receiving a fee from the investor. This enables the bank or mortgage company not only to relend the funds that had been committed to the mortgages but to continue the customer relationships as well. In many cases the home buyers are not even aware that the loans on their homes have been sold.

Mortgage pools are originated by certain government agencies, banks, and other private mortgage lenders. The originator of a pool moves a block of mortgages from its balance sheet and issues securities that represent ownership shares in the pool. The buyers of these securities become joint owners of the pool of mortgage loans and receive pro rata shares of the principal and interest payments made on the loans. Because of this treatment of payments, these securities are termed "passthroughs."

The Federal National Mortgage Association (FNMA) is the largest single investor in mortgage loans. This federally sponsored agency, known as Fannie Mae, is charged with providing liquidity to the mortgage market by buying loans when mortgage credit is in short supply and selling loans when funds are plentiful. For the most part Fannie Mae has been a buyer and has accumulated over $100 million in mortgage loans, many of which were originated by commercial banks. Fannie Mae has also issued a large amount of passthrough securities.

The agency most heavily involved with passthroughs is the Government National Mortgage Association (GNMA), often referred to as Ginnie Mae. GNMA was given the responsibility of issuing guarantees of passthroughs backed by pools of FHA and VA mortgage loans. Such mortgage-backed securities, when guaranteed by GNMA, bear the full faith and credit pledge of the federal government. These securities are sold in the open market and have been purchased by pension funds, individuals, banks, and other financial institutions. GNMA securities can be originated by any mortgage company or mortgage lender that is authorized to make FHA loans. Banks, therefore, participate in this type of lending either directly or indirectly. Another agency, the Federal Home Loan Mortgage Corporation (FHLMC), or Freddie Mac, issues passthroughs based mainly on conventional mortgages.

Bank of America, in 1977, offered the first private mortgage pool and passthrough certificates issued by commercial banks. These certificates were offered in accordance with the rules and regulations of the Securities and Exchange Commission. These certificates are not obligations of the bank but, rather, represent partial ownership of mortgages in a pool. In arrangements of this kind, the pool of conventional mortgages that are privately insured backs the certificates, and all payments to holders of the certificates are made out of mortgage payments from the underlying pool just as is the practice in GNMA-guaranteed passthroughs. Numerous other banks and savings associations have followed Bank of America's lead in offering passthroughs.

The liquidity of the mortgage market has been enhanced further in recent years by the issuance of large volumes of collateralized mortgage obligations (CMOs). The CMO is a bond backed by a pool of mortgages. Unlike passthroughs, the issuer of the CMO continues to own the mortgages, and the CMOs are direct obligations of the issuer, as would be true of any other bonds it might have outstanding. Most CMOs are assigned the highest rating by the bond rating agencies because, when issued, they are backed by mortgages valued at 180 percent or more of the face value of the CMOs. Investor demand has been strong in recent years, so CMOs have helped increase the liquidity of the mortgage market.

TYPES OF RESIDENTIAL LOANS MADE BY COMMERCIAL BANKS

Commercial banks make FHA, VA, and conventional first mortgage loans on residential properties. They also make second mortgage loans (discussed below), but these usually are made for purposes other than to facilitate purchase of the real estate serving as collateral. FHA loans are insured by the Federal Housing Authority, VA loans are guaranteed by the Veterans Administration, and conventional loans are neither insured nor guaranteed by the federal government. Private mortgage insurance may, however, be required by some banks on certain conventional loans. Of the residential mortgage loans made by commercial banks, most are conventional loans.

Several factors are responsible for the rapid increase in conventional loans relative to FHA and VA loans over the years. From the lender's standpoint, FHA and VA residential loans have some disadvantages. First, some bank officers do not look favorably on the low down payment. The owner's lack of equity may be conducive to nonpayment and default during periods of financial stress. The down payment may be as little as 3 or 4 percent of the purchase price under a FHA loan, and VA loans often require no down payment. The cost of the FHA insurance is also considered to be a detriment by some. The annual charge is one-half of 1 percent of the loan balance. Another reason some commercial banks favor conventional residential real estate loans over FHA and VA mortgages is the minimum of red tape in making, supervising, and foreclosing on the loans in the event that such a step must be taken. Probably the most important reason has been the comparatively low rate of interest allowed on FHA and VA loans. The rate of interest on FHA and VA loans usually is set below other market rates. Banks, as well as other lenders, can compensate for this spread between rates by charging *points*. One point equals 1 percent of the face value of the mortgage. Charging one point on a 30-year fixed rate mortgage has the effect of increasing the yield over the life of the loan by one-eighth of 1 percent. However, when this is done, the discount must be absorbed by the seller of the house, which means that the seller will suffer a reduction in his or her proceeds. Another factor contributing to the increase in conventional loans is the availability of private mortgage insurance similar to FHA. For example, a bank that otherwise would lend no more than 80 percent of appraised value under a conventional loan might lend 90 percent if private mortgage insurance were obtained for that amount of the loan exceeding 80 percent of value. Finally, VA loans were a product of World War II, and with the decline in the number of eligible veterans over the years, the demand for such loans has declined.

SIGNIFICANT STEPS
IN RESIDENTIAL REAL ESTATE LENDING

Because of their long maturity, fixed rate residential real estate loans are subject to a significant amount of interest rate risk and, since many things can happen to the borrower before the loan is fully repaid, all mortgage loans are subject to a considerable amount of credit risk. These risks have prompted many banks to develop expertise in this area and to establish real estate loan departments.

Credit Analysis of the Borrower

The first concern of a commercial bank in making a residential real estate loan is the creditworthiness of the borrower. The borrower must have the ability and the determination to pay. In this respect, credit analysis of real estate loan customers does not differ materially from the analysis of other types of consumers. In real estate lending, however, a more thorough analysis is made because of the nature of the loan; it is larger and its maturity is longer than in short- and intermediate-term consumer loans. The size of the loan in relation to the value of the property should also be considered in a thorough credit analysis. Many years ago, a loan equal to 50 percent of the appraised value of the property was normal, but in recent years a loan equal to 80 to 90 percent of the appraised value is quite common. When the loan-to-value ratio was relatively small, greater reliance could be placed on the value of the property as a source of repayment in the event of a default. Now it is necessary to rely more heavily on the borrower's ability to meet the terms of the loan agreement.

Banks are interested in the amount and stability of an applicant's income. Monthly payments on a mortgage are sizable and due with regularity for a large portion of a borrower's working years. In fact, monthly housing expenses are normally the largest single item in the family budget. A person who has an uncertain income probably will have difficulty obtaining a loan to purchase a home.

Appraisal of Property

A very important step in residential real estate lending is the appraisal of property offered as security for a loan. This is important since the ability of the borrower to pay may not continue as hoped and predicted, and the bank may have to look to the value of the house for repayment. The objective of such an appraisal is to arrive at the market value of the property—a difficult task since many factors influence the value.

Appraisal of residences is complex because some qualities are intangible. For example, the architecture or style can cause one house to have a higher value than another even though they are quite similar in other respects. Location, type of construction, and arrangement of rooms influence the value. A split-level house has less appeal to some purchasers than does a house on one level; houses far from the traffic flow are demanded by more buyers than are those located on a thoroughfare.

The neighborhood in which a house is located also influences its market value. Houses near an industrial area appeal less to some than do those in a residential district where all the houses are similar in appearance and construction and are occupied by middle-income families.

Houses located near schools, churches, parks, and playgrounds are especially appealing. The availability of services such as police and fire protection, sewers, and street lighting is a factor that must be considered in arriving at the market value estimates of residential properties.

Although real estate appraising is not an exact science, it must be done to carry out a real estate lending program effectively. Its success depends on the ability and experience of the appraiser and the use of such tools of appraising as adequate records of residential sales, new construction permits, sales prices of existing and newly constructed houses, population movements, depreciation and obsolescence factors, the supply of houses, and potential demand for housing. The appraiser must examine all the factors that influence market value and convert them into an estimated valuation of one specific house.

Small banks frequently rely on members of their board of directors to perform this function. Some banks permit the officer or officers concerned with real estate loans to do the appraising; others may employ independent professional appraisers, especially if appraising a particular piece of property presents unique problems. Many large banks that make sizable amounts of real estate loans have professional appraisers on their staffs.

Several methods of appraisal are employed by residential real estate appraisers, the most common of which are cost and market data. In the cost method, the appraised value is the product of the reproduction cost of a house less depreciation. The value of the land or lot is arrived at by comparing it with similar parcels of land in the area. The appraiser estimates the cost of constructing the house, usually on a square foot basis, and then subtracts from this figure the "used up" portion of this value. Consideration is also given to the intangible factors mentioned earlier. The market data method compares the house being appraised with similar houses sold recently whose actual market is known. This method, like the cost method, is not easy since all houses are not alike and other factors must be considered. Both methods have limitations and can be used successfully only by persons who have had considerable training and experience.

It is essential to make the appraisal as accurate as possible, for this is the basis of the mortgage loan. For example, if a bank agreed to loan an amount equal to 80 percent of the appraised value of a house appraised at $50,000 but worth only $42,000, it would be lending $40,000 or approximately the full current market value of the house. Should a default occur, assuming stable real estate prices, it would be doubtful that the bank could avoid some loss by the time all the costs of foreclosure and sale were considered. If the house were appraised at $35,000, however, the borrower might go to another lender, since the bank would be willing to lend only $28,000 on a house that was entitled to a loan of $33,600. Poor appraising can be expensive to a bank or any other lender. If appraisals are too high, the bank's risks are increased; if too low, borrowers will seek their loans elsewhere.

TERMS OF RESIDENTIAL REAL ESTATE LOANS

Real estate loan agreements and security instruments differ significantly from other types of bank loans. This is largely because of the maturity and size of real estate loans. Consequently, a considerable amount of investigation and document preparation is necessary in real estate lending.

Enforceable Lien

Since the property that secures a real estate loan may have to be sold to satisfy the loan if the borrower is not able to pay it in later years, an enforceable lien is absolutely essential. Securing such a lien may involve considerable time, effort, and expense both to the lender and to the borrower. Real estate is transferred by a legal document called a *deed*, and an enforceable lien can only be given by a person who has legal title to the property. The bank, as lender, must be sure that no prior liens on the property exist, such as unpaid taxes and mechanics' liens, which take precedence over a mortgage. This requires either the services of an attorney or the acquisition of a title insurance policy. From an examination of an abstract, which is a recorded history of the property, an attorney can usually determine the lawful owner. He or she will give what is known as an attorney's opinion, which identifies the legal owner and sets forth any outstanding claims or encumbrances against the property.

If there is any cloud on the borrower's title, it must be cleared up satisfactorily before a loan will be made. In some areas, lenders rely on title companies to investigate the property and determine who is the legal owner and whether any liens exist, and to insure the lender against loss should some person later prove that he or she has title to the property or that there were liens or claims against it.

Mortgage

In commercial bank lending on residential real estate, a loan is evidenced by a note and a real estate mortgage, or, in some areas, by a trust deed. Some states regard the mortgage as a document that transfers legal title of the property to the mortgagee or lender as security for a debt. If the debt is paid as agreed, the transfer becomes void. Other states regard the mortgage as a document that gives the mortgagee a lien on the property to secure the debt. This lien can be exercised by the mortgagee only if the borrower defaults on the debt. Whatever the mortgage concept, however, the mortgage is the basic security for real estate loans in this country.

A real estate mortgage usually includes several covenants that the borrower agrees to fulfill and that, basically, are similar to those found in term loan agreements employed in business lending. First, the mortgagor agrees to repay the principal sum with interest as set forth in the note. Another covenant states that the borrower will pay all taxes, special assessments, and other charges levied on the property. In many cases these special tax funds are held in escrow by the bank. However, in some states, where lenders are required to pay interest on escrowed funds, escrows may not be required. Further, the mortgage generally requires the borrower to keep the property in good repair and not use it for any unlawful purpose. It may also prohibit making substantial alterations or additions to the property without the express permission of the lender. The mortgagor is required to keep the property fully insured against such risks as fire and windstorm and to assign the policies to the bank.

These covenants are important and, in many instances, have proved necessary to maintain the lender's economic interest in the property. They can be invoked if they are being violated by the mortgagor. Covenants are defensive devices in that they are designed to protect the lender against excessive wear and tear on the property, undue hazards, the possibility of claims being levied against the property, and changes that will decrease its market value. If they are not complied with, the lender's interest in the property may be lessened; in the event that foreclosure and sale of the property are necessary, the lender may sustain substantial loss.

Mortgages usually contain an *acceleration clause*: if the borrower fails to make principal and interest payments or to comply with any of the covenants, the full amount of the loan becomes immediately due and payable. The need for such a clause is obvious. Finally, the mortgage must be recorded in the proper public office to protect the lender's interests from subsequent claims by third parties. The cost of consummating a real estate loan is quite high and is usually borne by the borrower.

From what has been said it may appear that, in the event of nonpayment, the foreclosure and sale of property is a relatively simple process. This is not the case. Each state follows the principle that every mortgage carries a *right of redemption* before foreclosure can be effected. This borrower's equitable right of redemption permits a mortgagor to redeem the mortgaged property by paying the debt within a certain period of time prior to the foreclosure sale. It is designed to temper the harshness of the law that permits the taking of a borrower's property.

Statute also gives the mortgagor a right to redeem after the sale. The redemption time varies from two months to two years after the foreclosure sale. During this period, depending on state law, the borrower may occupy the property if the rent is paid to a court-appointed receiver, and the purchaser of the property does not receive a deed until after the statutory term has expired. Since foreclosure proceedings are time consuming and the property may decline in value, banks are reluctant to foreclose, except as a last resort. The mortgagor is given every opportunity to pay or to transfer the property to another buyer.

Repayment Provisions

Most residential real estate loans are payable on an amortized basis with principal and interest combined in a single, uniform monthly payment. An example of a portion of an amortization schedule for a 30-year loan in the amount of $40,000, at 9.5 percent interest, is presented in Table 13-1. In this example the monthly payment of $336.35 consists of two parts, principal and interest. At the end of the first month, most of the payment, $316.67, is for interest and only $19.68 is allocated to the reduction of the principal. As additional payments are made, the amount allocated to interest declines because the amount of the loan is constantly being reduced, and the amount for reduction of the principal increases. At the end of 15 years and one month, for example, the monthly payment of $336.35 is divided into $254.97 for interest and $81.38 for principal payment, and the balance of the loan is $32,125.10.

With over 80 percent of the original balance remaining after 15 years, the interest rate risk of such loans is very high. To reduce this risk, one step taken by banks and other lenders is to encourage shorter maturity loans. A 15-year loan, for example, with the same rate and for the same amount as the loan illustrated in Table 13-1, would require a monthly payment of $417.69. However, because of the lower risk to the lender, the 15-year loan probably would carry a somewhat lower interest rate than the 30-year loan.

TABLE 13-1   Terms on an Amortized Mortgage Loan
Amount of loan: $40,000; Time outstanding: 30 years; Interest rate: 9.5 percent

Time			Monthly Payment		
			Interest	*Principal*	**Balance Due**
Year	*Month*	**Payment**	*Portion*	*Payment*	**on Loan**
0	1	$336.35	$316.67	$ 19.68	$39,980.32
0	3	336.35	316.35	20.00	39,940.48
0	9	336.35	315.39	20.96	39,817.15
5	6	336.35	303.49	32.86	38,302.44
10	3	336.35	284.84	51.51	35,928.16
15	1	336.35	254.97	81.38	32,125.10
19	6	336.35	212.75	123.60	26,749.50
24	6	336.35	137.96	198.39	17,228.60
29	0	336.35	32.65	303.70	3,820.78

ADJUSTABLE RATE MORTGAGES

The most significant step designed to reduce the interest rate risk in mortgages has been the broad adoption of alternatives to the fixed rate mortgage. The most important of these is the adjustable rate mortgage (ARM). The ARM transfers most of the interest rate risk to the borrower. Banks have used adjustable, or floating, rates in commercial lending for many years, but their widespread use in mortgage lending followed the high interest rates of the late 1970s and early 1980s.

ARMs make up approximately half the home mortgage loans made in recent years.[2] The ARM rate is reset at the end of each stipulated adjustment period, perhaps six months. The rate is reset according to changes in an index, such as the market rate on certain maturities of Treasury securities. The ARM rate is set above the index by a margin determined when the loan was granted.

ARMs frequently are made at low "teaser" rates for the first adjustment period. At the end of the period the rate is reset at the stipulated margin over the index, and the home buyer's monthly payment may rise sharply. The term "payment shock" has been used to describe home buyers' reactions when the increases are large. This has encouraged the use of "caps," which limit how high the interest rate, or monthly payment, can rise.

SECOND MORTGAGES

Second mortgage loans made by banks normally are for purposes other than to help finance the properties that serve to secure the loans. Such a loan usually is made against the equity a home buyer has built up over several years, and the proceeds may be intended for any reasonable purpose. Thus these are consumer loans, according to purpose, but they are classified as real estate loans due to the form of collateral. Second mortgage lending has been important to banks and other lenders in recent years.

Activity in second mortgage lending intensified with the passage of the Tax Reform Act of 1986, particularly in the so-called "home equity loan."[3] The new law gradually eliminated the tax deductibility of interest on consumer loans but continued the deductibility of interest on loans secured by borrowers' primary or secondary residences. An exception is

---

[2] John L. Goodman, Jr., and Charles A. Luckett, "Adjustable-Rate Financing in Mortgage and Consumer Credit Markets," *Federal Reserve Bulletin* (November 1985), pp. 823–835.

[3] Danial M. Clark, "Home Equity Taps the American Dream," *ABA Banking Journal* (April 1987), pp. 50, 52, and 54.

the interest on loan amounts that exceed the cost of a home. Thus the new law encouraged homeowners to borrow against their homes for consumption purposes, such as the purchase of a car. In one popular form the home equity loan provides the eligible homeowner a line of credit that he or she may draw on simply by writing a check.

TRUTH IN LENDING

Real estate loan transactions are included in the Truth-in-Lending Act, which is discussed in greater detail in the following chapter. In fact, a major portion of the act is concerned with the borrower's right of rescission, which is applicable mainly to home mortgages and home improvement loans. The right of rescission allows a borrower to cancel a credit arrangement within three business days if his or her residence is used as collateral for the credit. This provision allows the borrower time to contemplate the purchase, shop for better credit terms, or cancel a home improvement project that may have been foisted on him or her by a high-pressure salesperson. However, a first mortgage to finance the purchase of a borrower's residence carries no right of rescission, although a first mortgage for any other purpose and a second mortgage on the same residence may be canceled. The borrower may cancel the credit transaction and the transaction that predicated the credit application by signing and dating a notice of such a decision. All credit transactions where the right of rescission is applicable are required by the act to include in the borrower's papers two copies of a cancellation form. Before furnishing copies of the notice to the customer, the lender is to complete the copies with the name of the lender, the address of the lender's place of business, the date of consummation of the transaction, and the date, not earlier than the third business day following the transaction, by which the customer may give notice of cancellation. In case of an emergency, a homeowner may waive the right to rescind a transaction provided that he or she has determined that a three-day delay in performance of the lender's obligation would jeopardize the welfare, health, or safety of persons or endanger property he or she owns or for which he or she is responsible. All other conditions relative to the Truth-in-Lending Act, including the effective annual interest rate, disclosures, finance charges, penalties, and liabilities as discussed in previous chapters, apply to real estate transactions.

MOBILE HOME LOANS

The demand for mobile homes has increased in recent years for several reasons. They are less expensive than conventional housing and are usually sold with complete furniture packages. As larger units have become available, this type of housing has been more widely accepted. During periods of tight money, it has often been easier to obtain financing for a mobile home than for a single-family residence, because during such periods more buyers are attracted by shorter maturities and higher interest rates on loans for mobile homes.

Mobile home financing has changed dramatically. Originally, financing was secured through finance companies with limited participation by commercial banks. Then the Housing and Urban Development Act of 1968 provided for FHA and VA guarantees on mobile homes with maturities of 12 years or less. As a result, savings and loan associations, mutual savings banks, and commercial banks increased their activity in mobile home lending.

In many respects the sale and financing transactions involving mobile homes are similar to those involving automobiles. New mobile homes are normally sold by dealers who show them on display lots, and frequently the inventory is financed by banks. The financing of individual units is arranged at the time of sale by the dealer, and the note or paper is transferred to a bank. Since the bank is a third party to the sales transaction, the bank may require a *limited liability clause* or a reserve in the agreement with the dealer. Briefly, a limited liability clause requires the dealer to stand behind the borrower's loan in the case of default, whereas the purchase reserve involves the bank holding a percentage of the selling price until the mobile home is paid for. Additional protection for the bank is also required in a comprehensive mobile home insurance policy. This type of policy parallels the protection found in a traditional homeowner's policy. A second type of insurance is referred to as a *vendor's single-interest policy*. It can protect the lender and/or dealer from such losses as disappearance of the home, inability to repossess the unit, and collision. The basis for such coverage is an impairment of the lender's security interest. The establishment of such insurance plans protects the interest of the lender. Many commercial banks that make mobile home loans employ the services of companies that specialize in insuring and processing such loans. For a small fee, usually a percentage of the monthly payment, the insurance company provides a default insurance policy similar to private mortgage insurance for other homes. In the event of default, the insurance company pays the bank and proceeds to repossess the mobile home.

LAND DEVELOPMENT AND CONSTRUCTION LOANS

Commercial banks are relatively large lenders for land development and the construction of industrial, commercial, residential, and farm buildings. Land development loans provide a line of credit to the developer for the construction of streets, sewers, and other public utilities to prepare building lots for house sites or resale. Banks usually lend no more than 75 percent of the appraised value of finished lots and are quite selective in making land development loans. Land development loans require considerable supervision. The loan agreement includes a release mechanism that sets forth when, how, and at what price lots may be released. Moreover, the agreement specifies the amount of money from the sale of each lot that must be applied to the loan. Land development loans can be quite risky, since repayment often depends on the sale of the developed lots. The history of such financing indicates that some developments have been very popular while others have been financial failures. An experienced, reliable, and financially sound developer is very important. Commercial banks are interested in a land developer who fully discloses the essential facts regarding the lots that are for sale. The reason is, of course, that this activity has attracted unscrupulous operators. Real estate history is replete with incidents of selling lots under water, miles from modern transportation and utilities, and on the sides of mountains. Government regulations and more responsible people in the land development business have reduced such unethical practices. However, it is still possible to sell lots under water, but that fact must be revealed to the prospective purchaser.

One reason for providing land development loans is to get an inside track on financing the houses when the development is completed. Not only are residential loans desirable from the standpoint of collateral and income, but they frequently result in a deposit relationship for the lending bank.

Construction loans to contractors arise when the ultimate owner of a building may not be known at the time of construction, or when the owner is not able to provide enough financing or is concerned only with the finished product. For example, a builder specializing in single-family residences may have 50 or more houses under construction at one time. Obviously, a considerable amount of financing is required during the construction period. As another example, a business firm, individual investor, or a group of investors might agree to purchase an office building or a manufacturing plant, but first someone must finance and construct the building. It is during this construction period that bank credit is extended.

A construction loan assumes many characteristics of a commercial loan. In determining the amount to be loaned, the banker takes into account the estimated construction costs, the estimated market value of the completed building, and the managerial and financial ability of the contractor. Normally, construction loans are advanced in installments as the building progresses. As is true of all lending, risk is ever present in construction lending, which is the major reason for very close supervision.

The lending officer of a bank must be knowledgeable in many areas—construction costs and materials, the value of a location, demand for buildings, and the like. Unforeseen and adverse developments can occur. Weather may delay construction; strikes and a shortage of skilled labor at unpropitious times can be expensive and frustrating. The delivery of materials can become slow and even unavailable at times. Construction costs can rise as the general level of prices spiral upward. Environmental legislation and interpretations by regulatory bodies can cause construction moratoriums. Demand for the finished product may also change, especially in speculative construction. These factors and others can adversely influence the ability of the contractor to complete the project.

The administration of a construction loan is quite involved. A performance or *completion bond* may be required of the contractor. Such a bond guarantees that the contractor will fulfill the existing contract, that is, complete the building. Should the contractor default, the insurance company or surety protects the policyholder against the loss involved up to the bond penalty. A completion bond insures the property owner that the project will be completed free of liens. However, completion bonds do not protect a bank in the event of default on repayment of the loan. Other documents that may be required are title insurance, a survey, fire and casualty insurance, a building permit, an environmental impact study, and so on. An important document is the *letter of commitment*, which is a contract or pledge by a long-term lender to make the permanent loan, called the take-out loan, on the property when it is completed in accordance with all specifications. While the construction loan on, say, an office building might be suitable to its needs, a bank might not be in a position to finance the long-term loan because of its size, length of time to maturity, and the fact that this type of loan does not meet the established liquidity requirements. The permanent investor might be the company for whom the building was being built, an insurance firm, or possibly a pension trust.

NONFARM, NONRESIDENTIAL REAL ESTATE LOANS

Commercial banks make a variety of nonfarm, nonresidential loans that may be secured by properties such as stores, shopping centers, apartments, warehouses, and industrial buildings. These loans are called *income property loans*, and it is not uncommon for commercial banks to have a section devoted to this kind of lending within its real estate loan department. The income property term derives from the value of these properties, which is established by their ability to produce an income stream. In arriving at the value of such properties, the lending officer estimates the future potential gross income from the property and calculates the expenses of operation required to arrive at the net income. The next and final step is to select a proper capitalization rate and a capitalization technique for estimating the value of the property.

Because of the liquidity needs of commercial banks, the maturity of income real estate loans seldom exceeds 15 years, and the preference is for even shorter maturities. Income property loans are frequently made with a balloon payment at maturity. At maturity, this is paid in full or, in some cases, the amount may be refinanced at the rate of interest then prevailing. This arrangement reduces monthly, quarterly, or annual payments and permits the borrower to increase cash now. The loan-to-value ratio of an income property loan is usually low. Bankers are sensitive to real estate loans that contain an inordinate amount of risk, and correctly so.

Another factor that enters into income property loan considerations is the deposit relationship. Frequently, large real estate loans do not result in deposit balances in proportionate dimensions; consequently, such loans are not looked upon with favor by commercial banks. Banks prefer to make real estate mortgage loans to business firms that are depositors rather than to out-of-community firms that carry their deposit balances elsewhere. Banks also place greater emphasis on the creditworthiness of the borrower than do other income property lenders.

FARM REAL ESTATE LOANS

Banks hold about one-tenth of the debt secured by farm real estate, which totaled $106 billion at the end of 1985. It should not be assumed that the amount of credit secured by farmland was used exclusively for the purchase of land and buildings. To be sure, part of this credit was used to purchase fixed assets, but a large portion was used for current operations and the purchase of machinery. Although the proceeds of farm loans may be used for other purposes, a large portion of such loans is secured by real estate since it is the most common asset available. The irregularity of farm income and the feeling that land is a sound investment have contributed to the heavy reliance on real estate as security. Banks have not been attracted to farm real estate lending because of the maturity of the loans and the risks involved. The maturity of most loans is relatively long, since the purchase of a farm usually requires the working lifetime of a farmer. For this reason, the Federal Land banks that specialize in loans to farmers for the purchase of real estate are authorized to make loans for a 40-year period. Because of their liquidity needs commercial banks are not in a position to make loans of this maturity; therefore, individuals, life insurance companies, and Federal Land banks are the big farm real estate lenders.

MORTGAGE BANKING

Mortgage banking is an intermediation process that brings real estate borrowers and lenders together. Mortgage bankers generally utilize borrowed funds to originate and close loans on commercial properties as well as government-guaranteed and conventional residential mortgage loans, which are then sold to various financial institutions and/or government agencies. In originating and packaging the loans, mortgage banking companies provide a beneficial service by attracting capital to a capital-deficient area to finance residential construction at slightly higher, but acceptable, rates. The mortgage banker generally sells the loans outright in packages of $1 million or more, usually with the mortgage company servicing the loans, that is, collecting the monthly payments, escrow funds, and so on and making payment to the holders of the mortgage. A fee of .375 percent is normally charged for this service. Banks lend to mortgage bankers, which, in many cases, are owned by the holding companies that own the banks providing the loans. Some of the advantages to a commercial bank in being affiliated with a mortgage banking company can be understood when it is realized that mortgage companies are not limited to the geographic area of the bank, need not limit sales to the parent bank, and have a limited interest rate risk exposure because of the short time between the originating and the selling of the mortgage.

QUESTIONS

1. What factors have been responsible for the increase since World War II in bank loans secured by residential real estate?
2. Why must conventional loans conform more and more to the requirements established by the secondary market?
3. What is the relationship between the price and the yield on a mortgage loan? Explain "points."
4. What factors are important in evaluating the creditworthiness of an applicant for a residential real estate loan?
5. What are the steps in the appraisal process for residential and income properties? What are the different approaches to property appraisal?
6. Why is the appraisal of property important in making residential real estate loans? Why is such an appraisal often more difficult than that for a loan secured by an automobile or by stocks or bonds?
7. How do the long maturity characteristics of fixed rate residential real estate mortgage loans subject lenders to increased (a) interest rate risk and (b) credit risk? Explain.

8. What is a construction loan and what factors of risk are associated with such a loan?
9. What is an adjustable rate mortgage (ARM), and why has its use increased in the 1980s?

SELECTED REFERENCES

AMERICAN INSTITUTE OF REAL ESTATE APPRAISERS. *The Appraisal of Real Estate*, 8th ed. Chicago, 1983.

BANK ADMINISTRATION INSTITUTE. *Residential Mortgage Lending*. Park Ridge, Ill., 1985.

CLARK, DANIAL M. "Home Equity Taps the American Dream." *ABA Banking Journal* (April 1987), pp. 50, 52, and 54.

DENNIS, MARSHALL W. *Mortgage Lending Fundamentals and Practices*, 2nd ed. Reston, Va.: Reston, 1983.

————. *Residential Mortgage Lending*. Reston, Va.: Reston, 1985.

GOODMAN, JOHN L., JR. "Adjustable-Rate Financing in Mortgage and Credit Markets." *Federal Reserve Bulletin* (November 1985), pp. 823–835.

WIEDMER, JOHN P. *Real Estate Finance*, 4th ed. Reston, Va.: Reston, 1983.

14

LOANS
TO CONSUMERS

Consumer loans are made to finance consumption, as compared with loans made for productive purposes or for the purchase of assets that produce a flow of funds, such as stocks and bonds. Consumer loans make possible the consumption of goods and services in advance of the consumer's ability to pay; as a result, consumers can enjoy a higher standard of living. Such loans are made for a multitude of purposes, including the purchase of automobiles, household appliances, furniture, medical services, vacations, and so on. Although the maturities of consumer loans vary, they are usually made for a period of less than five years. With the rise in consumer incomes and expenditures, consumer credit, including that provided by commercial banks, has been growing rapidly for many years.

CLASSIFICATION OF CONSUMER CREDIT

Of the total amount of consumer credit extended by commercial banks, more than 80 percent is made on an installment basis. The remainder is classified as single-payment loans. Both lenders and borrowers have discovered that repaying a certain amount of the debt each month or payday is more convenient than accumulating the funds and retiring the total debt at one time.

Installment Consumer Credit

Commercial banks have played a dominant role in consumer lending for many years. At mid-1987, banks held 45 percent of the installment credit of the nation (see Table 14-1). Banks have increased their share of all categories of installment credit over the years with the single exception of automobile credit. The reason for this development has been due primarily to the financing of automobiles by "captive" finance companies at relatively low rates of interest in conjunction with an aggressive sales campaign by automobile companies in the early 1980s. An area dominated by commercial banks is revolving credit or what might be termed credit card credit. The dominance of revolving credit by banks stems from the popularity of bank credit cards such as Visa and MasterCard, the increased acceptance of bank credit cards by retailers, and the desire of consumers to limit their credit cards to only a few, of which one is a bank card.

The classification "Mobile home" in Table 14-1 includes the financing of mobile homes, trailers, campers, self-propelled motor homes, and similar vehicles. Although several reasons could be given for classifying mobile homes as real estate credit, the consumer credit statistics collected and published by the Federal Reserve System place these loans under the general heading of consumer credit. Several factors have been responsible for this practice, two of which are accretion and tradition. The financing of trailers came into being before mobile homes were financed by banks. Since trailer financing was similar in some respects to the financing of automobiles, such loans were placed in the same department. When banks entered the field of mobile home financing, these loans, too, were placed in the installment loan department because of their similarity to trailer financing. Also, the legal documents used in the financing of mobile homes are more like those used in trailer and automobile financing than those in real estate financing. Moreover, the fact that mobile homes are more easily moved than are houses had something to do with their being considered consumer loans. Finally, the maturity of mobile home loans normally is shorter than that for home loans. Although the maturity of mobile home loans varies, they usually range from 6 to 10 years compared with a maturity of 25 to 30 years for real estate loans. Mobile home credit is almost equally divided among three lenders: commercial banks, finance companies, and savings institutions.

The category "All other" in Table 14-1 includes loans for the repair and modernization of owner-occupied dwellings and personal loans. Personal loans are made for a variety of purposes, such as the consolidation of debts and the payment of medical, education, or travel expenses, personal taxes, and insurance premiums. Such loans satisfy the need for relatively large amounts of borrowed funds for the purchase of durable commodities that can best be repaid on a monthly or installment basis.

TABLE 14-1 Consumer Installment Credit, October 1987 (in millions of dollars)

| | Major Holders | | By Major Type of Credit | | | | | | | |
| | | | Automobile | | Revolving | | Mobile Home | | All Other | |
	Amount	Percent of Total	Amount	Percent of Total	Amount	Percent of Total	Amount	Percent of Total	Amount	Percent of Total
Commercial banks	$270,936	44.7	$105,479	40.7	$ 92,419	64.5	$ 8,462	32.9	$ 64,576	36.2
Finance companies	143,118	23.6	98,219	37.9	0	0	8,610	33.5	36,289	20.4
Credit unions	84,207	13.9	42,212	16.3	2,301	1.6	0	0	39,694	22.3
Retailers	40,848	6.7	0	0	36,416	25.4	0	0	4,432	2.5
Savings institutions	63,546	10.4	13,186	5.1	8,445	5.9	8,617	33.5	33,298	18.8
Gasoline companies	3,691	.6	0	0	3,691	2.6	0	0	0	0
Total	$606,346	100.0	$259,096	100.0	$143,272	100.0	$25,689	100.0	$178,288	100.0

NOTE: Items may not add to totals because of rounding.

SOURCE: Board of Governors of the Federal Reserve System, *Federal Reserve Bulletin* (February 1988).

Terms of Consumer Installment Credit

The terms of consumer installment credit are presented in Table 14-2 for selected dates. Consumer loan rates are among the highest found in all lending institutions. As was pointed out in Chapter 10, the reasons for the relatively high rates are the costs encountered in making and administering loans, the risks involved, the quality of the collateral supporting loans, and the maturity of the loan contract. In recent years the interest rate charged by finance companies on new cars was less than that found at banks, and it was for that reason primarily that the share of automobile credit held by banks declined. Because of the increase in the cost of automobiles, the maturity of new car loans has increased and so has the loan-to-value ratio. The loan-to-value ratio for used cars was slightly more than for new cars. The reason for this is the very large first-year depreciation on new cars. The amount of credit advanced by banks annually is substantial (see Table 14-2). Automobile purchases constitute the largest single category of expenditures financed by consumer installment credit. Loans on automobiles account for about 40 percent of the total nonmortgage installment credit of the nation. The maturity of automobile loans has increased in recent years as the price of automobiles has gone up. If the length of the contract had not increased, the monthly cost of automobiles would have risen also and sales would have declined, as many potential buyers would have been driven from the market. Unfortunately, as the length of the contract increases, so does the risk of nonpayment.

The interest charge for personal loans is slightly higher than for automobiles primarily because of the collateral supporting the loan. The automobile in our society is considered a necessity; consequently, the risk of nonpayment of an automobile loan is less than for personal loans,

TABLE 14-2 Terms of Consumer Installment Credit, August 1987

Interest Rates (percent)		Other Terms*	
Commercial banks		Maturity (month)	
48-month new car	10.37	New car	52.1
24-month personal	14.22	Used car	45.4
120-month mobile home	13.24	Loan-to-value-ratio	
Credit card	17.85	New car	93
Auto finance companies		Used car	98
New car	9.63	Amount financed (dollars)	
Used car	14.53	New car	11,374
		Used car	7,763

* At auto finance companies.
SOURCE: Board of Governors of the Federal Reserve System, *Federal Reserve Bulletin* (February 1988).

which normally are supported by less marketable collateral. Mobile home rates are higher than found in single-family houses primarily because of the location of many mobile home parks and the economic life of the structure. Mobile home parks usually are not located in areas as attractive and as highly valued as are single-family houses, and they are normally not as well built as houses constructed of conventional materials. Moreover, the market for mobile homes is not as large as for conventional housing.

Of all consumer rates, the highest is for revolving credit. Again, the reason is due to the risks involved. Credit card loans are unsecured, and the cost of administering revolving credit is relatively high. Costs associated with revolving credit are for funds, credit card processing, which includes numerous credit checks with credit reporting agencies and other creditors of the applicant, fraud, and collection losses.

In other types of lending there is normally more direct contact with the borrowing customer than with cardholders. This is an important ingredient in any kind of lending. There are advantages of a lender knowing the customer's employment record, liabilities, and financial status and progress. Once a credit card is issued, the contact may become infrequent unless the customer has some form of deposit relationship with the bank.

Frequently the interest rates charged by banks and other lenders that extend revolving credit in some form are questioned by public officials. This was the case in the early 1980s when most interest rates fell substantially, but credit card rates changed very little. This disparity led to the assertion that revolving credit rates were excessive in view of the decline in funding costs of card issuers. Bankers hastened to point out, however, that the cost of funds only represented about 40 percent of the overall costs of operating credit card plans and the remaining costs did not vary with the cost of money. As a result of the inflexibility of credit card interest rates, the Congress debated the issue, and several bills were considered that would have imposed a nationwide rate ceiling on credit card accounts. After much discussion the concept of an interest rate ceiling was dropped, but legislation requiring greater disclosure regarding rates and terms to consumers was enacted.

Studies of this issue show that a ceiling, as proposed by the Congress, would have adversely affected the availability of revolving credit and the profitability of credit card plans. Many observers do not recognize the costs involved in a credit card operation. The evidence that credit card rates are not excessive in relation to other types of lending has been the conclusion of several studies on the subject. An excellent study on this subject was conducted by officials of the Board of Governors of the Federal Reserve System.[1] The evidence that credit rates are not excessive in

---

[1] Board of Governors of the Federal Reserve System, "The Economic Effects of Proposed Ceilings on Credit Card Interest Rates," *Federal Reserve Bulletin* (January 1987), pp. 1–13.

relation to other types of lending is presented in Figure 14-1, which shows net earnings before taxes on various types of credit. Note that the annual net earnings of bank credit card plans before taxes averaged 1.9 percent on balances outstanding from 1972 through 1985. Over the same period, average net returns on other major types of bank lending were significantly higher. The percentage for real estate mortgages was 2.3, for consumer installment debt 2.4, and for commercial and other loans 2.8 percent.

It is obvious from Figure 14-1 that the earnings on credit cards have varied over the years, and in 1980 banks experienced losses. Evidence suggests that the return on credit card plans typically has been low and that on credit plans in general has been negative. Thus, it seems that credit card plans could not absorb significant reductions in income over the long run. Studies have shown that a maximum ceiling rate would have a widespread impact on other credit card operations and credit card customers. Banks might make adjustments because of a ceiling that would erode some of the benefits now provided cardholders and impose costs on other consumers. In an effort to recapture revenue, banks might raise the annual credit card fee or reduce the length of the interest fee grace period that cardholders enjoy in that payment is not due for several days or weeks after the billing date. A user fee could be employed rather than an annual fee and established at a level so that the price cardholders pay would reflect the cost of the service provided. Should this avenue be pursued, it would affect the credit cardholder who uses his or her card for convenience only, that is, pays as soon as a monthly bill is received.

FIGURE 14-1   Net Earnings before Taxes on Various Types of Bank Credit

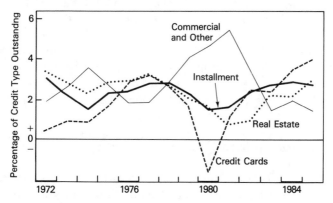

NOTE: This figure is based on annual data from the Federal Reserve's Functional Cost Analysis.

SOURCE: Board of Governors of the Federal Reserve System, "The Economic Effects of Proposed Ceilings on Credit Card Interest Rates," *Federal Reserve Bulletin* (January 1987), p. 2.

Credit standards could be raised in an effort to reduce fraud and collection costs. However, should this be done, revolving credit would be denied some customers. It is frequently pointed out that the interest rate on revolving credit in some states is lower than in others. This is true, but in those states studies have shown that fewer people are eligible for credit cards. A Federal Reserve study shows, for example, that fewer families in Arkansas, where a low ceiling exists, held credit cards than in those states with less restrictive credit card ceilings. It seems, therefore, that the credit card interest rates should be left to the free market.

Noninstallment Consumer Credit

Commercial banks are by far the largest single holders of noninstallment consumer credit. Although this amount, which approximated $66 billion at the end of 1986, has increased over the years, the percentage increase has been less than for installment credit. Noninstallment loans are made for the same variety of purposes as are installment loans and are not as large generally. The majority are not made in excess of 12 months.

ORIGIN OF CONSUMER LOANS

Commercial banks may make consumer loans directly to borrowers who apply for credit at the bank. The banks also purchase the notes of consumers from retail dealers of commodities who have sold goods to consumers or from those who provide consumer services. Commercial banks purchase the paper of automobile dealers, furniture stores, and, to a limited extent, retailers in household appliances such as refrigerators, stoves, washing machines, dryers, and televisions. The notes and supporting documents are usually referred to as *dealer paper.* These methods of lending have given rise to the terms *direct* and *indirect,* or *purchased,* loans. Sometimes, lending indirectly is referred to as *installment sales financing.* Indirect financing by commercial banks has increased in recent years. Banks have also initiated programs involving the purchase of consumers' obligations for dental and medical services and financing insurance premiums.

Reasons for Indirect Lending

The commercial banking practice of indirect consumer lending has developed for several reasons. Marketing methods and the ways that consumers shop for durable goods have encouraged its use. Most consumers shop first and then make their financial arrangements, a procedure encouraged by retailers who offer to sell on credit to increase sales. Since many retailers are financially unable to carry all their accounts receivable, they look to financial institutions as a source of credit. Most durable consumer goods are sold on terms that are readily acceptable to lending institutions. Indirect financing also provides an opportunity to obtain a volume of loans without a substantial increase in operating expenses. Direct lending involves loan interviews; this is an expensive process since it requires the time of trained personnel and various overhead expenses. Purchasing dealer paper is less expensive than lending directly. In addition indirect lending has certain advantages over direct lending that appeal to some banks. Loans purchased from some dealers may be more secure than direct loans since, in most cases, the dealer endorses the paper. If the dealer has substantial net worth, this arrangement adds financial strength to the notes purchased. The dealer may also be responsible for a certain amount of loan supervision, such as following up on delinquent accounts, repossession, and sale of repossessed merchandise, all of which save a bank considerable time and expense.

Dealer Reserves

Most banks that engage in indirect financing provide for a dealer's reserve, which is held by the bank to protect both the dealer and the bank against losses that may arise on installment paper. Such reserves are usually created from the difference between the amount charged the dealer by the bank for discounting the paper and what the dealer charges the purchasers for financing the contract. It may be likened to a finder's fee for originating the contract and completing the paperwork associated with the loan. This reserve is important not only to the bank as a safety fund but also to the dealer, since it may represent a large part of his or her profit. On an automobile contract of $5,000 with a maturity of 36 months, for example, the reserve might approximate $300.

Most reserve agreements provide that the balance will accumulate until it reaches a certain percentage of the dealer's outstanding paper. When the reserve exceeds this stipulated percentage, the excess is paid to the dealer. The amount of the reserve required of dealers varies with the risk involved. For reliable dealers with years of satisfactory experience who generate a very desirable automobile paper from the standpoint of down payment, maturity, and credit investigation, a bank might require that the reserve be a percentage equal to 3 to 5 percent of the outstanding paper. For dealers in household appliances, the percentage might be established at double or triple this amount.

Significant Factors Involved
in Indirect Lending

Since the purchase of dealer paper involves accepting the credit judgment of a dealer, many commercial banks have established standards to which dealer paper must conform. These standards may take the form of a gentleman's agreement or of a more formal document known as a *dealer agreement* entered into by the bank and the dealer that sets forth the conditions that will govern the purchase of dealer paper. Banks do not knowingly purchase the paper of a dealer who is dishonest or who follows practices that are unethical. The dealer must also have an acceptable net worth and sound business and credit judgment.

Indirect financing has certain pitfalls, which explains why some commercial banks do not engage in this type of financing and others follow strict procedures. First, the bank may never see the customer and is not, therefore, in a position to make a personal appraisal. Second, the attitude of some people who purchase durable goods on installment contracts is different from the attitude of those who borrow directly from a commercial bank. Bank borrowers generally take the attitude that the obligation must be repaid. But some consumers who buy from a retailer feel the debt can be wiped out by returning the merchandise if it proves unsatisfactory or if they are unable later to meet the payments. Disputes between buyers and sellers that impinge on the repayment of obligations are not completely foreign. Finally, when the lender does not interview the borrower, the chances of fraud, forgery, and misrepresentation are greater. For these reasons commercial banks closely scrutinize the contracts submitted to them for purchase, especially if the dealer who endorses the paper is weak financially.

Commercial banks have initiated several plans for financing dealer paper, each with certain advantages and disadvantages for the bank. The most common plans have become known as *full recourse, nonrecourse,* and *repurchase.* Under a full-recourse plan, the dealer gives an unconditional guarantee on all notes or paper sold to the bank. If some of the paper becomes delinquent, the dealer is required to pay off the note, and various arrangements can be made as to when. This plan involves less risk to the bank than do the other plans, assuming the dealer is sufficiently strong financially to pay off the delinquent accounts. Since the dealer is required to stand behind all contracts, the dealer has an interest in seeing that only sound sales are made. It is assumed also that adequate supervision will be exercised over the accounts, since not doing so may result in losses to the dealer. Moreover, in case of "skips" and delinquencies, the dealer will take steps to see that the purchaser is located and the installments paid. Many dealers favor this plan too, since the bank usually grants a lower interest rate than would be available under a plan requiring no endorsement.

A nonrecourse plan does not require the dealer's endorsement; consequently, the dealer has no liability once the paper is sold to the bank. Since the bank is assuming greater risk under this plan, it is usually more selective of the paper purchased, and the dealer receives no part of the carrying charge as a reserve or the bank will discount the paper at a higher rate than under a full-recourse plan. Because of this, many dealers do not look with favor on this plan. Although some dealers from whom banks purchase contracts do operate under a nonrecourse plan, these dealers have an excellent record of generating satisfactory paper.

If a dealer is financially strong and responsible, a repurchase plan has some advantages. This is a form of nonrecourse or limited recourse agreement that provides for dealers to repurchase the net unpaid balance when the loan is past due and the goods are repossessed by the bank and delivered to the dealer within a prearranged period of time. For example, if the past-due period were established at 90 days and the bank failed to repossess the merchandise within that period, the dealer would have no liability. Since the dealer assumes less risk under a repurchase plan than under full recourse, he or she is generally allowed a smaller participation in the finance income. Given the problem of repurchasing the contracts, the dealer would be encouraged to follow and maintain sound credit terms and to see that the customer made the payments as agreed. However, if the dealer were to go out of business, because of financial difficulties, the bank might encounter some trouble in liquidating all the accounts.

Credit Factors Involved in Indirect Financing

The credit factors involved in indirect financing are no different from those in direct financing. But since an unknown party has much to do with the indirect lending, banks are concerned about the evaluation for credit. Thus, they establish rules that they expect dealers from whom they purchase paper to follow. One of the most important is the determination of a purchaser's ability to pay for the merchandise. Banks insist that the dealer sell only to those who are employed, have a steady income, and have a record of repaying their obligations. Most banks require dealers to submit a credit application with each contract purchased and to secure a credit report from the local credit bureau.

Banks are also concerned with the down payment required on the merchandise and the maturity of the contract. Two golden rules of installment sales financing are that the down payment should be sufficiently large to establish a buyer's equity in the merchandise and a feeling of ownership and that the installment payments be sufficient to increase the equity established by the down payment at a faster rate than the merchandise depreciates. If the down payment and monthly payments do not accomplish these objectives, the purchaser may develop a feeling of renting the goods rather than of owning them. Experience with installment financing shows that most trouble is experienced with low down payment, long maturity contracts. Consequently, banks favor large down payments and short maturities.

Floor Planning

To merchandise such durable consumer goods as automobiles, washers and dryers, and televisions effectively, it is desirable to display them in a showroom or parking lot for customers to see and examine. This need has given rise to a form of financing known as *floor planning* or *flooring*. Although flooring is in reality a business loan rather than a consumer loan and could be discussed in the chapter on short-term lending, it is discussed here because it is closely related to indirect lending and is considered part of a dealer-financing plan. Flooring is seldom provided by banks as the only form of dealer financing. It is not regarded as the most desirable form of credit since it provides a lower rate of return and has a higher than normal risk. This type of dealer financing is provided primarily because it is an excellent means of obtaining dealers' contracts.

Flooring is a form of inventory financing reserved normally for the financing of goods that have several common characteristics. Such goods are easily identified and have a factory-inscribed serial number to facilitate identification. Only goods that have relatively high value and an established market in which value can be easily determined are floored. They are whole products, not parts that require assembly, and are goods on which valid liens can be given. Finally, they are goods with a sufficiently broad market so that no specialized demand will contribute to a high obsolescence rate.

Control of the inventory under a flooring arrangement may present a problem and, to a great extent, this creates the high risk. The major problem is to floor the correct amount of units. If the amount floored is too little, sales and profits will be down; therefore, the dealer becomes weaker financially than if there were a larger amount of sales and a high level of profitability. If too many units are provided, however, the inventory may become stale and eventually obsolete, especially if new models are introduced during this time. Providing the correct amount of inventory is difficult because of seasonal factors and economic conditions that constantly affect retailing.

Another problem encountered in flooring is the failure of a dealer to pay for all the items sold. This is referred to as *sold out of trust* and occurs frequently when a dealer runs into financial difficulties or forgets to pay off a unit that has been sold at retail. Should this occur, *double financing* results. This can become serious, especially if the goods are financed at or near inventory cost. In such a case, the dealer has no equity in the goods, and the bank might have a frozen loan on its hands. To protect itself against such developments, a bank engaged in flooring frequently checks the inventory of goods floored to determine whether they have been sold, to see that an adequate supply is on hand, and that inventory is maintained in an acceptable manner.

CREDIT CARDS

Credit cards have become an important vehicle of payment and credit in our society. One source estimated that at mid-1980 Americans were using 700 million credit cards, or more than three cards per person, to purchase nearly $300 billion worth of goods and services.[2] A survey conducted by Opinion Research Corporation in early 1987 found that 82 percent of those surveyed held some kind of credit card.[3] Of all the cards the most popular was Visa, which was held by 50 percent of the people sampled, followed by three department store cards—Sears, J. C. Penney, and Montgomery Ward. MasterCard was held by 45 percent of the people surveyed.

The popularity of credit cards is due to the many advantages they offer as a means of payment. These advantages have created two general distinct patterns of credit card use among cardholders—convenience and revolving credit. Many cardholders pay their outstanding balances in full each month; consequently, they incur no monthly finance charge. In fact, nearly half of the cardholders can be classified as convenience users. The remaining cardholders use credit cards as a source of credit and infrequently pay their entire outstanding monthly balance. Both of these uses have distinct advantages over cash, checks, and other means of payment. Convenience use minimizes the need to carry cash, allows the user to defer payment for goods and services for a short time, and establishes a favorable payment record that is important in credit evaluations. Revolving credit users realize the same advantages plus one other, namely, they increase their ability to purchase goods and services and in so doing avoid the red tape involved in obtaining a personal loan. Moreover, the credit card holder has considerable flexibility in the timing and amount of debt repayment.

It certainly appears that the use of bank credit cards will continue to expand. This expansion will probably be accompanied with improved technology that will make credit cards more appealing. A recent innovation is what has been termed the "smart card," which can be used for a variety of purposes. This card contains computer chips, which, it is hoped, will replace the magnetic strips on present-day cards. Although not widely held, the potential of a card of this kind may be quite far reaching not only for banking but for other purposes as well.

[2] Federal Reserve Bank of San Francisco, FRBSF Weekly Letter, December 27, 1985.

[3] The American Banker, May 26, 1987.

Commercial banks entered the credit card field in the early 1950s. They were not the first to issue credit cards; major oil companies had issued cards for years and department stores, travel, and entertainment cards were inaugurated prior to the banking industry's entry. Some banks encountered difficulties generating a sufficient volume of business to make the service profitable and withdrew from this type of installment lending. Although many banks throughout the nation contributed to the success of credit cards, the persistence of Bank of America has been note-worthy.

Several factors have motivated banks to enter the credit card field. It permits banks to offer new services to existing customers and is an excel-lent vehicle to attract new customers—individuals as well as retail mer-chants. Credit card plans increase opportunities for promoting other bank services also. Although not a deciding factor, many banks probably have entered into this area of consumer lending to keep abreast of develop-ments that may ultimately lead to an electronic money transfer system. In the final analysis, of course, banks have been motivated to adopt credit card plans because of the possibility of increasing profits.

Bank credit cards differ from check credit in several important as-pects. Credit card plans are not linked to a checking account as are check credit plans. Credit card plans involve a three-party arrangement—the cardholder, the bank, and a merchant. The embossed plastic card issued to consumers serves as evidence to merchants that a bank has granted a line of credit to the holder of the card. The card also serves as an accurate means of imprinting sales drafts. Retail merchants agree with the bank to accept the card for payment of goods and services. Merchants who have an account with a card-issuing bank may deposit their sales slips with the bank or with one of its agents and receive immediate credit to their ac-count, less a small discount. In a very real sense, the bank is financing the merchants' accounts receivable and, in so doing, relieves them of the costs involved in operating a credit department. If a merchant does not have an account with the bank but has a credit card clearing agreement with it, the bank is required to make payment to the merchant by check for the sales drafts. Regulation B of the Board of Governors of the Federal Reserve System, discussed in greater detail later in the chapter, prohibits any requirement that merchants have a deposit account with a bank with which they have a bank card clearing agreement.

For many years bank cards were issued at no cost to customers, but now an increasing number of banks charge an annual fee for a card rang-ing from $15 to $45. A customer of the bank is considered eligible for a card if he or she has a satisfactory deposit and loan relationship. Noncus-tomers are issued a card in anticipation of their becoming customers. Each card carries with it an assigned line of credit that may be changed, de-pending on how prudently the privilege is handled and whether the customer requests it. If payment is slow and some payments are in default, the card might be withdrawn or the established line of credit reduced to a level more in keeping with the cardholder's ability to pay. Cards are reissued periodically, which permits banks to reevaluate the cardholder's credit. It is not uncommon to raise the credit line of a cardholder on request and after satisfactory experience. The cardholder is billed monthly and has the option of paying the balance within a certain period—usually 25 days—without interest or on a revolving credit basis with a minimum monthly payment of $20. Because of rising costs, the free period is likely to be shortened. About a third of the bank card holders use the card merely as a convenience instrument, paying the bill immediately upon receipt. When this occurs, the bank's income is considerably less than if the charges were converted into a loan. It is for this reason that some banks levy a flat charge on the use of the card.

Most banks set a ceiling, sometimes referred to as a *floor limit,* on retail purchases; that is, they limit the size of a transaction that can be made without obtaining approval from the bank. Since most credit card operations are computerized, and banks have developed a rapid retrieval system for its customers' indebtedness and repayment records, approval can be provided the retail merchant in a matter of seconds via telephone. The ceiling may vary, depending on the type of store and its location as well as the type of goods and services purchased. A common ceiling at retail stores might be $50 to $100, but for airline tickets the limit might be $500. In addition to the purchase of retail goods and services, bank credit cards may be used for cash advances, that is, for receiving cash at the teller's window. Some banks also provide the overdraft feature by paying checks that overdraw the cardholder's account and adding the amount of the advance to the credit card bill.

In providing credit card services to customers, a bank has two alternatives. It can offer its own card by entering into a licensing or franchise agreement under which it becomes a participating or associate member with a group of banks or acts as an agent. Or it can offer another bank's card. If a bank decides to offer its own card, it must attract a sufficient number of merchants to make the program worthwhile for individuals to use the bank's card, and there must be a large enough group of cardholders to make it worthwhile for merchants to become associated with the plan. A credit card plan requires considerable volume if it is to generate a profit. If cardholders use the cards as a convenience and pay their bills within the allotted time before a service charge is applicable, the plan will be less profitable than if they pay on the installment plan and thus make full use of the service.

Although the cost of operating a credit card plan varies with the bank and the area to be covered, it is an expensive operation generally since considerable time, expertise, and promotion are required to make it successful. For this reason the number of bank credit cards has declined, and two national cards—VISA and MasterCard—command the bulk of the credit card business.

A popular arrangement in providing credit card services is through a franchised program in which the bank issues a nationally known credit card such as VISA or MasterCard. The major advantages of this franchised arrangement are that the bank receives a great amount of assistance on credit card marketing, processing, and promotion at a cost much less than if it attempted to set up its own credit card program. Some drawbacks remain. The bank agrees to handle the sales slips on any bank that uses the card, which contributes to a wider acceptance of the card. In this approach, however, some loss of identification for the bank occurs in that the name of the bank is not as conspicuously displayed as is the name of the credit card. However, it should be remembered that the name of the card and the fact that it is acceptable in many areas make it valuable and appealing to customers and merchants. The bank, in reality, has nation-wide scope in that its customers can use the card thousands of miles away from the bank and in foreign countries.

Sometimes several banks enter into what might be described as a cooperative agreement to provide a credit card program. Under such an arrangement, each bank issues its own credit card, provides for its own promotion, and signs up merchants; but the principal bank in the group provides the computer and accounting facilities. The "associate" members pay a fee for these services. The arrangement involves less expense than if each bank issued its own card. Small banks often enter into an agreement as a licensee with a larger card-issuing bank to accept the sales slips of retail customers and pass them on to the card-issuing bank. Small banks do this as a defensive measure: if they did not perform this service, the retail merchants would change their account to the card-issuing bank. Such agent banks are reimbursed for this service and, above all, they get to keep the account of the retailer, and their customers have the services of a credit card operation.

Nearly all banks provide credit card services, and thousands of foreign banks in over 100 countries are associated with the two national systems. VISA and MasterCard report that approximately 2 million merchants and over 4 million outlets accept either one or both cards. The number of credit card holders has increased significantly in recent years and now exceeds 75 million. Credit cards are a unique method of settling financial obligations and a firmly established banking service.

The most important problems associated with bank credit cards are lost and stolen cards. Cardholders are sometimes careless with their cards, and thieves are constantly on the lookout for them. It is not uncommon for cards to be removed from mailboxes, and it has been reported that even postal employees have been guilty of taking cards. It should not be assumed that bank credit cards are the only valuables stolen, however. Checks are removed from mailboxes, cash and currency are frequently taken, and the purse snatcher is still with us. Although banks in cooperation with merchants have done an excellent job in catching illegal possessors of credit cards, stolen cards still concern banks that provide this service.

Merchants have found credit cards advantageous. Travel-oriented merchants especially find that honoring bank credit cards is a useful method of attracting tourists. Although the discount charged by banks on merchants' charge slips varies, depending on the type and the amount of business generated, the average national charge is approximately 3.5 percent. This cost is considerably below the cost of operating a credit department, which has been estimated at an average of 5 to 6 percent of sales.

Credit cards are designed primarily for revolving credit at the retail level. Credit cards are not adapted to use with big-ticket items such as boats, automobiles, or expensive household appliances, which constitute a large portion of the consumer credit outstanding. Credit limits on most cards are normally below the cost of such items. Loans for the purchase of such expensive goods are usually well secured, and no arrangement has been designed as yet to provide security for such purchases when the consumer uses a credit card. For the time being, it seems that such large consumer loans will continue to be made on a closed-end basis.

A limitation to the use of credit cards is that the credit standards established by banks may not be consistent with those of merchants who agree to honor the cards. Some might be willing to extend credit to customers that banks would not. Of course, some low-margin retailers have been discouraged from signing up with bank credit card plans by the merchant discount. Although some food stores have accepted cards, the movement has not been widespread. Food chains have not accepted credit cards because of reluctance to encourage credit purchases of food and the fact that the cost of the discounted sales draft would reduce what is considered a low net profit margin. An increasing number of large department stores has joined bank credit card plans. Most, however, are reluctant to embrace a bank credit card plan since they are fearful that customer loyalty might suffer and that they would lose a strong marketing tool. Moreover, with their own credit card plans, they are in a position to tailor their credit plan to serve their customers' needs. With increased competition in retailing and the introduction of the discount store, which generally accepts bank credit cards, this attitude may also change. With credit card systems reducing their credit risk and with a discount charge of from 3 to 4 percent, which is considerably below the cost of operating a credit department, merchants are likely to reevaluate the cost of this service. Thus, we may see some large department stores accepting bank credit cards in the future.

As discussed earlier, many banks now provide an overdraft privilege associated with the bank credit card. For example, if a credit card holder were granted an overdraft privilege of $500, it would go into effect the moment a check was drawn that exceeded the balance in the account. The loan would become a bank card loan and would be repaid in accordance with the established rules governing credit card charges. Some interesting descriptions have been applied to this kind of arrangement. One bank refers to it as ACT, meaning automatic cash transfer, and another employs the descriptive term "Ready Reserve."

AUTOMATED TELLER MACHINES (ATMs)

ATMs, a natural outgrowth of bank credit cards, were introduced in the late 1960s and have been well received by bank customers. The rush to get to the bank before closing time is nearly a thing of the past since ATMs are usually open 24 hours a day. The popularity of ATMs is due to the convenience and flexibility they afford. A bank customer can secure cash, make a deposit or loan payment, transfer funds from one account to another, and secure information regarding his or her bank balance. As technology expands in this area, additional services will probably be added. It has been estimated that in 1986, 3.5 billion ATM transactions occurred. Many banks have developed shared ATM networks with other financial institutions. These networks can be either regional, national, or international. Because of the economies of scale and convenience to customers, the present trend is toward national and international coverage. There are several networks, such as Plus and Cirrus, that permit bank customers to withdraw cash throughout the nation and several foreign countries. When ATMs were introduced, they were usually located on the walls of the bank, but now they are found in airports, universities, grocery stores, and shopping centers. Although a reduction in operating costs was slow to develop, ATMs are now having a favorable impact on bank costs due, especially, to the introduction of a transaction fee imposed by many banks.

POINT-OF-SALE PAYMENT SYSTEM

The same basic technology that was responsible for bank credit cards, ATMs, and debit cards has also made possible the point-of-sale payments system commonly referred to as POS. This system involves the insertion of a bank credit or debit card into special electronic devices located at the retail counters of merchants for the purpose of transferring funds from the purchaser's account to that of the retailer. Such electronic devices could be connected with bank computers throughout the nation, an arrangement that could even be extended worldwide. In fact, the "electron" card introduced in the early 1980s and now being implemented will allow a holder to get instant cash from ATMs worldwide. Moreover, the card can be read electronically at computer-based registers in department stores and checkout counters at supermarkets. This development will contribute to lower distribution costs and increased convenience to the public.

Many benefits could derive from such a system, including the elimination of float, the use of tons of paper, the cost of handling such paper, and the writing of bad checks, which is of concern to retailers. Although there would be a reduction in some costs, there would be an increase in others, such as the cost of providing the devices, the means of transmission, computers, and so on. Even though such point-of-sale terminals are in place in a few areas of the nation, various factors have hindered large-scale development. The cost is of no little consequence not to mention the question of who should own and be permitted to use the facilities, government regulations, and the consumer's attachment to the use of cash and checks as a medium of exchange. Duplication of some elements of the system, such as transmission lines, would be uneconomic; consequently, in an effort to maintain a competitive environment, these should be available to users at reasonable cost. Even though several parties would benefit from such an arrangement, it is not easy to allocate cost. Due to many unresolved issues, some participants have been reluctant to move aggressively in this area. In the last few years, however, there has been renewed interest in this method of payment. Forerunners in the use of POS have been oil companies. At least one regional food chain is presently employing POS, and recently fast food companies as well as some national food chains and department stores have expressed an interest. Some observers are predicting increased activity in this area in the very near future.[4] A recent survey of debit card holders revealed that 26 percent indicated that they would be willing to use debit cards to pay electronically for goods and services at retail.[5]

REGULATION OF CONSUMER CREDIT

Consumer credit has been subject to more regulation than has any other type of credit provided by lending institutions. For many years the regulations centered on interest rates—the maximum amount that could be charged—but recently the emphasis has been on disclosure, discrimination, and billing.

[4] *The American Banker,* June 1, 1987.
[5] *The American Banker,* September 22, 1987.

Truth in Lending

The Truth-in-Lending Act covers three major areas. The first section is concerned with disclosure and requires creditors to provide customers with certain cost information, including the annual percentage rate of the finance charge on a consumer loan. Regulation of the advertising of consumer credit constitutes the second part of the act. The third part is concerned with rescission, which applies mainly to home mortgages and home improvement loans (discussed in the preceding chapter on real estate lending).

The Truth-in-Lending Act is primarily a piece of disclosure legislation. The law requires that certain information be presented in a standardized manner by all lenders. The objective of the law is to provide borrowers with data on finance charges so that they will be able to compare the cost of credit. Finance charges can be confusing, since several different methods are used to compute the interest rate on a loan. If a loan is based on simple interest, the borrower's interest for each period is computed on the unpaid balance of the loan. For example, if the loan is repayable in monthly installments and the stated annual rate is 12 percent, the interest cost each month is 1 percent of the unpaid balance at the beginning of the month. If the discount off the face method is used, the finance charge is computed on the total amount of the loan, and the borrower receives the face amount of the loan, less the finance charge. Thus, if the loan were a single-payment, one-year loan of $100 at a nominal interest rate of 10 percent, the borrower would receive $90, and the effective rate would be 11.1 percent. For many years a popular method of computing the finance charge of installment loans was known as the *add-on-method*. With this method, the finance charge is added to the principal amount of the loan and the total is divided by the number of payments to arrive at the amount of each payment. For example, if the principal amount of a loan were $100 and the nominal interest rate 10 percent, the total amount of the one-year loan would be $110. If the loan were repayable in 12 monthly installments, the amount of each payment would be $9.17, and the effective interest rate would be approximately 18.2 percent. The reason the effective rate is higher than the nominal rate is that with an installment loan the borrower does not have the use of the full amount of the loan for the entire year. Recently more and more banks are using the *simple interest method* of rate computation because it is easier for the borrower to understand.

The Truth-in-Lending Act applies to credit extended to all individuals for personal, family, household, or agricultural use, up to a limit of $25,000, unless the collateral is the borrower's residence. The most important requirement of this act is that the consumer be presented with a copy of the credit agreement, which contains the finance charge and the annual percentage rate along with other data. The finance charge includes all charges made in connection with the extension of the credit. Among the many charges that might be included are interest, loan fees, finder's fee, service charge, points, investigation fees, and premiums for life insurance, if insurance is required by the lender. Some costs associated with loan agreements are not included as part of the finance charge. These include taxes, license fees, certain legal fees, some real estate closing costs, and other costs that would be paid if cash were used instead of credit. The annual percentage rate (APR) is the finance charge expressed as an annual interest equivalent.

The advertising provision of the act requires as a general rule that terms be stated clearly, accurately, and conspicuously on all promotional material. All advertising must state the finance charge and the annual percentage rate, the amount of any required down payment, the dollar amount of the finance charge, and the number of installments or the period of payment. Although banks come under the advertising requirement of the Truth-in-Lending Act, they are certainly not singled out from other lenders. In fact, the advertising requirements will have a minimal effect on bank advertising.

Equal Credit Opportunity Act

The Equal Credit Opportunity Act, frequently referred to as ECOA, prohibits discrimination in any aspect of a credit transaction, including advertising, application forms and procedures, standards of creditworthiness, record keeping, and collection procedures. The act prohibits discrimination on the basis of sex, marital status, age, race, color, religion, national origin, or receipt of public assistance benefits. Although the Federal Reserve Board is responsible for promulgating regulations to implement the ECOA, enforcement has been placed in the hands of several federal agencies including the Federal Reserve Board, the Federal Deposit Insurance Corporation, the Comptroller of the Currency, and the Federal Trade Commission. Banks and financial institutions that regularly extend credit to individuals must comply with the provisions of this legislation.

Regulation B of the Board of Governors sets forth the requirements of ECOA. The regulations are far-reaching, even to the point of containing model application forms designed for use in a particular type of consumer credit transaction. Some significant provisions of this legislation are

1. Creditors may not ask for information about an applicant's spouse unless the applicant resides in a community property state, the spouse is to be liable for debt repayment, or the applicant chooses to rely on the spouse's income to repay the loan.
2. Creditors may not request information about a credit applicant's marital

status, nor can they demand information about childbearing capability or birth control practices.

3. A creditor cannot inquire whether any of the applicant's income, as stated in the application, is derived from alimony, child support, or support maintenance payments unless the creditor appropriately discloses to the applicant that such income need not be revealed if the applicant does not desire the creditor to consider such income in determining the applicant's creditworthiness.

Several significant rules must be adhered to in the extension of credit. Credit scoring systems that are statistically sound and comply with the regulations may be used as long as the age, sex, and marital status of an applicant are not adversely taken into consideration. The creditor cannot take into account a telephone listing of the applicant in evaluating creditworthiness. If an applicant requests unsecured credit and relies in part upon property to establish creditworthiness, the creditor may require the signature of the applicant's spouse or other person on an instrument necessary to make the property relied upon available to satisfy the debt in the event of default. Similar arrangements are in order if secured credit is requested. Creditors are required to notify an applicant of action taken on a credit request within 30 days. Notification can be given orally, but if the applicant requests written notification, it must be forthcoming.

Holder-in-Due-Course Doctrine

A development that has influenced the extension of consumer credit, especially indirect lending, has been the constant erosion of the holder-in-due-course doctrine. This long-standing principle relates to the legal treatment of negotiable instruments, such as promissory notes, executed between buyers and sellers. Under this doctrine a purchaser in good faith of a negotiable instrument acquires it free of any claims the maker of the instrument might have against the original holder. The purpose of the doctrine is to promote the free flow of trade. Without established standards of performance on the part of all parties concerned, commerce and trade would be precarious and fraught with uncertainty. As already discussed, the practice of indirect financing has developed over the years whereby a negotiable instrument is created at the point of sale and then sold to another party—the lender in the transaction. Abuses have crept into these transactions when sellers have sold faulty merchandise. The note or dealer paper that arises from such a transaction is then sold to another party, often a bank, who buys it in good faith, thereby becoming a holder-in-due-course and entitled under the law to collect from the maker of the note. Criticism of this practice has developed. In many instances the courts and state legislatures have denied the holder-in-due-course status to lenders, especially if they are knowledgeable about the transaction and have participated in the credit approval process. On the national level the Federal Trade Commission has gone even further and holds the protective clauses available under the holder-in-due-course doctrine as unfair trade practices and prohibits their use in consumer credit contracts.

When the holder-in-due-course principle is abrogated completely, banks and other lenders can protect themselves by purchasing dealer's retail paper only with full recourse and by requiring a reserve fund. Since commercial banks generally buy consumer notes only from responsible and financially sound dealers who stand behind their products, elimination of the holder-in-due-course doctrine from the retail area should have little impact on them. The demise of this doctrine is a result of the violation of an acceptable and desirable code of ethics by a few sellers. Without the holder-in-due-course doctrine, a buyer can return faulty merchandise to the dealer in certain circumstances and refuse to pay the promissory note, even if it has been purchased by a lender in good faith. In some cases buyers of merchandise do this even though they themselves have caused the damage to the product. Since these developments do occur, lenders tend to raise their credit standards to guard against such losses and, in so doing, limit the availability of consumer credit. Credit standards can be raised by refusing to purchase contracts from dealers who are weak financially and by scrutinizing each individual contract more closely.

Fair Credit Billing Act

The Fair Credit Billing Act is an amendment of the Truth-in-Lending Act and is purportedly designed to protect consumers from inaccurate and unfair billing. This amendment gives customers 60 days after billing to make a complaint in writing, and during this period no interest can be charged on the disputed amount. Complaints must be resolved within 90 days. Complaints arising from inaccurate and unfair billing before and after the introduction of this legislation have not been significant. Disputes usually arise when customers forget that they made certain purchases, but once they are presented with their signed sales drafts, the issue is cleared up quickly. Additional regulations applicable to credit cards have had the effect of increasing the liability of commercial banks that issue cards, and have resulted in increased costs. In many states a credit card holder is allowed to withhold payment and assert claims against the card issuer where shoddy goods and services have been delivered. This change also eliminates the holder-in-due-course protection that has for years been available to lenders. However, the amount of a claim under this provision may not exceed the amount of the sales draft, and the credit card holder must make a "good faith attempt" to obtain restitution from the merchant. The customer must also live in the same state where the purchase was made and/or within 100 miles of where the transaction occurred. The Truth-in-Lending Act also prohibits the issuance of unsolicited credit cards and places a limit of $50 on the liability of a credit card holder for unauthorized use of a credit card.

Regulation of consumer lending, as with all other types of lending, raises important questions regarding social justice and the availability of credit. It is desirable that an adequate amount of consumer credit be made available for the purchase of consumer goods if many individuals are to have a high and rising standard of living. If interest rates are kept too low by legal ceilings, or if the debtor-creditor-relationship is not fair and equitable, funds will not be made available or the laws will be violated.

Much of the concern about consumer interest rates and debtor-creditor relations stems from lack of knowledge about personal finances on the part of consumers and their occasional unwillingness to repay loans once they become financially strained. Through poor planning, some consumers buy goods they cannot afford, thinking that the monthly payments will be easy. Once good intentions are shattered, it is easy to blame the seller, the lender, or society in general for one's plight. Fortunately the great majority of consumers handle their obligations properly. As in any kind of regulation, the zeal to arrive at a perfect state in consumer lending must be tempered by the fact that it is for the majority that regulations are imposed. The scales of social justice must balance if we are to have an adequate flow of credit for consumer purposes and the proper functioning of our financial system.

LOANS FOR THE PURCHASE AND CARRYING OF SECURITIES

As pointed out in the beginning of this chapter, loans to purchase and carry securities are not classified as consumer loans. However, since they are made to individuals and are certainly not business loans, they are discussed here. Loans for the purchase of securities are highly regulated and, from the standpoint of liquidity and safety, are highly desirable, but they do require some supervision. Individuals who borrow to purchase securities and pledge them as security for a loan may get credit for this purpose from securities' dealers or commercial banks. The size of this category of loans made by commercial banks indicates that many purchasers of securities on margin prefer a bank as a source of credit.

Because of the belief that speculation was rife in the late 1920s and early 1930s and such behavior contributed to the Great Depression, Congress enacted the Securities Exchange Act of 1934, which empowered the Board of Governors of the Federal Reserve System to establish margin requirements. Margin refers to that portion of the purchase price or market value that represents the buyer's equity. Margin requirement is the difference between the market value (100 percent) and the maximum loan value. If, for example, the margin requirement is 40 percent, the purchaser must pay 40 percent of the price of the securities in cash and the remaining 60 percent may be borrowed. If the Board of Governors determines that there is excessive speculation in securities, the margin will be raised; when trading is more normal, the margin will be lowered.

Policing loans on securities is not always an easy task. If a borrower says that the borrowed funds are to be used for the purchase of an automobile or some other item and then uses them for stock purchase, the question arises as to whether or not the loan is subject to margin requirements. It is also possible that an applicant will pledge securities as collateral and use borrowed funds for some personal reason or even in his or her business. In instances of this kind, the overriding issue is a matter of intent. It is for this reason that a special form prepared by the Board of Governors of the Federal Reserve System must be signed by the borrower stating that the funds will not be used for the purchase of listed securities. Banks must watch closely the market value of pledged securities that support this kind of loan. Should more margin be required as the price of securities fluctuates, the borrower must be notified and must comply with the request that more margin be provided. If the borrower is not in a position to comply, the bank has no other alternative but to sell the securities and pay off the loan.

The amount of loans held by banks for the purchase and carrying of securities fluctuates greatly, due in large part to the margin requirements established by the Federal Reserve authorities. Recently this category of loans has varied from $10 billion to $20 billion.

QUESTIONS

1. What are the social and economic implications of consumer credit? Evaluate them.
2. Although both single-payment and installment credit have increased, installment credit has increased more rapidly. Why?
3. Of all the plans initiated to finance dealer paper, which would you recommend to a bank and why? Which plan would you recommend to a dealer and why? What factors led you to these conclusions?
4. Do you agree with the statement "the introduction of bank credit cards has proved to be one of the most significant developments in banking and finance"? Why or why not?
5. Why does indirect lending exist? Does it have something to do with our method of shopping? Explain.

6. What are the advantages of a dealer's "reserve"?

7. The amount of bank card credit is much larger than bank check credit. Why? Which would you, as an individual, prefer? Why?

8. Do you agree that the potential use of bank credit or debit cards is great? Give reasons for your position.

9. What problems may our society encounter in changing to a cashless-checkless society?

SELECTED REFERENCES

AMERICAN BANKERS ASSOCIATION. "Bank Credit Cards: Over the Hill . . . or Climbing." *ABA Journal* (September 1981), pp. 185–187.

———. "Mastercard and Visa Air Their Differences in a Friendly Fashion." *ABA Journal* (November 1981), pp. 113–121.

CANNER, GLEN B., AND ANTHONY W. CYRNAK. "Determinants of Consumer Credit Card Use." *Journal of Retail Banking* (Spring/Summer 1986).

HARDWICK, LEO P. "Understanding the Debit Card." *The Bankers Magazine* (May–June 1982), pp. 41–47.

LONG, DONALD G. "The Business Case for Electronic Banking." *Journal of Retail Banking*, 24, no. 2 (June 1982), pp. 114–122.

SOLOMON, GREGORY M. "Strategic Implications of ATMs: Why Haven't All the Tellers Gone?" *Journal of Retail Banking* (Fall 1986).

SVIGALS, JEROME. "The Smart Card: A U.S. Status Report." *Journal of Retail Banking* (Spring 1985).

15

PROBLEM
LOANS

In the chapter on credit analysis, it was pointed out that commercial bank lending involves risks and that bankers enter into the lending process only after a careful analysis of the factors that have a bearing on the borrower's willingness and ability to repay an obligation. However, credit analysis has not progressed to the point where it is possible to predict with absolute accuracy whether or not a loan will be repaid as agreed. The willingness and ability of borrowers to repay may change after loans are made. This may be responsible for some loans presenting problems as far as collections are concerned and, in some instances, losses. Moreover, collection problems may also arise with some loans because of the inability of bankers to make a proper credit analysis, a hasty decision to lend without adequate credit information, or the failure on their part to accept the results of a credit analysis. Although the aim of commercial bankers is to make only good loans, it must be admitted that mistakes are made in the process of lending. Bankers are human, and they, like others, do not achieve perfection.

The number and dollar amount of loans that present problems to commercial banks are not known. That there are some is evidenced by the amount of losses and recoveries experienced by banks, although these are not, at present, of serious proportions. The problems that may arise with loans vary considerably in intensity and duration. Some may present minor problems from the very beginning of the loan, some problems may develop slowly and become chronic, and some may develop suddenly without any indication of trouble. Although problems may develop with some loans that may be classified as serious, they may be rehabilitated; others may develop into partial or absolute losses. The turn that problem loans may take obviously forces banks to devote considerable time to their supervision. Problem loans adversely affect a bank's liquidity and increase the possibility of loss. Losses are certainly not welcomed, since they result in a decrease in reserves and/or capital, which saps the financial strength of a bank. Losses reduce the ability of a bank to serve its customers and to contribute to the economic growth of the community.

Loan losses, recoveries, and reserves for loan losses are presented in Figure 15-1. A marked rise in loan losses occurred in the early 1980s. This rising trend was accompanied by an increase in the reserve for loan losses. As we have learned, this reserve is designed to care for potential loan losses and is transferred from current earnings; consequently, loan losses affect bank profitability. An excellent indicator of the seriousness of loan losses is to relate the amount of losses to the amount of loans outstanding, as in Figure 15-2. Note that loan losses as a percentage of loans have nearly tripled since the late 1970s, from 0.3 percent to 0.9 percent in the mid-1980s. A way to find out how well a bank or a banking system is prepared to care for loan losses, and in so doing protect the deposits of

FIGURE 15-1   Loan Losses and Reserve for Loan Losses

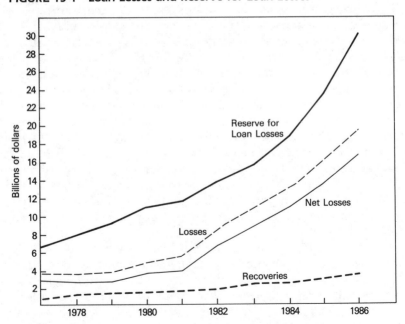

SOURCE: Federal Deposit Insurance Corporation, annual reports.

FIGURE 15-2   Loan Loss Reserves and Losses as a Percentage of Loans

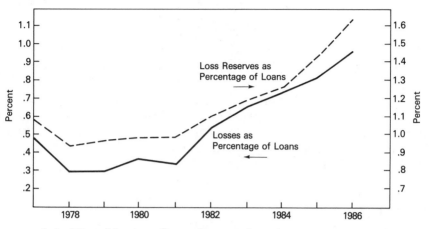

SOURCE: Federal Deposit Insurance Corporation, annual reports.

customers, is to relate reserves for loan losses to loans outstanding. This is also done in Figure 15-2. Note that the ratio of loss reserves to loans has paralleled the ratio of losses to loans and at the end of 1985 stood at 1.6 percent. This percentage exceeds the amount that regulatory authorities have encouraged banks to maintain. However, banks that have a substantial amount of substandard loans may be required to maintain higher reserves. In general, small banks have experienced greater loan losses than large banks due primarily to less diversification in the former's loan portfolio and the extension of credit to new business firms that normally have a higher incidence of failure. This fact is reflected in the failure rate of commercial banks. To be sure, some medium-sized and large banks that have engaged in lending abroad or are located in an area of the nation that has had a severe economic setback have experienced financial difficulties due to loan losses.

The economic environment has a great impact on the financial health of bank borrowers and on bank loan losses. In periods of prosperity borrowers perform well because incomes are relatively high, but in periods of recession the ability to pay is reduced. Normally, financial problems are encountered with some consumer loans soon after a recession is underway, but there is usually a lag in its impact on business borrowers. The degree of impact on both individuals and business firms that reduces their ability to repay obligations obviously depends on the seriousness of the recession and its duration. As the recession deepens, consumer purchases decline, which reduces the sales and level of income of business firms. Business inventories are increased reluctantly, which has an additional impact on the level of employment and income of both individuals and business borrowers. Inflation has a very unfavorable impact on business behavior. Rising prices result in a rising demand for more credit as the cost of materials, supplies, energy, and labor increases. As long as prices are rising, the money supply is increasing, and there is a demand for the output of business firms, debt is not a matter of great concern. However, once a deflationary period sets in, highly leveraged companies and individuals encounter financial difficulties. Relative to other outlays, the cost of debt service increases. Unlike incomes, debt does not decline in periods of adversity. It is fixed in dollar amounts. Debt does not vary with the purchasing power of money; consequently, it becomes more burdensome in the downturn—a burden that some borrowers cannot continue to bear; hence loan losses.

RECENT LOAN LOSSES

Net loan losses—losses minus recoveries—declined in the last part of the 1970s as the economy recovered from a recession. This pattern is normal in that loan losses usually increase during a recession and immediately thereafter and decline once economic growth is resumed. The trend in the first half of the 1980s departed from this usual pattern because of special national and world economic conditions that adversely affected particular borrowing sectors, namely, agriculture, energy, real estate, and foreign lending. In the latter part of the 1970s and early 1980s the agricultural and energy sectors borrowed huge amounts that could not be serviced when conditions subsequently deteriorated.

The high inflation rate with which the country had struggled for several years was finally brought under control. Even though this was a positive development for the economy as a whole, it resulted in a decline in the value of farm real estate, and along with the price of oil there was an increase in delinquencies and defaults on bank loans. In the parts of our country that had witnessed the energy boom and bust, the loan problems spilled over into the real estate industry, especially in the area of downtown office buildings. Small agricultural banks suffered most, as is evidenced by the number of bank failures.

In general, banks with assets of less than $100 million had the highest relative level of loan losses during this period. Problems in foreign lending stemmed from the cartelization of oil production in the Near East in the early 1970s, followed by a decline in the exports of debtor nations. The foreign debt problem was concentrated primarily in the money center banks of the nation, which increased their reserves for loan losses in unprecedented amounts.

There was a distinct upward trend of loan losses after 1981. The ratio of charge-offs to total average loans reached 1 percent by year-end 1986, an unusually high level for the banking industry. Nonperforming loans also increased to approximately 2 percent of total loans, an equally high rate. In general, the highest percentage of nonperforming loans was found in the largest and smallest banks of the nation, reflecting the loan problems in agriculture and foreign lending.

Banks responded quickly and properly to their loan losses and potential loan losses by increasing their loan loss reserves. This is quite obvious from an examination of Figure 15-1. In 1980, for example, the loan loss reserve for all banks was nearly $10 billion, but six years later it had been increased to nearly $30 billion, up nearly 200 percent.

CAUSES OF PROBLEM LOANS AND LOSSES

Basically, problem loans are those that have not been written off but are at least 90 days past due, nonaccruing, or renegotiated. Although problem loans and losses are a result of many factors, they are basically the result of the unwillingness of borrowers to repay or of their inability to realize sufficient income to reduce or repay loans as agreed. It is difficult to say to what extent unwillingness to repay is a factor in the development of slow loans and of eventual loss to commercial banks. Many lenders, including some commercial bankers, insist that only an infinitesimally small percentage of the borrowers become unwilling to repay obligations once loans are granted. They contend that most loans are entered into in good faith and with good intentions. Although this may be true, there are a few who borrow from banks and elsewhere who have earned the title of "deadbeats" and who must be encouraged, and in some instances forced, to carry out the requirements of a loan contract. Some lenders, including some commercial bankers, contend that many borrowers have a little "larceny in their hearts."

The unwillingness to pay varies with the economic fortunes of some borrowers. In periods of prosperity, the willingness to repay is greater than in periods of adversity. Unwillingness to repay obligations is closely associated with economic depressions, periods of unemployment, and declining profits. It is during such periods that credit character is placed under severe strain. The complex that the lender is a Shylock seeking his pound of flesh develops during hard times, and it is during such periods that the lender, in the eyes of some borrowers, takes on the look of a villian. It seems, however, that the major reason by far for problem loans and possible losses is the inability of borrowers to realize income from normal business operations, employment, or the sale of assets.

Consumer Loans

The repayment of consumer loans, both short and intermediate term, and of residential real estate loans is closely associated with the level of employment and income. Practically all consumer loans are paid from the earnings of borrowers; therefore, any interruption of employment may place them in a position of not being able to pay. Interruption of employment may be a result of a variety of causes, such as the temporary closing of plants for repairs, permanent closing of factories due to the shifting of productive activities elsewhere or firms going completely out of business, sickness and accidents resulting in absence from work for various lengths of time, and even death. The cost of moving and getting established in a new community due to declining economic opportunities in an old location may result in some borrowers becoming slow in meeting their obligations.

In addition, the ability to repay consumer loans may be influenced by personal circumstances, such as sickness and death in the family, military service, accident, or divorce. Some consumer loans may present problems due to poor budgeting by the borrowers, such as the assumption of obligations that, when coupled with unforeseen contingencies, are in excess of income.

Loans for Productive Purposes

Loans that have been contracted for the financing of business and agricultural purposes can develop into problem loans and losses as a result of many factors: in fact, the causes are so numerous and vary so much with the state of the economy that it is impossible to list all of them or to classify those that are known in order of importance. Although some causes may arise outside the business, and some analysts have attempted to explain business failures in terms of internal and external causes, most can probably be laid at the door of management. The management of a firm has great responsibilities, which include the selection of goals of the business and the type of organization that will implement them, the selection of policies to be followed that will result in a reasonable return to the owners of the business, the control over the productive process that will result in salable goods and services, and the initiation of action and planning that will adjust existing policies and procedures to ensure continued successful operation of the business firm. If these responsibilities are not met, the ability to create income is reduced; consequently, the ability to repay bank loans is lessened.

Detailed information on loan losses in commercial banks on a nationwide basis and according to classification is not available. But studies that have been made covering selected areas indicate that bank losses are highest for the short- and intermediate-term consumer and business loan classifications, which make up a relatively large portion of the loan portfolio of banks. There are many reasons for loan losses, and all the reasons may not be applicable to all firms. Some lending officers point out that the single most important cause of loan losses is poor business management on the part of the borrower. Other major factors include what is commonly referred to as "poor economic conditions" combined with a too heavy reliance on debt. Fraud is not a major cause of loan losses, although this factor may be faced if relations between the bank and the borrower become strained and the cooperation with the principals involved deteriorates. This may also be true if liquidation of the firm becomes necessary.

Some insight into the causes of business failures and of loans held by commercial banks becoming problems may be obtained from the reports of Dun & Bradstreet, a firm that has been gathering data on business failures since 1857. Business failures, as counted by Dun & Bradstreet, are concerns that have ceased operations following bankruptcy or assignment for the benefit of creditors; have ceased operations with loss to creditors after such actions as execution, foreclosure, attachment, discontinuing operations leaving unpaid bills; have been involved in such court actions as receivership, reorganization, or arrangement; or have voluntarily compromised their obligations with creditors.

According to Dun & Bradstrret, over 90 percent of business failures are due to inexperience and incompetence. Under this general heading are listed two relatively important reasons: inadequate sales and competitive weakness. Other reasons listed under this broad category are heavy operating expenses, receivables and inventory difficulties, poor location, and excessive fixed assets. Neglect is another reason listed for business failure, as are fraud and such disasters as fire and flood, although these are not major ones.[1]

Business firms operate in a dynamic world; if they are to progress and avoid financial troubles, they must be prepared to change operations, to introduce new lines, and to make improvements in their goods or services to keep them competitive in the marketplace. Firms that do not will eventually experience a decline in sales and, hence, in profits. Rapidly developing technology makes present goods obsolete and present firms high-cost producers. Substitutes are continually being developed for many products that have dominated the market for years. Light metals, plastics, and synthetic fibers have made their presence felt in the market in recent years. Advertising and improved and more efficient marketing methods have been responsible for the success of many firms and for the decline in others.

The demand for goods and services is constantly changing. Consumers seek improved and better products and are influenced in their selection by advertising. An appreciable change in demand for a firm's products or services may be devastating. Marginal firms are usually more quickly and seriously affected by a change in demand than are those that

---

[1] Dun & Bradstreet, *Business Failure Record* (New York, 1986).

are highly profitable. Firms with large amounts of fixed capital and those that produce highly specialized capital goods are also adversely affected by a shift in demand.

For business firms to be successful they must be soundly capitalized. Management must have, among the many attributes that are necessary for the efficient operation of a business, a knowledge of production techniques, proper purchasing and selling policies, effective control over costs and expenses, desirable credit and collection policies, enlightened labor and personnel policies, alertness to change, and proper forecasting and planning. Firms that do not have attributes of this nature run the risk of encountering financial difficulties when the economic environment becomes stormy and unsettled. Under such conditions, those who have extended credit may have some problems. If such firms are not able to cope with the problems at hand, the financial road may become rough and rocky and losses to lenders may ultimately result.

Imperfect Lending Practices

Some of the problem loans and loan losses may be due to procedural breakdowns within the bank. Lending officers must bear some of the blame for problem loans according to two authorities who cite the following reasons:

1. Insufficient loan analysis pertaining to the borrower's management skills
2. Inadequate analysis of financial statements
3. Ill-conceived terms placed on loans
4. Poor review and audit of marginal loans
5. Overemphasis on bank profits and growth
6. Too lenient credit policies for personal friends or friends of directors and executive officers[2]

A bank examiner's view of the causes of problem loans should not be dismissed lightly since bank examiners have had years of experience with such loans. One examiner presents the following list of causes:

1. Incomplete credit information
2. Technical incompetence—inability to analyze financial statements
3. Anxiety for income—placing the desire for income above sound lending
4. Failure to obtain or enforce liquidation agreements—no clear-cut agreement governing loan repayments and a program of progressive loan liquidation
5. Competition—desire to have a larger loan portfolio than competing banks

   [2] Edmond E. Pace and Donald G. Simonson, "Solving Problem Loans," *The Journal of Commercial Bank Lending* (July 1977), p. 25.

6. Timidity—reluctance to demand performance in accordance with the contract
7. Lack of supervision—due in part to the lack of knowledge of the borrower's affairs
8. Overlending—loaning beyond the reasonable capacity of the borrower to repay
9. Poor selection of risks:
    a. Liberal lending to a new business
    b. Loans based on the expectation of completion of a business transaction rather than on net worth
    c. Loans for speculative purchase of securities or goods
    d. Loans inadequately collateralized
    e. Loans based on the size of the borrower's deposit rather than on net worth
    f. Loans for carrying real estate transactions based on equity ownerships
    g. Lending to borrowers with questionable moral standards
    h. Loans based on unmarketable stocks or bonds[3]

Indicators of Problem Loans

There are many indicators of problem loans, but there is no set pattern of frequency of occurrence of events leading up to a point where a loan could be declared a problem loan. In the area of business lending, one or more of the following would indicate financial trouble and serve as a "red flag" to the lending officer:

1. Delayed submission of financial statements.
2. Slowness in the ability to arrange plant visits and a deterioration in the rapport that has existed between the personnel of the bank and the borrower; a deterioration in the atmosphere of mutual trust and confidence.
3. Declining deposit balances and the occurrence of overdrafts and/or returned checks.
4. An unusual rise in inventories and an increase in trade payables.
5. An increase in receivables. This may indicate a lowering in the quality of the firm's products or services, a change in the terms of sale, or the sale to financially weak firms in an effort to increase sales and income.
6. Slow or delinquent loan payments to the bank.
7. Increase in fixed assets; expansion through merger or acquisition; talk of merger with another firm or the sale of assets.
8. Change in management or the resignation of key personnel; labor problems; change in the social behavior of the principles.
9. New financial arrangements or indebtedness.
10. Natural disasters such as a flood or fire.

[3] Robert A. Jacobsen, "A Bank Examiner's Loan Review," *The Journal of Commercial Bank Lending* (May 1973), pp. 49–51.

Since banks normally do not have as close a relationship with personal borrowers as with business borrowers, there are fewer indicators that financial problems may develop. The most significant and obvious indicator is loan delinquency. Others might be the decline in deposit balances of the borrowers and the writing of checks on insufficient funds. Prolonged strikes and unemployment due to unfavorable economic conditions do not contribute to the ability of borrowers to repay obligations on time. Unplanned and nonbudgeted items such as sickness or injury place a strain on family budgets, and marital problems are not conducive to financial stability. When problems such as these develop, many personal loan borrowers consider loan repayment a low-priority item.

Many bankers rate divorce as a major cause and indicator of problem loans, since both parties usually become reluctant to pay even though both have signed a note to the bank. Unfortunately, indicators of trouble with consumer loans are not as obvious as with some other loans. Information is expensive and difficult to collect and maintain to assure the bank knowledge of the ability and willingness to pay of each borrower. The success of farming and the ability of farm borrowers to repay obligations are very closely tied to many external factors. Unfavorable weather conditions (drought, too much rain, storms, hailstorms, etc.) can adversely affect the economic fortunes of the farmer and the farmer's ability to repay loans. A drop in price of farm commodities may also place farm loans in a hazardous position.

Once the danger signals that normally surround a potential problem loan are recognized, the first step that bank lending officers take is to determine through appropriate processes the seriousness of the problem. Obviously, to accomplish this task requires additional information and the cooperation of the borrowers. Such information is derived from financial statements, exhibits, and conferences with the borrower. The steps that follow will depend on the seriousness of the situation.

PERSONNEL CONCERNED
WITH PROBLEM LOANS

The personnel or department responsible for the handling of problem loans varies primarily with the size of a bank. In small banks, the officer or officers who made a loan that has developed into a problem usually handle it with the assistance of the bank's legal counsel.

Many banks, especially the large ones, take the position that a separate department staffed by trained personnel with considerable experience and expertise in handling problem loans should be concerned with all such loans, rather than the officers who made the loan originally. The reason for this position is that a fresh look at a situation of this kind is highly desirable. Moreover, the lending officer who made the loan may have developed such a close personal relationship with the borrower that a scientific and unbiased analysis may be difficult, and the necessary firmness in handling the loan may be lacking. This attitude is widely held and is supported by the fact that surveys on this subject show that approximately 60 percent of the banks do have a separate department concerned with problem loans exclusively. These departments have achieved an enviable record in the handling of problem loans.

Although loans are normally written off when they are 90 days past due, this action does not terminate collection efforts. Seldom do banks turn over their problem loans to collecting agencies. When borrowers move to other states, it may be necessary, however, to rely on this type of collection.

PREVENTION OF PROBLEM LOANS AND LOAN LOSSES

Commercial banks are very much interested in the preventive steps and precautionary measures that may be taken to reduce the number and dollar amount of problem loans, because of the costs involved in their supervision and collection as well as the impact of losses, should they occur, on their financial structure. As soon as it is evident that a borrower has encountered financial problems, bank management takes steps to correct the situation and protect the bank's interests. One of the following steps or a combination might be taken to rescue the borrower and restore financial health:

1. *Counseling.* Bank personnel may help with advice on a variety of topics such as sales, collections, production, and so on. The bank may also bring in consultants for advice and counsel.
2. *Addition of capital.* The bank may suggest that the owners of the firm provide more capital. If the concern is a corporation, the firm might be encouraged to sell additional stock and thus provide for an infusion of new capital.
3. *Merger.* The bank might encourage the borrower to merge with another. This would be recommended only after careful study and evaluation of all the influencing factors. If the business is a single proprietorship, a partner might be suggested.
4. *Reduction of expansion plans.* If expansion plans are on the drawing board, the borrower might be advised to drop them if possible until the firm has improved its financial position. Such plans might be diverting needed funds from current operations.
5. *Encourage the collection of slow receivables.* This might be done by encouraging an improvement in the collection program and/or the addition of personnel specialized in this area. It might also involve an examination of the credit policy of the firm.

6. *Improve inventory control.* It is not uncommon for business firms to have excess inventories sometime during the business cycle. The firm might be encouraged to offer some items at a discount and thus increase sales. This would increase the cash flow and place the firm in a position to meet its loan payments.

7. *Obtaining additional collateral.* Although the borrower may be skeptical of this move, it may be advantageous to both parties. The bank is less likely to call the loan and in fact may be in a better position to restructure the loan and thus make it easier for the borrower to make loan payments. It would, of course, be to the advantage of the bank since its financial position would be strengthened.

8. *Obtaining guarantees.* If the borrower cannot raise additional funds, a guarantee from a major stockholder, a supplier, or a purchaser of the final product might be possible.

9. *Debt restructuring.* The bank might restructure the loan by lengthening its maturity and reducing the monthly payments or even eliminate principal payments for a period of time. The bank may also recommend a longer-term lender or participate with another lender and thus reduce its risk.

10. *Increase the amount of the loan.* Normally banks are reluctant to advance additional funds, although it is an attractive and easy solution. It should only be done after all the conditions made by the bank have been met and it is clear that the firm can be placed on the road to recovery.

HANDLING PROBLEM LOANS

In handling problem loans commercial banks have two broad choices—workout or liquidation—and, within each choice, there are various alternatives. As the term implies, a *workout* is a process of working with the borrower until the loan is repaid, in part or in full, and not relying on legal means to enforce collection. *Liquidation* is forcing borrowers to comply with the terms of the loan contract and employing and exhausting every legal means to accomplish this objective.

The major factors that will influence the selection of the choice that banks will follow in handling loans that present collection problems and possible loan losses are the reputation that a bank will acquire in enforcing collection, the borrower's honesty and attitude toward the debt, the borrower's financial strength and ability to repay the obligation even though considerable time may be necessary, the value of the borrower to the bank, the costs involved in collecting and rehabilitating the borrower, and which method will net the bank the greatest return on the funds that have been extended and are in jeopardy. A final factor that must be given consideration is the attitude of other creditors, of which there may be many. In an out-of-court settlement, the arrangement is only binding upon those who accept the plan. A sole dissenter can make a plan unworkable.

These creditors must be convinced that they will receive more by cooperating with a proposed plan than by going it alone.

Handling problem loans, like granting credit, is more an art than a science, and to what extent these factors influence the decision of bank management in handling specific problem loans, it is difficult to say; all certainly have a bearing. The honesty of the borrower, attitude toward the debt, and willingness to repay are probably the most important factors that influence the steps that a bank will take in regard to problem loans. If the borrower is dishonest, and there has been evidence of fraud or shady dealings or the borrower does not feel morally bound to repay an obligation, the only avenue a bank can follow is to expedite collection by whatever means possible, with a minimum of loss. To do otherwise, when the actions and attitude of the borrower are to "beat" the bank, is too risky. Also, if the borrower has lost the will to exert every effort possible to make a comeback, the bank is forced to collect. If, however, borrowers who are in financial trouble recognize and accept the fact that the debt should be repaid and have the will to undergo sacrifices to repay the debt, banks can afford to be more lenient in effecting collection. They can, possibly, enter into some kind of workout arrangement rather than liquidation. Many bankers contend that their first and most important task, in handling problem loans that may be bordering on losses, is to develop an attitude to repay on the part of the borrower and to create an atmosphere of mutual trust between the bank and the borrower. It is only then that a satisfactory workout arrangement can be arranged and carried out.

A problem loan does not necessarily mean that all is lost, that the borrower has come to the end of the line, and that, if a bank has extended credit, the loan will not be repaid in whole or in part. But it does imply the inability to pay in accordance with the loan contract and possible insolvency. There are, however, various degrees of financial distress or insolvency. Insolvency in a bankruptcy sense is interpreted to mean that a firm's liabilities exceed its assets and, consequently, that its net worth is negative, that it cannot pay its obligations, and that, in the foreseeable future, there will be little, if any, change in its financial condition.

Although some firms may not be insolvent in this sense, since their assets exceed their liabilities, they may not be able to meet their current obligations. A financial predicament of this kind may be a result of a shortage of working capital or of a drop in the market price of a firm's finished product or of its general assets, which cannot be converted into cash easily and quickly without some loss. If given sufficient time, however, the firm would be able to meet all its obligations. Obviously, a more liquid condition depends, in part, upon the amount of time necessary for the market price of the firm's assets to increase, for collections on its accounts receivable, and for the sale of some of its inventory of finished products. A firm that is experiencing a financial condition of this type may be said to be temporarily insolvent or financially embarrassed.

Workout Arrangements

When bank borrowers are financially embarrassed, banks can afford to, and usually do, enter into a workout arrangement, assuming, of course, that the borrower is honest and his or her attitude toward the debt and repayment is satisfactory. This is especially true if the borrower has a sizable equity in the business, some valuable fixed assets, an organization that is capable of creating income sufficient in amount to repay the loans that are questionable, as well as other loans that may be necessary to keep the firm in business, and has indicated, in the past, evidence of sound management. If, however, the borrower is insolvent in a bankruptcy sense, it would be foolish for a bank to do more than proceed along lines of liquidation.

Most loans that become a problem in commercial banks are handled on a workout basis; that is, borrowers are permitted to work out of their financial difficulties and repay their obligations to the bank as quickly as possible. For productive loans, such as business and agricultural, the payments on the loans should not be of sufficient size to reduce the borrower's ability to create income. In the case of consumer loans, the payments should not be so large that the borrower's productive efficiency would be impaired. The borrower should not, figuratively speaking, be dispossessed and thrown into the street.

In a sense, the workout method of handling problem loans might be described as a rehabilitation or austerity program imposed on borrowers with their consent and cooperation. Since a workout arrangement is not a legal device, it may take several forms and may vary from one loan to another. The bank "plays it by ear" and adopts a program that best suits a particular situation. The steps may include advice on many topics affecting the borrower's ability to create and earn income, extending or redrawing the loan contract to reduce the size of the loan payments, the advance of additional funds in an effort to place the borrower in a stronger financial position, the bank taking an active participation in the business, or even the bank taking over the business and operating it until it is assured that the loan will be repaid.

Consumers might be advised to exercise a closer watch over the household budget, encouraged to take another position that offers greater opportunities, or advised to sell some consumer goods—an expensive boat, a second or third car, membership in an exclusive club—that has been a drain on ability to pay. In other words, it would be a matter of getting the idea across that the borrower really doesn't have to "keep up with the Joneses." It would not, however, include the advice to sell the only car in the household when the breadwinner has to drive to a job several miles from home and no public transportation or "share-a-ride" is available. The bank might advise that the expensive house be sold and other living arrangements be made.

For a business firm, advice might include the recommendation that an expansion program be halted, a reevaluation of its sales policies, reduction in the salaries of some managers, the addition of a new product, the purchase or sale of another firm, and many other changes—all designed to reduce expenses, increase sales and income, and, hence, increase the borrower's ability to repay the debt. The advice might consist of recommendations to dispose of certain operations that are not profitable or for which the outlook is not very bright. This could very well involve the sale of assets and the renegotiation of contracts. Some have referred to this as an "unwinding operation."

Sometimes, borrowers, due to unforeseen events such as sickness and accident, are not in a position to repay their consumer loan or to make an installment payment. Under such conditions, the situation may best be handled by an extension of the loan or by redrawing the loan contract so that the installment payments are more closely related to the borrower's income. Sometimes, business borrowers may be unable to pay because their purchasers are not in a position to pay as promptly as they once were. This situation, if of a temporary nature, might be handled like the consumer loan, by an extension or by remaking the loan contract.

Sometimes, business firms, due to poor management, may be in such poor financial condition that the best solution would be for the bank to take an active part in the management of the business. If, for example, a business is pledging its accounts receivable as security for a loan and, for some reason, encounters financial difficulties, the bank may place a representative in the business to ensure that the payments that are received are applied to the reduction of the loan or are expended for some purpose that will increase debt repayment ability.

In some few instances, the bank may remove the head of the firm from the active direction of the business and operate the business itself. This, of course, is done when the present manager is incompetent, there is some evidence of dishonesty, and this method appears to be the only logical solution to a bad situation. Management of a business firm by a bank may include the handling of all accounting and finance functions, such as the purchasing of raw materials and supplies, the sale of goods, the payment of bills, and the handling of all funds.

Banks might find it desirable to advance additional credit to business borrowers that have financial problems, for it may be the only way that a sizable amount of the original loan can be recouped. Business firms that are not operating are not of much value, and in many instances specialized machinery, plant, and real estate have limited marketability.

Before funds are advanced to a business firm that is in financial difficulty, there must be a market for the firm's product or service and a sufficient amount of viable assets to ensure that the firm can meet a satisfactory output. If additional assets must be purchased, the bank will certainly require that these assets be pledged to secure the loan.

In fact, when any loan reaches the problem stage, banks immediately take steps to secure a mortgage and a security agreement on every available asset belonging to the borrower. In the event that some assets have already been given to another lender as collateral for a loan, a second mortgage is taken. Banks are prohibited from making a loan secured by a second mortgage instrument, but once a loan is made and trouble develops, they are permitted to take a second mortgage. This is usually referred to as a DPC—debt previously contracted.

Liquidation of Problem Loans

If it becomes obvious to a bank that a workout arrangement is not feasible, liquidation, which may take one of several forms, may be decided upon as the best way of handling a loan that has become a collection problem. When this method is selected, it means that the bank has decided after carefully weighing all of the factors mentioned that the possibility of the borrower improving his or her financial condition is remote, that an extension of the loan contract or the advancement of additional funds would be hazardous, and that the bank will recoup a larger percentage of the funds advanced by this move than by any other.

Liquidation, in many cases, is pursued only after a workout arrangement of some form has been tried but has not proved successful. Liquidation is usually entered into quickly only in those cases where the unwillingness to repay is obvious, fraud or some dishonest act has been detected, an act of bankruptcy has been committed, the financial condition of the borrower is hopeless, or the will to repay is not present.

Banks do not desire a liquidation process, for it usually results in ill will on the part of the borrower and of the endorser, if there is one, and, sometimes, in long and tedious legal proceedings. If the loan is secured, there may be a period of time in which the borrower may permit the collateral to depreciate considerably through misuse or poor maintenance. Moreover, when collateral is sold at a foreclosure sale, it frequently does not bring what may be termed a fair market price. In the event, however, that the amount realized from the sale of the collateral is not sufficient to extinguish the debt, the bank may receive from the court a *deficiency judgment*. Such a judgment places the bank in a position to recover the additional amount, if the borrower has assets.

There are several ways of carrying out a liquidation. Bank personnel may do it with the help of the bank's legal counsel or the department that is concerned with problem loans, which is found in larger banks, and has personnel on the staff with expertise in this area. Finally, a professional liquidator, of which there are many throughout the country, could be employed to handle the liquidation. Normally, a professional liquidator is employed in those instances where the business has a large number of items that must be sold, such as a furniture store or a large factory. If the asset to be liquidated is a house or several large pieces of equipment, bank personnel can handle such an undertaking.

A form of liquidation is the *repossession* of such durable consumer goods as automobiles and, in some instances, capital goods sold on a conditional sales contract and purchased from a dealer. This process merely involves taking the merchandise in full payment of the debt and then proceeding to sell it at a price that, it is hoped, will cover the debt. In the event such finance paper had been purchased from a dealer with recourse, the bank usually provides in the dealer agreement for a different arrangement. In this case, the bank agrees to place the goods on the dealer's premises, and the dealer then pays the bank the amount of the unpaid balance on the contract. If the dealer provides for a reserve to be accumulated out of the various contracts sold the bank, the loss, if any, would come from this reserve.

In the event a bank decided to use every legal means to collect on an unsecured loan, a *judgment* would be secured from the proper court. This judgment would permit the seizing and selling of property belonging to the debtor in the amount sufficient to satisfy the judgment or the *garnishment* of wages in an amount permitted by law. In some cases, the borrower may not have sufficient property, and the process of garnishment is not an entirely satisfactory arrangement. The employer does not welcome the role of collector and the employee may lose his or her job. Consequently, this process might be futile.

Although the borrower may not have sufficient assets to pay the indebtedness at the time of foreclosure, the judgment is a recorded claim that must be paid in the event sufficient assets are ever accumulated, assuming, of course, that the statute of limitations is not effective. A judgment, for example, becomes a lien on real estate that may be owned by the borrower. It must be satisfied before a clear title can be given to a purchaser in the event it is transferred to another party.

If the bank is one of a number of creditors, all of which want their money and are in as strong a relative position as the bank, a creditors' committee may be formed. This arrangement is short of full bankruptcy and may result in a workout situation. The major creditors agree to take over the firm and manage it so that they will receive their funds. Sometimes, the creditors agree to extend funds to the firm in an effort to keep it operating. Usually a representative of the bank chairs the committee and carries out the policies agreed upon by the creditors. In many instances, the major creditors that are members of the creditors' committee are forced to pay off the minor creditors. Sometimes these minor creditors find themselves in an enviable position in that they can literally demand their money from the creditors' committee or force the borrower into involuntary bankruptcy. Blackmail is an ugly word, but such action borders on this. A creditors' committee may proceed to liquidate the firm, but this may not necessarily be the objective, which may be to rehabilitate the firm and return it to a sound and productive status. In this sense, it may be very similar to a workout arrangement. But seldom does a creditors' committee have a similarly happy ending.

A business in financial distress may assign its assets to the creditors. Under this arrangement, the assignment is made to a trustee, who liquidates the business and divides the assets among the various creditors. If the business is a single proprietorship or partnership, the personal assets of the principals will also be assigned to the trustee. An assignment has some advantage over an equity receivership in that the trustee has considerable latitude in disposing of the assets of a business. There is no definite time limit placed on the trustee regarding the sale of assets or how they must be disposed of. If an assignment is accepted when the price of the various assets is relatively low and the marketability is not great, they can be withheld until a more favorable market exists. The trustee may also sell the assets or the whole business to another going concern and thus realize more from the liquidation process. Since an assignment is an act of bankruptcy, it may be the factor that is responsible for involuntary bankruptcy proceedings brought about by one of the creditors taking the position that liquidation is not proceeding in the way that it should.

Bankruptcy

Bankruptcy provides two basic forms of relief for debtors—liquidation and rehabilitation. Chapter VII of the Bankruptcy Act is directed toward liquidation of business firms and Chapter XI to reorganization, that is, reorganizing the firm in such a manner that it can continue operations with the hope of becoming a profitable operation once more.

Bankruptcy may be voluntary or involuntary. It is the last resort from the standpoint of creditors. The possibility of a bank or any other creditors receiving a substantial amount of its loan from this liquidating process is practically nil. In many instances, it is employed when creditors cannot come to a satisfactory agreement regarding the steps that should be taken to receive as much as possible in return for funds advanced, when some minor creditor refuses to go along with a cooperative arrangement, or when the borrower refuses to work with the creditors in trying to solve a most knotty financial problem.

With the liberalization of the provisions of the Bankruptcy Reform

Act of 1978, an increasing number of individuals and business firms are seeking protection under the provisions of this act. The question of exemptions was left entirely to the states prior to 1978. However, with the introduction of the Reform Act of 1978, the debtor now may choose the exemptions that are listed in this act, those listed under other federal laws (such as social security, veterans' benefits, etc.), or those listed under the laws of the state of domicile. The exemptions listed under the federal statutes are in many instances more liberal than are those of many states; consequently, individual debtors accept the federal exemptions. Many observers of these developments seem to think that the increased exemptions have encouraged individuals in increasing numbers to go through bankruptcy proceedings.

Business firms are attracted to Chapter XI of the Reform Act because of its provisions for reorganization of the business firm so that it may continue as an operating entity during which period it is protected from its creditors. Although only limited experience has been registered under this act, it appears that creditors may receive less than previously from bankrupts and may have to wait for years before they realize much on the funds advanced to business borrowers who seek protection under this provision. Should the number of filings for bankruptcy continue to rise, banks and other lenders may reevaluate their policies and restrict the extension of credit to marginal borrowers.

QUESTIONS

1. What is the impact of loan losses on the following: bank assets, capital, surplus, reserve for loan losses, prestige of the bank, public relations, loan policies, loan personnel?

2. Have you noticed a news item about a financially troubled firm or a business failure recently? If so, relate the circumstances surrounding the development.

3. There are many ways of handling problem loans from the standpoint of organization, administration, and the involvement of personnel. What sort of arrangement would you recommend as the most efficient? Why?

4. Various reasons are given for business failures. If you were asked to list the most important, how would you respond? Why?

5. It is sometimes said that a bank never makes a bad loan and that loans go bad only after the loans are made. Analyze this reasoning.

6. Why do banks become apathetic about problem loans once they are accepted by a court of bankruptcy?

7. Where does the fault lie in problem loans—the business firm or the bank? Defend your position.

8. Although both consumer and business loans that develop into problem loans are related to the business cycle, consumer loans are more closely related. Why?

9. How would you define a problem loan?

SELECTED REFERENCES

BANK FOR INTERNATIONAL SETTLEMENTS. *Recent Innovations in International Banking.* Prepared by a Study Group Established by the Central Banks of the Group of Ten Countries. Basel, Switzerland, March 1986.

BAUGHN, W. H., AND C. S. WALKER. *The Bankers' Handbook,* rev. ed. Homewood, Ill.: Dow Jones-Irwin, 1978, pp. 602–610.

BRICK, J. R. *Bank Management, Concepts and Issues.* Richmond, Va.: Robert F. Dame, 1980, pp. 77–97.

CONWAY, FRANCIS X., AND WILLIAM A. SIEGENTHALER. "Loan Loss Reserves: Tax, Regulatory, and Adequacy Issues." *The Journal of Commercial Bank Lending* (September 1987), pp. 4–15.

DUN & BRADSTREET. *Business Failure Record.* New York. Annual.

MARTIN, K. D. "Problem Loan Signals and Follow-up." *The Journal of Commercial Bank Lending* (September 1973), pp. 660–667.

NOSKER, J. L. "The Examiner's Viewpoint." *The Journal of Commercial Bank Lending* (September 1975), pp. 35–45.

NOAH, M. G. "Bankruptcy: One Bank's Response." *Journal of Retail Banking,* 3, no. 3 (September 1981), 15–22.

PACE, E. E., AND D. G. SIMONSON, "Solving Problem Loans." *The Journal of Commercial Bank Lending* (July 1977), pp. 668–675.

SODERBERG, R. K. "Assistance to Financially Troubled Companies." *The Journal of Commercial Bank Lending* (November 1974), pp. 629–640.

16

THE INVESTMENT ACCOUNT: POLICIES AND MANAGEMENT

The lending activity provides most of the typical bank's income, but the second largest income source is the securities portfolio. The secondary reserve was defined in Chapter 5 as consisting primarily of high-quality, short-term securities that can be converted to cash on short notice. Banks also invest in longer-term, less liquid debt securities, however, and the portfolio of these notes and bonds is referred to as the *investment account.*

CHARACTERISTICS OF THE INVESTMENT ACCOUNT

A relatively small amount of personnel time is involved in managing the investment account. The investments of a bank with 20 loan officers may be handled in an hour each day by one of the bank's senior officers. Although there are exceptions, lending is a face-to-face activity with some degree of negotiation. Investing is impersonal, with the bank choosing from an array of available securities, the terms of which it had no part in designing. In lending, the borrower usually initiates the transaction, but in investing the bank takes the initiative. The bank is either the major creditor or one of a few creditors of a borrower, but in investing, the bank normally is one of many creditors.

The difference between secondary reserve securities and investment account securities is in the degree of liquidity. An asset is liquid if it can be converted to cash in a very short time. In this sense, many securities in the investment account are as liquid as those in the secondary reserve. Liquidity has another dimension, however, in that a liquid asset undergoes little fluctuation in value. The more distant the maturity date of a credit instrument, the more its market value will change with a change in interest rates. Therefore, U.S. government bonds that mature in 20 years are less liquid than are short-term bills due within 90 days, even though both are issued by the Treasury and the investor can sell the bonds as easily as the bills. The bonds are more burdened with interest rate risk.

Credit (default) risk also influences the liquidity of a security. Credit risk results from the possibility that a creditor will not pay interest and principal when due. The typical investment account contains a larger proportion of securities with some degree of credit risk than does the typical secondary reserve, although it must be stressed that banks do not deliberately invest in high-risk securities in either account. However, the higher degree of credit risk in the investment account does contribute some illiquidity in comparison to the secondary reserve.

Management may consider those securities with maturities of 12 months and less as belonging to the secondary reserve and all others as falling into the investment account. Therefore, assets constantly move from the investment account to the secondary reserve. For example, a U.S. government note purchased today and maturing five years hence would be placed in the investment account today. But four years from now, it would be considered part of the secondary reserve, assuming that twelve months is the dividing line.

The investments comprising the investment account make up a significant part of the assets of most banks. Nationwide, securities average about 16 percent of total assets. Perhaps three-fourths of these would fall into the investment account classification. Small banks hold much larger proportions of their assets in securities than do large banks. For example, banks with assets of less than $100 million hold an average of about 28 percent of their assets in the form of securities.

OBJECTIVES OF THE INVESTMENT ACCOUNT

The objectives of a commercial bank's investment account are to provide the bank with diversification, income, tax benefits, and a liquidity backup for the secondary reserve. It is doubtful whether all the deposits of a commercial bank or the commercial banking system could be placed in desirable loans. It would also be unwise, since such a practice would violate one of the fundamental principles of investment—diversification.

In the event a small bank followed such a practice, it would be relying heavily on the fortunes of the local economy. Prudent banking dictates that a bank acquire some of its assets from sources other than the area where it generates its loans. Large banks are able to obtain geographic diversification in their loan portfolios, so they usually have less need for securities to serve this objective than do local banks.

The income requirement of the investment account normally is higher than that of the secondary reserve. Pursuit of that higher income results in a sacrifice of liquidity, because in most economic periods the more liquid assets produce lower yields. This does not mean high-risk assets are deliberately placed in the investment account, because neither the regulatory bodies nor most bank managements would allow such an approach, but it does mean that the longer maturities used in the investment account do build in a higher level of risk than exists in the secondary reserve.

If bank management feels uncertainty about this liquidity versus income trade-off, it should lean in the direction of liquidity, because the investment account should serve as a buttress to the secondary reserve. If the secondary reserve is drawn down to meet deposit withdrawals or increased demand for loans, it must be replenished in a short period of time to restore adequate liquidity to the bank. If generating funds by increasing liabilities—perhaps large certificates of deposit—does not replenish the secondary reserve, then the sale of investment account securities may be required. If such sales are required, it is usually during a period of tight money and high interest rates when the prices of debt securities are depressed. During such periods disintermediation becomes a problem for many banks.

Banks have held a large part of the investment account in the form of municipal bonds and notes. These securities have contributed a significant tax benefit primarily because the interest they pay is exempt from taxation by the federal government. The Tax Reform Act of 1986 removed much of this benefit, however, so it can be expected that banks will reduce their commitment to municipals.[1] A second tax benefit of the investment account results because of the ability of banks to choose the time to sell bonds with losses and thus offset other income when management feels it is most beneficial to do so. This benefit also has been reduced by the Tax Reform Act of 1986.

---

[1] On April 20, 1988, in *South Carolina v. Baker*, the U.S. Supreme Court ruled that federal taxation of the interest paid on municipal securities is not prohibited by the Constitution. Although there is presently no indication that Congress will enact legislation providing for the taxation of municipal bond interest, this Court decision may create a situation that will contribute to the possibility of further reducing the role of such securities in bank portfolios.

THE RISKS INHERENT
IN THE INVESTMENT ACCOUNT

The risks inherent in the investment account of a commercial bank are *credit risk, market risk,* and *interest rate risk.* The credit risk of a security arises from the probability that the financial strength of the issuer will decline so that it will not be able to meet its financial obligations. Credit risk on obligations of a governmental unit is a product of the character of the debtor or *obligor,* the economy supporting the obligations, and the tax and borrowing power of the unit. When speaking of the character of the obligor, we are thinking in terms of the attitude of public officials and the people toward debt repayment. The attitude of the people is important, for it is from them that public officials derive their strength and mandate. Occasionally, political upheavals in other areas of the world have resulted in the repudiation of debts of governments.

The debt-paying abilities of governments change. This is true of nations as well as of local governments. The strength of an obligor's economy becomes very important when the obligation is a revenue bond, which is supported by special revenues such as those from an electric power plant or a sewer facility. The tax and borrowing powers of governments are essential for a high credit rating on general obligation or guaranteed bonds. Maximum tax rates limit a government in supporting its debt. Some governments are limited in their borrowing activities, which might become very important if sufficient funds were not available from taxes for the payment of principal and interest.

Securities of the federal government are considered free of credit risk because of the government's great taxing and borrowing powers and the strength of the economy from which it derives its funds for the repayment of its obligations. State and local securities are not in the same enviable classification since there have been some defaults in past history, the economies of these governments are not as strong as the total economy, and their taxing and borrowing powers are not comparable. However, it is not our intention to imply that only the obligations of the federal government are acceptable assets to be placed in the investment account since many bonds issued by states and local units of government are excellent investments.

Market risk refers to the possibility that unforeseen changes in the securities markets or the economy may reduce the investment appeal of certain securities so that their sale is possible only at large discounts from earlier values. For example, an economic recession might cause investors to avoid the bonds of small public bodies even though the debt-servicing abilities of such issuers had not declined.

Although an asset may enjoy low credit and market risk, it is still subject to interest rate risk, that is, the risk that market value will decline due to interest rate increases. This phenomenon is the result of the contractual rate of interest a bond carries when it is issued and the relative freedom of market rates to move up and down. A federal government bond, for example, which was issued in 1960 with a 3.5 percent coupon rate and a 1998 maturity lost considerable value in later years because of the rise in interest rates after 1960. Ordinarily, the more distant the maturity date of a credit instrument, the greater the interest rate risk.

BOND PRICES, YIELDS, AND MATURITIES

The rate of return on a fixed income obligation may be stated in terms of the *coupon rate*, the *current yield*, or the *yield to maturity*. The coupon rate is simply the contractual percentage of par value the issuer must pay. A bond carrying a 10 percent coupon pays the holder $100 per year (assuming a par value of $1,000) regardless of the prevailing market rate of interest. The current yield is obtained by dividing the coupon return by the market price. This ratio is more applicable to measuring the rate of return received on preferred stock than on bonds, since it ignores any difference between price and maturity value. The yield to maturity concept provides the best measure of returns on fixed income investments. This measure considers the coupon rate, maturity value, purchase price, and time to maturity.

The yield to maturity concept can best be explained by a simple computation. Assume that a bond is purchased bearing a coupon rate of 12 percent and maturing in 20 years. If the bond is purchased at par (100 percent of face value) at a time when the current market rate of interest is 12 percent for comparable quality bonds, its market price is $1,000 (assuming par value of $1,000). In this instance, the yield to maturity is the same as the coupon rate. However, if the cost of this bond is 92.93 (bond prices are stated in percentages of face value) or $929.30, the yield will be greater than 12 percent. It is obvious that at maturity the bond will be redeemed for $1,000.00 and will have appreciated $70.70 at that time. In computing yield to maturity, however, this increase should be spread over the life of the bond. During the holding period it will produce an annual interest payment of $120.00, and appreciation will amount to approximately $3.54 per year ($70.70 ÷ 20 years), so the annual income is $123.54.

To determine the yield, the average investment must be ascertained. This figure can be found by taking the initial investment of $929.30, adding to it $1,000.00 (the maturity value of the bond), and dividing by 2 to arrive at an average investment of $964.65. The annual return of $123.54 on the bond divided by the average investment gives a yield to maturity of 12.81 percent.

On the other hand, if the bond had cost $1,125.50, we would have to consider the premium of $125.50 in determining the yield. This amount would have to be written off over the 20-year period. We would not consider all the $120.00 interest as current earnings, therefore, but would charge off $6.27 per year from the interest income, which would leave a net of $113.73. We would determine the average investment by adding $1,125.50, the price paid, and $1,000.00, the redemption amount. Dividing by 2 would give us $1,062.75. This amount divided into the net return would give a yield of 10.70 percent.

The formula we have used to determine the approximate yield to maturity in this example is

$$\text{Yield to maturity} = \frac{\text{annual dollar return from coupon} \begin{array}{c} + \text{ annual accumulation} \\ \text{or} \\ - \text{ annual amortization} \end{array}}{(\text{current market price} + \text{par value})/2}$$

This formula produces approximations only. For bonds selling close to face value it gives reasonably accurate results, but for bonds selling at large discounts or large premiums this formula produces a significant error because it ignores the compounding effect that results as the receipt of coupon payments over time gradually amortizes the premium or accumulates the discount. Of course no one who works with bonds makes calculations by hand. Several manufacturers produce desk-top or hand-held calculators programmed to make calculations pertaining to financial instruments, including yield to maturity calculations and others specifically applicable to bonds. When a financial calculator is used to compute the yields to maturity of the bonds in the examples cited, they are found to be 13 percent for the discount bond and 10.49 percent for the premium bond. While the formula we used does not produce precisely accurate yields, it does demonstrate how bond discounts and premiums influence bond yields.

Prior to the introduction of financial calculators, the *yield book* was relied on by virtually everyone who was involved in the bond market, and it is still employed by those who, for whatever reason, do not use a financial calculator. This book contains bond tables from which it is a simple matter to determine a bond's yield when price, coupon rate, and maturity are known.

Bond prices and bond yields are inversely related. When bond prices are low, bond yields are high; when bond prices are high, yields are low. Investors who purchase bonds when interest rates are low face the risk of a decline in value if rates increase. On the other hand, market appreciation will occur when interest rates fall.

This relationship between bond prices and yields means that the market value of commercial bank investment portfolios fluctuates with changes in interest rates. Assume that a bank purchases $10,000,000 worth of 12 percent, 20-year bonds at par. Shortly thereafter the market rate of interest rises to 14 percent. If the bank is forced to sell the bonds, the increase in the rate of interest results in a capital loss to the bank of $1,333,000, since the bonds would sell for only 86.67, or $8,667,000.

When this happens, bank management may feel *locked in*. The bank does not want to sell the bonds and take a huge loss. The alternative is to hold them until maturity or until interest rates decline, causing prices to increase. Even if the bonds recover in price, however, the bank has still suffered an opportunity loss because it could not invest or lend the locked-in funds during the period of high interest rates.

Banks devote extensive attention to avoiding or minimizing such price declines in the investment account, for it must be a major source of liquidity during periods of credit stringency when interest rates tend to rise most. In many cases banks have little choice but to take losses on bonds to restore their primary and secondary reserves if deposits have declined or it is necessary to meet increased loan demands. Obviously, the interest rate risk is of great importance to bank portfolio managers.

The degree of interest rate risk associated with bonds normally varies with the length of their maturities. The shorter the maturity, the more stable the price; the longer the maturity, the less stable the price. For example, if the market rate of interest moves from 12 to 14 percent, the price of a 20-year, 12 percent bond would drop to 86.67, but a 3-year, 12 percent bond would drop to only 95.23. This is a sizable difference, and it explains why short-term securities are frequently more attractive to some investors, especially commercial banks, than are long-term obligations. However, one point of qualification should be made: interest rate increases (or decreases) often vary for different maturities. As an example, the rate change on 3-year maturities could be much greater than that on 20-year maturities. In fact, it is usually true that interest rate changes are greater for the shorter maturities.

INVESTMENT POLICY

Every commercial bank has an investment policy, whether it is recognized or not. Even though a written statement of investment policy is desirable, not all banks have them. The main objectors to a written investment policy are those who feel that the economic environment of banking changes so rapidly that a formal, written statement would become dated within a short time. It is true that banking operates in a changing environment, but changes do not occur so rapidly that they cannot be incorporated into a written policy.

The basic factors that will determine the objectives of a bank's investment policy are its income and its liquidity needs and management's willingness to accept risk. But risk is not limited to the investment account, and the risk generated by an aggressive investment account may be offset by conservative policies elsewhere. For example, a bank with a relatively large secondary reserve is in a better position to take more risk in its investment account than is one with a small secondary reserve. Moreover, a bank that has a portfolio of high-quality loans and relatively stable deposits can assume more risk in the investment account if it so chooses than can a bank without these characteristics. From the standpoint of the welfare of the bank's market area, it might be preferable for the bank to pursue an aggressive lending policy and a conservative investment policy. This would mean a willingness to make loans in its home area, which might be considered somewhat risky but which would, for the most part, benefit the community. The higher risk in the loan portfolio would be countered with a very liquid investment portfolio.

Approaches to the problem of determining what proportions of a bank's total assets should consist of loans and investments and what the makeup of each of these classes of assets should be were discussed in Chapter 5. Once its size is determined, investment policy should describe the makeup of the investment account with the intent of making it as productive as possible within acceptable limits of risk.

Diversification

One of the acceptable methods of reducing risk in the investment portfolio of a commercial bank is by *diversification*—a basic and important rule of any investment policy. Diversification means holding an assortment of securities rather than very few. The diversification policy should consider maturity, geography, type of security, and type of issuer. Risks may not be completely avoided by diversification, but they can be reduced.

A commercial bank is most concerned with quality and maturity. Quality is not the problem it once was because of the large amount of U.S. Treasury and agency securities that are now available to commercial banks. The objective of quality diversification is to minimize the risk that the obligors might not meet their obligations as agreed. Therefore, diversification is more important when investing in securities of a lower quality.

Commercial banks hold a sizable amount of the municipal debt of the nation, and here diversification becomes important. States and their political subdivisions differ considerably from an economic standpoint. Some are industrial, some commercial, some agricultural, while others are fairly well diversified. Some are heavily in debt; others, only lightly. When investing in municipal bonds, a commercial bank should not duplicate its loan portfolio. Loans are of local origin generally, and, as a result, a great part of the bank's assets depends on the economic stability of the local community. Therefore, the investment account affords a means of hedging against any economic instability that may strike the local trade territory. Another factor to be considered in investing in local municipal obligations is that during a recession a bank may make loans to the municipalities for current operating purposes. If securities of these municipalities are held in large amounts, the pyramiding of credit extension in this manner would be unsound. Although there have been few defaults of municipal securities in recent years, local units of government are not immune to financial problems. This fact was evidenced by the financial problems of New York City and a default by the city of Cleveland in the 1970s.

Maturity diversification is also desirable. The goal here is to keep the interest rate risk of the investment portfolio consistent with the income and liquidity objectives of the bank. As we have seen, securities that may not have any credit risk fluctuate considerably in price as interest rates change so that gains and losses frequently result when sales are made. The risk of significant loss dictates that banks stagger maturities in their investment portfolios. As various issues mature, the funds can be reinvested in other securities that best fit the investment portfolio if they are not needed elsewhere.

The investment policy should set forth the manner in which maturities are to be structured. One approach used by many banks is to *ladder* maturities, a process that involves the investment of an equal amount of funds in securities that mature each year up to, say, ten years. Thus, one-tenth of the portfolio would mature in one year, one-tenth in two years, one-tenth in three years, and so on. Funds released from maturing securities are reinvested in the longest maturity category. This approach offers the advantages of simplicity, ease of management and supervision, and a usually stable earnings performance; but it precludes shifts in maturity schedules that might increase returns due to changes in the structure of interest rates. Under a pure ladder of maturities approach, no effort is made to forecast interest rate movements. Many banks modify this approach and restructure maturities when their rate forecasts indicate that benefits—either production of profits or avoidance of losses—will result from such restructuring.

Forecasting Interest Rates

Forecasting interest rate movements is far from being an accurate process. If confidence is placed in a forecast of declining rates and the bank lengthens its maturities, a severe loss of liquidity and perhaps serious losses could result if interest rates subsequently rise. The process of forecasting interest rates begins with understanding the existing rate structure. This structure is depicted by a *yield curve*.

A yield curve is a graphic presentation of yields to maturity for a certain class of securities that differ only as to maturity dates. It is prepared by plotting each issue's yield on the vertical axis of a chart and its maturity date on the horizontal axis. A smooth curve best depicting the overall yield structure of the securities is then fitted to the plotted points. Some points will be above the curve and some below. Since the curve represents the market in a given class of securities at one point in time, its shape may change significantly within a short time span. Yield curves may be constructed for any class of marketable debt instruments, but usually the curve of U.S. government securities receives most attention because of the number of issues and the absence of credit risk. The U.S. Treasury, each quarter in the *Treasury Bulletin,* publishes the yield curve for Treasury issues. Figure 16-1 shows the yield curve for U.S. Treasury securities as it appeared on March 31, 1987.

The shape of the yield curve at any point in time is determined by a number of influences, including Federal Reserve monetary policy and maturity preferences of borrowers and investors, but it also indicates the expectations of investors. A declining, or inverted, yield curve exists when short-term interest rates are higher than long-term rates. If a preponderance of investors believed that the inverted shape would be permanent, they would simply place all their investments in the shortest maturities. However, the inverted shape can only exist because a sufficient number of investors expect rates of all maturities to decline, and they want to "lock in" the prevailing long-term yields.

An increasing yield curve indicates that investors believe that interest rates will soon rise. Thus, investors reason that it would be better to take a low return in the short run and to purchase long-term securities when the yield increases and the prices of the longer-term securities are lower. However, those expectations of higher interest rates are not necessarily borne out, and an increasing, or upward-sloping, yield structure such as that in Figure 16-1 may prevail for many months. Such a yield structure indicates ample liquidity in the economy, usually because the rate of economic growth is slow or negative in the case of economic recession. Such conditions may continue for months or years. The economy had been in a period of slow growth for many months preceding the date of the yield curve in Figure 16-1.

An upward-sloping yield curve such as that in Figure 16-1 usually exists when interest rates are low, at least in relation to experience in recent years. Such a yield structure presents a trap for bond investors, including banks. The yields on short maturity instruments are so low that there is a temptation to buy longer maturities in order to increase yields. If, as we have seen, interest rates subsequently rise, the declines in value will be much greater in the longer maturities.

An investment strategy that has been adopted by a number of banks and that relies heavily on yield curve analysis is the *barbell* maturity

FIGURE 16-1 Yields of Treasury Securities, March 31, 1987 (based on closing bid quotations)

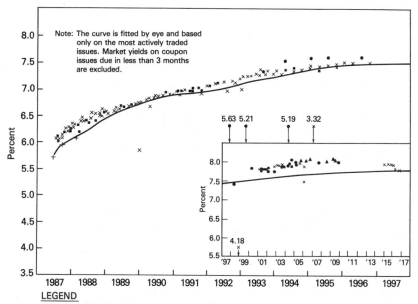

LEGEND

x Fixed maturity coupon issues under 12%.
▪ Fixed maturity coupon issues of 12% or more.
● Callable coupon issues under 12%.
▲ Callable coupon issues of 12% or more.
+ Bills. Coupon equivalent yield of the latest 13-week, 26-week, and 52-week bills.

Note: Callable issues are plotted to the earliest call date when prices are above par and to maturity when prices are at par or below.

SOURCE: *Treasury Bulletin* (Spring 1987), p. 39.

structure. This approach places a significant portion of the portfolio in long-maturity bonds and retains the balance in short maturities with few, if any, bonds maturing in the intermediate range. The two "bulges" at the short and long ends of the maturity structure give this strategy its name.

Under a barbell strategy, the amount invested in long-term bonds and the timing of those investments depend on the level of long-term rates and the direction in which those rates are expected to move. If long-term rates are expected to decline, a heavy commitment to the long end of the barbell is made. If rates at the short end of the yield curve are expected to be stable or declining, the short end of the barbell might include maturities of as much as three or four years, but if short-term rates are expected to rise, the short end of the barbell may consist of maturities so short that they are considered part of the secondary reserve.

If the bank is accurate in its interest rate forecasting, the barbell structure should be more beneficial than the ladder of maturities structure. The continued popularity of the laddered approach suggests that many bankers do not place a high degree of confidence in interest rate forecasts.

Quality Requirements

The quality of the securities that make up the investment portfolio is so important that it must be mentioned in the statement of policy. High quality implies marketability and safety of funds, whereas low quality implies the opposite, even though the return may be greater. Investment officers must have some standards to guide them in their selection of securities, just as loan officers must have some criteria regarding the quality of loans that should be sought by the bank. A bank may wish to state in its investment policy that a certain percentage of its investments must consist of U.S. government securities, since they are virtually risk free if they are of relatively short maturity. The quality of municipals may be stated in terms of an acceptable rating by private rating agencies or of a quality considered suitable by the board of directors.

Managerial Responsibilities

A statement of investment policy should designate the person responsible for handling the investment program. This is fundamental to the efficient operation of an investment portfolio, in that "too many cooks may spoil the stew." This person should be capable, well trained, and above all, cognizant of the bank's responsibilities to the community. One fault of many department heads in any organization, including banks, is the feeling that their responsibilities and activities should take precedence over other departments in the organization. The investment department must realize that its activities are subordinate in nature. Loans to customers, along with the primary reserve, come first in priority. The sale of a bond at a loss may be a hard blow to the investment department, but if the same funds can be employed more profitably in loans, the sale decision may be wise. Commercial bank management is a team undertaking, and the investment officer should be given full authority for the operation of the department, consistent with the investment policy established by the board of directors. If the size of the investment portfolio warrants it, this person should devote full time to this important function and have capable personnel, facilities, and materials available to help carry out the policies.

An important influence on the management of an investment portfolio is the pledging requirement imposed by governmental units. Most governments—federal, state, and local—require commercial banks to hold securities of certain amounts and classifications to secure their deposits in those banks. For example, a state may require that its deposits be secured by obligations of the U.S. government, federal agencies, or the state itself in amounts totaling no less than 110 percent of those deposits. A bank that anticipates holding a significant volume of the state's deposits should establish in its investment policy the manner in which the pledging requirement normally will be met. The policy should also recognize the immobility that such a pledging requirement injects into the investment portfolio. The investment manager may be prevented from making advantageous portfolio switches because of the frozen nature of pledged securities. The portion of the investment portfolio immobilized by such a pledge can reach 50 percent or more at some banks during periods when they have become somewhat illiquid in their effort to satisfy loan demands.

Since the board of directors is responsible for the proper investment of the bank's funds, periodic reports regarding the investment portfolio should be prepared for the board's use in evaluating investment management and establishing investment policy. These reports should be informative, clear, and concise. The board of directors is basically interested in the quality, diversification, and maturity schedule of the investments and an appraisal at periodic intervals.

The investment policy of a bank should be reviewed occasionally and modified as economic conditions change. It is impossible to state how frequently this should be in terms of months or years. It should be reviewed as developments occurring inside or outside the bank dictate. For example, if interest rates increase or decrease after several months or years of stability, a review is in order. If loans, in strong demand for months, decrease, the policy should be reviewed.

Trading

Trading can refer to "making a market" in certain securities or to buying and selling securities actively in the hope of profiting from short-term movements in prices. *Making a market* is the practice of a bank investment department, or any other underwriter, who acts as a merchant standing ready to buy or sell a particular issue at established bid and ask quotations. Commercial banks are permitted to underwrite municipal issues and commonly make a market for them, which is an acceptable function of an underwriter. A few large banks also have dealer departments that make a market in U.S. government securities. Banks that conduct dealer activities in securities have committed a certain amount of capital in support of such operations, and the securities involved are segregated from the investment account and are designated *trading account securities*.

Active trading of investment account securities in the hope of realizing profits is a practice that calls for close and continuous awareness of the securities markets, skillful trading techniques, and probably some good luck to achieve success. Before contemplating the practice of trading, a commercial bank should consider the objectives of the investment portfolio. As we have seen, the principal objectives are to provide liquidity and income commensurate with the risks involved; a bank that engages in trading extensively, consciously or unconsciously, is placing greater emphasis on income than liquidity as its investment goal.

An activity that may be classified as trading and that should be considered at times by any bank portfolio manager is termed *tax swapping*. It was mentioned earlier in this chapter that banks may feel "locked in" to securities that have declined in market value as a result of a sharp rise in interest rates. However, if a bank feels that it can tolerate a loss in the current year—perhaps loan interest has been very good—then taking a loss by selling a depreciated security may result in significant tax savings. The swap element results if the bank replaces the security sold with another of somewhat similar maturity. The bank cannot repurchase the same or an essentially identical security, or the loss on the sale will be disallowed for tax purposes. However, purchase of a similar security will keep the investment portfolio in approximately the same composition as it was previous to the sale, but with the added benefit of the tax loss. The dollar amount of the tax loss may be offset in the future as a result of gains in the replacement security, but the bank will experience a net benefit because it has had the use of the dollars saved on taxes during the interim.

Hedging

Hedging was discussed in Chapter 6 as a tool a bank might use in its asset-liability management program. One instrument that may be used to hedge is the financial futures contract.

Futures contracts, whether they pertain to commodities such as wheat and copper or to financial instruments such as Treasury bills and bank CDs, are relatively complex. Essentially these forward contracts call for the delivery of a stated amount (and specified quality in the case of commodities) of the commodity or financial instrument on a specified future date. The futures contract itself can then be traded (various futures exchanges are involved in the issuance and trading of futures contracts) until its expiration date.

A brief example of a hedge will suggest the possible benefits of financial futures. Perhaps a bank anticipates a rise in interest rates over the next six months and a corresponding increase in loan demand, both due to a rapidly expanding economy. The bank wants to be prepared to expand its loans to strong borrowers by that time and in particular to meet the credit needs of its long-time customers.

The bank holds in its investment account $5 million par value of U.S. Treasury bonds due in five years. The bonds could be sold now and the funds placed in Treasury bills with maturities matching the times when need for funds is anticipated. This would avoid the decline in market value that the bonds would experience if rates do in fact rise. The bank is reluctant to sell the bonds now, however, for two reasons. First, the bonds were purchased at a time when interest rates were lower than at present, so sale would incur a loss. If sale can be postponed six months, the bank will be in a new tax year, when it is anticipated that taking the loss will be much more advantageous. Second, the bank's interest rate forecast may not materialize. If the bank sells the bonds yielding, say, 9 percent at their present price, and buys Treasury bills yielding, say, 6 percent, it will lose a significant amount of income.

To avoid selling the bonds now and also to protect itself from a decline in the market value of the bonds if interest rates do rise, the bank could establish a *short hedge*. The bank would sell Treasury bond (or other financial instrument) futures contracts in sufficient amount to provide the desired hedge. If, as projected, interest rates rose during the ensuing months, the bonds would have declined in value, but the futures contracts (from the bank's standpoint of having sold contracts) would have appreciated. When the funds were needed, the bonds would be sold and the futures contracts closed out through the purchase of matching contracts. If the hedge is well designed, the gain on the futures contract can approximate the loss on the bonds during the period of the hedge. Seldom if ever is a hedge perfect; nevertheless, if properly set up, the bank would have its funds when needed and would take the loss on the bonds in the desired year.

The hedge entails some costs, of course, and had interest rates declined rather than risen, losses would have developed in the futures contracts. However, the bonds would have appreciated during that time. Thus, the hedge neutralized the bank's position during the time the hedge was in place.

DETERMINING THE ORGANIZATION
OF THE INVESTMENT DEPARTMENT

The size of the investment or bond department of a commercial bank depends on the size of the investment portfolio; the functions performed by the department, such as underwriting, trading, and services performed for customers; and the types of securities purchased and held in the investment portfolio. The investment function requires an analysis of the credit and interest rate risk of the assets to be purchased, an evaluation of the bank's ability to assume the degree of risk found, and, once they are placed in the investment portfolio, continual assessment of the securities.

A lack of organization is sometimes found in some smaller banks, but most large banks have people skilled in various phases of the investment program with funds budgeted for research and analysis. Such specialists have a wealth of materials in the form of information from investment services and financial and economic data that have bearing on various securities. Small banks generally do not have ready access to most of these aids. The investment function may be performed by any of the officers, who may also make loans and, possibly, perform additional administrative duties. Because of lack of time for specialization, the personnel in a small bank usually do not acquire the acumen of those who handle the investment accounts in larger institutions.

In many small, and some medium-sized, banks, the trust and investment functions are combined. There are arguments both for and against this kind of organization of course. The most important argument in support of this combination is that both departments are concerned with the analysis of various securities; therefore, it is economical from a personnel standpoint to combine both functions in the same department. The most potent argument against it is that greater opportunity exists for self-dealing than if the two functions are separate and distinct. In the event that these functions are combined, safeguards should be established to avoid direct as well as indirect self-dealing as far as trust funds are concerned. Complete separation of these functions is the ideal situation.

Many large banks make their own analysis of the securities purchased; the investment department determines whether the issue in question meets the specific needs of the bank. Other banks may rely on outside sources for this analysis. However, outside sources are not as aware of the bank's investment requirements as are those associated with it who have probably participated with the board of directors in the formulation of the policy.

The small bank may employ several means of overcoming its lack of proficiency in investment portfolio management. It can abstain from purchasing issues that require elaborate analysis and concentrate on credit risk-free securities, which would mean heavy purchases of U.S. government obligations. This may be desirable from the standpoint of safety and liquidity, but the bank may forgo considerable income if the practice is followed for a long period. Many small banks follow this practice, however, coupled with the purchase of local municipals.

Small banks also utilize various statistical services. Many are worthy of consideration, but the small bank should not rely on them exclusively. Rating agencies do not always agree on each security, and they are as subject to error as others. Some people hold that rating agencies follow the market rather than lead it. Relying exclusively on ratings means that some small but high-quality issues would never be purchased.

A final means that many small banks employ is to utilize the services

17

INVESTMENT
SECURITIES

The investment activities of commercial banks are closely regulated for the same reason as are lending activities: to assure safety of depositors' funds. There are many limitations as to which securities are acceptable in the eyes of state and federal regulatory authorities. We will discuss the most important of these that apply to national banks.

INVESTMENT REGULATIONS PERTAINING TO NATIONAL BANKS

The investment activities of national banks are regulated by law[1] and by regulations of the Comptroller of the Currency. Generally, national banks are prohibited from investing in equity securities. There are minor exceptions to this rule, however. National banks must belong to the Federal Reserve System and are required to own stock in their respective regional Federal Reserve banks. Also, a bank can own stock in an amount up to 15 percent of its capital and surplus in the corporation that operates its safe deposit business, and it can own stock in amounts equal to its capital in the corporation that owns the buildings in which the bank is located. With the permission of the Board of Governors of the Federal Reserve

[1] Title XII of the U.S. Code, Sec. 24.

389

System, banks may also invest an amount equal to 10 percent of capital and surplus in a foreign banking corporation. A bank may own stock in the Government National Mortgage Association, the Student Loan Marketing Association, and the Federal National Mortgage Association if that association buys FHA and VA mortgages from the bank.

For purposes of regulating the investment and underwriting activities of national banks, the Comptroller of the Currency has defined three classes of securities. *Type I securities* include obligations of the United States or its agencies or general obligations of any state of the United States or any political subdivision of any state. These can be purchased without limit other than the need to exercise prudence.

Type II securities include obligations of the International Bank for Reconstruction and Development, the Inter-American Development Bank, the Asian Development Bank, and the Tennessee Valley Authority, and obligations issued by any state or political subdivision or any agency of a state or a political subdivision for housing, university, or dormitory purposes. *Type III securities* are corporate debt instruments, including those convertible into common stock, foreign corporate or government bonds, and assessment and revenue bonds of states and political subdivisions issued for purposes other than housing or university dormitories. A national bank may invest in type II or type III securities in amounts up to 10 percent of capital and surplus for each obligor. However, this limit is reduced to 5 percent for all obligors combined when the bank's judgment is based on "reliable estimates" of the obligor's ability to perform rather than "adequate evidence." The distinction between types II and III securities is that the bank cannot underwrite or deal in type III issues.

Banks are expected to exercise prudence in the selection of their investment securities and to maintain credit files adequate to demonstrate prudence. Banks will become owners from time to time of corporate stocks pledged as collateral on loans that become uncollectable. These stocks must be disposed of within a reasonable time. In the view of the Comptroller, that generally is regarded to be no more than five years.

Banks may purchase debt instruments convertible into common stock or with stock purchase warrants attached, but they must reduce the cost of such securities by amounts equal to the value of the conversion features. This requirement discourages the purchase of such securities if they are selling far above their market values as pure debt instruments.

The National Bank examiners look closely at the investment account to determine the quality and hence the market value of the securities held. For this purpose, securities are placed in three categories: *investment securities, doubtful securities,* and *loss.* Investment securities, as the term implies, are those that meet the standards of quality laid down by law and the regulatory authorities. Doubtful securities mean that a credit problem exists and that the possibility of the obligor meeting interest and/or principal payments is questionable. Should a bank have doubtful securities in its portfolio, a portion of their book value is deducted by the examiner in his or her computation of the bank's adjusted capital and reserves. Securities are placed in the loss classification if, in the evaluation of the bank examiner, a loss exists; consequently, these securities must be written off.

DETERMINATION OF QUALITY

Regulatory authorities are concerned with the quality of the securities purchased by commercial banks. For example, the Comptroller's Office states that its definition of investment securities does not include investments that are "predominantly speculative." Quality, however, is difficult to define, recognize, and regulate. Many circumstances are responsible for the quality of bonds commonly purchased by commercial banks, but it is not always easy to recognize these circumstances when purchases are made. The investment of funds is not an exact science. There is no sure way to invest funds for long periods since many uncertainties face the obligors that issue securities commonly purchased by commercial banks. Almost any security is speculative to a degree; however, some are more speculative than others. Quality is, to a great extent, relative.

Marketability has been emphasized as a criterion for quality by regulatory agencies. This attitude raises the question of a definition of marketability. There are certainly different degrees, depending on the size of the issue, the creditworthiness of the issuing body, and general economic conditions; but, as a general definition, a marketable instrument is one that is actively traded and thus easily sold. Active trading usually results when both the issuer and the issue are large. Issues of the U.S. government are traded in an active market; those of a small country school district are not. Probably the difference separating the bid and ask quotations for a bond is as good a test of marketability as can be found. A small difference, or spread, indicates an active market for a bond.

Two private agencies provide most of the ratings of corporate and government securities. These agencies—Standard & Poor's Corporation and Moody's Investors Service—do not rate all issues but confine their ratings to those that have a relatively broad market.[2] In general, investors have great respect for these ratings, and so does the Comptroller's Office, which looks with favor on those securities rated in the upper four brackets. However, the Comptroller's Office recognizes that there are thousands

---

[2] Moody's ratings of bonds are abbreviated as follows:

Aaa	Best quality	Baa	Medium grade	Caa	Poor standing
Aa	High quality	Ba	Have speculative elements	Ca	Speculative in a
A	Upper medium grade	B	Lack characteristics of a		high degree
			desirable investment	C	The lowest rated

of issues of small localities outstanding that are not as marketable as rated issues but are of high quality and are eligible for a bank's portfolio.

To ensure high quality of the securities placed in the investment account by a bank, the Comptroller's Office requires that investment securities be supported by adequate credit files. Banks are prohibited from relying exclusively on the evaluation of others. The objective of this regulation is to encourage bank management to make desirable decisions regarding the investment portfolio. It is believed that this cannot be done intelligently unless adequate information about the issue and the obligor is available. This is desirable since banks, especially smaller ones, tend to rely on a city correspondent, an investment counselor, or a bond dealer, some of whom might have a special interest in certain issues.

CLASSIFICATION OF ELIGIBLE SECURITIES ACCORDING TO OBLIGOR

Eligible securities may be classified according to obligor: federal government, federal agencies, state and local units of government (municipals), and corporate securities. Although municipal issues make up the largest portion of commercial bank investment portfolios, as a single obligor, the federal government is by far the most important.

Federal Government Securities

Deficit financing of the federal government has created a huge national debt. This debt is represented by various classes of U.S. Treasury securities.

Treasury Bills. Bills are short-term securities with original maturities of three, six, or twelve months. Because of their short maturities and high marketability, Treasury bills are the most liquid of all U.S. government securities and meet the liquid asset needs of banks very well. Bills are discount instruments; that is, the investor does not receive separate interest payments, but instead earns interest income by paying a price below the face value of the bill and receiving face value at maturity. If the bill is sold before maturity, the seller receives less than face value but will have earned interest income if the bill is sold for more than was paid for it. This should be the case unless interest rates have risen sharply since the purchase date.

Because Treasury bills are issued in tremendous volumes, an active and efficient secondary market exists. Thus banks are not limited to purchasing newly issued bills and, in fact, buy most of their bills in the secondary market. A given bill may be bought and sold several times while it is outstanding. Because of their superior quality and tremendous volume, yields on Treasury bills are pivotal rates in the money market. Changes in bill rates will likely affect rates on other types of short-term obligations since investors continually compare the relative attractiveness of investment alternatives.

It is customary to speak of Treasury bill yields, although bills are quoted on a bank discount basis. The computation of Treasury bill discount, price, and equivalent bond yield follows.[3]

> **Let** A = **number of days to maturity**
> B = **discount basis expressed as percentage**
> C = **discount from par in dollars**
> P = **dollar price**
> Y = **investment return**

To find the discount on a Treasury bill due in 347 days on a 9 percent discount basis, let

$$C = \frac{A}{360} \times B$$
$$= \frac{347}{360} \times 9\%$$
$$= \textbf{8.675\%, or \$8.675 discount per \$100 maturity value}$$

The price of the bill will be quoted in the market as

$$P = \$100 - C$$
$$= \$100 - \$8.675$$
$$= \textbf{\$91.325 per \$100 maturity value}$$

The investment return, or equivalent bond yield, will be higher than the discount-basis return because the discount is expressed as a percentage of $100 and not as a percentage of the $91.325 actually invested and because bond yields are computed on a 365-day year while bill discounts and prices are based on a 360-day year. The bond equivalent yield is computed as follows:

$$Y = \frac{\$\ 8.675}{\$91.325} \times \frac{365}{347} = \textbf{9.99\%}$$

Treasury Notes and Bonds. Treasury notes are issued with maturities of from one to ten years. Bonds may have any maturity but are usually issued with maturities of ten to thirty years. Notes and bonds are issued with specified coupon rates. Several issues of bonds are callable prior to maturity. For example, the 8.50 percent bonds of 1994–99 mature in 1999

---

[3] *The First Boston Corporation Handbook of Securities of the United States Government and Federal Agencies and Related Money Market Instruments,* 29th ed. (New York: First Boston Corp., 1980), pp. 63–65.

but may be called in, or any time after, 1994. The bond will be called, of course, only if market rates at the time of call are below the coupon rate.

Issuing Treasury Securities

Commercial banks are involved in the issuance of U.S. Treasury obligations through their participation in the *auctions* of Treasury bills, notes, and bonds. Bills are issued through auctions conducted by the Federal Reserve banks. The auctions normally take place each week on Monday, with delivery and payment on the following Thursday. Competitive bids are entered by investors on a basis of 100, with the highest bid accepted first, then the next highest, and so on, until the desired amount has been sold. For example, a bid of 98.914 would be filled entirely before any bills were granted to a bid of 98.913. Investors who do not wish to enter competitive bids may enter noncompetitive tenders. In this case, investors are assured of having their orders filled but must pay the average price as determined from the accepted competitive bids. Only relatively small amounts—usually no more than $1 million—may be purchased on a noncompetitive basis.

A Treasury offering of notes or bonds may be on an auction or a subscription basis. If the auction process is followed, it is similar to a bill auction except that bids are in terms of yield instead of price, with the lowest yield bid receiving the full amount of its order before the next highest bid receives any securities. Noncompetitive orders are usually accepted for relatively small amounts. If the subscription process is followed, all terms of the forthcoming issue are set in advance (amount to be sold, maturity and call dates, coupon rate, and price). The subscription process has been used infrequently in recent years.

The Dealer Market

The secondary market for U.S. Government securities is maintained by approximately 35 business organizations that buy and sell securities for their own accounts. These organizations, termed "primary dealers," may be commercial banks, but more than half are nonbank securities dealers. Most of the nonbank dealers conduct a wide range of investment activities. Primary dealers are authorized to trade directly with the Federal Reserve System. Other investment firms and banks also buy and sell Treasury securities, but they cannot deal with the Federal Reserve and often depend on primary dealers as the source of the securities they sell.

The spread between a dealer's bid and asked price represents the gross profit of a trade. When dealers want to increase their trading volume or reduce their holdings of a particular issue, spreads between bid and asked prices are narrowed. The spread on a highly demanded issue is quite small because of competition between dealers.

Government Agency and Related Issues

The obligations just discussed are direct obligations of the U.S. government. In addition to these securities, various government agencies and related organizations issue obligations in the securities markets not guaranteed by the U.S. government. Among the most important of these agencies are the Federal Home Loan Banks, Government National Mortgage Association, Federal National Mortgage Association, Farm Credit Banks, and Student Loan Marketing Association. Some agencies borrow through both short-term and long-term securities. The securities in this group, termed "agencies," do not include passthrough securities (discussed below).

Yields on government agency and related issues normally are above those on Treasury issues. The spread varies with money market conditions, investor preference, and the features of the particular issue that affect its liquidity. Agency and related issues make up approximately one-fourth of bank securities holdings.

Municipal Securities

Municipals.   This is a broad term employed in financial circles to include securities issued by states and their political subdivisions and, sometimes, even the obligations of territories and possessions of the United States. The political subdivisions of states whose obligations are classified as municipals are cities, counties, towns, boroughs, and villages. State and local governments may also create various types of districts with the authority to issue obligations classified as municipals, such as school, road, water, library, and sanitary districts. Municipal securities are difficult to classify as to source of payment because of the many variations that exist. The usual classifications are general obligation, revenue, and assessment; but, not too infrequently, one finds an obligation with some features of two or all three of the classifications.

General Obligation Bonds.   The most common type of municipal security is the general obligation or, as it is sometimes called, the *full faith and credit* obligation. The term full faith and credit means that the full taxing power of the obligor is pledged to ensure payment of the obligation; technically, such securities have a tax lien on all taxable property within the obligor's domain up to 100 percent of the property. The term also means that the issuing body will exert every effort to collect taxes to pay the principal and interest on the obligations. From a credit standpoint, general obligations are the best type of municipal security and are the most sought after of all municipals by investors, including commercial banks. The creditworthiness of general obligations is also recognized by bank regulatory authorities.

Revenue Bonds.   Revenue bonds are obligations issued by publicly owned business agencies or authorities. The principal and interest are payable solely from the earnings of the business. Examples of revenue bonds are the obligations issued by municipally owned waterworks, electric power departments, and sewer districts or toll bridge and toll road authorities created by states. The issuance of revenue bonds stems from the debt limitations that were imposed on municipalities when they had fewer proprietary functions than they now have. If municipalities have used up their ability to issue general obligation bonds, revenue bonds provide an alternative method of financing revenue-producing facilities. The quality of revenue bonds is not usually as high as that of general obligation bonds.

Assessment Bonds.   Assessment bonds are obligations that have been issued to finance a particular improvement, such as the pavement of a street or the installation of a sewer. Such obligations are payable from the proceeds of a specific assessment based, for example, on frontage footage or on some other measure levied against each piece of property located in the area that receives the benefit. In some cases local governments may agree to make up any deficit that occurs, however, and if this should happen, assessment bonds would assume the characteristics of general obligation bonds.

Hybrid Bonds.   In addition to general obligation, revenue, and assessment bonds, there are municipal obligations that possess features of one or more of these securities. In a sense, these bonds are hybrids. The full faith and credit of the issuing government could be added to a revenue bond. In this instance, it would be relied on only in the event that revenue from the public utility was insufficient to pay the principal and/or interest. This type of bond would certainly be of a higher quality than if only one source of funds were available to support it. It would therefore command a lower interest rate in the market.

Some states have issued general obligation bonds payable primarily from the revenue derived from particular taxes, and others have issued bonds with no pledge of the full faith and credit of the state but with only the pledge of the revenue from a particular tax. These bonds are sometimes referred to as tax revenue bonds. Industrial revenue bonds are issued by a local governmental body to finance facilities used by private industry. These bonds are secured by, and derive interest and principal payments from, lease payments made by the private enterprises that use the facilities.

Public bodies frequently issue short-term *anticipation notes* to provide temporary funds until receipt of the proceeds from a new bond issue, tax revenues, or other anticipated income. Another form of short-term, tax-exempt security that many banks purchase is the *project note*. These notes are issued to provide construction funds for urban renewal, neighborhood development, and low-cost housing projects. They are issued under agreement with the Department of Housing and Urban Development, are sold through auctions by that agency, and are guaranteed by the U.S. government.

Municipals and the 1986 Tax Reform Act

Banks invest relatively less in municipals than in past years, although these securities still make up over one-fourth of securities held by banks. As discussed in the previous chapter, a bank gains diversification of assets when it acquires municipals from various locations. However, the overwhelming appeal of municipals has been their exemption from federal income tax on interest payments. In addition, most states that have an income tax have exempted the interest paid by municipals issued within their borders.

Municipals became much less attractive to banks with the passage of the 1986 Tax Reform Act. The act disallows deduction of the cost of funds invested in municipals by banks and other financial intermediaries, thus essentially eliminating the shelter benefits of municipals. The rule covers municipals purchased after August 7, 1986. An exception is that 80 percent of the carrying cost can be deducted on municipals "qualified for investment by financial intermediaries." These are certain issues of municipalities that do not issue more than $10 million of such bonds during a calendar year.

Whether or not investment in a qualified municipal will provide tax shelter benefits depends on the yield of the security, the cost of funds to the bank, and the bank's marginal tax rate. For example, for a qualified municipal selling at par with no state tax implications, if it is assumed that

A qualified municipal will yield 6 percent
The bank's average cost of funds before tax is 8 percent
The bank's marginal tax rate is 34 percent

then

$$\frac{.06 - (.08 \times .20 \times .34)}{1 - .34} = .0827, \text{ or } 8.27 \text{ percent}$$

This rate is then compared to rates available on fully taxable securities of similar risk to determine which is the most appropriate to purchase.

Passthrough Securities

The reduced net after-tax returns available from municipals have led banks to increase investment in other types of securities, including those representing ownership interest in mortgage pools, termed *passthroughs*. Passthroughs were mentioned in Chapter 13 as one of the innovations that added liquidity to the market for residential mortgage loans. Here the passthrough is considered as a vehicle for bank investment.

The passthrough was originated by the Government National Mortgage Association (GNMA or Ginnie Mae) in 1970. The GNMA passthroughs are based on residential mortgage loans guaranteed by the Federal Housing Administration or the Veterans Administration. To originate passthrough securities, a lender first segregates a pool of mortgages with the same interest rate and approximate maturity and places them under the supervision of a trustee. Then certificates representing shares of ownership in the pool are sold to investors. GNMA, which is an arm of the federal government, guarantees the certificates, so they are as free of default risk as Treasury securities.

The name "passthrough" results because the original lender continues to collect interest and principal payments on the loans in the pool and distributes both monthly on a pro rata basis to certificate holders. If a borrower does not make payment, it is replaced by GNMA.

The Federal Home Loan Mortgage Corporation (FHLMC or Freddie Mac) also sponsors passthroughs much like GNMA's, except that the pools are made up of conventional mortgages. Although FHLMC guarantees payment, unlike GNMA its guarantee is not directly backed by the federal government. Thus FHLMC passthroughs are slightly more risky than GNMA's and carry slightly higher yields.

Passthroughs have been issued as well by banks and other financial intermediaries that are independent of GNMA and FHLMC. These are based on mortgages that carry private mortgage insurance and thus are of high quality even without the backing of a government agency.

Passthroughs of all types provide yields higher than those on Treasury securities and thus have appeal to many banks. Although yields are higher, the investor in a passthrough is not certain what earnings rate will be realized, even if the passthrough is held until it is completely paid off. That is because the principal payments on mortgage loans, which, along with interest payments, are passed through to certificate holders monthly, are somewhat unpredictable as to amount. When loans are prepaid, usually as the result of new financing when homes are sold, large amounts of principal are distributed to certificate holders. The remaining book value represented by their certificates is correspondingly reduced. Investors try to estimate prepayment rates before buying passthroughs, but success is limited because prepayments depend on such conditions as the state of the economy and the level of interest rates. If interest rates are high, prepayments tend to be much less than when interest rates are low. Prepayments are most likely in pools made up of high-rate loans when interest rates fall because homeowners are eager to refinance such loans.

Prepayments may influence realized yields positively or negatively. If, for example, a certificate based on a pool of 8 percent mortgages were purchased at a discount to yield 10 percent, a high rate of early payoffs would increase the effective yield to more than 10 percent. The opposite would be true if a certificate based on a pool of 12 percent mortgages were purchased to yield, say, 11 percent and early prepayments were experienced. The yields quoted on certificates based on low-rate mortgages are, consequently, lower than the yields on certificates based on pools of high-rate mortgages.

Collateralized Mortgage Obligations

The collateralized mortgage obligation (CMO) was originated in 1983 by the Federal Home Loan Mortgage Corporation and since has been issued in great numbers by banks and other financial institutions. Rather than owning a piece of a pool of mortgages, as in the case of a passthrough holder, an investor in a CMO owns a bond collateralized by a pool of mortgages. The value of the mortgages typically is far greater than the face value of the bonds issued; thus CMOs usually carry the highest rating of the rating agencies.

Several maturities of CMOs are issued based on a single mortgage pool, the most common arrangement being four classes.[4] All principal payments initially go to the shortest maturity class. When that class of bonds is retired, all principal payments go to the next class, which had received interest only until all of the first maturity class was retired. The final class is similar to a zero coupon bond in that it receives no principal or interest until all prior classes are retired. Then it receives all cash flows until it too is retired.

The shortest maturity class may have a stated maturity of two to five years when issued, but due to gradual retirement of bonds as principal payments are made on mortgages, average life of the bonds would be one to three years. Other classes will have longer average lives, with that of the final class projected to be 15 to 25 years.[5]

---

[4] Janet Spratlin and Paul Vianna, *An Investor's Guide to CMOs* (New York: Salomon Brothers, 1986).

[5] Ibid.

REMICs

The real estate mortgage investment conduit (REMIC) was authorized by the 1986 Tax Reform Act. The issuers of REMICs can structure them in passthrough form or bond form, in both cases with multiple maturity classes. The underlying mortgages may be segregated into risk classes and REMICs issued based on default risk as well as with different maturities. The REMIC has numerous flexible characteristics that give it appeal to banks both as an investment vehicle and, from the issuer's standpoint, a means to add liquidity to mortgage portfolios.

Other Securities

Other issues, principally of corporations, may be purchased if they meet the tests of quality. These may include commercial paper, corporate bonds, and issues backed by asset pools other than mortgages. For example, securities have been issued backed by automobile loans and commercial loans.

BANK UNDERWRITING
OF MUNICIPAL SECURITIES

Unlike U.S. government securities, which are issued without the services of an underwriter, municipal securities are issued through a competitive bidding process in which commercial banks and other underwriters compete for a given issue. The underwriter offering the bid with the lowest interest cost to the issuer is awarded the right to market the issue. Member banks are prohibited from underwriting assessment bonds or revenue bonds for other than housing, university, or dormitory purposes.

From a bank's standpoint, the most important part of the underwriting process is the preparation of the bid. The announcement of a new bond issue is made in the form of a published *invitation to bid*. The invitation describes the issue and informs prospective bidders of procedures to be followed in submitting bids. If the issue is small, a bank may bid on it without forming an underwriting syndicate. On large issues, syndicates consisting of a number of banks and other underwriters will be formed to spread the risk of underwriting and assist in marketing the issue. For large issues, for example from $100 million to $250 million, a syndicate may include as many as 100 banks and other underwriters, and several syndicates may bid on the issue. Prior to making its bid, an agreement is drawn under which the syndicate spells out the responsibilities and liabilities of syndicate members if a bid is successful.

The first step in determining the bid is *scaling*, that is, determining the reoffering scale, which is the list of yields investors will be offered by the underwriter on the various maturities of the issue. The reoffering scale is determined by conditions in the municipal securities market. The underwriter scales presently outstanding issues of municipal securities of the same quality rating as the one on which the bid is being prepared by listing the yields at which the various maturities of these issues are trading in the market. This process is, in fact, the development of a yield curve for a particular quality group of municipal securities. The underwriter will plan to offer the new issue to the public at yields equal to or slightly higher than those available in the open market.

The next step is the determination of the *coupon structure*—the coupon rates that will be assigned to the various maturities of the bond issue. The coupon structure is not the same as the reoffering scale because the underwriter usually will sell some of the bonds at a price above par and some below par. Setting the coupon rate above or below the scale will result in an offering price somewhat below or above par.

The coupon structure is determined in part by what the market will consider attractive, but it is also a factor in the bidding strategy. Putting the highest coupon rates on the shortest maturities results in a lower net interest cost to the issuer. The calculation of the net interest cost as an amount and as a rate is demonstrated in Table 17-1, which depicts a hypothetical bond issue and a bid by the underwriter of 100.50, or $1,005 per $1,000 bond. The bid price determines the net interest cost and, of

TABLE 17-1 Computation of Net Interest Cost to Issuer

Amount	Coupon Rate	Years to Maturity	Bond Years	Coupon in $	Total Interest
$ 50,000	.060	1	50	$60	$ 3,000
50,000	.060	2	100	60	6,000
50,000	.060	3	150	60	9,000
50,000	.060	4	200	60	12,000
100,000	.058	5	500	58	29,000
100,000	.058	6	600	58	34,800
100,000	.058	7	700	58	40,600
100,000	.058	8	800	58	46,400
100,000	.058	9	900	58	52,200
100,000	.058	10	1,000	58	58,000
100,000	.058	11	1,100	58	63,800
100,000	.058	12	1,200	58	69,600
100,000	.058	13	1,300	58	75,400
150,000	.040	14	2,100	40	84,000
150,000	.040	15	2,250	40	90,000
150,000	.040	16	2,400	40	96,000
150,000	.040	17	2,550	40	102,000
$1,700,000			17,900		$871,800

course, that bid resulting in the lowest net interest cost will be the one accepted.

The formula used to calculate net interest cost is

$$\frac{\text{Net}}{\text{interest}} = \frac{\text{total interest cost for the life of the issue less premium}}{\text{total number of bond years}}$$

$$\frac{\text{Net}}{\text{interest}} = \frac{\text{total interest of \$871,800 less premium of \$8,500}}{\text{17,900 bond years}}$$

$$\frac{\$863,300}{17,900} = \$48.229 \text{ net interest cost per \$1,000 bond per year}$$

$$\frac{\$48.229}{\$1,000} = 4.8229\%$$

This formula gives the net interest cost per bond year. It should be noted that bond years are calculated by multiplying the number of years a maturity group will be outstanding by the number of bonds in the group.

The underwriting spread is the difference between the bid and the price at which the underwriter will offer the bonds to the public. The spread is the underwriter's gross profit. If the underwriter is confident of a rapid sale of the issue or if much of it has been presold to investors before the bid is determined, the underwriter will consider the risk of buying the issue to be small and will be more aggressive by entering a bid with a small spread—perhaps $8 or $10 per bond. If the issue is not expected to be very attractive or if the underwriter has been unsuccessful in prebid selling efforts, the bid will be made with a much larger spread, perhaps $16 or $18 per bond, to compensate for the greater selling effort that will be required in case the bid is successful.

Besides the underwriting spread from which the bank will derive its profit if the issue is sold as planned when the bid is made, a bank may derive benefit also from public deposits resulting from its underwriting efforts. If it is a participant in an underwriting, a bank may have a deposit stemming directly from the sale of the issue. In addition, if the bank is known for its willingness to make bids on issues of governmental units in its region, the goodwill generated may result in sizable public deposits.

TRENDS IN BANK INVESTMENTS

Bank investments have changed significantly over the years, both in relative amount and composition (see Figure 17-1). Investments as a percentage of total assets have declined substantially since reaching a high point during World War II. This high level was the result of U.S. government borrowing to finance the war and the dearth of loan demand during the war years. Banks participated heavily in financing the war by increasing

FIGURE 17-1   Investments of Commercial Banks, 1950–86

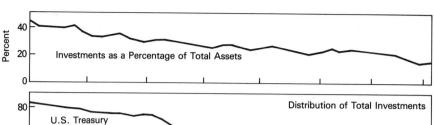

SOURCE: *Federal Deposit Insurance Corporations, annual reports, and Federal Reserve Bulletins.*

holdings of U.S. government securities from $22 billion at the end of 1941 to $91 billion at the end of 1945. The entire investment account totaled less than $100 billion in 1945, but this equaled 62 percent of bank assets.

Bank securities holdings approximated one-half billion dollars by mid-1987, but this was only 18 percent of bank assets. A major reason for the relative decline in securities is that loans have offered better earnings opportunities, and with increased reliance on liability management, banks have felt less need to hold investment securities for liquidity purposes.

QUESTIONS

1. The Comptroller's regulations refer to a process called "overtrading" as an improper investment practice. Overtrading results when a bank engages in a "swap" of one security for another, receiving a price well above market for the security it is eliminating while paying a commensurately higher price for the security it acquires. Why would such a practice have appeal to portfolio managers, and why would the Comptroller consider it inappropriate?

2. How much emphasis should be placed on the ratings of the private rating agencies in selecting municipal bonds for a bank's investment portfolio?

3. Should national banks be allowed to invest in corporate common stocks such as those listed on the New York Stock Exchange?

4. How do Treasury bills differ from Treasury notes?

5. When a bank sells bonds at a loss, it can deduct those losses without limit from other income in determining federal income taxes. How does this differ from the way individuals and nonfinancial corporations must treat such losses?

6. Look at the government bond quotes in the *Wall Street Journal*. What does a quote of, say, 98.14 convert to as the dollar price of a $1,000 bond or note?

7. Notice in the government bond quotes that the yields to maturity for certain long-term bonds, such as the 3's of February 1995, are much lower than other issues, for example, the 8⅝'s of August 1993. Why is this?

8. Notice that the spread—the difference between bid and ask quotations—varies from one Treasury bond to another. Why?

9. Except for a few specified types, banks cannot underwrite revenue bonds, yet they are allowed to acquire such issues for their portfolios. Why do you suppose this restriction on underwriting exists?

10. What is the difference between marketability and quality as these terms apply to debt securities? Can a security be high in one and low in the other? If so, give examples.

SELECTED REFERENCES

COOK, TIMOTHY Q., AND TIMOTHY D. ROWE, eds. *Instruments of the Money Market*, 6th ed. Federal Reserve Bank of Richmond, 1986.

"A Farewell to Municipals and Other Tax Effects." *ABA Banking Journal* (February 1987), pp. 35–36.

FIRST BOSTON CORPORATION. *Handbook of Securities of the United States Government and Federal Agencies and Related Money Market Instruments*, 29th ed. New York, 1980.

LAMB, ROBERT, AND STEPHEN P. RAPPAPORT. *Municipal Bonds*. New York: McGraw-Hill, 1980.

LEVINE, SUMNER N., ed. *Financial Analyst's Handbook I: Portfolio Management*. Homewood, Ill.: Dow Jones-Irwin, 1975, chaps. 6, 9, 11, 12, 13, 15, 29, 30, and 33.

"Mortgaged-Backed Securities Come to the Fore." *ABA Banking Journal* (February 1987), pp. 31–32.

ROSS, IRWIN. "Higher Stakes in the Bond-Rating Game." *Fortune*, April 1976, pp. 132–142.

SHERWOOD, HUGH C. *How Corporate and Municipal Debt Is Rated*. New York: John Wiley, 1976.

SINKEY, JOSEPH F., JR. *Commercial Bank Financial Management in the Financial Services Industry*, 2nd ed. New York: Macmillan, 1986.

STIGUM, MARCIA L., AND RENE O. BRANCH. *Managing Bank Assets and Liabilities*. Homewood, Ill.: Dow Jones-Irwin, 1982.

URNIKIS, MARIAN S. "The New Tax Law: What It Means for Your Bank." *ABA Banking Journal* (November 1986), pp. 56, 59, 63, and 65.

18

TRUST SERVICES OF COMMERCIAL BANKS

Property ownership gives rise to the need for property management services; and managing property for others, in virtually all its forms and under various arrangements, is the business of trust departments. The users of trust department services include individuals, businesses, charitable organizations, and governmental units. The assets managed by trust departments are maintained separately from the assets belonging to the bank, and thus trust assets do not show up in bank balance sheets.

Providing a trust service results in a *fiduciary* relationship, that is, one party acting for the benefit of another in matters coming within the scope of their relationship and, in most instances, involving the holding of property commonly administered by the trustee for the benefit of a third party or parties. In general, the services of a trust department may be classified into three broad areas: the settlement of estates, the administration of trusts and guardianships, and the performance of agencies. Trust services are detailed, highly technical, and "legalistic," so our approach will be cursory and very general.

ADVANTAGES OF A CORPORATE TRUSTEE

Trust services may be performed by individuals or corporations, including the trust departments of commercial banks. Because of the advantages that a corporate trustee should have over an individual acting in this capacity, most trust services are performed by bank trust departments. These advantages are experience, permanence, financial responsibility, responsiveness to obligations, specialization, group judgment, impartiality, and adaptability. Most of these advantages emanate from the professionals employed, given that the trust department is sufficiently large to include an appropriate number of qualified experts. Permanence is a product of the corporate form. Since a corporation in general has perpetual existence, capable and efficient personnel can be employed to carry out the provisions of the trust and other trust services to which the corporation is obligated. Individuals may die or become incapacitated or for other reasons—personal or business—find it impossible to perform the services of a trustee.

Many trusts and trust services involve large sums of money and/or property. People who create trusts or have other trust services to be performed are interested in the financial capacity of the trustee. Few individuals have sufficient funds to assure the creator of a trust that they are financially able to meet this test. Trust services and trust agreements must be carried out punctually and with dispatch; consequently, bank trust departments usually are more responsive to their obligations than would be an individual who has many other obligations.

A very important advantage that many corporate trustees have over an individual is group judgment, since several technicians—specialists in the fields of law, investments, and taxation—are normally in a better position to render sound judgment and advice than is a single individual. Corporate trustees are also better qualified to act impartially than are individuals. Finally, a corporate trustee with specialists in various fields is more adaptable than is an individual who cannot be expert in all required skills.

The value and importance of these advantages may be offset at least partially in some trust departments. Almost 65 percent of the trust departments in the United States have less than $25 million in assets under management. Few trust departments of this size can afford to employ the wide range of experts required to administer trust accounts of all the various types discussed later in this chapter. Many small trust departments consistently experience low or negative profits, so compromises must be made in the number and caliber of employees.

Even very large trust departments often have difficulty generating good levels of profit, so in some of these, the expertise of capable employees may be diluted by excessive work loads.[1] In addition, it is very difficult to systematize many aspects of trust administration because each account has unique features. Some efforts to systematize and thus stream-

---

[1] Robert J. Person and Steven D. Blecher, "Planning for Profits: A Must for Trust Departments," *Trusts & Estates* (February 1980), pp. 47–50.

line trust management, such as lumping accounts together for investment management purposes, may result in customer dissatisfaction.

DEVELOPMENT AND REGULATION
OF TRUST SERVICES IN COMMERCIAL BANKS

Trust functions were first performed by individuals and insurance companies in this country, and it was not until the demand for fiduciary services became great that corporate trustees were organized. Although state banks have performed trust services for many years, national banks are relative latecomers to the field. Not until 1913, with the passage of the Federal Reserve Act, were national banks granted the right to perform fiduciary services. At the present time, approximately 4,200 banks provide trust services, many of which use the word "trust" in the name of the bank. All banks do not offer trust services since the demand is not great in every area of the country and the cost of operating a trust department is quite high. Trust services are concentrated in banks located in areas where there is centralization of both wealth and population. For example, of total trust assets held by insured commercial banks, almost 17 percent is held by four New York City banks.

Since handling trusts and performing trust services involve a great deal of social responsibility, society has seen fit to regulate the performance of these services very closely. Only a few states permit banks, by virtue of having a charter to carry on commercial banking activities, to render trust services also. Most states require that a state bank must first obtain a special permit or license from the proper state authority to operate a trust department. State banks that are members of the Federal Reserve System must also receive permission from the Board of Governors to perform trust services. In addition to a special permit or license, most states require state banks to make a special deposit of securities with the state treasurer or some other designated state official to guarantee the faithful performance of their duties as a trustee. Trust activities of national banks are under the supervision of the Office of the Comptroller of the Currency. Although this office does not require the pledging of securities or other assets, if national banks operate in states that require the pledging of specific assets, they are obliged to comply with state law.

TRUST SERVICES PERFORMED
FOR INDIVIDUALS

Space does not permit the discussion of all the trustee services rendered to individuals by commercial banks. Only the major functions will be mentioned, which include the settlement of estates, the administration of trusts, serving as guardian and conservator of estates, and performance of agency services.

Settlement of Estates

The property of deceased persons must be distributed in accordance with law. Some persons die *testate*, that is, leaving a will that declares their wishes regarding the disposition of property. Others may die *intestate*, leaving no will. In such cases state laws direct who is to receive the decedent's property. Unless negligible in size, estates must be settled by an executor or administrator under the direction of a court of law. A person dying testate appoints in the will an executor to carry out his or her wishes—often the trust department of a commercial bank. The person who settles an estate in which no will existed is called an administrator and is appointed by the court; this responsibility too may fall to the trust department of a commercial bank. In addition to serving as executors and administrators of estates, trust departments may serve in two other capacities: as *administrators with the will annexed* or as *administrators to complete the settlement* of an estate. An administrator with the will annexed exists when a will names no executor or when the one named is unwilling or unable, by law or otherwise, to serve or has died. In these instances, the court will appoint one. An administrator to complete the settlement of an estate exists when an executor or administrator of an estate dies, resigns, or is removed before the estate is fully settled.

The Uniform Probate Code, which was first adopted in Idaho in 1971 and has since been adopted in various forms by several other states, uses the term "personal representative" in place of executor and all the various administrator designations. The Uniform Probate Code was an effort to simplify and bring uniformity to the complex estate settlement process and its state-by-state variations.

The basic duties of an administrator or executor are to obtain court authority to act, assemble and safeguard the assets of the estate, pay administrative expenses and debts of the estate, pay taxes due, distribute the net estate, and render personal services to members of the family. Since property must be distributed in accordance with law, a will must be probated, that is, proved to be the last will and testament of the deceased. The administrator or executor will receive from the court *letters testamentary*, an official document that provides authorization to proceed with the settlement of the estate. Assembling the assets of an estate may be a meticulous and time-consuming process. Bank accounts must be located, brokerage accounts closed, safe deposit boxes opened and the contents surveyed and removed, and life insurance policies collected. If real estate, growing crops, or livestock are part of the estate, they must be inventoried and cared for. Business interests might have to be supervised and continued in operation, and household furniture and heirlooms inventoried and protected. The executor or administrator may have to offer a variety of personal services to the family of the deceased person. Funeral arrangements might become a responsibility. In many instances, the immediate cash needs of the family prove to be a major problem. Obviously, serving as administrator or executor requires special skills and tact.

Safeguarding the assets of an estate may become an enormous task. An appraisal must be made by persons skilled in this type of work; if there are perishable goods they must be cared for and disposed of with a minimum of loss. If a business has to be sold, timing of the sale is important to secure a satisfactory price; the same is true of the sale of securities. Real property might have to be insured, rented, and cared for so that it does not become nonproductive or decline in value. The administrator or executor must arrange for payment of all debts, taxes, and administrative costs of the estate. Funeral expenses, appraiser's and attorney's fees, and court costs must be met.

The next step in settling an estate is to distribute the assets. If a person dies intestate, distribution must be carried out in accordance with the law; that is, so much of the assets will pass to the living spouse, children, grandchildren, and so forth. If there is a will, its provisions must be followed, assuming that they are not in conflict with the laws governing the distribution of property.

Administration of Personal Trusts

One of the most important functions performed by trust departments of commercial banks is the administration of personal trusts. A trust arises out of an agreement between the creator of the trust and a trustee and involves the transfer of property from the creator, or trustor, to the trustee who holds title to and administers the property for the benefit of the trustor, a beneficiary, or beneficiaries. A personal trust may be created by inclusion of provisions in a person's will. The will contains the terms of the trust, names the trustee, and provides instructions to be followed by the trustee to hold and administer property and distribute its income to designated beneficiaries. This is commonly referred to as a *testamentary trust*. A person may create a *living trust* during his or her lifetime. In this method, the creator enters into an agreement with the trustee, say, the trust department of a commercial bank, and delivers to it certain properties. The trustee holds, invests, and disposes of the income and principal in accordance with the agreement. In most cases, the creator retains some control over the trust, including the authority to amend or revoke. In some cases, the trust is irrevocable, however, and the creator has no control over it. When an irrevocable trust is created, the creator has, in fact, made a gift of the property, and normally it cannot be reclaimed. In some instances, the trust is irrevocable for a certain period, after which it becomes revocable. A basic reason for the establishment of an irrevocable trust in past years was to gain tax advantages, but the 1986 Tax Reform Act removed most of these benefits.

Other reasons besides potential tax savings exist for the creation of a personal trust, whether through one's will or with a trust agreement while one is living. A trust allows the owner of property to control its disposition and the distribution of income earned from the property long after death. A trust can relieve the beneficiary, perhaps an aged spouse, of the burden and responsibility of caring for the property and yet allow him or her to enjoy the benefits of the property. The beneficiaries may be children who are unable to care for the assets; possibly the beneficiary is a spendthrift, and the creator feels that if the property were to be given in one lump sum, it would soon be consumed irresponsibly and the beneficiary would then live in poverty. In other cases, the beneficiary might be incompetent or otherwise incapacitated.

Other factors may influence the creation of a trust. Assets placed in a living trust ordinarily do not go through probate on the death of the creator. If the trust does not continue after death, the trust assets are distributed by the terms of the trust. Thus, the period of probate, which at times might extend four or five years after death, is avoided. The probate fee is also avoided. As the living trust is a private agreement between the creator and the trustee, the nature and extent of trust assets are never made public. Probating an estate is a matter of public record, however, and all assets going through probate are disclosed. Thus the privacy afforded by a trust may be valuable to many families.

The attorney of the creator of the trust normally draws the trust agreement or the will containing the provisions of a testamentary trust. However, one or more officers of the trust department may have been instrumental in convincing the individual that a trust was needed and may have suggested many of the terms of the trust. Most larger trust departments have one or more officers who have responsibility for developing new trust business, and to do so, they must be skilled in estate planning. On many occasions, the attorney for an individual may decide to invite the new business trust officer to advise on how best to construct the terms of the trust. In such cases the bank will almost certainly be named trustee.

Serving as Guardian and Conservator of Estates

In most states a minor is considered legally incapable of managing and holding property. When a minor inherits property, a guardian is appointed to hold it for his or her benefit; frequently, this responsibility falls to the trust department of a commercial bank. Guardianships are often required as well for persons judged legally incompetent.

As the term implies, a conservator of an estate has the objective of preventing the wasting of an estate. This arrangement usually arises when a property owner becomes physically incapacitated and is unable to care for and manage property. Guardianships and conservatorships are created by a court of law, and the fiduciary must perform them in accordance with statutory law and under the jurisdiction of the court. Trust departments of commercial banks perform these functions, but they do not constitute an appreciable part of their business.

Performance of Agencies

Trust departments perform agency services for individuals, the most important of which are custodian, managing agent, and attorney-in-fact. An agency differs considerably from a trust. In a trust, title to the trust assets is transferred to the trustee; in an agency arrangement, the title to the property does not pass to the agent but remains with the owner. An agency exists when a person, referred to as the *principal*, authorizes another, called the *agent*, to act on his or her behalf. An agency is a contractual arrangement, and before acting in this capacity, a trust department of a commercial bank requires an agency agreement between the two parties or a letter of instructions from the principal. Agencies are generally less structured than are trusts and can be terminated with less formality.

One form of agency is a custodianship. In a custodianship, the trust department accepts and cares for certain properties. For example, securities are accepted, and the trust department collects the income and notifies the customer of all collections. In addition, arrangements can be made for the trust department to collect the principal on matured bonds, notes, or mortgages; exchange securities; and even buy, sell, receive, and deliver securities.

A managing agency is an enlargement on the custodianship. Not only does the trust department have the authority to hold securities and collect the income but it also has the authority to manage the principal's investments or business affairs. The trust department can be given the authority to pay various bills for the principal, make recommendations on the purchase and sale of securities, pay taxes, renew insurance policies, receive income from all sources, and exercise stock rights. It would be difficult to mention all the services that can be performed by a managing agency since they are tailor-made arrangements and can be all-inclusive, if such is desirable. It is possible, under a managing agency, for a person to enter into an agreement where his or her total investment portfolio is handled by a trust department while sojourning for a year on the Riviera.

An attorney-in-fact is one who has been given authority by a principal to do certain legal functions on behalf of the principal. Attorneys-in-fact are agents and frequently exist under a custodianship and managing agency arrangement. An attorney-in-fact is created by the principal giving to the trust department the *power of attorney*. Trust departments usually receive and prefer special powers rather than general powers. Such special powers include the right to draw checks; endorse notes, checks, and other documents requiring endorsement; borrow funds; assign stocks and bonds; and execute deeds and leases. Sometimes a trust department acting in the capacity of custodian or managing agent is also appointed as an attorney-in-fact.

TRUST SERVICES PERFORMED FOR BUSINESSES

Most trusts established by corporations are for pension, profit sharing, and stock bonus purposes; for bond issues; for redemption and sinking funds; and for the issuance of collateral trust bonds or certificates. Many businesses have established pension and profit-sharing plans and stock bonus trusts to provide security for their employees' old age and retirement, stimulate higher productivity on the part of the work force, reduce labor turnover, care for employees who become incapacitated, and enable employees to participate in the ownership of the firm.

The various plans designed for the benefit of employees may take several forms, but usually when the trust department of a commercial bank accepts a trust of this type and it is a self-funded plan, the trust department invests the funds, keeps records on how much each employee is to receive, and makes payments to employees in accordance with the trust agreement. If the plan is operated on an insured basis, the trust department purchases individual annuity contracts for each employee covered by the plan out of the contributions made by the employer. Employee benefit plans are not limited to private corporations, of course, and the administration of public plans—those for city, county, state, fire and police departments, and other public employees—constitutes an important part of trust business.

Employee benefit plans of all types are an important part of trust business. Of the $945 billion of trust assets at the end of 1985, almost $395 billion were in employee benefit accounts. The competition to be trustee and investment manager—often the functions are separated—of large corporate or public employee benefit plans is intense. In such a competition, a trust department may find the potential customer is being courted by several other trust departments or bank holding company investment subsidiaries from various parts of the United States, by investment counselors, and by insurance companies. In such competitions many factors are important, but investment philosophies and performance records usually receive primary attention. If the bank's trust department is not named investment manager, it may still be named trustee and perform all functions except investment management. In some cases a trust department may act as trustee for a large corporate retirement fund that has several investment managers.

A common trust function performed by commercial banks is that of trustee in connection with a bond issue or what is usually referred to as *trustee under indenture*. When corporations borrow money for long periods, bonds, notes, or debentures are generally issued. If these securities are secured, the trustee under the indenture usually has legal title to the assets on which the lien is imposed, acts on behalf of the bondholders, and has the power to foreclose on the pledged property should the obligor default on the payment of principal or interest. Many activities are performed with this type of trust, including the transferring of ownership of securities; making payments of interest and principal; releasing mortgaged property; handling sinking funds that have been created for the redemption of bonds; and maintaining records and making reports to bondholders, the issuing corporation, regulatory bodies, and stock exchanges. If the securities issued are collateral trust bonds, the trust department holds title to the stocks and bonds pledged as security. In some instances the trustee may issue equipment trust certificates, which are credit instruments secured by equipment such as railway cars and engines. Title to the equipment is transferred to the trust department, and the railroad pays a rental for the use of such equipment to the trustee, who in turn makes payment to the holders of the certificates.

Trust departments perform several agency functions for business firms. They serve as transfer agents, concerned with transferring the ownership of a corporation's stock. Serving as an exchange agent is very similar to being a transfer agent. When performing this service, the trustee receives one kind of securities and delivers another type in accordance with a prearranged plan. The exchange might involve a stock split, a stock conversion, a combination of two or more business firms, or the distribution of securities arising out of a reorganization. In the capacity of a registrar, trust departments are responsible for seeing that stock is not issued in excess of the amount authorized. Since a trustee cannot act in the capacity of both a transfer agent and registrar for stock listed on the New York Stock Exchange, there is an independent check on the shares of stock issued by a corporation. Corporations with many stockholders are not particularly interested in handling payment of dividends on their stock because of the great volume of intermittent work; therefore, they turn to the trust department of a commercial bank to serve as a dividend-disbursing agent. The trust department receives payment from the corporation when dividends are due and in turn prepares the checks and mails each stockholder the dividend payment. Trust departments perform several other similar types of agencies for corporations such as acting as agent for the redemption of preferred stock and subscription warrants.

Many large trust departments are very competitive in offering investment management services separate from other trust services. Serving as investment management agent for employee benefit accounts is an important source of business for such trust departments. Another agency activity important to some trust departments is the provision of cash management services to business firms. The purpose of these services is to keep the temporarily idle working capital funds of businesses earning as high a rate of return as possible commensurate with safety and daily liquidity. This is accomplished through investment in high-quality money market instruments, repurchase agreements, and money market funds.

TRUST SERVICES PERFORMED FOR CHARITABLE INSTITUTIONS AND OTHERS

Trust departments of commercial banks provide trust services for parties other than individuals and businesses. They may serve as trustees of community trusts that derive their funds in the form of gifts and bequests. These trusts are created for purposes such as promoting research; assisting schools, charitable, and benevolent institutions; care of the sick, aged, and needy; aiding in the rehabilitation of victims of alcohol and narcotics; care of wayward or delinquent persons; public recreation; and improving working conditions. Trusts are established by civic clubs to award scholarships to students. Many of our educational institutions receive portions of their income from trusts that have been created for such purposes by wealthy people. The same is true of many of our hospitals, art centers, orphanages, and homes for the aged.

Trust departments also perform agency functions for parties other than individuals and businesses. They act as investment management agents for endowment funds. Trust departments sometimes act as agents for municipal and state governments, serving as paying agents for the bonds issued and sometimes countersigning the bonds, which authenticates them. As paying agents, they are also in a position to see that the correct amounts are issued.

RESPONSIBILITIES OF TRUST DEPARTMENTS

A considerable amount of responsibility is involved in performing trust services. The basic duties and responsibilities of trust departments to the parties they serve have been laid down by statutory law, government regulations, and court decisions over the years; because of the extent of this subject matter, space does not permit a thorough analysis. One outstanding work on trust services has stated that "the basic responsibilities of a trustee are (1) to be faithful, (2) to conform to instructions, (3) to be competent and (4) to be diligent."[2] Faithfulness, in the performance of trust services, implies many things. The trustee should be loyal to the creator and beneficiary and never be motivated by self-interest. Reasonable charges for the performance of services offered are acceptable, but the use of trust funds for personal gain is absolutely prohibited. A trusteeship is an agreement involving confidence and trust; and the trustee is legally bound to adhere to the agreement, must have high standards of honesty and business conduct, and is expected to defend the agreement if necessary.

A trust department must follow the instructions and terms of the trust agreement, will, court order, or agency agreement under which it performs. It cannot accept a responsibility and then decide that other actions would be better. This does not mean, however, that in the case of some unusual events changes could not be made. It may be necessary in some situations for the trustee to go to court and seek changes in the provisions of a trust if the trustor is deceased or incompetent.

Individuals and businesses who use trust services and the courts expect and are entitled to a high degree of competence. Trust departments cannot plead ignorance or forgetfulness. Trustees are required and expected to exercise constant diligence to accomplish the objectives of a trust or agency agreement.

These responsibilities are great, but it must not be assumed that trustees are guarantors. They cannot perform miracles, nor are they expected to do so. They are, however, guarantors if losses arise because of their own negligence. A trustee who leaves securities out of the vault that should obviously have been kept there or fails to collect interest on a bond as instructed would be held liable. In general, a trustee is charged to use a degree of diligence, prudence, care, and management that persons of discretion and intelligence would have used in the performance of a similar task.

POTENTIAL LIABILITIES
OF TRUST DEPARTMENTS

Trust departments assume great liability in the administration of trusts. When losses occur, the court may impose a *surcharge*, that is, require the fiduciary to pay to the beneficiary either the asset or assets that were lost,

---

[2] American Institute of Banking, *Trust Department Services* (New York: American Bankers Association, 1954), p. 172.

plus the income that would have been earned or an amount equal to the damage suffered. In other words, a surcharge restores the beneficiary's interest to what it would have been if the fiduciary had not failed in the performance of duty. The major reasons for surcharging are as follows:

Breaches of trust for which fiduciaries are always held liable are:

1. Fraud, such as misappropriation of the corpus or income for the benefit of others than the heirs or beneficiaries. This type of breach is not only surchargeable against the fiduciary, but makes him liable also to criminal prosecution.
2. Failure to pay taxes due.
3. Failure to reinvest trust funds for an unreasonable length of time, thereby causing loss of income to the trust.

Acts of negligence or omissions of duty include:

1. Making an unauthorized investment that gives rise to loss (*State* v. *Washburn*, Conn. 187, 34 Atl. 1034 [1896]).
2. Failure to diversify investments as authorized by the instrument or law, when this failure results in undue losses to the trust (*West* v. *Bialson*, 365 Mo. 1103, 293, S.W. 2d 369 [1956]).
3. Carelessness in permitting an agent or co-trustee to breach the trust instrument, which causes losses to the trust fund (*Cred* v. *McAleer*, 275 Mass. 353, N.E. 761 [1931]).
4. Failure to collect rents or other income when due, thereby depriving the trust of income.
5. Retaining securities or other assets for an unreasonable time after they fall below the standards for trust investment, or holding too long securities that when received in the trust, were ineligible for investment of trust funds (*Babbit* v. *Fidelity Trust Co.*, 72 N.J. Eq. 745, 66 Atl. 1076 [1907]).[3]

TRUST INVESTMENT POLICIES AND OBJECTIVES

Obviously one of the great responsibilities of a trustee in handling trusts is to invest funds properly. Each individual trust account has its own unique features and requirements, so each account should have its own specific investment objective. A high level of safe, secure income may be most suitable for a $100,000 trust managed for the benefit of a 90-year-old widow, while the pursuit of growth through a portfolio consisting mostly of a diversified portfolio of common stocks may be suitable for a 40-year-old businessowner with a large income. Whatever the nature of the trust

---

[3] *Financial Handbook*, 4th ed., rev. printing, edited by Jules I. Bogen. Copyright © 1968 The Ronald Press Company, New York.

account, the trust department should seek the highest return it can attain within the constraints limiting the selection of investment assets. Many constraints may be imposed on the investment of trust funds by law, by the trust contract itself, by the type of trust, and by the underlying investment philosophy of the trust department. Trust agreements may specifically state what investments shall be made and held. Others may state that the investment function shall be carried out in accordance with state law, and finally, some agreements make no provision regarding this matter whatsoever. In some accounts, the investment responsibility is shared with another party who could be the creator of the trust, a cotrustee, or beneficiary. In a few accounts, the trust department has no investment authority.

For years trustees operated under *legal lists,* that is, lists of investments spelled out in the laws of the various states as being eligible for investment by trustees. However, with the passage of time it became evident that governments had no monopoly on investment knowledge and judgment and that to attain the objectives of many trust agreements greater freedom should be given to trustees. Because of this feeling, practically all states have liberalized such laws and have introduced what is commonly called the *prudent man rule.* The prudent man rule is an outgrowth of various court decisions and has been adopted either by court decision or by statute. It was well defined in the famous court decision of *Harvard College and Massachusetts General Hospital v. Francis Amory* in 1830 when the Supreme Judicial Court of Massachusetts said:

> All that can be required of a trustee to invest is that he shall conduct himself faithfully and exercise a sound discretion. He is to observe how men of prudence, discretion and intelligence manage their own affairs, not in regard to speculation but in regard to the permanent disposition of their funds, considering the probable income, as well as the probable safety of the capital to be invested.

In justification of this reasoning the court stated:

> Trustees are justly and uniformly considered favorably, and it is of great importance to bereaved families and orphans that they should not be held to make good losses in the depreciation of stocks or the failure of the capital itself, which they held in trust, provided they conduct themselves honestly and discreetly and carefully, according to the existing circumstances in the discharge of their trusts. If this were held otherwise, no prudent man would run the hazard of losses which might happen without any neglect or breach of good faith.[4]

[4] 26 *Massachusetts Reports* 447.

While prudent man statutes are at the state level, the federal government made an entrance into the area of trustee investment standards with the passage of the Employee Retirement Income Security Act of 1974 (ERISA). While ERISA pertains only to the administration of private retirement plans, and thus does not directly affect other trust business, it sets forth a prudent man standard that all trust departments must observe in the investment of private retirement fund assets. Many have called it a "prudent expert" standard, since it calls for evaluation of trustees against trustees. Section 404 of the act states that the trustee shall exercise "the care, skill, prudence, and diligence under the circumstances then prevailing that a prudent man acting in like capacity and familiar with such matters would use in the conduct of an enterprise of a like character and with like aims."

Trust departments are charged with using good judgment and diligence in making investments of trust funds, with due regard to both the safety of principal and the production of income. Although this concept may appear somewhat vague, it becomes more concrete when one considers the problems of actual investment. Trustees should not err on the side of safety by investing exclusively in short-term U.S. government securities, nor should they emphasize income and possible gains to the extent of placing all the funds in securities with great credit risk. Trustees must "hew a fine line"—they must employ diversification and prudence in investing and perform consistently with the objectives of their numerous trust agreements and managing agencies.

The Pursuit of Investment Performance

The majority of trust departments are small, and typically their approach to investment decision making can be considered risk averse. They give more consideration to avoiding large losses than to seeking quick, large gains and assuming the attendant risk. Most large trust departments are more performance oriented and have staffs of security analysts and portfolio managers whose goals are to produce high levels of investment returns, presumably using professional skills to control risk. Investment management is a separate, and often lucrative, service for large departments.

The competition to manage large investment portfolios is extensive and intense. This competition has been centered on the large and growing portfolios of employee benefit plans since the passage of ERISA in 1974. Due to its potential penalties for investment management errors, it produced a significant increase in the demand for professional managers. In addition to trust departments—or in some cases the investment management subsidiaries of bank holding companies—professional investment managers include investment counselors, mutual fund organizations, and insurance companies.

Successful selling of investment management services depends largely on convincing customers that performance will be better than that of competitors. The perception developed in recent years that trust departments, particularly in managing common stocks, do not produce performance equal to that of other categories of investment managers. Whether or not this perception was ever accurate, recent surveys indicated it has not been valid in recent years.[5]

Common Trust Funds

A common trust fund is a single trust made up of funds drawn from a number of smaller trusts, each of which acquires a share of the principal and income of the common trust fund in proportion to the amount invested. Participation in the common trust fund is represented by units. Units are issued to participating trusts at net asset value and redeemed at net asset value at various predetermined evaluation dates. Since a trust department performs no selling function, no charge is imposed when a trust invests in units of a common trust fund. The income of a common trust fund is exempt from taxation to the fund. However, income distributed to the participating trusts is taxable to each according to its applicable tax bracket.

The major problems associated with handling small trusts are diversification of investments and costs of administration. All trusts need diversification, which is difficult to achieve with small trusts. Small trusts, too, may require just as much of a trust department's time as do large ones; hence, the costs of administration become important. The common trust fund is an answer to both these problems. It was the need for efficiency in the handling of small trusts that brought about broad usage of common trust funds in the 1930s and 1940s. However, when Regulation 9 of the Comptroller of the Currency was originated in 1962, replacing Regulation F of the Board of Governors of the Federal Reserve System as the main regulatory instrument for national bank trust departments, it removed the size limit on the amount of participation a trust could have in a common trust fund. The only size limitation imposed by Regulation 9 is that no trust can hold more than 10 percent of the units of a common trust fund.

A much more significant restriction is that trust departments are not allowed to invest agency accounts in common trust funds. The wording of Regulation 9 expressly limits their use to the capacities of trustee, execu-

---

[5] Thomas S. Stewart, "Data Denies 'Myth of Mediocrity,'" *Trusts & Estates* (May 1987), pp. 35–38.

tor, administrator, or guardian. Thus an investment management agency opened by a trust department cannot be placed in what may be the most carefully managed portfolios in the department: the common trust funds. Various attempts by the trust industry to remove this limitation have brought the response that such use essentially would make common trust funds into mutual funds. Objections naturally arose from that industry as well as certain regulatory bodies.

The earliest common trust funds were almost all balanced funds. These portfolios consisted of stocks and bonds in some relatively constant ratio, say, 40 percent stocks and 60 percent bonds, and most trust departments had only one fund. All trusts that participated in the fund had no choice as to asset mix. Over the years, trust departments developed separate funds for various categories of assets. Now a trust department may have two or more stock funds, each different in its emphasis on seeking growth or income; a taxable bond fund (or a bond and mortgage fund); a municipal bond fund producing income exempt from federal income taxes; a money market fund composed of short-term, highly liquid assets for temporary placement of money; and any number of even more specialized funds. With a variety of common trust funds, a given trust can have its investments tailored to its own needs by placing whatever amount seems appropriate in each of two or more funds.

AMOUNT AND MAKEUP OF TRUST ASSETS

Table 18-1 shows the important categories of trust assets under various management arrangements held by financial institutions at the end of 1985. Of the $945 billion in assets, $905 billion was under the management of bank trust departments.

The table shows that common stocks was the largest single category of assets, making up 42 percent of the total. This percentage is not a result of trust departments' investment policy. It should be recalled that trust departments do not have investment control over many of the accounts they hold, and in some, such as estates in probate, assets are simply held pending distribution.

TRUST DEPARTMENT ORGANIZATION

Many different organization plans have been created for trust department operations, depending on the amount and kind of trust business performed. Reference has already been made to the requirement that trust work be kept separate from commercial banking activities. In large banks that have a substantial amount of trust business, this requirement has resulted in an entirely separate department located in quarters apart from

TABLE 18-1 Trust Assets of Financial Institutions (in thousand of dollars)

		Trusts and Estates			Agencies		Total
		Employee Benefit	Personal Trusts	Estates	Employee Benefit	All Others	
Non-interest-bearing deposits—Own	1	$ 406,567	$ 665,879	$ 103,399	$ 242,628	$ 516,392	$ 1,934,865
Non-interest-bearing deposits—Other	2	17,223	82,759	6,339	155,873	274,937	537,131
Interest bearing deposits—Own	3	2,306,951	5,214,558	820,957	385,982	1,769,665	10,498,113
Interest-bearing deposits—Other	4	12,959,812	3,385,550	389,973	2,216,719	5,160,737	24,112,791
U.S. government and agency obligations	5	48,318,648	39,434,627	2,332,168	36,640,101	43,893,152	170,618,696
State, county, municipal obligations	6	684,371	42,996,294	1,298,755	91,782	20,049,671	65,120,873
Other short-term obligations	7	5,999,097	9,710,145	1,662,965	1,417,044	7,885,655	26,674,906
Other notes and bonds	8	47,345,787	17,255,926	1,816,116	8,962,770	29,622,927	105,003,526
Preferred stocks	9	22,186,699	13,783,815	401,267	21,266,860	18,698,420	76,337,061
Common stocks	10	94,563,306	165,676,235	6,195,056	69,406,930	63,493,623	399,335,150
Real estate mortgages	11	2,211,518	4,013,496	437,587	505,318	1,560,310	8,728,229
Real estate	12	3,952,246	19,932,476	3,152,278	1,450,489	3,849,905	32,337,394
Miscellaneous	13	8,935,151	5,305,120	728,514	2,058,188	7,182,111	24,209,084
Total discretionary assets	14	$249,887,376	$327,456,880	$19,345,374	$144,800,684	$203,957,505	$945,447,819
Total number of discretionary accounts	15	269,406	870,649	83,429	25,643	154,712	1,403,839

SOURCE: *Trust Assets of Financial Institutions—1985* (Washington, D.C.: Federal Financial Institutions Examination Council, 1986), p. 31.

the other banking activities. However, in small banks with a small amount of trust business, this is not feasible or physically possible. In many small banks that have trust powers, one officer may perform all the trust work along with other duties.

In very large banks where the amount of trust work is counted in the millions of dollars, the trust organization becomes quite detailed and specialized. For illustration, a hypothetical organization chart for a large trust department that might be found in a large bank is presented (see Figure 18-1). The executive trust officer is responsible for the successful and efficient operation of the department and concerned primarily with the formulation and implementation of trust policy, along with other administrative officers of the bank and the trust department. The trust committee, which must review and approve the activities of the trust department, is composed of members of the bank's board of directors and chaired by the bank's board chairman in many cases. The trust committee may include other bank officers who have applicable skills. The committee reports to the bank's board of directors.

In our hypothetical example, the work of the trust department has been divided into six broad divisions or areas of operation. The trust administration division is concerned with estate settlement, the administration of personal and pension and profit-sharing trusts, guardianships and conservatorships, and personal agencies such as custody and agency management. The corporate trust division handles bond indentures, stock transfer and registration, and acts as a paying agent. The service section serves all divisions that need legal advice, tax and investment information, and real estate management. The operating section is responsible for accounting, auditing, filing, safekeeping of the properties held by the trust department, and providing teller services. The business development section handles advertising, personal representation and contacts, and estate planning.

FEES OF TRUST DEPARTMENTS

Trust departments of commercial banks are compensated for their trustee services by fees that are in many instances, especially in settling estates, established by statute or by probate courts. Most other fees, however, are negotiated. Trustee fees may consist of annual charges on the income of a trust, annual commissions on principal, and, in some instances, a commission collected on the principal when the trust is terminated. Fees are far from uniform throughout the country, and the variability makes generalization hazardous. However, rates normally charged for handling personal trusts range from .5 to .75 percent of the principal annually. For a managing agency consisting of stocks and bonds similar to those held by

FIGURE 18-1 Hypothetical Organization of a Trust Department of a Large Commercial Bank

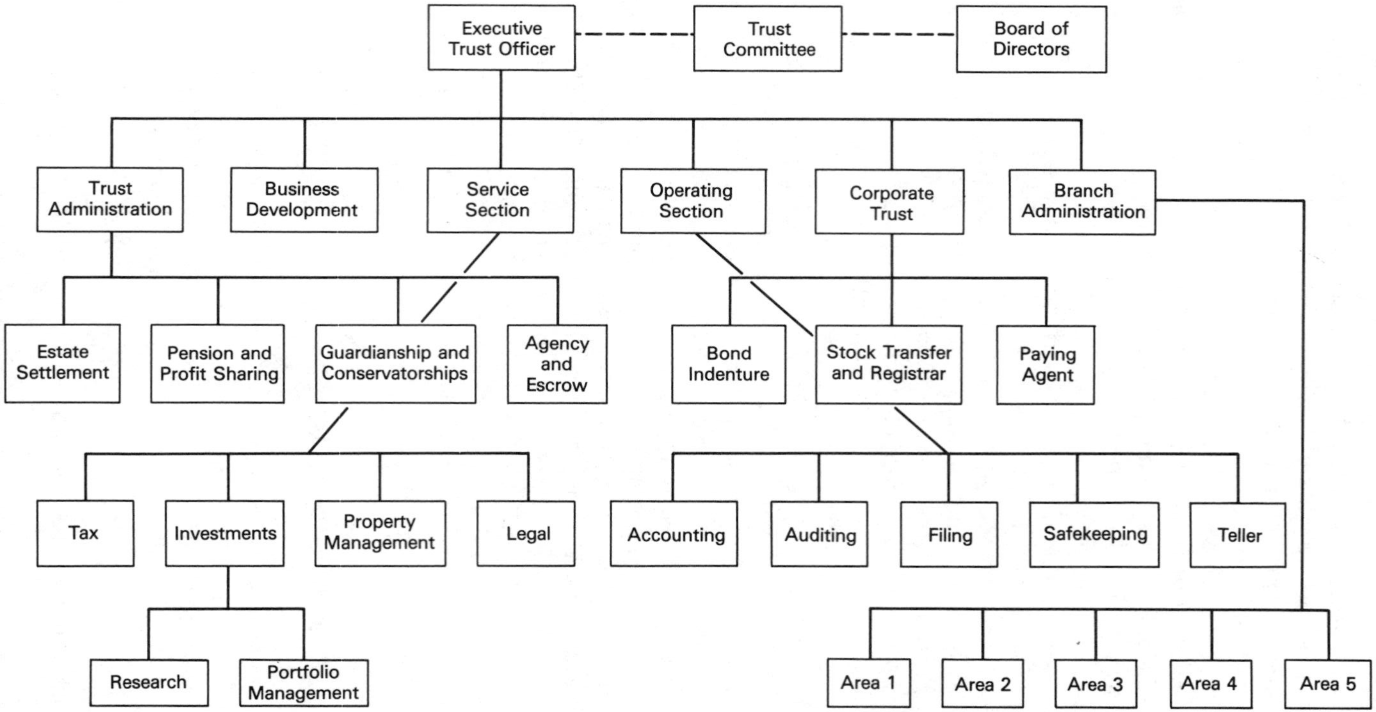

personal trusts, the cost would be about the same. If the agency consisted of mortgages, notes, and contracts involving some additional supervision and expense, the cost would be slightly higher; if the trust department's function were to manage real estate properties and a business involving even greater activity, the fee would be still higher. For the performance as executor or administrator, the charges permitted by most states are graduated. An example might be 7 percent on the first $1,000 of property for which the executor or administrator is responsible, 4 percent of the next $9,000, 3 percent on the next $40,000, and 2 percent on all above $50,000. Thus, for serving as executor or administrator of an estate of $50,000, the charge would be $1,630; for one of $400,000, the charge would be $8,630.

It is an accepted fact among commercial banks that a substantial volume of trust business is necessary before a trust department is a profitable undertaking. This is because of the relatively large amount of fixed expense or overhead that trust departments must have in the form of capable personnel. Even though a trust department may have only a small amount of trust business, its ability to perform must be assured. The liability involved in providing trust services is too great to settle for inefficient personnel. Trust services are highly personal, and as a result the cost of operating a trust department closely parallels the cost of personnel. Some banks probably operate their trust departments at a loss but feel that their services will not be complete without trust services, and some probably operate at a loss but do not realize it because of the absence of an adequate system of cost accounting. The production of adequate profits from trust departments appears to be an ongoing problem that will not be easily resolved.

QUESTIONS

1. Why is probate normally required for a will?
2. Why might a person name a bank trust department as executor of his estate rather than, say, his cousin Bob or Aunt Lucy?
3. What are some reasons for the concentration of trust assets in banks in the eastern United States?
4. How does a trust differ from an agency?
5. How can the investments of a trust be tailored to the specific needs of that trust and still consist entirely of common trust fund units?
6. What are some possible conflicts of interest resulting from the trust department being part of the bank?
7. What may be some of the major reasons for the low profitability of many trust departments?

8. If trust business is not very profitable for many banks, why would those banks continue to have trust departments?

9. From what sources, besides other bank trust departments, would the most competition for the various types of trust business be likely to come?

SELECTED REFERENCES

AMERICAN BANKERS ASSOCIATION. *Trust Fact Book.* Washington, D.C., 1980.

AMERICAN INSTITUTE OF BANKING. *Trust Functions and Services.* New York: American Bankers Association, 1978.

FEDERAL FINANCIAL INSTITUTIONS EXAMINATION COUNCIL. *Trust Assets of Financial Institutions—1985.* Washington, D.C., 1986.

GREEN, DONALD S., AND MARY SCHUELKE. *The Trust Activities of the Banking Industry.* Chicago: Association of Reserve City Bankers, 1975.

KENNEDY, JOSEPH C., AND ROBERT I. LANDAU. *Corporate Trust Administration and Management,* 2nd ed. New York: New York University Press, 1975.

KENNEDY, WALTER, AND PHILIP F. SEARLE. *The Management of a Trust Department.* Boston: Bankers Publishing Co., 1967.

MACE, MYLES L., AND CHARLES T. STEWART. "Standards of Care for Trustees." *Harvard Business Review* (January–February 1976), pp. 14–16 ff.

STEPHENSON, GILBERT THOMAS, AND NORMAN ADRIAN WIGGINS. *Estates and Trusts,* 5th ed. New York: Appleton-Century-Crofts, 1973.

Trusts and Estates. Monthly, all issues.

U.S. COMPTROLLER OF THE CURRENCY. *Regulation 9: Fiduciary Powers of National Banks, Collective Investment Funds, and Disclosure of Trust Department Assets.* Washington, D.C.: Government Printing Office.

19

INTERNATIONAL BANKING

In addition to the usual domestic activities of commercial banks with which we have thus far been concerned, many banks provide international banking services. Although not as important in dollar amounts as the domestic side of banking, international activities of commercial banks have grown phenomenally in recent years. The types of international services offered by banks have expanded, the volume of services has increased, and the number of banks providing these services has multiplied. Some banks that specialize in international banking have in recent years derived half or slightly more than half of their profits from international banking. International banking includes all those services demanded by customers engaged in international trade, investment, and travel and in reality is an extension of the services provided in domestic banking.

In providing international banking services to customers, several avenues are open to banks. They may have an *international department* that specializes exclusively in international banking services. A bank with an international department would have several strategically located correspondent banks in foreign countries through which the various services would be provided. Banks may have branches and/or subsidiaries located abroad through which the international services are offered. With this type of arrangement, a much broader array of services can be provided. Although a bank with an international department is able to engage in international banking, a bank with branches abroad has greater flexibility and is in a position to provide more personalized services. A branch and/or subsidiary arrangement, for example, would be better to accept and service deposits (a large part of which would be denominated in the money of the host country) of foreign nationals and Americans abroad. Moreover, the bank with branches abroad would, in general, be in a better position to lend to (or invest in) business firms, governments, and individuals in foreign countries.

A final arrangement is termed a *representative office*, where a representative is maintained abroad to give financial advice and assist customers in their borrowing and depositing activities with the domestic bank. A representative office does not accept deposits or make loans abroad. It may be maintained because the country in which it is located has not granted a franchise for the establishment of a branch or the domestic bank has not yet decided to establish a branch, possibly because of insufficient banking business to maintain a full-fledged branch. In other words, it may be an interim arrangement.

DEVELOPMENT
OF INTERNATIONAL BANKING

International banking is a recent development in the United States. For many years the financing of international trade was dominated by European institutions. From the twelfth to the midsixteenth centuries, banks in Italy were supreme in the area of international finance. Banks in Belgium and Holland then became important, and soon after the establishment of the Bank of England, Great Britain became the center of international finance—a role that was maintained until World War II. Banks in the United States were slow in entering into the financing of international trade primarily because of the lack of capital and the great need for domestic financing. Also, the momentum of an early start on the part of European banking houses was of no little consequence. Finally, the early prohibitions against national banks establishing foreign branches and the acceptance of bills of exchange precluded a large part of the banking system from financing international commercial transactions. Although state-chartered banks were free to engage in international banking, as were private unincorporated banks, the aggregate amount conducted by these institutions was not great prior to World War I.

With the passage of the Federal Reserve Act in 1913, the door was open to American banks to engage in financing international transactions. Member banks were permitted to accept bills of exchange arising from international transactions. Moreover, banks with capital and surplus of $1 million or more were permitted to establish branches abroad. Although these provisions were significant, the development of international banking was slow. The volume of acceptances did not increase to significant proportions, and during the three years following the enactment of the Federal Reserve Act only one national bank established branches abroad. To stimulate further expansion in the area of international finance, the Federal Reserve Act was amended in 1916 to permit national banks to invest in corporations engaged principally in foreign banking. These corporations had to enter into an agreement with the Federal Reserve Board regarding the type and manner of activities, and from this arrangement they became known as *agreement corporations*. The Federal Reserve Act, however, did not provide for the federal chartering of agreement corporations, and this was not conducive to an increase in this type of international banking institution.

The Edge Act

An additional inducement to the development of international banking was the enactment by Congress in 1919 of the Edge Act, authorizing the Board of Governors of the Federal Reserve System to charter corporations for the purpose of engaging in international and foreign operations abroad. Two types of corporations were permitted to be established under this act—banking and financing. Banking corporations were authorized to hold demand and time deposits of foreigners and to acquire equity investment in foreign corporations engaged in banking. Financing corporations were permitted to invest in foreign corporations other than banks but were not permitted to accept deposits. Both types of corporations could buy and sell foreign exchange; receive checks, drafts, bills, acceptances, notes, bonds, coupons, and other securities for collection abroad; and buy and sell securities for the accounts of customers abroad.

This approach to international banking was confusing, and the logic of such an arrangement was debatable. Finally, in 1963, financial and banking corporations were permitted to merge all functions into one corporation. Regulations covering these corporations, organized under Section 25(a) of the Federal Reserve Act as amended, are spelled out in Regulation K of the Board of Governors of the Federal Reserve System. When such a corporation has aggregate demand deposits and acceptance liabilities exceeding its capital and surplus, it is considered to be "engaged in banking" and subject to the rule limiting loans and investments to one person or organization to 15 percent of its capital and surplus. Otherwise a corporation is considered an investment corporation and may lend or invest up to 50 percent of its capital and surplus to one person or organization.

Since 1963 the number of Edge Act corporations has increased substantially. In the 1960s several banks from outside the state of New York formed Edge Act affiliates and located them in New York City. In the

1970s the trend was toward the formation of Edge Act offices in other areas of the country. Nearly 150 Edge Act corporations are in operation, with out-of-state banks having established offices in New York, Los Angeles, Miami, Houston, Chicago, San Francisco, New Orleans, Wilmington, and Norfolk. These offices were formed in these particular cities because of the increase in the demand for various financial services arising out of the financing of foreign trade. While they are limited to financing foreign commerce and investments, these offices are a means of bypassing the prohibitions in the United States on interstate banking. An Edge Act corporation may act like a branch office in many ways and provides a presence for an out-of-state bank in direct competition with banks domiciled in the cities named above, competing for the international banking business that is available in those cities.

International Banking Facilities

Recently the Board of Governors of the Federal Reserve System authorized U.S. banks to establish *international banking facilities (IBFs)* as adjuncts to the regular banking facilities of U.S. banks, Edge or Agreements corporations, or U.S. offices of a foreign bank. These facilities are limited to accepting deposits from non-U.S. residents and other IBFs, and all deposits transactions must be in minimum amounts of $100,000. These deposits are exempt from reserve requirements and interest rate ceilings. Such funds obtained as deposits cannot be used domestically but may be used to make foreign loans. These IBFs cannot issue negotiable certificates of deposits, bankers' acceptances, or other bearer instruments. To ensure that deposits will not be used as "transaction balances," they must have a maturity of two days. IBFs were permitted in an effort to increase the attractiveness to foreigners of dollar-denominated deposits to give banks a greater role in the recycling of OPEC surpluses. It was hoped that the establishment of such facilities would make it possible for U.S. banks to recapture a portion of the Eurocurrency market lost to foreign banks because of Regulations Q and D. The size of this market had been estimated at $2 trillion at year-end 1987. By that time, approximately 540 banking institutions had formed IBFs and assets of such facilities amounted to nearly $200 billion.

Expansion Abroad

At the present time, American banks have a great network of international banking facilities throughout the free world. Approximately 150 banks in the United States have an international banking department. The number of correspondent banks abroad that are associated with U.S. banks in providing these international banking services varies but is in the thousands. Branch offices of U.S. banks are widely distributed throughout the world. About 45 percent of all overseas branches are located in Latin America and the Caribbean. In terms of volume of assets, branches in the United Kingdom account for more than one-third of all assets of foreign branches, and those in the Bahamas and Cayman Islands offshore banking centers account for about 30 percent.

Several factors have contributed to the expansion of offshore branches in the Bahamas and Cayman Islands. One of the most important was a series of restrictions introduced in the 1960s by the federal government on the outflow of funds designed to correct our current balance of payments problem. The *interest equalization tax* (*IET*) levied a tax on foreign equity and debt issues purchased by U.S. residents. This piece of legislation was also applicable to long-term bank loans to foreigners. In addition to this tax, voluntary limits on bank lending abroad were adopted under the *voluntary foreign credit restraint* (*VFCR*) *program*. The Federal Reserve System also adopted measures (Regulation M) to stem the inflow of funds from foreign branches of U.S. banks during the tight money period of 1969. These restrictions curbed the activities of banks, which responded by establishing branches in the Bahamas and the Cayman Islands. Another factor that contributed to establishing branches in these islands was Regulation Q, which limited the amount of interest that banks could pay on time deposits. Although the capital control programs were removed in early 1974 and Regulation M was eliminated in 1978, the branches were well established because of other advantages of such locations. These included lower costs of operation and freedom from other regulations, particularly reserve requirements, interest rate ceilings, and deposit insurance. These locations also offer a choice to some depositors who may have some concern that their accounts may be blocked or expropriated.

Many of these branches were established solely to avoid the many regulations applicable to deposits and taxation. They are, for all purposes, "shells" in the sense that there are usually no banking facilities established abroad comparable to a full-service branch. Banks maintaining such branches as "shells" generally conduct all the banking business from the head office located in the United States. With the authorization of IBFs and the removal of Regulation Q, this avenue of expansion has slowed in recent years. In fact, some have ceased operations because IBFs can accomplish the same objectives. Thus IBFs are a substitute for shell operations.

At the present time 316 banks have 1,904 branches abroad that hold assets in excess of $400 billion, an amount that approximates 15 percent of all commercial bank assets. The customers of foreign branches are more widespread in their geographic distribution than are the branches themselves, but nearly one-half of all assets of foreign branches are amounts due from customers in Europe, about one-fifth from customers in Latin America and the Caribbean, and the balance from other areas.

In addition to branches abroad, other methods are employed in extending foreign banking services. Some U.S. banks have a minority interest in foreign banks, that is, own stock in foreign banks, and a few banks provide foreign banking services in consortia with other banks. Bank of America, for example, has joined with Banque Nationale de Paris, the largest bank in France; Banca Nazionale del Lavoro, the largest bank in Italy; Barclays Bank, the largest bank in Great Britain; the Dresdner Bank (Germany); the Banque de Bruxelles (Belgium); and Algemene Bank Nederland (the Netherlands) to form a new banking organization that is known as Société Financière Européenne. Another example of this type of organization is the International Commercial Bank owned by Irving Trust of New York; First National Bank of Chicago; Commerzbank. A.G., Düsseldorf; National Westminister Bank, Ltd., London; and the Hong Kong and Shanghai Banking Corporation of Hong Kong.

In recent years, most of the expansion of U.S. banks has been by acquiring subsidiaries, in consortia, and joint effort rather than by branching. Several factors have been responsible for this development. In the first place, foreign countries are generally more inclined to accept the entry of American banks if the undertaking is in conjunction with nationals of the country. Part of this attitude stems from nationalistic pride; also, domestic bankers are less likely to be critical of this type of arrangement than of a branch of a U.S. bank. Many foreign countries do not admit branches of American banks freely. They normally do so only if such a business venture is advantageous to the economic development of their country. A host country does not look with favor on a branch entry if the state in which the head office is located does not have a reciprocal arrangement for branches of the host country's banks, and some American states are not noted for their willingness to accept foreign branches. In 1961, New York relaxed some of its restrictions on foreign branches when the authorities of such countries as Brazil, Venezuela, the Philippines, and Japan threatened to impose restrictions on American banks. California also liberalized its banking laws in 1964 as they applied to foreign banks, although it still does not permit the operation of foreign branches. In many instances, expansion by branching or by establishing a new subsidiary abroad is an expensive and time-consuming process. Opening a new office would require an outlay for building and equipment and the training of personnel. Moreover, it might take considerable time to develop a clientele. Expansion by acquisition of a subsidiary and the other methods would normally require less initial outlay, and the operation would start with some already established customer relationships. Therefore, a profitable undertaking would probably be realized in a relatively short time, which, of course, might not always be the case with a new branch abroad. In addition, the ownership of a subsidiary corporation limits the liability of the parent bank. The establishment of a branch office may expose the entire assets of the parent to liabilities arising from the operation of the branch. The reluctance of many banks to assume this additional risk has thus favored other forms of organization for offices in foreign countries.

The establishment of branches abroad depends in large part on the attitude of foreign countries in regard to competition from foreign banks. Those countries that need capital and the expertise of lending and investing in general welcome U.S. banks with open arms and permit a wide array of banking services. Some countries, however, permit entry somewhat reluctantly and limit the banking activities of foreign banks, and others even prohibit the entry of foreign banks. In recent years, a rising tide of nationalism in many countries has slowed down the expansion of American banks abroad. Canada, for example, has objected to the ownership of a bank by Citibank of New York, and after much discussion an agreement was reached whereby the U.S. bank reduced its ownership to 25 percent. This is an interesting development since several U.S. states permit Canadian banks to operate freely. In banking, as in many other areas, reciprocity is more illusory than real. The rise of nationalism that has slowed down U.S. expansion has encouraged some banks to purchase an interest in foreign banks. Some countries, however, limit the percentage of foreign ownership. In 1973, two countries liberalized their attitude toward the entry of U.S. banks. Japan, which had permitted only two banks to operate branches for a number of years, approved the entry of eight additional U.S. banks; and the U.S.S.R. permitted two banks to establish representative offices. This change in attitude resulted from increased trade with Japan in recent years and the opening of trade relations with the U.S.S.R.

REASONS FOR THE GROWTH
OF INTERNATIONAL BANKING

Several factors have been responsible for the growth of international operations by U.S. commercial banks in recent years. The growth of the United States economically and financially in the postwar period certainly cannot be overlooked. The general worldwide reduction of tariffs and the dismantling of other restrictions imposed on international trade and payments contributed to the growth of world trade, which in turn stimulated international banking. The growth of exports and imports of the United States has been phenomenal in the post–World War II period.

The dollar value of trade flows, including such items as merchandise and service exports and imports, in the past two decades has increased tenfold. Capital flows, which include such movements as investments and securities purchases between countries and bank claims to and on foreigners, have increased nearly twentyfold during the same period. All of these international movements approximated $1.5 trillion in 1987. Foreign investments require numerous financial transactions, which are handled almost exclusively by American banks. Since American business firms prefer to deal with banks with which they are acquainted and which understand their operations, banks were encouraged to follow business firms abroad. Likewise, the recent rise in investments by foreigners in the United States has been followed by an increase in the activity of foreign banks in the United States, especially from Japan, Korea, Europe, and to a lesser extent the Middle East and Latin America.

The relatively liquid position of banks at the beginning of the 1960s also contributed to their expansion into foreign markets. A liberalization of our restriction on the entry of foreign banks into certain states contributed to the expansion of branches abroad in the early 1960s. A final factor has been the technological advances in transportation and communication. With improvements in air travel, wire transfer, and so on, the task of maintaining constant surveillance of foreign markets and overseas operations has become less burdensome and much more efficient.

In addition to these factors, there has been a rapid growth of some developing countries. Moreover, the imbalance in world payments, due in large part to the 1973–74 oil price increases, contributed to the increased role of commercial banks in the recycling process.

INTERNATIONAL SERVICES OF U.S. BANKS

Although many international banking services are similar to those provided by banks on the domestic level, some differences make them unique and therefore require elaboration. The uniqueness of international finance has been responsible for many of the activities performed in the international department of a bank. For example, the international department usually has separate divisions such as bookkeeping, credit information, and business development. Because of the many activities and services offered by the international department, it is frequently referred to as a bank within a bank. The implication of such a statement, of course, is that a customer can find all the services required for the successful implementation of his or her international activities within this single bank department. The variety of activities performed and the services offered arise primarily from the differences that exist in monetary standards, business practices, and languages among the various countries that engage in foreign trade.

One of the interesting but not unusual activities of an international department, for example, is that it maintains its own bookkeeping department. This is because deposits are received from foreigners—banks, business firms, and some individuals. The foreign department of a bank also will carry accounts in banks in foreign countries. Foreign accounts in American banks are almost always denominated in American dollars, and the deposits of American banks in foreign banks generally are denominated in foreign currency. Foreign deposits in American banks are usually in the form of demand deposits, but frequently time deposits are carried as well. Many services are provided by banks that engage in international banking. We will discuss the most important.

TRANSFER OF FUNDS

Several methods might be employed in transferring funds between various parties living or traveling in different countries. Most of the funds, especially those from business transactions, are transferred by air remittance, cable remittance, and foreign drafts. Transferring funds via air mail is a relatively simple procedure. The customer of an American bank, for example, who wanted a certain amount of funds transferred to a party in England would pay the bank the amount in cash or by a check drawn on his or her account. The bank in turn would send an air mail letter instructing the bank in England to pay the exact amount to the party designated in the letter. The letter would specify the details of the payment: amount, name and address of beneficiary, name of the sender, and authorized signatures. Immediately on receipt of these instructions, the foreign bank would proceed to verify the signatures of the officials who had been authorized to sign for the bank and contact the beneficiary to make payment. The funds (denominated in pounds) would be deducted from the American bank's account in the foreign bank. A fee would be charged by the American bank to cover the expenses incurred by both the American and the foreign bank in this transfer of funds.

Sometimes it is necessary to transfer funds more quickly than by letter. Under such conditions the transfer would be made by cable or by telephone. Since it is impossible to verify signatures by this method, authenticity of the message would be verified by code or test-key arrangement. Obviously, this method of verification would be prearranged, although the code or key would change from day to day to ensure secrecy.

A draft is a very common method employed in transferring funds to another party in a foreign country. A foreign draft is a negotiable instrument drawn by a bank on a foreign correspondent bank. Drafts are normally employed when the customer of a bank wants to have an actual negotiable instrument to mail to the beneficiary abroad. When a draft is issued, the American bank sends the foreign bank a special *letter of advice* that includes all the salient details of the draft. Since the draft is not paid until the letter of advice is received, it serves as a protection against fraud.

Commercial banks aid in the transfer of funds by selling traveler's checks. Although only a few banks issue traveler's checks, most banks sell them for domestic and foreign use. For years the traveler's checks of U.S. banks have been acceptable in most foreign countries. Because of this almost universal acceptance abroad, tourists rely heavily on this instrument that results in the transfer of funds from this country to another.

FINANCING INTERNATIONAL TRADE

One of the most important functions performed by U.S. banks engaged in international banking is to finance exports and imports of the United States and trade between foreign countries. Just as domestic trade requires various financing methods, there are several ways of financing international trade. They are *cash in advance, open account, documentary collection,* and *letters of credit.* Of all these methods, the most important is the letter of credit.

Although terms of cash in advance involve little risk and are highly advantageous to exporters, they are not very popular as a means of financing foreign trade because of the many disadvantages presented to the foreign buyer. The buyer is forced to have a considerable amount of working capital tied up for long periods of time and is also at the mercy of the exporter because of the possibility of the shipment of inferior merchandise, delayed shipments, and even bankruptcy of the exporter. Nonpayment of foreign accounts arises many times out of unstable economic and political conditions, which are frequently encountered, and the difficulty in obtaining adequate credit information about foreign customers. Thus the cash-in-advance method of settlement is used primarily when the risk of not receiving payment is quite high.

Sales on open account reverse the risk exposure entailed in terms of cash in advance. Just as cash in advance presents some disadvantages to the foreign purchaser, the open account presents similar disadvantages to the exporter. If the foreign purchaser is slow in paying his or her bills, the exporter will experience a drain on working capital, which ultimately will adversely affect the latter's turnover. The chief objection to this method of financing is that the exporter does not have any negotiable instrument evidencing the obligation, which would become very important in the event of a dispute over delivery, loss, or quality of product. Open-account financing has one great advantage, however—it is very simple. Moreover, it is a way of avoiding financing and service charges incurred with other credit arrangements. Sales on an open-account basis are used when exporters are dealing with buyers they know very well who are located in well-established markets. This method is also used when sales are made to foreign branches or subsidiaries of domestic concerns. In times of peace and stability in the foreign exchange market, sales on open account tend to increase, but when economic and political clouds gather, less reliance is placed on this method.

Bills of Exchange

While widely accepted in domestic trade, terms of cash in advance and on open account are less widely employed in foreign trade because of their many disadvantages. Consequently, heavy reliance is placed on bills of exchange and letters of credit as methods of payment, both of which involve the services of commercial banks. A *bill of exchange* is an unconditional order in writing addressed by one person to another, signed by the person giving it, and requiring the addressee to pay a certain sum of money to order or to bearer on demand, or at a fixed or determinable time. To illustrate this type of financing, let us assume that Dixie Textile Company, an American importer, has agreed to purchase some woolen goods from John Bull Ltd., an exporter in England. The English exporter prepares the goods for shipment and delivers them to the shipping company for delivery to Dixie Textile Company in the United States. The exporter then executes a draft, or a bill of exchange, that directs the American importer to pay, say, $100,000 for the goods.

The exporter must take this instrument along with the other documents necessary for the transaction to the bank, which we will assume is a branch of Barclays Bank in London, and request the bank to send these documents to its correspondent bank in the United States. On receipt of these documents, the American bank makes a presentation to the buyer for payment. Once the buyer has paid the bank, all the documents are turned over to the importer, who, in turn, goes to the dock to claim the goods. The U.S. bank in this situation is acting only as an agent and performs a collection function. For this service the bank is paid a fee by the English bank, which normally varies from .1 to .25 percent of the amount of the bill of exchange or a stated dollar charge. Obviously, this example may have many variations. If, for example, the goods have to be examined and approved for entry into the United States by the Department of Agriculture or another government agency, Barclays Bank might instruct the bank in America to deliver the documents against trust receipts that stipulate that payment for the goods would be made after they have cleared inspection.

Letters of Credit

A letter of credit is a financial instrument issued by a bank on behalf of one of its customers, which authorizes an individual or a business firm to which it is addressed to draw drafts on the bank for its account under certain conditions as set forth in the document. In a letter of credit, the financial strength or credit of the bank is substituted for that of the bank's customer simply because the credit of the bank may be more substantial and more widely known. Another reason for heavy reliance on the letter of credit is that it is a desirable way of establishing certain quality standards or classifications that the goods must meet. Finally, it permits the seller to receive almost immediate payment for his or her goods, as soon as they are shipped; as a result, the cost to the importer is less than if the seller had to wait for payment for an extended period. Irrevocable letters of credit are used in international finance and, as the name implies, cannot be changed without the consent of all parties concerned.

Risks are numerous in international trade—accidents at sea, strikes, riots, and civil commotions in port cities—all of which can cause damage to ships and their cargo. Typically, many documents are necessary to complete an international transaction, and these must be specified in an application for a letter of credit. Several copies of a commercial invoice are needed for office use, and customs' invoices are required before some goods can be brought into this country. Probably the most important document stipulated in an application for a letter of credit is the negotiable *on-board ocean bill of lading*. This document is a receipt that the cargo was received and was loaded on board ship. Whoever holds the on-board ocean bill of lading has title to the goods. Therefore, the bank must have this document before payment is made.

After an importer has completed arrangements for the issuance of a letter of credit by his or her bank, it is usually forwarded by the issuing bank to the beneficiary's bank abroad. The receiving bank is instructed to deliver the letter of credit to the beneficiary. After receipt of the letter of credit, the foreign exporter arranges for the shipment of the goods to the American importer in accordance with the terms of the letter of credit. When the exporter has prepared all documents required and has delivered the goods to the ship, the documents are then attached to a draft and submitted to the exporter's bank along with the letter of credit. If the documents are in order, the bank then negotiates the draft and forwards the documents to the bank in the United States. The handling of the draft at this point depends on whether it is a sight or a time draft. If it is a sight draft, which means that it must be paid on sight, the bank pays the draft immediately. Several procedures could be employed in transferring the funds to the exporter's bank. The U.S. bank could merely credit funds to the exporting bank's account if the foreign bank carried a correspondent account with the bank in the United States. If it did not carry an account and the U.S. bank carried an account with the foreign bank, a transfer from the importing bank to the exporting bank could be effected. The U.S. bank could also order the transfer of funds from its account in another bank in the exporting bank's country to the bank that originated the draft. Whatever method is employed, the funds would be paid to the exporting bank within a very short time, and this bank would then transfer the funds to the exporter of the goods.

Banks that issue letters of credit may be paid in cash—a simple transfer from the customer's account to the bank. If, however, the importer does not have all or a part of the funds, a loan must be negotiated from the bank. This loan could be unsecured, assuming the borrower has sufficient creditworthiness, or it could be a loan secured by the goods just imported. If these goods are ready for sale, they could be released to the importer on a trust receipt. As they are sold, the loan is repaid, or they might be placed in a warehouse, with the warehouse receipts serving as collateral for the loan. Whatever the arrangement, the importer receives the order bill of lading that gives him or her title to the goods. If the goods were to be used in further manufacture, a different kind of loan might be made and with a longer maturity.

Bankers' Acceptances

Drafts authorized by a letter of credit may have various maturities. A sight draft, as we have said, must be paid when received. If the draft is drawn for 180 days, let's say, we would have an additional step in our financial transaction, that is, the creation of a bankers' acceptance, which is a draft that has been accepted by the drawee bank. The draft is changed into an acceptance by stamping the word "accepted" across the face of the draft, the signature of a bank officer who has been authorized to sign such documents, and a brief description of the transaction that gave rise to it. The bankers' acceptance can be returned to the drawer, who could hold the instrument until it is due to be paid and then present it to the accepting bank for payment. Bankers' acceptances are seldom disposed of in this manner, however, since the drawer of the original draft is not in the financing business and would, therefore, prefer to have his or her money immediately for the operation of the business.

An exporting bank could authorize a U.S. bank to sell the acceptance in the market. Since the acceptance market is old and well established, such a request would ordinarily present no problem. The U.S. bank could buy its own acceptance, which is not uncommon, especially when loan demand is relatively low. Acceptances are sold at a discount, and the difference between their price and the face value is the return received by the buyer.

Acceptance financing is a well-established form of financing, and bankers' acceptances in the money market are considered a prime asset. This high regard stems from the maturity and security of the acceptance. The maturity of bankers' acceptances usually will be for a maximum of

180 days,[1] which definitely places them in the category of a highly liquid asset. They are of high-quality credit, since they are the promise to pay of a well-regarded bank. Finally, they are eligible for discount at a Federal Reserve bank if they conform to the standards established by law. The high value placed on bankers' acceptances as an asset in the money market is reflected in their yield. Although the yield on acceptances fluctuates, the yield on prime acceptances generally is slightly above that on 90-day U.S. Treasury bills and about the same as the rate on commercial paper. The fact that bankers' acceptances can be discounted at a Federal Reserve bank is quite important and is one reason for banks holding them in their investment portfolios and considering them part of their secondary reserves.

The creation of bankers' acceptances by commercial banks is closely regulated by the Federal Reserve System; moreover, their use is limited. The total value of bankers' acceptances that a bank can create must not exceed 50 percent of the bank's capital and surplus unless prior approval from the Federal Reserve System has been obtained, and under no circumstances can the amount exceed 100 percent of these two capital items. They are also subject to the 15 percent lending rule previously discussed in the chapters on lending; that is, the amount of acceptances drawn by a single drawer is limited to 15 percent of the bank's capital surplus. The Federal Reserve Act limits the use of bankers' acceptances to the exportation and importation of goods as just discussed, the domestic shipment of goods, and the storage of readily marketable commodities, provided that a bank obtains a warehouse receipt or other comparable document as evidence of the transaction. These restrictions on bankers' acceptances stem from the fact that their creation is similar to the creation of demand deposits via the lending function, and such monetary creation is closely regulated by the central bank.

Although bankers' acceptances can be used in financing the domestic shipment of goods, they are somewhat cumbersome because of the documentation required and are therefore not widely used for this purpose. Their usage has grown, however, especially in tight money periods when loanable funds are less plentiful than in normal times. They are used extensively in financing the storage of readily marketable goods in foreign countries. In addition to these three basic uses of bankers' acceptances, they are also used to alleviate seasonal shortages of dollar exchange in those countries that rely heavily on a single crop or a few specialized exports. Several one-crop countries need dollar exchange for the purchase of machinery and material before a crop is harvested, processed, and sold in international trade. Under such conditions, banks in those countries can draw drafts on American banks and thus obtain dollar

---

[1] Bankers' acceptances may have maturities exceeding 180 days, but longer maturities are not eligible for rediscount with Federal Reserve banks.

exchange that will be repaid after the crop is exported. This type of financing is closely regulated by the Federal Reserve System. Any member bank may accept drafts for this purpose if the country is on the list that has been approved by the Board of Governors of the Federal Reserve System. The maturity of these acceptances is limited to three months. Member banks may accept drafts only in an amount equal to 10 percent of the drawee bank's unimpaired capital and surplus, and total drafts accepted may not exceed 50 percent of the bank's capital and surplus. Most of the dollar exchange is created for Latin American countries, particularly for the coffee crop.

Export Financing

In our discussion of the use of letters of credit, an example was given involving the importation of goods into the United States. Letters of credit also are employed in the exportation of goods from the United States. Foreign purchasers may ask their bank for a letter of credit for the same reasons that our importers requested its use when importing from a foreign seller. Although foreign importers may not want to use letters of credit when purchasing goods from a financially responsible U.S. exporter, the American exporter may nevertheless insist on their use for several reasons. The foreign purchaser may not meet the credit standards of the American exporter; therefore, the exporter may demand a bank obligation to eliminate the credit risk, although additional cost is involved. If the exchange situation in the buyer's country indicates that a delay might occur in the transfer of payment to the United States despite the financial responsibility of the buyer, the exporter may insist on a letter of credit. In fact, if the exporter considers the risk of nontransfer of funds to be quite high, he or she may ask the bank to add its confirmation to that of the foreign bank before agreeing to the transaction. In an arrangement of this kind, the U.S. bank adds its confirmation to that of the foreign bank to honor drafts and documents that are presented in accordance with the terms of the credit. However, confirmed letters of credit are not common, especially in times of international political and financial stability. Since the U.S. bank is providing a service that reduces the risk against which the U.S. exporter wants to be protected, obviously this service must be charged for.

COLLECTIONS

An important bank service that contributes to the flow of international trade is making collections. This is the process of presenting an item to the maker or drawee for payment. In the area of domestic banking, this is sometimes referred to as *clearing checks*, that is, routing the checks that have been deposited in bank A to the maker of the check who has an account in bank B, several miles from bank A. Domestic checks are cleared or collected through the facilities of the Federal Reserve System, the correspondent banking system, and local clearinghouses. In the area of international banking, only one of these arrangements exists for clearing items—the correspondent banking system.

The international items collected by banks may be *clean*, that is, without documents attached, or *documentary*, which means accompanied by documents. Such items as checks, traveler's checks, and money orders drawn on banks or agencies are usually clean items and are normally exchanged at a bank for local currency. An American traveler, for example, may cash a personal check or a traveler's check for $100 in a Paris bank. The funds are paid to the American tourist in French francs, and the check is then airmailed to the French bank's correspondent, let's say in New York, which credits the French bank's "due to account" either for immediate credit subject to final payment or as a collection, which means that the procedure will be credited to the "due to account" when payment is carried out.

Clean collections are relatively simple and do not present many problems. Documentary collections are a bit more complicated and are at present more important as far as international trade is concerned. These collections cover both exports and imports and may be in the form of either sight or time drafts. We have already had an example of an international financial transaction that required a collection effort, namely, the importation of goods under a letter of credit that required an American bank to collect funds from the importer and return the funds to the bank abroad. We have also had an example of the collection under a bill of exchange. In this example the bill of exchange was due at sight and the documents were sent to the U.S. bank, which was asked to release the documents only after payment had been made. Frequently exporters will ask their banks to provide them with blank drafts and collection instructions, which they will use in their international dealings. The amount of collections outstanding is relatively large when compared with acceptances.

FOREIGN EXCHANGE MARKET

International payments necessitate converting one currency into another. The French exporter of rare wines to a buyer in the United States is not interested in dollars but in French francs, and the U.S. exporter of machinery to a purchaser in Italy wants dollars rather than liras. Whether the foreign transaction involves the purchase or sale of goods, tourism, or capital movements for investment purposes or interest arbitrage, there is a need for the exchange of currencies of the various countries. This demand is met by the foreign exchange market, which is dominated by commercial banks. Although the foreign exchange market is one where money is exchanged, there is no central marketplace such as the one for stocks and bonds on the New York Stock Exchange or for grains on the Chicago Board of Trade. The foreign exchange market is a mechanism rather than a place. The market is very informal and has no fixed hours. In the United States it is composed of approximately 25 banks and a few foreign exchange brokers. Outside the United States the major participants are the central banks of various countries and large commercial banks. Trading is done by telephone or telex. The foreign exchange market has no written rules of trading. Its activity is conducted under principles and a code of ethics that have evolved over time. The major framework of the market is a system of direct communications among its participants.

Making a Market

Many banks throughout the nation provide facilities for handling foreign exchange but only a few make and maintain a market—take a position or maintain an inventory in foreign currencies. These banks are really the hub or foundation of the foreign exchange market. Only a few are in this category, most located in New York City. The West Coast market is growing, however, with the establishment of Edge Act affiliates of New York banks and offices of several foreign banks. Although many other banks provide their customers with foreign exchange services, they arrange for this service through these very few banks. A bank located in Harrisburg, Illinois, for example, that needs 6,320 West German deutsche marks for a customer who must pay a German exporter for a new printing machine would probably arrange for these funds from a bank in St. Louis or Chicago. Most banks have access to daily quotations of the various foreign currencies. Although the price of currencies may change frequently, a current quotation can be obtained by making a telephone call to a dealer in foreign exchange.

To provide customers with foreign exchange services, some American banks must hold foreign exchange inventories in the form of deposits with foreign banks. These deposits or inventories are maintained by the purchase and sale of balances owned by both foreign and domestic banks, individuals, and business firms. Inventories may also be augmented by the purchase and sale of bills of exchange, traveler's checks, bond coupons, dividend warrants, and other assets denominated in foreign currencies. How much of an inventory and the variety of currencies held depend on the amount of activity a bank has in a given currency. Obviously, the largest percentage of its inventory will be in those currencies that are in greatest demand. High on the list would be the pound sterling, the Canadian dollar, the Japanese yen, and the West German mark. In other words, the inventory would contain the currencies of those countries with which we trade, in which we invest, and in which Americans tour.

TABLE 19-1   Foreign Exchange Rates (currency units per dollar)

Country/Currency	1984	1985	1986	1987 Feb.	Mar.	Apr.	May	June	July
1 Australia/dollar[1]	87.937	70.026	67.093	66.77	68.17	71.19	71.42	71.79	70.79
2 Austria/schilling	20.005	20.676	15.260	12.833	12.905	12.739	12.574	12.793	12.996
3 Belgium/franc	57.749	59.336	44.662	37.789	38.029	35.562	37.091	37.712	38.329
4 Brazil/cruzeiro	1841.50	6205.10	13.051	18.08	20.56	22.59	n.a.	n.a.	n.a.
5 Canada/dollar	1.2953	1.3658	1.3896	1.3340	1.3194	1.3183	1.3411	1.338	1.3262
6 China, P.R./yuan	2.3308	2.9434	3.4615	3.7314	3.7314	3.7314	3.7314	3.7314	3.7314
7 Denmark/krone	10.354	10.598	8.0954	6.8939	6.9166	6.8388	6.7333	6.8555	7.0179
8 Finland/markka	6.007	6.1971	5.0721	4.5556	4.5102	4.4227	4.3604	4.4281	4.4882
9 France/franc	8.7355	8.9799	6.9256	6.0760	6.1091	6.0332	5.9748	6.0739	6.1530
10 Germany/deutsche mark	2.8454	2.9419	2.1704	1.8239	1.8355	1.8125	1.7881	1.8189	1.8482
11 Greece/drachma	112.73	138.40	139.93	133.88	134.68	133.502	133.35	136.06	139.313
12 Hong Kong/dollar	7.8188	7.7911	7.8037	7.7952	7.8017	7.8023	7.8049	7.8080	7.8090
13 India/rupee	11.348	12.332	12.597	13.062	12.924	12.8224	12.666	12.837	13.01
14 Ireland/pound	108.64	106.62	134.14	145.93	145.54	147.49	149.59	147.25	144.99
15 Italy/lira	1756.10	1908.90	1491.16	1297.74	1305.90	1292.96	1290.80	1316.50	1337.96
16 Japan/yen	237.45	238.47	168.35	153.41	151.43	143.00	140.48	144.55	150.29

	C9	C8	C7	C6	C5	C4	C3	C2	C1
17 Malaysia/ringgit	2.3448	2.4806	2.5830	2.5418	2.5230	2.4861	2.4759	2.5078	2.5414
18 Netherlands/guilder	3.2083	3.3184	2.4484	2.0592	2.0731	2.0447	2.0154	2.0490	2.0814
19 New Zealand/dollar[1]	57.837	49.752	52.456	54.815	56.333	57.751	57.639	58.686	59.644
20 Norway/krone	8.1596	8.5933	7.3984	7.0067	6.9335	6.7781	6.6632	6.7147	6.7632
21 Portugal/escudo	147.70	172.07	149.80	141.62	141.48	140.339	139.18	142.12	144.51
22 Singapore/dollar	2.1325	2.2008	2.1782	2.1410	2.1418	2.1350	2.1202	2.1176	2.1183
23 South Africa/rand[1]	69.534	45.57	43.952	47.97	48.21	49.55	49.87	49.41	48.52
24 South Korea/won	807.91	861.89	884.61	857.38	856.11	845.00	832.53	818.39	811.81
25 Spain/peseta	160.78	169.98	140.04	128.62	128.86	126.975	125.28	126.33	126.97
26 Sri Lanka/rupee	25.428	27.187	27.933	28.662	28.823	28.902	28.988	29.171	29.405
27 Sweden/krona	8.2706	8.6031	7.1272	6.5016	6.4202	6.3210	6.2606	6.3482	6.4466
28 Switzerland/franc	2.3500	2.4551	1.7979	1.5403	1.5391	1.4968	1.4705	1.5085	1.5365
29 Taiwan/dollar	39.633	39.889	37.837	35.056	34.681	33.863	32.354	31.226	31.114
30 Thailand/baht	23.582	27.193	26.314	25.933	25.881	25.695	25.629	25.779	26.041
31 United Kingdom/pound[1]	133.66	129.74	146.77	152.80	159.23	162.99	166.66	162.88	160.90
MEMO									
32 United States/dollar[2]	138.19	143.01	112.22	99.46	98.99	97.09	96.05	97.78	99.36

[1] Value in U.S. cents.

[2] Index of weighted-average exchange value of U.S. dollar against the currencies of ten industrial countries. The weight for each of the ten countries is the 1972–76 average world trade of that country divided by the average world trade of all ten countries combined.

SOURCE: *Federal Reserve Bulletin* (September 1987).

Exchange Risks

Providing a market in foreign exchange is not without risk, and it is for the assumption of risks that a charge is imposed in the form of a spread between the bid and ask prices of currencies. The risks involved in foreign exchange trading stem from the fact that the exchange rates of the various currencies are subject to change as a result of a country's economic health and political stability. A country with a favorable balance of payments, for example, would have a stronger currency in the exchange markets than would one with a negative balance. The United States, for example, has experienced huge trade deficits in recent years, and the dollar has declined to very low levels against the currencies of such countries as Japan and West Germany (see Table 19-1). The depressing effect of a country's trade deficit on its currency can be offset somewhat by central bank purchases, but that solution is temporary, at best. In time the country must find solutions to its trade deficit.

Maintaining a position in another country's currency is risky. For example, on September 29, 1987, the Japanese yen declined 1.5 percent against the dollar. A U.S. bank with yen deposits and currency totaling $100 million would have lost $1.5 million that day. Such short-term movements are common and may reverse themselves in a short period. Over longer periods, however, major changes in exchange values may take place. As shown in Table 19-1, a huge decline took place in the Brazilian cruzerio from 1984 to 1985, leading to currency reform. In September 1986, the Mexican peso was approximately 700 to the dollar. Just over a year later it was more than 1,600 to the dollar. A U. S. bank that carried an inventory of constant size in pesos during that period would have lost nearly 60 percent of the dollar value of the inventory.

A bank that deals in foreign exchange must limit its exposure in the various currencies and carry on a sufficient volume of business so that losses tend to be offset by gains. Moreover, managers of foreign exchange departments must be alert not only to changes in exchange rates but also to the causes of those changes so that steps may be taken to reduce risk. In major currencies, banks or bank customers can reduce risk with transactions in the forward exchange market.

Spot and Forward Rates

In general, two classes of transactions are made in the foreign exchange market—*spot* and *forward*. Spot transactions are for immediate delivery; forward transactions are for delivery on some specified future date. The spot rate and the forward rate will differ because of market forces, expectations for inflation, and so on. If the forward rate is above the spot rate, the difference between the two is termed a *premium*. If the reverse is true, the difference is a *discount*. For example, if at the same time on the same day the spot rates in the final column of Table 19-1 prevailed, the forward rates for the Japanese yen and the Canadian dollar might have been as shown in Table 19-2.

In our hypothetical examples, the yen is selling at a sharp premium to the dollar in the forward market. In other words, it takes more dollars to buy a specific amount of yen for forward delivery than for spot delivery. The Canadian dollar is selling at a slight discount to the U.S. dollar in the forward market in our example.

The rationale for forward markets lies in the exchange rate risk inherent in all international commercial and financial transactions. As long as spot rates fluctuate, even within narrow limits, risk is involved for those who expect to convert one currency into another. An American exporter who sells goods to a purchaser in England for sterling payable in three months is concerned about the rate at which the sterling claims can be converted into dollars. Let us assume, for example, that the goods were sold for [£]100,000 on October 22, 1988, when the spot rate for the pound was $1.6965. If the pound were at the same quotation on January 22, 1989, the American exporter would receive pounds from the purchase that could be converted into 169,650 U.S. dollars (100,000 times 1.6965). Let us further assume that if this price were received, the exporter would realize a profit of $24,900 on this transaction. However, if for some reason or reasons a pound were worth only 1.5735 on January 22, 1989, the American exporter would only receive 157,350 (100,000 times 1.5735) U.S. dollars after the conversion. This unforeseen development would be upsetting to the exporter, since the profit would be reduced to a mere $12,600. Thus, because of a drop of less than $0.13 in the price of the pound, the profit is cut by nearly 50 percent. Of course, it could be reasoned that if the pound had increased in value to, say, $1.8075, the profits would have increased by $11,100. This is indeed correct, but the issue that is now raised is whether assuming this risk is really a logical or legitimate function of the person who exported the goods. It probably is not, and this person should stick with his or her trade and let someone else assume the risk that arises because of changes in exchange rates.

TABLE 19-2 Hypothetical Spot and Forward Rates

	Japanese Yen		Canadian Dollar	
	Per U.S.$	*U.S.$ Equiv.*	*Per U.S.$*	*U.S.$ Equiv.*
Spot rate	150.29	.006654	1.3262	.7540
30-day forward	147.51	.006779	1.3316	.7510
90-day forward	142.01	.007042	1.3376	.7476
180-day forward	140.88	.007098	1.3457	.7431

The American exporter could be protected in this particular transaction by entering the forward exchange market. This could be done by entering into a contract with a commercial bank in which the exporter promises to deliver, at a stated future date, pounds in exchange for dollars at the market price existing for forward pounds at the time the contract was initiated. If we assume that on October 22, 1988, the 90-day forward rate was $1.6996, then once the sale transaction is completed, the exporter is ensured of receiving $169,960 for the goods, which is only $310 less than on the day the sale was made. Now if the pound were to drop to $1.5735, the deal looks good. Thus, for giving up $310 the exporter is protected against a possible loss of $12,300 or more. The student here might raise a question concerning the wisdom of entering into a contract with the exporter whereby the English importer has three months to pay for the goods. This is because the importer does not have the funds; if the American exporter insisted that payment be made at the time of sale, the English importer might purchase the goods from another exporter who would be willing to extend credit. Competition is a great motivator, and in our example, the exporter is able to compete because the forward exchange market makes possible the removal of exchange risk.

INTERNATIONAL LENDING

As in domestic operations, the greatest amount of income in international banking is derived from lending. Banks that engage in international lending do so through any one or a combination of an international department, branches, or other types of organization involving locations abroad. The bulk of foreign lending is done by those U.S. banks with locations in foreign countries, however. Banks with an international department only concentrate their efforts on financing international trade by extending credit to domestic customers for the production of goods that will be exported abroad or by lending to domestic firms for the purchase of goods from abroad that will be sold domestically or used in the further production of goods and services in this country. In reality this is domestic rather than international lending, however. Moreover, the amount of foreign loans made by affiliates of U.S. banks, those banks that are owned jointly with foreign banks, and banks abroad in which U.S. banks have a minority interest is not known. Data are available, however, on the amount of loans made by foreign branches of U.S. banks. At year-end 1987, the loans of branches of U.S. banks abroad amounted to approximately $250 billion.

Risks of International Lending

In many respects, lending abroad is similar to lending domestically. The credit principles discussed in previous chapters are certainly not ignored. In addition to these basic factors, three others play a very important role in the granting of credit to foreign borrowers: *currency, country,* and *regulatory risks.* The currency risk is concerned with convertibility and the stability of the monetary unit of the borrower's country. A bank is interested in the monetary unit being convertible and the loan being repaid in a medium of exchange of the same value as when the loan was made. This might not be realized, however, in the event of inconvertibility or the devaluation of the monetary unit in which the loan is repaid. In other words, a risk exists because of changes that might occur in the convertibility of a currency or in its exchange rate. As long as a country has its international payments and receipts in approximate balance or has sufficient international reserves to cover a deficit in its balance of payments, the currency risk is minimal. If, however, the country does not have an equilibrium in its balance of payments and does not have sufficient reserves, its currency may decline in value; thus, the amount repaid would purchase fewer dollars in world markets. Moreover, if a country's international payments persistently exceed its receipts, it may establish exchange controls. Should this come about, the borrower who may be financially sound otherwise might have difficulty in securing funds to repay the bank.

Closely associated with these risks that must be considered in international lending is country risk or what is sometimes referred to as *political risk.* Country risk includes the uncertainties arising from political and economic developments with a host country that will influence the ability and willingness of borrowers to meet obligations as agreed. An economic recession is obviously a country risk as is a political upheaval of some kind and degree that adversely affects the free flow of commerce and income to individuals and business firms as well as tax revenues of various levels of government. Expropriation of property and expulsion from a host country is not an unknown happening.

In international lending, consideration would have to be given to such items as the country's internal and external debt, for if external debt were exceptionally large and economic developments were such that tax revenues were insufficient in amount to meet the principal and interest payments, steps such as additional taxation might be taken that would reduce the ability of the borrower to repay the loan to the bank. A risk that must be considered is the imposition of restrictions, which might prevent the delivery and acceptance of merchandise. Some foreign importers are required to secure an import license from their government to import goods, and this privilege might be canceled after goods are purchased and shipped. Rebellion, civil commotion, and war are hazards that may be encountered in international lending. In this general area, a most significant risk is concerned with the expropriation of property. U.S. banks have been forced out of several countries, including Spain, Cuba, Chile, and some other South American countries.

Although banks in the United States encounter regulatory risks at home, such risks abroad are sometimes greater. Regulatory risks abroad are that a country will impose or change drastically reserve requirements, capital/asset ratios, special taxes, and a variety of other regulations that would hamper banking activities. Such regulations are usually imposed when the host country encounters financial and economic difficulties. Currency restrictions frequently accompany the imposition of regulatory limitations. Some of these risks can be reduced or eliminated by various clauses in loan agreements that allow the added cost of the restrictions to pass through to the borrower.

In recent years, international lending by banks has come under close scrutiny because of the worldwide recession, the heavy indebtedness of nations, and the rescheduling of foreign debts by several countries. As previously mentioned, foreign lending has mushroomed since the early 1960s. The foreign debts of developing countries alone increased sixfold since 1973, from $100 billion to approximately $640 billion a decade later. Of this amount about half is owed to U.S. and European commercial banks. The size of foreign debts of countries is not as important as the cost of servicing these international obligations. Although there is no absolute rule regarding the amount of money that a country should devote to debt service, a generally accepted rule of thumb is an amount equal to 20 percent of a country's income from exports. According to this measurement, many countries in the early 1980s were spending far in excess of this percentage. Because of burdening debts many countries have been forced to reschedule their debts, that is, reduce the amount of principal and/or interest presently scheduled to be repaid in the immediate future.

Several factors have contributed to the financial plight of developing countries. The worldwide recession is an underlying cause. Economic recessions result in declining exports followed by the depletion of foreign currency reserves. The "oil shock" of 1973 and 1974, when oil prices were raised to unprecedented levels, ushered in an age of slower industrial growth. Many of the developing countries followed very liberal monetary and fiscal policies, which contributed to rising costs, high rates of inflation, social unrest, and a decline in their competitive position. To maintain the economic strides that had been made in rising output, investment, and living standards, the developing nations resorted to increased borrowing. Funds were available from the World Bank and the International Monetary Fund. Moreover, the private international banking system, which had received large deposits from the OPEC countries, was eager to make funds available to needy nations. Some observers contend that banks were overly eager for growth and income; consequently, they were too liberal in their lending.

The foreign debt problem is a serious one and its impact can be widespread. Countries that have foreign debt problems frequently resort to policies that are upsetting to international trade and worldwide financial relations. They sometimes engage in such policies as devaluation, exchange controls, restrictions on capital flows, tariffs, and the nationalization of various businesses. When these developments occur, banking institutions are adversely affected. A bank's liquidity and income are materially affected, and losses from loans are liable to occur.

The collection of foreign debts differs from those incurred domestically in that the legal avenues to enforce repayment are not always available. The host country may reduce or even eliminate some or all of the legal steps that are taken for granted in domestic lending. Since much of the foreign debt of U.S. banks has been extended to governments or government institutions, very little can be done to effect collection. Governments are sovereign powers and in the final analysis immune from the law. To be sure, if foreign governments do not repay obligations and take steps to block repayment, their credit among world nations is tarnished; but, frequently, in the short run, little consideration is given to this fact. In many instances, creditors are forced to wait. From past experience with foreign debts, it will take some time before the problem is completely solved. Many foreign loans held by U.S. banks may become classified as problem loans, and some losses are a distinct possibility. Unfortunately, recent experience with foreign lending may result in a reluctance on the part of banks to expand in this area in the immediate future.

Types of Loans

Foreign borrowers include individuals and business firms just as in this country. Commercial banks also, either individually or jointly, may extend credit for short periods to central banks, a practice that is not followed in the United States. These funds may be used by a central bank to make credit available to other commercial banks or may be employed in the central bank's foreign exchange operations. Banks abroad may have deposits from central banks and extend credit to central governments, neither of which is done in this country. If the U.S. Treasury needs funds, it borrows in the money and/or capital markets via the issuance of securities. This, of course, is done abroad; but in some countries, particularly where the money and capital markets are not as well developed as here, government borrowing from commercial banks is not uncommon. Loans to governments might be made directly or indirectly through central banks or foreign banks. In some countries, especially in developing areas, the government may be the strongest and most financially responsible borrower. In many cases, the borrowing government will in turn make the funds from U.S. banks available to local borrowers through various government agencies or development banks.

The purpose and type of loans made to foreign business firms do not differ greatly from business loans made in the United States. U.S. banks generally do not, however, make as many term loans abroad as they do domestically; it is not uncommon, especially in making loans with a relatively long maturity, for an American bank and a bank abroad to participate with a bank located within a third country in making the loan. In this way the risk is reduced, and at the same time the U.S. bank has acquired some expert judgment on the part of the local banker. Because of our huge investments in foreign countries in manufacturing, mining, and other forms of business enterprise, many American firms abroad look to U.S. banks and branches for credit. Since American bankers have great knowledge of American firms, it is in this area of lending that they excel. Although U.S. banks abroad make personal loans, they do not engage in personal lending to the extent that they do in this country.

Just as in this country, foreign loans may be unsecured or secured, and the type of collateral taken as security varies. Since most of the loans in dollar amount are made to large business concerns, governments, and banks, a larger percentage of foreign loans is made on an unsecured basis than is the case domestically. This is especially true of those banks that do not have branches abroad. Unsecured loans might take the form of authorizing foreign banks or trading companies to draw drafts on U.S. banks up to a prearranged amount or merely signing a note supported by a loan agreement. Banks are interested in reducing the risks of lending, and this is done to some extent by diversifying their lending among several countries rather than concentrating it in one single country. It is not uncommon for several banks to form a syndicate to participate in a large loan to a borrower in a single country. The bank that negotiates the loan, the lead bank, is responsible for the investigation of the risks involved, the actual drawing up of the loan agreement, collecting the interest and principal on the loan and disbursing the proceeds among the participating banks, and other supervisory activities that might be involved during the course of the loan. Some banks have sustained losses by relying on information provided by the lead bank or syndicate manager. While the syndicate manager has certain responsibilities[2] to the participating banks, each bank should evaluate the risks independently and not rely solely on the lead bank.

Insurance and Guarantees

Banks are able to reduce their foreign lending risks by loaning to exporters who insure their trade credits with the Foreign Credit Insurance

---

[2] A. D. Calhoun, Jr., "Eurodollar Loan Agreements: An Introduction and Discussion of Some Special Problems," The Journal of Commercial Bank Lending (September 1977), pp. 27–31.

Association (FCIA). This is a voluntary organization of more than 60 stock and mutual insurance companies throughout the United States that provides insurance coverage up to a certain percentage of the trade credit against nonpayment arising from credit losses and losses from political hazards. Political risks are reinsured through the Export-Import Bank, which is described below. The FCIA makes a thorough credit investigation of the foreign purchaser as well as the political risk in the purchaser's country. In general, the insurance covers up to 90 percent of the credit risk and up to 95 percent of the risks from the political hazards. Insurance premiums paid by the exporters vary with a rating established for each country and foreign borrowers but average approximately.5 percent of the sale price. FCIA provides coverage for both short-term credits, which are defined as those up to 180 days' maturity, and intermediate-term credits from 180 days up to 5 years.

A government institution that will sometimes guarantee foreign loans made by commercial banks, in addition to other activities in the area of international lending, is the Export-Import Bank (Exim Bank). The Exim Bank deals primarily with risks beyond the scope of private capital or that private lenders are unwilling to assume because of the high risks involved. The bank extends credit to foreign buyers to purchase material and equipment produced or manufactured in the United States. The bank's role in international finance may take the form of direct loans, participation in loans with other lenders, or guaranteeing loans. The Exim Bank's guarantee program is very similar to the insurance provisions of the FCIA. This international financial institution tends to operate in the area of capital loans and in relatively large amounts rather than in working capital loans. Moreover, it is more interested in financing capital equipment, such as commercial airplanes or generators for a hydroelectric installation, than consumer goods.

Eurodollar Lending

Eurodollar lending derives its name from the source of funds rather than from differences in lending techniques. Branches of U.S. banks abroad originate deposits in their locales and normally lend these funds in the same areas. In recent years there has developed what is referred to as *Eurodollar deposits*. These dollars are purchased by banks and loaned to business firms and governments; hence, the term *Eurodollar lending*. Eurodollars originate from dollar deposits with U.S. banks that are acquired by foreigners and redeposited in banks outside the United States. For example, a French bank with a surplus of francs might exchange them with the French central bank for dollars that have accumulated because of a surplus in the French balance of payments. The French bank could then deposit these funds in a London bank and receive a stipulated rate of interest. These same funds could, in turn, be reloaned to another bank in Switzerland, which could make the funds available to a producer of steel in Spain. Since the origin of this kind of deposit was in Europe and most of these deposits are found there, the market has been termed the Eurodollar market. Other currencies have also become part of the Eurodollar market such as the pound sterling, yen, deutsche mark, French and Swiss francs, and the guilder. Dollars account for about 70 percent of the market, however. There are similar developments in Asia and other parts of the world; hence, the term *Asian dollar.* Hong Kong and Singapore are the centers of this market. The trading center for Eurodollars is London. The rate paid for Eurodollars is referred to as the London interbank offered rate, usually shortened to LIBOR.

Several factors have been responsible for the rise in Eurodollars: American aid abroad after World War II, a rise in our imports, and during the last few years, our substantial deficits. Moreover, the high esteem placed on the value of the American dollar in international transactions contributes to an increasing number of countries tying their currencies to the American dollar and expressing their reserves in dollars. Eurodollar lending has also been encouraged by the reserve requirements placed on bank deposits in the United States, the insurance on deposits, and the taxation of corporate income. U.S. banks must maintain a certain amount of their deposits as reserves at Federal Reserve banks and pay a fee to the FDIC for the insurance of deposits. This is not required of all foreign banks; consequently, the lending of funds in American banks must be done at a slightly higher cost than if the funds were held abroad and not returned to the United States. The fact that income is taxed when returned to the United States also encourages both lenders and borrowers to maintain funds outside the continental limits of the United States where such income is not taxed, or if taxed, the rate is considerably lower. Although in the last few years there have been changes in the taxation of corporate income earned abroad, for many years this was an important factor contributing to the establishment of foreign branches and to the rise in the Eurodollar market as well.

Eurodollar lending is in relatively large amounts—ranging from a minimum of $1 million to as much as $1.5 billion. Usually a larger international bank puts together a Eurodollar loan and then proceeds to find other banks that would like to participate in that type of credit. Once the banks agree to the terms, rate, repayment schedule, and so on, the loan is consummated. The rate that is agreed upon is a certain amount above the LIBOR rate on the date the funds are advanced. If the rate offered on the loan is not of sufficient amount above the LIBOR rate, the loan would not be granted. Sometimes this type of lending is referred to as *spread banking,* indicating that the crucial factor in engaging in this kind of lending is the spread between the cost of funds on the one hand and rates paid on the other. In addition to an interest payment, participants in Eurodollar loans sometimes receive a fee such as one-eighth to one-half of 1 percent of the amount of the loan. Occasionally there is a flat fee. The managing bank is not responsible for the soundness of the Eurodollar credit. Each participant must make its own decision on the credit worthiness of the borrower. Because of the volatility of rates, the interest rate on loans is adjusted every six months. The maturity of most Eurodollar loans varies from five to ten years. Eurodollar loans are made to a wide variety of businesses throughout the world. Such loans have been made to the government of Malaysia, a subway system in Brazil, the central bank of Mexico, an oil monopoly in Venezuela, Mobil Oil of Indonesia, and so on. Eurodollar lending has shown rapid growth. The pool of funds from which loans are made is quite substantial. At year-end 1987, for example, it was estimated that Eurodollar deposits were over $2 trillion.

FOREIGN DEBT CRISIS OF THE 1980s

A brief discussion of the foreign debt crisis of the early 1980s, involving the underdeveloped countries of the world, might be helpful in demonstrating the risks of international lending.

Hazards of Foreign Lending

Bank lending officers are placed in a position of analyzing a potential borrower under past and present conditions— analyzing management skills, earnings record, financial position, payment experience, and the like—and then projecting that borrower into a future environment, which the banker is not positive will exist. If the environment remained the same as at the time credit was granted, the process of bank lending would be relatively simple. The environment in the future is the unknown in the lending equation. Foreign lending is more hazardous than domestic lending because of the currency, country, and regulatory risks. The future may present pitfalls so remote that to consider them seriously when credit is granted may appear ludicrous. Costs may rise and fluctuate wildly, improved technology may adversely affect a firm's or country' s competitive position, the supply of labor and materials may be interrupted, economic growth and foreign trade may decline, political upheaval and war may occur, and tariffs may be erected; consequently, income may decline to a level where scheduled repayments are impossible. In the United States, economic activity is conducted in a competitive economy with which lending officers are familiar. In a world economy, administered prices and cartels are frequently encountered. It is difficult to predict a cartel's action. In 1970, for example, who expected the creation of OPEC in 1973 and its behavior thereafter?

Contrary to popular opinion, international loans are unlike private domestic loans. Private loans are in many instances secured, and all are supported by an enforceable contract. Should the borrower not pay as agreed, collateral can be seized and sold in satisfaction of the debt. Should the collateral be insufficient to pay off the loan or if the loan is not supported by collateral, a judgment can be secured from the proper court of law. The debtor must honor the judgment. An additional means of effecting payment is through bankruptcy laws, whereby the debtor's assets are turned over to the creditors by a bankruptcy court. These legal enforcement mechanics made possible the modern credit system.

Such legal arrangements do not exist in international lending. Circumstances are very different for bank loans made to developing countries. Practically all of the loans that we are discussing were made to or guaranteed by governments. Nations are sovereign powers, and borrowing and lending are not within the jurisdiction of a court of law. International loans are normally not supported by collateral, and there is no access to a bankruptcy court. Although the assets of a government could be seized, it is not feasible; and should this be carried out, it would be in the form of "gunboat diplomacy." To be sure, this has happened in some parts of the world, but it is frowned upon politically, and world opinion seems to side with the debtors rather than the creditors in such cases.

From a practical standpoint we must conclude, therefore, that there is no workable way of enforcing the fulfillment of an international loan such as we have been discussing. There are, however, some forces that support repayment, such as ethics, peer pressure, and the recognition that if a country does not pay it will have difficulty in obtaining credit again, not only from the present creditors but from lenders from other countries who view the nonpayment behavior from afar.

Causes of Debt Crisis

The foreign debt crisis of the 1980s was the result of liberal lending policies on the part of world banks and a world economy upset by an energy crisis brought on by the OPEC cartel. When the loans were made, the world economy was characterized by low interest rates and rapidly expanding markets. Under such circumstances the lenders did not foresee the unfavorable developments that made the underdeveloped countries unable to repay their loans. Developing countries, sometimes called the Third World, are interested in improving their lot. However, when sufficient funds are not available internally to accomplish this worthy objective, they must rely on foreign borrowing. The crisis had its beginning in the late 1960s, when borrowing by the underdeveloped countries increased sharply, and by the early 1970s, the external debt had reached $100 billion. The energy crisis of 1973–74 accelerated the size of this debt since the very large increase in the cost of imported energy led to a sharp rise in the balance of payments deficits of these countries from nearly zero in 1972 to $32 billion by 1975. A country's balance of payments deficit is financed either by foreign capital inflows or by borrowing from abroad. Private direct foreign investment in the developing countries is not high by any measurement; consequently, borrowing was a likely avenue of financing. World banks at the time were flushed with so-called "petrodollars," money that had flowed to them from the OPEC countries that was a product of their balance of payments surpluses. Bank loans rose sharply from $35 billion in 1973 to $63 billion two years later, when total indebtedness soared to $165 billion.[3]

Even after the energy emergencies receded in the mid-1970s, the recycling of petrodollars and the desire for bank loans by the undeveloped countries continued. Loans were used not only to finance oil-related deficits but economic development as well. The ease of securing loans contributed to some economically wasteful expenditures and in some instances to the financing of current consumption. Easy borrowing also contributed to inflation, which had the effect of undermining the confidence of many residents to such a degree that a flight of capital occurred. Many times the money that left the developing countries was invested in nonproductive projects abroad or deposited in world banks to be relent to the same countries. By 1980 the total foreign debt of the 104 developing countries that report to the World Bank had climbed to $540 billion, of which $210 billion was owed to international banks.[4] U.S. banks held a large portion of this debt, most of which was concentrated in the Latin American countries.

Signs of Trouble

Although it was recognized by many that the burden of the Third World countries had climbed to unprecedented heights, it was not until 1981 that signs of trouble began to appear. Many of these signs were not predictable and obviously not expected when credit was extended. With a total debt of $88 billion, Mexico declared to the world that it was unable to meet its repayment obligations. This declaration started a chain reaction, and within a year 30 countries had followed the trend, including the major countries in Latin America.

Impact of Heavy Indebtedness

The ensuing developments are evidence of what can go wrong and the need for a margin of safety in bank lending. The very sharp increase in

---

[3] Federal Reserve Bank of Chicago, *International Letter*, No. 555 (February 1986).
[4] Ibid.

oil prices by OPEC in 1979–80 contributed to a severe recession throughout the world. The demand for the products of developing countries
dropped and world commodity prices declined by 27 percent, adversely
affecting the income from the sale of raw materials. Due to the great inflow
of funds from borrowing, the rate of inflation soared and created great
social and economic problems.

With the high rate of inflation and overvalued currencies, foreign
goods became more attractive and the balance of payments deteriorated
rapidly. The current account deficits of these nations more than doubled
in four years. The only way to service a foreign debt other than by borrowing is to experience a surplus of exports over imports. Because of a series
of unfortunate developments, this arrangement was denied the debtor
nations; consequently, their capacity to service the debt was not possible.
Another unfortunate development for the Third World countries was the
sharp increase in interest rates in the United States during the three-year
period 1980–82, which increased the carrying cost of the debt of the
developing countries by approximately $40 billion.

It is fairly obvious that because of all these adverse developments the
Third World countries could not meet their obligations—hence the "foreign debt crisis." By 1983 nearly 50 countries had asked for a rescheduling of debts. The IMF reported that some $480 billion was owed by coun-
tries that were experiencing payment difficulties and more than half of the
$797 billion of developing countries' debt was in jeopardy.[5] When the
debt crisis was recognized in the summer of 1982, developing countries
owed banks throughout the world $268 billion, of which U.S. banks held
37 percent, or approximately $100 billion. Although the debt was widely
held by hundreds of U.S. banks, the concentration was in a few of the
larger banks of the country. Of the 15 largest banks in the nation, these
questionable loans exceeded the capital of some banks by as much as 150
percent. This concentration was highly significant since should a default
on this debt occur, these banks would be technically insolvent because
their capital was insufficient to offset these losses.

Some Improvement

For bankers to arrive at the correct strategy under such conditions is
not easy. It is obvious that the borrowers could not meet their scheduled
payments. Therefore, demanding payment would be futile. There are no
courts to render a decision or to force payment. Fortunately for the banks
there were some developments that temporarily improved their position—actions by international lending agencies and by the U.S. Treasury
and the Federal Reserve System, the adoption of austerity programs on the

---

[5] Ibid.

part of the debtor nations, and some recovery in the world economy. The IMF and the World Bank extended funds to some Latin American countries on condition that steps would be taken to reduce the rate of inflation and revitalize their economies and thus improve their ability to service their debt. The U.S. Treasury and the Federal Reserve System extended some short-term credit to several Latin American countries. The austerity programs adopted by some countries were successful, and the rise in economic activity contributed to a decline in the aggregate current account deficits from $67 billion in 1981 to $8 billion in 1984. Moreover, the economic growth in debtor countries rose in 1984–85, which raised personal income and reduced some of the political tensions that had become more noticeable during the trying times of the early 1980s.

Trouble in Latin America

Although the complete collapse of the Third World countries was averted, the financial problems are still present. Most of the problems of U.S. banks are centered in Latin America, where the five largest debtors in mid-1987 owed world banks $202 billion of which $72 billion, or 37 percent, was held by U.S. banks. Citicorp held the largest Latin American debt of $11.7 billion, followed by Manufacturers Hanover Corporation, Bank of America, Chase Manhattan, and Chemical of New York. A large portion of the foreign debt is not now being handled according to acceptable principles. Some countries have suspended interest payments, and some have suspended not only interest payments but principal payments as well. Since U.S. banks are not in a position to effect payment, most have increased their loan loss reserves, which was also followed by Canadian and British banks that had extended credit to the underdeveloped countries. Many suggestions were made to improve the situation, including one from the U.S. secretary of the treasury. He suggested that the debtor nations restructure their economies in an effort to provide economic growth and thus encourage foreign investment and that private world banks and government-sponsored world financial institutions make additional funds available. This suggestion was not received enthusiastically. It soon became obvious that some banks throughout the world have become more and more reluctant to advance additional funds; consequently, the public sector may be forced to play a greater role in the debt crisis.

Some banks sold loans in a secondary market at a substantial discount, which improved bank liquidity and provided banks with greater portfolio flexibility. Although such action does not eliminate losses, we are likely to see more of this in the future. In fact, regulatory authorities may permit banks to amoritize their losses over a number of years.

In an effort to solve the debt problem, some banks have engaged in debt equity swaps, that is, exchanging debt held for investments in private firms in the debtor countries. This procedure has been approved by the Board of Governors of the Federal Reserve System. Although a debt equity swap may be better than holding a nonconforming loan, it may not be the perfect solution for a variety of reasons. Among these reasons are that (1) the amount of desirable investments in debtor countries is limited, (2) the sovereign control of natural resources presents a problem and developing countries may be selling their productive resources at depreciated prices, and (3) the shift in demand for local credit is likely to place upward pressure on local interest rates. Also there might be an impact on domestic monetary policy. This would be true if the authorities of a developing country were unwilling to neutralize the monetary policy of the foreign debt conversion. If the foreign debt, for example, is exchanged directly with the central bank for local currency, the money supply would be increased; consequently, there would be an expansionary impact. If, however, the foreign debt is exchanged for local debt and then converted into domestic currency in a secondary market, this would not be true. Finally, exchanging debt for equity does not eliminate an outflow of funds since dividends replace interest payments, assuming that dividends are paid.

Despite the shortcomings of swap arrangements, seven developing countries including Argentina, Brazil, Chile, Mexico, and the Philippines have introduced debt equity swap programs. The conditions under which these programs operate differ. Mexico, for example, limits its debt equity swaps to certain industries such as tourism and other nonstrategic areas while Chile imposes fewer restrictions, permitting foreign investment in all industries except petroleum and uranium. Although much interest has been shown by debtor nations in this method of handling their foreign debt, by mid-1987 debt equity swaps amounted to only $6 billion, a very small fraction of the total debt of Latin American countries. One study concluded that if five of the developing countries that had already adopted swap programs were more aggressive, the total debt could have been reduced by approximately $24 billion and that the debt service requirements could have been reduced by about $8.5 billion over a five-year period.[6] It seems, therefore, that such programs as now constituted are not the solution of the debt crisis of the 1980s. However, should many of the restrictions that have been imposed by the debtor nations be liberalized or removed, the possibility of the success of such programs would be greatly improved.

Mexico offered a unique swap arrangement involving U.S. government bonds in early 1988. Under this plan Mexico offered to swap 20-year bonds, which carried a slightly higher interest rate than the existing Mexican debt, for bank loans. Such bonds would be backed by zero coupon

---

[6] T. A. Layman and T. F. Kearney, "Debt for Equity: A Solution to the LDC Debt Crisis? Part 2," *The Journal of Commercial Bank Lending* (February 1988), p. 42.

bonds purchased from the U.S. Treasury. Banks were required to tender the Mexican bank loans at a discount. Although this plan attracted some attention, it fell short of expectations. The various plans thus far advanced for meeting debt requirements on the part of several debtor nations cannot be termed a financial success, but their originality and the intentions of the countries involved must be complimented.

Debt Crisis of the 1980s Not the First

It should not be assumed that this debt crisis of Third World countries is the first. In the past 200 years there have been four major world debt crises, including the present one, namely, 1822–41, 1850–80, 1929–40, and 1980. In all of these periods Latin American countries were involved, and the same conditions were present. One author summarized the conditions as follows:

> Downturns in the economic environment involving commodity price declines, protectionism and slumping world trade, and attendant financial instability were crucial in every wave. Unproductive use of capital due to poor policy decisions such as using borrowed funds to finance showcase projects or government corruption was a factor in each wave. Political crises also were involved.[7]

The number and frequency of Latin American countries involved in debt crises stem, in large part, from a lack of administrative experience and the use of borrowed funds. Latin American countries have had less experience in administrative guidance and financial support than many other countries in a colonial system since they received their independence earlier than most other countries. Moreover, the Latin American countries have used borrowed funds for less productive purposes, such as budget deficits, the purchase of arms and munitions, and a variety of luxury projects. They have also not been free of corruption in government activities. Banks, it seems, failed to examine the history of lending to underdeveloped countries and debt crises. The often quoted statement seems appropriate here: "What we learn from history is that we do not learn from history."

Who Is to Blame?

Not only were banks at fault in this debt crisis but so were the debtor nations. Banks exercised poor management and lacked foresight. They apparently did not build into the lending equation the possibility of a drastic change in the economic environment of the borrowing countries—

---

[7] Shaheen F. Dil, "Debt and Default: 200 Years of Lending to Developing Countries," *The Journal of Commercial Bank Lending* (April 1987), p. 45.

which did occur and resulted in the inability to pay—or if they did, the margin was not sufficient. Moreover, many banks in the 1970s entered international syndicated lending that had no long-term interest or expertise in the field.

The borrowing countries did not comprehend and project their capacity to repay, nor did they visualize a decline in world trade and a rise in inflation and its impact on living standards and the balance of trade. Moreover, the debtors had no contingency plans to meet their contractual obligations. In every period of debt crises, borrowing countries have tended to borrow in excess, which makes them highly susceptible to the risk of changes in world interest rates.

The Outcome?

Predicting the outcome of the Third World debt crisis is not easy. Despite the willingness of some Latin American countries to discuss the debt problem with lenders, the World Bank and the IMF, it appears that banks will struggle with this problem for years. It is not exclusively a short-term problem of liquidity and temporary cash shortage, but one of the basic inability to repay. Bank losses will undoubtedly rise, and the ability of banks to loan and move aggressively in the marketplace will be lessened. The credit rating of countries that defaulted on their obligations will be adversely affected for a long time. Some banks are presently reluctant to lend directly to the debtor countries or even to finance those business firms that have an interest in dealing with them. In this kind of environment trade will not flourish, and economic growth will be impeded. The debt crisis of the 1980s is not a proud chapter in world development.

Since we believe that the solution to the debt crisis will take years to solve, international institutions and countries that have an interest in a solution should take steps to encourage production and free trade among the undeveloped countries and all nations. Debts are repaid from income, not penalties. We may see some aid from the public sector since it is not available from private sources. Debtors must demonstrate greater interest in the administration and the use of borrowed funds. Caution must be exercised in the event there is a movement for governments to assume part or all of the Third World debt. Unfortunately, banks will probably be more closely policed and regulated in this area of lending.

QUESTIONS

1. What different organizational arrangements are used by American banks to meet the needs of their customers for international banking services?

2. Discuss the factors that caused U.S. banks to be relatively uninvolved in international banking activities prior to World War II.

3. How can an American bank effectively engage in interstate banking in connection with its international banking activities?

4. What is the meaning of reciprocity as it applies to international banking offices?

5. How would tourists traveling abroad assure themselves of sufficient funds for expenses and purchases without the risks of carrying large amounts of the currency of each of the nations they expect to visit?

6. Define each of the following terms: (a) letter of credit, (b) bill of exchange, (c) bankers' acceptance, (d) bank draft, (e) spot exchange, (f) forward exchange, (g) on-board ocean bill of lading, (h) floating exchange rates.

7. Where is the foreign exchange market located? How does it operate?

8. How do the risks of international lending differ from those of domestic lending?

9. Evaluate our lending performance during the early 1980s. As a lending officer, what would you have done differently?

SELECTED REFERENCES

BAKER, J. C. "Is the International Banking Act of 1978 Working?" *The Bankers Magazine* (May–June 1982), pp. 15–19.

BANK FOR INTERNATIONAL SETTLEMENTS. *Recent Innovations in International Banking.* Prepared by a Study Group Established by the Central Banks of the Group of Ten Countries. Basel, Switzerland, April 1986.

CALHOUN, A. D. "Eurodollar Loan Agreements: An Introduction and Discussion of Some Special Problems." *The Journal of Commercial Banking* (September 1977), pp. 23–43.

DIL, SHAHEEN F. "Debt and Default: 200 Years of Lending to Developing Countries." *The Journal of Commercial Bank Lending* (April 1987), pp. 38–48.

GOODMAN, LAURIE S. "Bank Lending to Non-OPEC LDCs: Are Risks Diversifiable?" *Quarterly Review*, Federal Reserve Bank of New York (Summer 1981), pp. 10–20.

GRABBE, J. ORLIN. *International Financial Markets.* New York: Elsevier, 1986.

KORTH, C. M. "The Evolving Role of U.S. Banks in International Finance." *The Bankers Magazine* (July–August 1980), pp. 68–73.

LAYMAN, THOMAS A., AND TIMOTHY F. KEARNEY. "Debt for Equity: A Solution to the LDC Debt Crisis? Part 1." *The Journal of Commercial Bank Lending* (January 1988), pp. 33–45.

———. "Debt for Equity: A Solution to the LDC Debt Crisis? Part 2." *The Journal of Commercial Bank Lending* (February 1988), pp. 23–43.

LEWIS, MERU, AND KERWIN T. DAVIS. *Domestic and International Banking*. Cambridge, Mass.: MIT Press, 1987.

MADDEN, JOHN T., ET AL. *America's Experience as a Creditor Nation*. New York: Prentice-Hall, 1937.

ZWICK, C. J. "Miami—The New International Banking Center." *The Bankers Magazine* (January–February 1982), pp. 19–24.

INDEX